# Gallipc

In January 1915, Imperial Russia appealed to her allies for help against the seemingly invincible Central Powers. Churchill, as First Lord of the Admiralty, overrode the advice of his First Sea Lord, the aged Fisher ('Damn the Dardanelles – they will be our grave!'), and persuaded the Cabinet, unversed in war, to sanction a naval expedition to force its way to Constantinople. It was to eliminate Turkey from the war and thus sustain Russia's war effort.

The campaign, which veered from the brink of victory to final resounding defeat, was one of the most interesting in modern history. It saw the end of an era in Britain; after Suvla it would never again be possible to recruit a volunteer army as had Kitchener in 1914. It also saw the emergence into full statehood of Australia and New Zealand (where the story of Anzac has rightly become part of the modern *Zeitgeist*), and the beginnings of modern Turkey under Kemal Atatürk; he first appears on the historical stage at Gallipoli.

Michael Hickey traces the complex roots of catastrophe to the remoteness of war leaders in London, the chaotic operations of under-equipped and incompetent admirals and generals on the spot, and the extraordinary diversity of the Allied troops. Closely familiar with the battlefields and the straits, he unfurls a panorama of tenacity and heroism in conditions sometimes reminiscent of the Crimean War. By drawing on official papers, diaries and letters – many never published before – he gives an awe-inspiring impression of what it was like for the luckless fighting men who did their best but also, in the words of one of them, were 'beaten in the end by our own leaders'.

**Colonel Michael Hickey** served in the Army Air Corps, flying operationally in Korea, Malaya, East Africa and the Near East as well as in Germany. He taught at the Royal Military College of Science, was a Defence Fellow at King's College, London, and was later Director of the Museum of Army Flying. His most recent book is the critically acclaimed *The Unforgettable Army*, on Slim and his 14th Army in Burma. He and his wife have two sons and live in Hampshire.

*Cover illustrations*: (above) Landing at Gallipoli, 26 May 1915 (*Illustrated London News* Picture Library); (below) Australian troops charging a Turkish trench just before the evacuation at Anzac (Q13685, Crown copyright, Imperial War Museum)

# GALLIPOLI

## Michael Hickey

JOHN MURRAY
*Albemarle Street, London*

First published in 1995
by John Murray (Publishers) Ltd,
50 Albemarle Street, London W1X 4BD

Paperback edition 1998

A catalogue record for this book is available from the British Library

ISBN 0-7195-6142 6

Maps by Venture Graphics, Chislehurst, Kent

Typeset in 11/13pt Palatino by Servis Filmsetting Ltd
Printed and bound in Great Britain by
The University Press, Cambridge

# Contents

# Illustrations

The author and publishers would like to thank the following for permission to reproduce photographs: Plate 1, The Vale and Downland Museum Centre, Wantage; 2, 3, 4, 6, 7, 9, 10, 13, 18, 24, 25, 26, 27, Imperial War Museum, Crown copyright; 5, 11, 17, 19, 20, 28, Private Collections; 8, Liddle Archive, Leeds; 12, Illustrated London News Picture Library; 14, 23, Regimental Collection, Serle's House, Winchester; 15, Astley Collection, Liddle Archive, Leeds; 16, Gowans Collection, Liddle Archive, Leeds; 21, Mrs W. Begbie; 22, Mrs B. Campion.

# Foreword

I HAVE BEEN drawn to writing this book for many years. As a small boy
I heard my father and his contemporaries talking about their service
in the Great War of 1914–18, and it was apparent to me even then
that they had undergone experiences which their descendants have
mercifully been spared. It was my father's lot to serve as a platoon
commander on the Western Front in a Kitchener battalion of his
county regiment, the Cheshires, and he was lucky enough to escape
with wounds which at least ensured he would never return to the
trenches, but which resulted in his relatively early death. Many of his
friends from the village near Chester where his father was rector
served on the Western Front and elsewhere including Gallipoli,
where three battalions of the Cheshires found themselves in 1915.
Few of them returned.

As a parson's son in several Cheshire parishes my father grew up
in a world whose social stability seemed immutable. At Dukinfield,
a mill town on the Lancashire border, he remembered lying in bed on
winter mornings, hearing the factory hooters summoning the work-
force, and the sounds of hundreds of pairs of iron-shod clogs on the
glistening cobble-stones of the street outside as the men trudged in
silence to another day of grinding toil. The working population was
gregarious; as they moved daily to their work-place, so they gravitated on Saturday in a companionable herd to the football ground
where they stood muffled and cloth-capped on the terraces, cheering
their team on. It was only natural, therefore, when challenged by
Kitchener's fearsome stare on that famous poster to volunteer for his

New Army, that they should obediently troop down to attest and join collectively, as 'pals', 'sportsmen', and other categories proclaiming their social groupings. There were even 'public schools' battalions, in which the nation's potential leaders served and died prodigally in the ranks.

The men who joined the New Army saw nothing unusual in their readiness to volunteer. Society was still stratified and biddable; men looked to the 'gentry' for a lead and the gentry duly obliged; the yeomanry and territorials had long been commanded in this way; now, from the industrial towns of the North, came forth the ironmasters' and mill-owners' sons to form the new officer caste. Their rudimentary training in the Officers' Training Corps at their grammar and public schools was better than nothing at all, and they duly gravitated to the officers' mess as raw subalterns. In battle they would prove alarmingly brave, but their lack of military knowledge would kill them and their men by the thousand before the war was much older.

Much has been written about the senior officers, sailors and soldiers, charged with the command of the Dardanelles expedition. Many fully deserve the scorn heaped on them. Others deserve a more charitable reappraisal. In this book I have not sought to make excuses or indeed bore the reader with strings of sensational value judgements. It is, however, worth recalling that the professional officer corps of the pre-1914 army was accustomed to dealing with only one category of man: the short- and long-service regular soldier, whether in the British or Indian army. By the spring of 1915 Britain was fighting its first continental war since 1815 with three different types of army: the remains of the pre-war regulars; the Territorial Force and yeomanry; and the first-fruits of Kitchener's appeal for volunteers. In 1916 these three categories were to be joined by conscripts. Few if any of the generals had ever come across the citizen soldier as represented by the territorials, and none had ever seen a Kitchener volunteer. Many simply did not know how to treat them, for it quickly became apparent that these men did not react instinctively to the stimuli long employed for bringing regulars to fighting pitch.

The New Army men came from a much wider social spectrum; they included the desperately unemployable, but also professional men – solicitors, barristers, bank clerks, skilled artisans and mechanics – who could not be treated like cattle or conditioned to respond instantly to abrupt orders. A great deal of the blame for the fiasco following the Suvla landings must be attributed to this; the men had simply not been trained or conditioned for the peculiar circumstances attendant on an amphibious landing and were totally disorientated. Their training, for nearly a year, had been directed towards trench warfare on the Western Front and when confronted by a very different situation at Gallipoli they were lost.

The Australians and New Zealanders at Gallipoli were altogether different. Their view of life was entirely unlike that of the urbanized Britons of the territorials and New Army units. The two newly-minted nations were already sensing their identity and Gallipoli was its first true manifestation. Their soldiers were scornful of 'authority' unless the man giving the orders had shown himself to be worthy of their obedience. Outwardly their appearance suggested indiscipline on a heroic scale; but those making this accusation failed to note the perfect discipline displayed by the Australian infantry in their boats as they were rowed towards the shore on 25 April 1915. Their silence in the face of destiny is one of the most awesome features of this campaign. Similarly, no ill-disciplined unit would have been obedient unto death as were the officers and men of the Light Horse at the Nek, or the Australian and New Zealand brigades ordered to 'fix bayonets, slope arms, and quick march to Krithia'.

The appalling casualties suffered in many of the actions at Gallipoli do not bear comparison with anything in our nation's recent history. Again and again, battalions were all but wiped out; the trauma inflicted on the survivors must have been terrible, but there were relatively few cases of what was then known as 'shell shock', and there were certainly no 'counsellors' available to help those who would now be described as undergoing 'post-operational stress syndrome'. Those who were unnerved had to work it out for themselves, helped when necessary by their officers, chaplains and more robust comrades. Those who failed – and there were some – could be summarily court-martialled and shot; the sentence was frequently carried out down on Suvla beach, and in a sinister copse behind the lines at Helles. Gallipoli was not a friendly place for those of delicate susceptibilities.

I have sought to present the tale from the viewpoint of individuals who played their parts at all levels, whether in Whitehall, as senior officers, or as smaller players in a tragedy which produced heroism of astounding proportions. I have acknowledged many sources in the Bibliography at the end of the book but would especially like to thank those who have freely given their advice or made various documents available for study and generously granted permission to use them as I saw fit:

Dr Iffet Ozgonul of Ankara University, for her invaluable insights on modern Turkish history and as an encyclopaedic companion on two tours of the battlefields; Mr Alan Dowell of Linlithgow; Lieutenant-Colonel John Darroch of the former Royal Hampshires' regimental headquarters, Winchester; Mrs Joan Begbie for permission to quote from her late husband's personal memoir; Major Dick Mason and Mr Alan Clark of the Royal Scots headquarters and museum; Coralie Ovenden of the classics department, Winchester College, for her tactful correction of my erroneous ancient history; Mr Harry Foot of the Museum of Army Flying; Miss Lella Raymond for the quotations from her father's book, *Tell England*; Mrs Evelyn Baldwin for the loan of photographic material; Mr Nigel Steel of the Department of Documents, and the staff of the Reading Room, Imperial War Museum; Dr Correlli Barnett and the staff of the Churchill Archive, and the Master and Fellows of Churchill College, Cambridge, for permission to quote from the Fisher and Jack Churchill papers; Patricia Methven, Kate O'Brien, the archivists, and the trustees of the Liddell Hart Archive, King's College, London, where I seemed to be encamped for much of 1993–4; Frances Lumley, for information concerning her grandfather, 'One-arm Sutton'; Mr David Saunders, editor of *The Gallipolian* – a rich vein of anecdotage as well as scholarship; the staff of the Royal Naval Submarine Museum, Haslar; Mrs Brenda Campion for use of her father's memoir of service in the Yeomanry; Colonel Ross Harding, late Australian Staff Corps, for forty-five years of friendship, advice, and invaluable help in my researches at Canberra; the librarians and staff of the Prince Consort Library, Aldershot, for their unending courtesy and patience; Major John Hallam of the Lancashire Fusiliers headquarters and museum, Bury; the staff of the Tameside Local Studies Library, Stalybridge, for access to the Manchester Regiment's archives; Mrs Rachel Lambert for permission to use the memoir of her late father, Brigadier-General Frank Maxwell VC; Mr Barry Lyndon for information concerning his late father's service at Suvla; Mr Peter Liddle, creator of the eponymous archive at Leeds University; Mrs Edith Philip and her colleagues at the library of the Scottish United Services Museum; Mr M. G. Little and the staff of the Royal Marines Museum; Major Bob Astles of the Cheshire regimental museum and headquarters; Miss Susan Milward for permission to use her grandfather's diary; Mandy Little, my energetic agent; Howard Davies and Roger Hudson for their reading of the typescript and invariably constructive suggestions; and finally, Grant McIntyre, Gail Pirkis and John Murray, whose encouragement and advice have helped to make the writing of this book such a rewarding experience. My wife and family have, as always during my extended literary confinements, been remarkably tolerant.

I dedicate the work to the enduring memory of my father's generation, who gave so much and who were so cruelly cheated by the politicians who, from places of safety, sent them to something much worse than hell.

*Kings Worthy, 1995*

# The Theatre of Operations

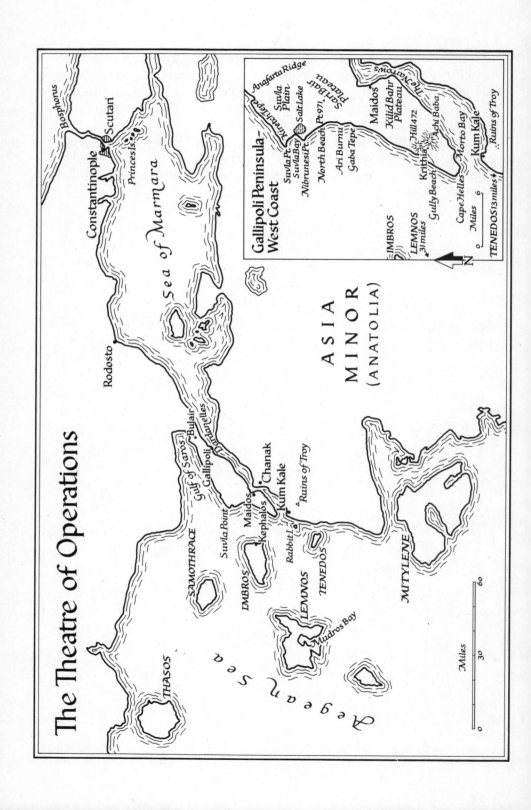

Bosphorus

Scutari

Constantinople

Princes Is.

Sea of Marmara

Rodosto

Bulair

Gulf of Saros

Gallipoli

Dardanelles

Suvla Point

Maidos

Chanak

Kephalos

Rabbit I.

Kum Kale

Ruins of Troy

SAMOTHRACE

IMBROS

LEMNOS

TENEDOS

THASOS

Mudros Bay

Aegean Sea

MITYLENE

ASIA MINOR (ANATOLIA)

Miles
0    30    60

### Gallipoli Peninsula—West Coast

Anafarta Ridge

Kiretch Tepe

Suvla Plain

Suvla Bay

Salt Lake

Anzac

Sari Bair Plateau

Pt.971

Suvla Pt.

Nibrunesi Pt.

North Beach

Ari Burnu

Gaba Tepe

Maidos

Kilid Bahr Plateau

Krithia

Hill 472

Achi Baba

The Narrows

Gully Beach

Cape Helles

Morto Bay

Kum Kale

Ruins of Troy

IMBROS

LEMNOS 31 miles

TENEDOS 13 miles

N

Miles
0    6

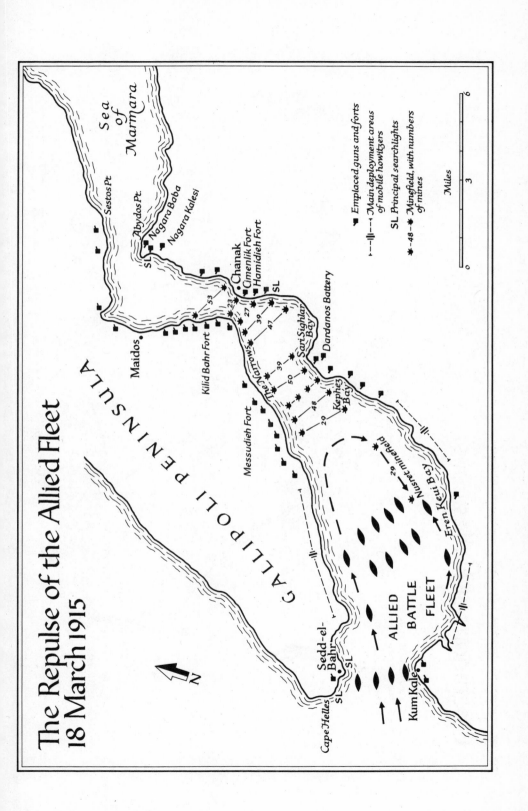

The Repulse of the Allied Fleet
18 March 1915

Sea of Marmara

GALLIPOLI PENINSULA

Sestos Pt.

Abydos Pt.
Nagara Baba
Nagara Kalesi

SL

Maidos

Chanak
Cimenlik Fort
Hamidieh Fort

53
23
27
39
47

SL

Kilid Bahr Fort

Sari Sighlar Bay

Dardanos Battery

39

The Narrows

50

48

Messudieh Fort

29

Kephez Bay

Nusret minefield

29

Eren Keui Bay

ALLIED

BATTLE

FLEET

Cape Helles

Sedd-el-Bahr

SL

SL

Kum Kale

N

■  Emplaced guns and forts

⊢–⊩–⊣  Main deployment areas
of mobile howitzers

SL  Principal searchlights

✳–48–✳  Minefield, with numbers
of mines

Miles

0        3        6

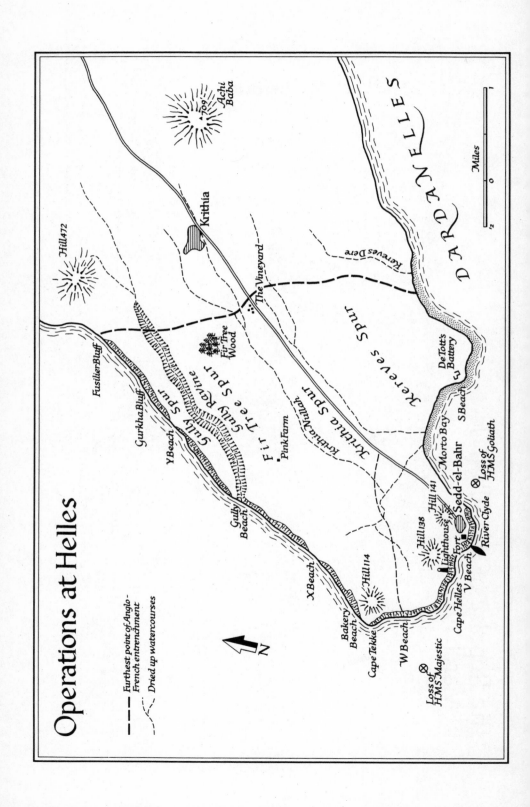

Operations at Helles

--- Furthest point of Anglo-French entrenchment
····· Dried up watercourses

N

DARDANELLES

Achi Baba
·709

Krithia

Hill 472

The Vineyard

Kereves Dere

Fir Tree Wood

Fusilier Bluff

Gurkha Bluff

Kereves Spur

Y Beach

Fir Tree Spur

Gully Spur

Krithia Spur

Krithia Nullah

Gully Ravine

De Tott's Battery

S Beach

Pink Farm

Gully Beach

Morto Bay

Sedd-el-Bahr

Hill 141

Loss of H.M.S. Goliath

X Beach

Hill 114

Bakery Beach

Cape Tekke

W Beach

Hill 138

Fort
Lighthouse

V Beach

River Clyde

Cape Helles

Loss of H.M.S. Majestic

Miles

0    1    2

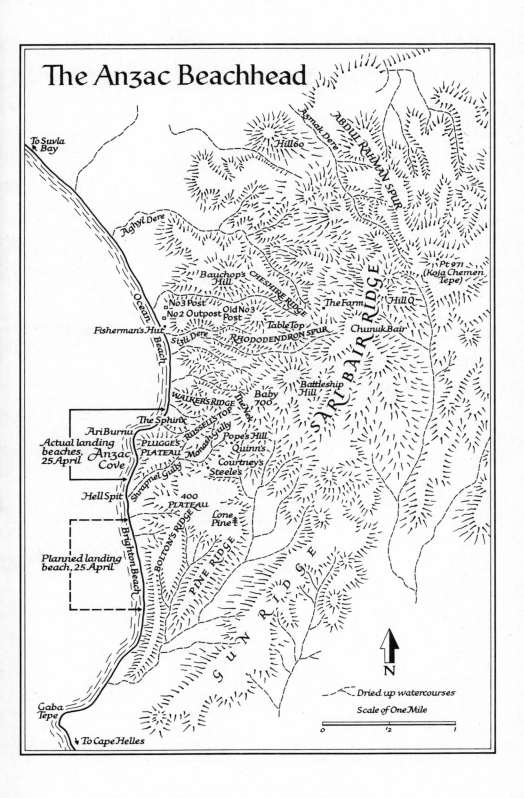

# The Anzac Beachhead

To Suvla
Bay

Aghyl Dere

Hill 60

Asmak Dere

ABDUL RAHMAN SPUR

Ocean Beach

Bauchop's
Hill

CHESHIRE RIDGE

Pt 971
(Koja Chemen
Tepe)

No 3 Post

No 2 Outpost

Old No 3
Post

The Farm

Hill Q

Fisherman's Hut

Sizli Dere

Table Top

RHODODENDRON SPUR

Chunuk Bair

SARI BAIR RIDGE

WALKER'S RIDGE

RUSSELL'S TOP

The Sphinx

Baby
700

Battleship
Hill

The Nek

AriBurnu

Actual landing
beaches,
25 April

Anzac
Cove

PLUGGE'S
PLATEAU

Monash Gully

Pope's Hill

Quinn's

Courtney's

Steele's

Hell Spit

Shrapnel Gully

400
PLATEAU

Lone
Pine

Brighton Beach

BOLTON'S RIDGE

Planned landing
beach, 25 April

PINE RIDGE

GUN RIDGE

Gaba
Tepe

To Cape Helles

N

Dried up watercourses

Scale of One Mile

0    ½    1

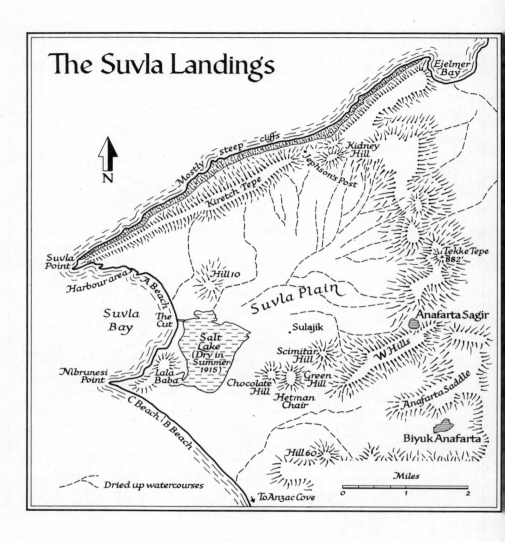

# The Suvla Landings

N

*Ejelmer Bay*

Mostly steep cliffs

*Kiretch Tepe*

*Kidney Hill*

Jepisson's Post

*Tekke Tepe 882'*

*Suvla Point*

Harbour area

*A Beach*

*Hill 10*

*Suvla Plain*

*Suvla Bay*

*The Cut*

*Sulajik*

*Anafarta Sagir*

*Salt Lake (Dry in Summer 1915)*

*Scimitar Hill*

*W Hills*

*Nibrunesi Point*

*Lala Baba*

*Chocolate Hill*

*Green Hill*

*Anafarta Saddle*

*Hetman Chair*

*C Beach*  *B Beach*

*Biyuk Anafarta*

*Hill 60*

- - - Dried up watercourses

*Miles*

0    1    2

↓ To Anzac Cove

# Prelude to Battle

IN 1915 THE British railway system was working to the limit of its capacity in support of the war effort. The main lines radiating out from London to the North were under particular strain; the busiest of these for many years had been the route linking London with Scotland via the Midlands and thence up the west coast, through the industrial areas of Lancashire, then on over the steep climbs of the Border country and into Scotland near Gretna.

The double track line from Carlisle to Glasgow was subject to particularly high traffic levels, for it was used by trains of several companies, all vying for the lucrative passenger and freight custom between England and Scotland. The track was owned by the Caledonian Railway north of the border and apart from its own trains it carried those of the London and North Western, North British and Glasgow and South West railway companies. There were numerous traffic agreements and elaborate precautions had been taken to ensure the highest standards of safety. On the morning of 22 May 1915, however, these failed with disastrous results.

A few miles north of Carlisle at Quintinshill, just inside the Scottish border near Gretna Green, one of several relief loops had been constructed; its function was to clear the main lines for express traffic by shunting local passenger and freight trains into sidings so that express trains on the London–Glasgow route could pass through without loss of time. The loops were controlled from a signal box. On the morning of the 22nd, the night dutyman should have been relieved at 6 a.m., but a lax practice had developed by mutual agreement between the two men concerned and the day relief arrived at the signal box nearly half an hour late. A leisurely handover then began, as the two men discussed the morning news and made tea.

Whilst they were doing this, several trains were approaching Quintinshill. From the south came the two main-line overnight expresses from Euston to Glasgow, on the 'down', or northbound line. They were running late, and in order to give them a clear road the night signalman had shunted a row of coal wagons on to the 'up' loop, and a laden goods train on to the 'down' loop. Both loops were now occupied, so when the morning Carlisle–Glasgow commuter train arrived on the 'down' line, it had to be accommodated on the 'up' main line, out of the way of the two expresses, which were both running late, ten minutes apart.

The first of these passed through without incident at 6.38 just as the empty coal wagons entered the 'up' loop. Now, only the 'down' main line was clear of traffic. According to well-tried safety procedures the signals on the 'up' line should have been set at 'danger', but the two signalmen, gossiping as they completed their paperwork, failed to observe this precaution; indeed, when offered an unscheduled 'up' train a few minutes later, they accepted it without question.

This unscheduled train had left Larbert in the small hours. It carried half a battalion of the Royal Scots, *en route* to Liverpool where they were due to embark for the eastern Mediterranean as part of the expeditionary force already in the field with the grand objective of taking Constantinople and knocking Turkey out of the war. Having accepted the troop train without even looking out of his window to where its line was occupied by the displaced commuter train, the signalman now accepted the second north-bound Glasgow express and set all the main-line 'down' signals to 'clear'.

The troop train was approaching Quintinshill from the north at 70 m.p.h. and the express was minutes away at a similar speed. The commuter train, of three coaches and a milk van, stood on the 'up' track with all its brakes on. The troop train driver's line of sight was partly obscured by the goods train standing in its loop. Behind him he had no less than twenty-one coaches of various types containing 563 officers and men of the 7th Royal Scots, a territorial unit recruited in the Leith and Edinburgh area. Its battalion HQ, signals section and two rifle companies were aboard.

The driver had only a few seconds in which to react to the situation which now confronted him; his last action was to apply full emergency braking, but at such a speed this barely arrested the train's progress. With a deafening explosion it charged head-on into the commuter train, instantly telescoping from a length of 213 to 67 yards of splintered wreckage. Both the engines exploded and the contents of their fireboxes were spewed out in all directions. The tender of the commuter train's engine was hurled across the 'down' main line. Immediately a fierce fire broke out, fuelled by the gas cylinders under every coach, which were used for lighting, and by the shattered woodwork from which all the rolling stock was built.

Survivors, deeply shocked, began to extricate themselves from this holocaust; the signalman, aghast, set all signals to danger. He was too late; barely a minute after the collision, the London–Glasgow express, hauled by two large locomotives at full speed, came into view. It ploughed into the flaming wreckage at 60 m.p.h., hit the upturned tender of the commuter train, and ground to a halt within a few yards, its first three coaches telescoped.

The fire raged for twenty-four hours as the local population, alerted by the colossal detonations of successive crashes, did what they could to succour the injured and comfort the survivors. When the flames died down the unrecognizably charred remains of the victims were recovered; 215 officers and men of the Royal Scots had been killed and a further 191 injured. Only five officers and 52 men were unscathed and able to answer the trackside rollcall. Ten civilians died. The two signalmen were duly convicted on charges of manslaughter.

Most of the survivors were sent on leave and thus missed the boat that sailed with the rest of the shattered battalion. Edinburgh and Leith were plunged into mourning. Those who survived, and followed on to Gallipoli later, had little or no inkling that an even more appalling fate awaited them on that ill-starred peninsula.

At such a tale, who could forbear to weep?

Virgil, *Aeneid*, tr. Joseph Addison

# PART ONE

## *The Dire Straits*

# 1

# Kitchener's Army

'I wish', quoth my uncle Toby, 'you had seen what
prodigious armies we had in Flanders.'

Sterne, *Tristram Shandy*

THE BOER WAR of 1899–1902 administered a salutary shock to the
British military establishment. Following Kitchener's eventual
victory over a numerically inferior but far more mobile enemy, far-
reaching studies were carried out in Whitehall and at the Staff
College, by then under the command of the able and perceptive
Major-General Henry Rawlinson, a staff officer under Kitchener in
the Sudan campaign of 1898 and destined to be the highly successful
commander of the 4th Army in France later in the Great War.

The basic problem, it was agreed, was that the British army lacked
a professional General Staff on the lines created a century earlier in
Prussia, whose military academies and staff schools had turned out
generations of rigorously trained officers destined to fill the highest
staff appointments as well as key field commands. In Prussia the
army was regarded as the school of the nation, its ranks manned by
conscripts whose subsequent reserve obligations provided the state
with a huge pool of readily mobilized manpower. In Britain, owing
to a deep-seated objection to any form of standing army or compul-
sory military service, the only reserves had been those accruing from
manpower released from colour service in the regular army, the
volunteers, the militia and the yeomanry.

The steady decline of British power in the face of fierce international competition, the rise of Germany as a world power, and the
growing hostility of other powers prompted the Anglo-French
accord, the *Entente Cordiale*, of 1904 which aimed to assemble a body
of new friends. This alliance also subsumed Russia, in an attempt to

contain the Central Powers and to discourage lesser parties from aligning themselves with Germany. Imperceptibly, a 'European' strategy was beginning to supplant the old imperial one. This brought further problems, however. A whole-hearted commitment to European alliances demanded the ability to field a very large army for continental campaigning, a concept from which Britain had shrunk since 1815.

The Secretary of State for War in Campbell-Bannerman's Liberal government was R. R. (later Lord) Haldane, who applied a lawyer's mind to a sweeping reform of the army impelled by its shortcomings in South Africa. One of his innovations was the creation of a General Staff. Another was the reorganization of the several reserve forces into a Territorial Force capable of taking the field alongside the regulars. He recognized that a large conscript army can only be created in a democracy through the consent of an electorate convinced by a government prepared to make the issue an electoral platform. The Liberals were adamant that this would not be the case as long as they formed the government. Haldane therefore had to apply sweeping reforms to the existing voluntary forces, if only to raise manpower for home defence and release regular forces for operations in Europe.

By carefully reorganizing the regulars Haldane managed to create an expeditionary force for service in Europe. His proposals went before the House of Commons in July 1906; they included the provision of six infantry divisions and four cavalry brigades, which were to be formed into a cavalry division on mobilization. The expeditionary force would comprise 150,000 men of whom a third were to be regulars. The remaining two-thirds were to be drawn from regular reservists recalled to the colours, from the newly created Territorial Force, and the yeomanry, now almost the only surviving remnant of the ancient militia.

The militia had been in existence well before the Napoleonic Wars, a voluntary force recruited for home defence as well as a fertile recruiting-ground for the regular army. The yeomanry, also a volunteer force, existed as a form of mounted militia. It thrived in the rural counties and was officered by the knights of the shire and landowning gentry. These encouraged their estate workers to enrol, and the annual yeomanry camps were a uniformed migration of English rural society, with all its delicate social gradations: the gentry in the officers' mess, the yeoman farmers in the sergeants', and the ordinary tenants, artisans and labourers in the ranks. Besides these were the volunteers, a product of French invasion fears, first in Napoleonic times, but more recently in the period following the Crimean War.

The newly created Territorial Force embraced the yeomanry and most of the old volunteer units. Responsibility for running the territorials was handed over to county associations, thus maintaining the connection with the mediaeval shire levy or *posse comitatus*. Enlistment was for an initial four-year term with obligatory periods of training at local drill halls as well as a duty to attend annual camp. A total of fourteen infantry divisions and fourteen mounted brigades were created overnight, all earmarked for home defence, though individuals could opt to serve overseas on mobilization. The establishment of the Territorial Force was fixed at 302,199 officers and men, but this total was never achieved in the years prior to the war. The peak strength, attained in 1911, was 276,000. A private member's bill to introduce a measure of compulsion into the force was rejected in the House of Commons without even being put to the vote.

Haldane's reforms were watched closely by one of Britain's foremost soldiers. Herbert Kitchener was born in Ireland in 1850, the son of an eccentric father who scorned bedclothes and required his family to use old newspapers instead. Herbert and his brothers were educated in Switzerland until he entered the Royal Military Academy at Woolwich in 1868. Fluent in French and German and already well travelled, he stood apart from the herd, and he awed his contemporaries from then on. He loved to travel, especially alone, in the Middle East, and quickly mastered Arabic and Turkish. In his work as surveyor and map-maker he acquired a deep knowledge of the countries where his destiny was to lead him, and was well-equipped professionally for his greatest moment – the defeat of the Mahdi and his followers at Omdurman in 1898 which avenged the death of Gordon, Kitchener's hero and pattern, at Khartoum in 1884.

Kitchener's character was well-nigh impenetrable and few could ever claim intimate acquaintance with him. Only his ADCs in India, Frank Maxwell VC and Victor Brooke (brother of a future Chief of the Imperial General Staff), were privy to his confidences or bold enough to chaff him.

Haldane's reforms had taken place by the time Kitchener arrived back in London in the autumn of 1910. He felt cheated of his great ambition to be Viceroy of India and it did not improve his temper to be told that he had been selected as Commander-in-Chief in the Mediterranean. When he paid his duty call on King Edward VII to receive his field marshal's baton, the monarch told him that he thought the Mediterranean command was 'a damned rotten billet' and agreed to let Kitchener turn it down, so exciting the new field marshal that he left his baton in the throne room, which greatly upset the King. A week

later the King was dead, and Kitchener was appointed to command
the troops at the coronation of his successor George V. He was introduced into the House of Lords as Viscount and entered into the frenetic
social round of that coronation summer of 1911.

He was particularly sought out by the Liberal Prime Minister,
Herbert Asquith, who, whilst aware of the field marshal's affinity
with the Conservatives and Unionists on the opposition benches,
was fascinated by him. He also knew that Kitchener, thwarted in his
viceregal ambition, had called in at Constantinople on his way home
the previous autumn, from where he had written to his friend and
confidante Lady Salisbury, telling her of his alarm at the spread of
German influence there: 'We are out of it altogether, as the present
ambassador does nothing and the German is allowed to do as he
likes.' A new ambition stood in his sights. He wanted to be ambassador to the Sublime Porte, believing that he had the qualifications to
apply sufficient pressure on the Grand Vizier and Ottoman court to
counterbalance the influence of the Young Turks and the German
ambassador. There was one drawback; if Kitchener was to make any
headway in securing the political influence he sought at Constantinople he would have to be provided with huge sums of money for
disbursement as bribes at all levels of the Ottoman system. The
Germans had been doing this for years to buy the support of key
officials, the press and politicians, but Grey, the high-minded Liberal
Foreign Secretary, was unwilling to play that game.

Instead, in September 1911 Kitchener was sent to Egypt as British
Agent, where he soon established good relations with the majority of
the senior Egyptian officials as well as earning the respect of the
British military commanders. He had bought a house in England and
quickly settled to an annual routine which took him home for the
summer season; he now enjoyed high society and the attentions of
titled hostesses. In the summer of 1914 he followed this pattern,
intending to return to Egypt in early August. One of the many social
functions he attended was the Household Cavalry Ball at the
Knightsbridge Barracks officers' mess, where Osbert Sitwell, another
guest, described his appearance in a memorable passage:

> One only saw him, for his partner sank into insignificance since, what-
> ever his faults or his merits, his genius was sufficient to concentrate
> attention on him to the exclusion of all others in his neighbourhood . . .
> the colour of his face was tawny beyond sunburn, and pertained to the
> planet Mars . . . A large square frame, with square shoulders, square
> head, square face, a square line of hair at the top of a square forehead

. . . a slightly unfocussed glance which seemed almost in its fixity to possess a power of divination . . . He could claim kinship to the old race of German generals, spawned by Wotan in the Prussian plains, and born with spiked helmets ready on their heads . . . not an English leader of patrician type, such as Wellington, but one from the class that had, since the Reform Bill, monopolized power.

The summer of 1914 lived on in the memories of those who experienced it and managed to survive the next five years. At Oxford the undergraduates slept out in Christ Church meadows to escape the heat of their rooms. At Henley, a crew from Harvard University won the Grand Challenge Cup; the entire crew reappeared at the regatta half a century later in 1964 and to thunderous applause rowed down the course for a final time. Few of the British oarsmen who had lost to this crew in 1914 were still alive in 1918.

The murder of the Archduke Franz Ferdinand and his wife by Serbian nationalists in June 1914 led the Austro-Hungarian government to declare war on Serbia, and set in train a series of treaty obligations extending far beyond the Balkans. Russian began to mobilize as an act of Slav sympathy with Serbia; within days, Germany had declared war on Russia and France. On 4 August, Britain declared war on Germany in accordance with her obligations to France and Russia, and followed this by extending the declaration to Austria-Hungary on 12 August. All over Europe, nations were rushing to arms. Although under no obligation to do so, the self-governing dominions of Canada, New Zealand and Australia declared their immediate support of the motherland.

On 4 August, Kitchener had already set off for Dover on his way back to Egypt but to his great annoyance he was taken off the boat and rushed back to London that afternoon on the Prime Minister's orders, for Asquith was aware that his Cabinet, though highly gifted intellectually, lacked any experience in the conduct of war. Kitchener was formally appointed Secretary of State for War and thus took his seat in the Cabinet as an apolitical soldier, the first to do so since General Monck earned his place in the inner council of Charles II by restoring him to the throne in 1660.

Despite Haldane's attempts at its reform the army was in no state for a major continental war. Staff talks between the British and French General Staffs however had been going on in great secrecy for some years and these enabled the small British Expeditionary Force (BEF) to cross rapidly to France. It consisted of only 150,000 men in one cavalry and six infantry divisions. A further 60,000 regulars were still overseas garrisoning the empire and arrangements had to be made to get them home, to be replaced by territorials, providing these agreed to serve overseas.

The Territorial Force was theoretically capable of almost unlimited expansion and many of its battalions began to form second battalions as volunteers came in. Kitchener, however, had a low opinion of the existing system. Almost alone in the hierarchy he foresaw a protracted war lasting anything up to four or five years, which would demand more than a small regular force and the voluntarily recruited territorials, neither of which was capable of expansion on the scale required. He also held the French army in contempt and expected the Germans to 'walk through them like partridges'.

At once he announced his intention of calling for thousands of volunteers for a New Army, one which would be separate from the regulars and territorials: to this new third army, supplementing the regulars and territorials, a fourth army was to be added in 1916 with the introduction of conscription. It was Kitchener's original intention to give his 'New Army' units no more identity than a numerical title, as was the case in continental armies, but he was dissuaded from this by the General Staff. Thus it was that the Kitchener, or 'service', battalions were recruited on a local and county basis, becoming battalions of the relevant county regiments.

To create this New Army an artist of genius drew the famous poster showing Kitchener pointing towards the reader and fixing the world with a disturbing stare, given its unearthly quality by the cast in one eye. The response was immediate. So great was the surge of patriotic enthusiasm in the first few weeks of the war that the administrative system was overwhelmed. The factories and mines were deprived of key workers, particularly skilled artificers, and the war industries were adversely affected. Young men from every occupation and social class came in their thousands to be given a cursory medical examination and to be kitted out in whatever clothing was available. Stocks of khaki soon ran out and blue serge, surplus to General Post Office requirements, was put to use. Many volunteers went without proper uniforms for weeks, and there was a great shortage of tentage, boots, weapons and junior leaders. Elderly retired officers were recalled to command the new battalions and the junior officers were appointed with little attempt at rigorous selection. It was enough to have served in the Officers' Training Corps whose detachments in the public and grammar schools had, since the 1870s, given a modicum of military training to the young men destined – it was hoped – to provide the officer corps of the volunteers.

Opposition to Kitchener from some quarters of the army establishment was not slow in surfacing. An early opponent was Sir Henry Wilson, Deputy Chief of Staff in France. He had been publicly rebuked by Kitchener several times in the past, most recently for his indiscreet conversations with unauthorized persons about the BEF's transportation plans for the move to France. Wilson, one of the most intelligent officers of his day and a fluent French linguist (which contrasted notably with the almost monoglot General French, his chief) was a born intriguer. He now embarked on a destructive war against Kitchener who, he told French, detested the BEF, the regular army and the territorials, and would now bleed the BEF of all its best young officers and NCOs for use as instructors for the New Armies, which he described as 'shadow armies for shadow campaigns and unknown and distant dates'. This was the start of a relentless struggle between the 'Western' school, represented by French and his staff, and what would become the 'Eastern' school, once plans for the Mediterranean Expeditionary Force had been revealed. It was a battle which would cost the nation dear.

French, carefully briefed by Wilson, was soon highly critical of Kitchener, accusing him of starving the hard-pressed BEF of reinforcements, so badly needed after the battles of the autumn and subsequent deadlock at Ypres. After the repulse of the Germans on the Marne in early September, French had become wildly optimistic and pressed Whitehall for every spare unit and man, forecasting that an advance of only fifty miles would result in the collapse of the German lines of communication and the precipitate retreat of their routed armies back across the Rhine. Kitchener, however, had his friends in high places. Churchill, though an old friend of French, took the War Minister's side, urging him to stand his ground against the blandishments of Wilson and the other 'Westerners'. Meanwhile the old regular army was dying in its shallow trenches before Ypres, even as French called for reinforcements in an offensive he could not mount.

Churchill re-established relations with French by suggesting a series of amphibious landings on the captured Belgian coast in order to turn the German right flank. Kitchener turned these plans down flat. Churchill then produced another idea, one of which French would certainly not approve: the outflanking of the Central Powers by landings in the Dardanelles, aimed at taking Constantinople with an Allied force and foiling German strategic plans. Churchill was supported in this by the influential Secretary to the War Council, Sir Maurice Hankey, himself a former Royal Marines officer. The seeds of disaster were being sown.

# 2

# *Fisher's Fleet*

Had anyone suggested that fighting efficiency lay in
knowing how to shoot the guns and not polishing
them, he would have been looked at as a lunatic and
treated accordingly.

Naval officer of the 1890s, quoted in
Robert Massie, *Dreadnought*

IN BRITAIN, WAR with Germany was not unexpected. The creation of
the Kaiser's High Seas Fleet, in progress since the early years of the
century, was seen as an overt challenge to British naval supremacy.
Fortunately, the Royal Navy had been in good hands as the threat
materialized.

In 1860 a revolutionary warship had been launched in Britain
which, though it never fired a shot in anger, changed the face of
naval architecture and tactics. This was the ironclad, HMS *Warrior*.
Although her main armament was arranged to fire in broadside, as
in Nelson's day, and a full set of sails was carried, she was the first
warship in the world to be constructed completely of iron. One of her
earliest gunnery officers was John Arbuthnot Fisher. Born in Ceylon
in 1841, he was destined to be the most controversial and influential
officer to serve the Royal Navy since Horatio Nelson, and would
exercise a significant influence over the early conduct of the
Dardanelles campaign.

Fisher's speciality was gunnery. After his service in *Warrior* he
went to the navy's Spartan gunnery school, HMS *Excellent*, to which
he was to return many times during his later service. By 1870 he had
been noted for accelerated promotion and in 1872 was back at
*Excellent*, this time for experimental work on the new torpedo, a
weapon held in derision by his conservative superiors and colleagues but one in which he saw immeasurable potential. He was an
innovator, and as such rapidly made enemies; he was also combative
by nature and throughout his life engaged in vendettas of remarkable

venom with those he saw as his opponents. In 1882 he had been captain of HMS *Inflexible*, the most powerful battleship in the navy, at the bombardment of Alexandria. From 1890 on he spent fourteen years ashore: as captain of the gunnery school, then Director of Ordnance and Torpedoes at the Admiralty and, following promotion to Rear-Admiral in 1890, as Third Sea Lord and Controller of the Navy. He was thus continuously engaged with naval technology and was recognized as a master of his profession. All-importantly, he understood the intricacies of the Admiralty itself, and the ways in which politicians carried out their business.

The Naval Defence Act of 1880 had been a milestone as far as modernization of the service and naval construction was concerned. Fisher was on hand to take advantage of the huge opportunities he saw for rebuilding the fleet, which he considered hopelessly outdated and stagnant. He forced the adoption of water-tube boilers; anyone rash enough to gainsay him felt the full force of his acid tongue and with it the ruin of his career. As the building programme took shape in the 1890s under his close scrutiny, he also became something of a public figure. His experience of the political machine enabled him to shine at the Hague Conference of 1899, initiated by Tsar Nicholas II with the aim of arms limitation and setting up a form of international arbitration to pre-empt war. All recognized his encyclopaedic grasp of naval technology and he used his considerable histrionic powers to make the best of every public speaking opportunity. Following this success he was appointed Commander-in-Chief of the Mediterranean Fleet, Britain's greatest naval command at the time.

Fisher came as a considerable shock to his new command, which considered itself an élite force; its elegant battleships and cruisers, with their black hulls, white superstructures and buff funnels, looked more like yachts than engines of war; spit and polish was everything, and the social life of the officers when ashore at Malta was dazzling. Fisher played a full part in the social junketings but when at work he left nobody in any doubt as to what he wanted. He specialized in unheralded inspections of ships which often ended in the summary dismissals of captains and shoals of officers. He encouraged original thinking by setting prize essays, especially to see what his junior officers' opinions were, and he warmly commended those whose unconventional ideas appealed to him. The younger officers adored him, as did the sailors.

After two hectic years Fisher returned to London as Second Sea Lord; he was now in charge of the navy's personnel matters including training. This was his chance to prepare the service for the technical innovations lying ahead; he needed a well-educated navy and began by introducing new officer entry procedures, and set up a new cadet college at Osborne to which applicants were admitted from the age of 12.

On 21 October 1904, ninety-nine years to the day since Trafalgar, he assumed office as First Sea Lord. The Royal Navy was now his. He swept through the corridors of the Admiralty like a refiner's fire, hurling opposition aside as he prepared the fleet for the conflict he saw ahead. A hundred and fifty old warships were struck off the list. Flotillas of new destroyers were ordered, together with the beginnings of a submarine fleet. The most radical innovation, however, was Fisher's special brainchild: the all-big-gun battleship, powered by steam turbines. In great secrecy the first of these, christened *Dreadnought*, was laid down in the autumn of 1905, launched in the following March, and completed in December of that year. At a stroke, she rendered every other battleship in the world obsolete. A frantic naval race ensued as the other naval powers, notably Germany, sought to redress the balance and erode Britain's supremacy. Fisher also gave orders for the construction of a new category of capital ship, the battle cruiser. Whilst carrying a large-calibre main battery, the battle cruiser was far less heavily armoured than the dreadnoughts, giving it the speed to overhaul and destroy any armoured cruiser afloat. Fisher's rationale in ordering this type of ship was that on the outbreak of war it would be necessary to protect seaborne commerce from attacks by the fast German cruisers then under construction.

A cloud now appeared on Fisher's horizon. He fell out, not for the first time, with an old friend, the traditionalist Admiral Lord Charles Beresford. When Beresford moved on to the command of the Mediterranean Fleet in 1905 Fisher's vitriolic public attacks on his professional competence followed him. Private correspondence was leaked and the outcome was the sacking of Beresford; but although Fisher was raised to the peerage in 1909 as Admiral of the Fleet the Lord Fisher of Kilverstone, enough mud had stuck to him to ensure that his own resignation followed in January 1910.

As the war clouds gathered in 1914, the political head of the Royal Navy was the 39-year-old Winston Churchill, whose career to date had embraced soldiering, journalism and membership of both the principal political parties of the House of Commons. Having been offered a governmental post by the Liberals, he had weighed the possible advantages of joining their party as a means of furthering his political career, and had duly crossed the floor despite the opprobrium of his former colleagues in the opposition Unionist camp. He had come to the Admiralty from the Home Office and revelled in the new appointment, which he assumed in 1911.

The First Sea Lord was now Prince Louis of Battenberg. On the outbreak of war with Germany, a nationwide campaign of mindless xenophobia triumphed against all reason and pressure mounted for the resignation of the prince from the service he loved; with great dignity he departed in October 1914 to the accompaniment of an effusive but glib letter of appreciation from Churchill, described tartly in a *Times* editorial as a rhetorical document 'which compared ill with the brevity of Battenberg's letter of resignation'. Churchill could have taken his pick of a number of highly competent officers to succeed Prince Louis; he decided instead to take a bold step, inviting Fisher to emerge from retirement at the age of 73. The old sailor accepted. He and Churchill had known each other for some time; their relationship was one of mutual fascination and repulsion in almost equal parts; they certainly stimulated each other, and Fisher had been acting as Churchill's private and unofficial adviser at the Admiralty almost since he had become First Lord in 1911.

The rapid mobilization of the navy in August 1914 brought some unforeseen problems. As a long-term effect of Fisher's earlier pruning of the service and the scrapping of so many obsolete ships, there were now considerably more naval and Royal Marine reservists than seagoing berths. Churchill's solution was to form the Royal Naval Division, for service ashore. For the reservists of the Royal Marine Light Infantry and the Royal Marine Artillery (respectively the 'red' and 'blue' marines) this presented no great problem, as their colour service had prepared them to fight on land as much as on water. Some of them, however, were nearing their fifties and no longer medically fit for strenuous service. The naval reservists were not promising material for conversion to the infantry role, although the physically tough stokers showed that they could not only adapt to novel conditions but excel, once the necessary training had been given.

A large training depot was set up at the Crystal Palace in south London and the task of creating the naval division began. Before it could be completed, however, Churchill decided to send the raw formation to Antwerp, in a vain attempt to stem the German invasion of Belgium and buy time for the arrest of the seemingly irresistible advance of the Kaiser's armies across northern France. Some of the division's units were captured after a fitful resistance, others crossed into neutral Holland and were ignominiously interned for the duration, and about half the force was safely evacuated by sea back to England, where it resumed its training and received fresh drafts of raw volunteers from many quarters.

The successful novelist Compton Mackenzie came from his home on Capri to offer his services, and the poet Rupert Brooke, offered a naval commission by Churchill, applied himself diligently to the profession of arms. Other officer entries included the Prime Minister's sons Arthur and Herbert Asquith and the New Zealand-born Bernard Freyberg who had travelled back to England from Mexico to join and who was later to make a remarkable contribution to the Gallipoli campaign. Theirs was a dazzling company of talented young men whose academic and sporting achievements had already set them apart; few of them would outlive the war. A great camp was established on the downland above Blandford Forum in Dorset, where the division continued to train in the late autumn and early winter of 1914–15. Conditions were terrible but morale remained surprisingly high.

If the performance of the scratch naval division at Antwerp had scarcely enhanced Churchill's reputation, that of the navy itself had not been dazzling. On 22 September a British force off the Dutch coast had been attacked by a German U-boat which rapidly sent three elderly cruisers to the bottom with 1,600 officers and men. In October came another blow, when the brand-new super-dreadnought HMS *Audacious* hit a mine and sank. On the high seas, marauding German light cruisers were ranging far and wide, apparently dodging the attentions of the Royal Navy with impunity. The armoured cruisers of Admiral Graf von Spee's China squadron emerged from their base at Tsingtao, crossed the Pacific and destroyed Rear-Admiral Sir Christopher Cradock's squadron of old cruisers at Coronel off the Chilean coast. Churchill responded by ordering two battle cruisers to the south Atlantic, where they duly sank the *Scharnhorst* and *Gneisenau* off the Falklands.

As Fisher and Churchill warily renewed their acquaintance and began to work together, further woes beset the Admiralty; on 27 November the battleship *Bulwark*'s magazines blew up at Sheerness with the loss of 700 lives, and intermittent raids on the coast of northeast England by German cruisers caused some damage and loss of life, as well as indignation among the civil population at the Royal Navy's apparent inability to perform its historic role of defending the home country.

Very soon, however, the curious chemistry which characterized the meeting of these two minds began to show itself; Fisher and Churchill were both highly emotional, volatile and imaginative men and it was thus natural that they should be in constant discussion and argument over more effective ways of prosecuting the war against Germany. Fisher favoured a naval incursion into the Baltic, using a fleet of obsolete pre-dreadnought battleships, fitted with additional anti-torpedo protection, and monitors – flat-bottomed shallow-draught gunships capable of closing with coast defences in the treacherous shoals and sandbanks of the north German coast. The firepower thus deployed would be adequate, in Fisher's opinion, for the protection of an amphibious landing force carried in armoured craft fitted with bow doors, which could negotiate the shallows and beach themselves for the rapid landing of troops and guns. Without consultation, Fisher gave instructions for such craft to be designed and built in quantity.

The Baltic expedition never took place; apart from the practical difficulties of forcing an entrance through the narrows separating neutral Denmark and Sweden, the Russian armies assumed to be the beneficiaries of this scheme were in no state to offer battle on the Baltic coast after their crushing defeats at Tannenberg and the Masurian Lakes in September 1914. There would, however, be a use for the monitors and the landing craft before long, in the eastern Mediterranean.

# 3

# The Battleground

Stop, traveller! The ground you have just
trodden is the spot where an era ended
and where the heart of a nation beats.

Inscription on hillside above Kilid Bahr

FOR ALMOST FORTY centuries the area known in modern times as the
Dardanelles has played an important if fitful part in military history.
This is the point of access to the Black Sea from the Aegean – and
shipping attempting to enter the Sea of Marmara has to negotiate a
difficult passage between the European and Asiatic shores. The
Trojan Wars which took place here around 1200 BC had nothing to do
with the abduction of Menelaus' wife Helen by Paris, prince of Troy.
The reason for the prolonged siege and sacking of the city was a
quarrel over the rights of foreigners to pass through the Hellespont
or Dardanelles and trade with the inhabitants of the distant Crimea.
Once through the Narrows and the Sea of Marmara there was a
further defile to negotiate; the key to this, the Bosphorus, lay in the
hands of whoever possessed what is now Istanbul.

Istanbul is probably one of the world's most strategically significant capitals, making it through history the objective of successive
aggressor states. In 1453 the Ottoman Turks stormed the walls of
Constantinople under the energetic leadership of Mehmed II, the
'drinker of blood'. Mehmed was one of the men of destiny who feature
from time to time in world history; young, ruthless, cultured and
an instinctive tactician, he secured his empire by fortifying the
Dardanelles and the Bosphorus. His great Dardanelles fortresses still
stand: on the European shore facing across to Chanak is the amazing
heart-shaped Kilid Bahr ('Key of the Sea') and at Chanak itself, the
Cimenlik fortress. No ship passing through the Narrows was more
than 600 yards distant from their great cannon.

By the nineteenth century there were sultans who recognized the latterday weakness of the Ottoman system of government and tried to temper it by experiments in democracy and the adoption of European political, economic and military techniques. This conscious attempt at reform, known as the *Tanzimat*, was only fitfully applied and by the 1870s it was clear that the Ottoman Empire was approaching dissolution. As early as 1844 Tsar Nicholas I of Russia was referring to Turkey as the 'sick man of Europe' and suggesting an Anglo-Russian partition.

To generations of Turkish rulers, the perceived menace to national security had been from the north. Russia depended on free passage through the Bosphorus and the Dardanelles in order to export the grain surpluses of the Ukraine which formed a staple of her economy. At the same time, both Russia and Greece entertained hopes of recovering Constantinople for Orthodox Christianity. The Romanov tsars, as well as the German-bred royal house of Greece, had visions of a new imperial age based on Constantine's historic capital; the rival aspirations of the Greek and Russian Orthodox churches added to the frictions which affected international relations where Turkey was concerned.

Although attempts were made by the reformers of the *Tanzimat* to maintain the concept of a unified Ottoman Empire, rather than of a nation state 'Turkey', a sense of Turkish nationhood gained strength as the empire dissolved. In 1876 Sultan Abdulhamid II ('The Damned') ascended the throne. He was not greatly seized by a wish to democratize his empire but under the 'Midhat Constitution' of 1876 was forced reluctantly to accept certain changes limiting his power. After two years he re-established an absolutist style of government which was enforced until 1908. In that year came a revolution which changed the course of Turkish history.

During the last quarter of the nineteenth century a growing number of army officers, intellectuals and professional men had been formulating revolutionary political ideas. They called themselves the Committee of Union and Progress, better known as the 'Young Turks'. From places of exile in western Europe – mainly in Paris – they proclaimed a doctrine which set out to restore Turkey's national pride, arrest decay, and establish a more liberal constitution than that of the sultanate, with effective democratic control.

The leaders of the Young Turks were a remarkable group of men. Chief among them was a Macedonian regular soldier, Enver Pasha. In 1908, when the Sultan was forced to reinstate the Midhat Constitution, Enver was only 27. His principal supporters were also young: Mehmed Talaat Pasha (33) was before long to become Minister of the Interior; he was the political commissar of the Young Turk movement, and like most of the others destined to meet a violent death in the years immediately following the 1914–18 war. Ahmed Djemal Pasha, later to be Navy Minister, was 35. The most intelligent member of this group was probably the Thracian Jew, Mehmed Djavid Bey, who would become Finance Minister.

The revolution of 1908 coincided with a sudden downturn in Turkey's fortunes. There were rebellions in Albania, Kurdistan and Arabia. Bedouin attacks on the new Hedjaz railway threatened communications with the holy cities of Mecca and Medina. A revolt in the Yemen was fired by the resurgent Mahdist sect. Taking advantage of these diversions, reactionary forces in Constantinople, encouraged by Sultan Abdulhamid, staged a counter-revolution, which was quickly put down by the national assembly at the bidding of the Young Turks, who then called for the Sultan's abdication. He was succeeded by his younger brother, Mehmed V, but the empire continued to disintegrate. In 1910 Crete declared its independence and in 1911 the Italians, seeing their chance, went to war with the Ottomans, emerging victorious and in possession of Libya, Rhodes and the Dodecanese islands. In 1912 the Balkans erupted and in a brief but bloody war, notable for the ineptitude of the Turkish generals and the dogged gallantry of their troops, Turkey was deprived of most of her remaining European territory.

This woeful procession of military disasters gave the Young Turks the chance they needed to stage their bid for absolute power. Led by Enver, they moved on 23 January 1913. The Prime Minister was ousted and the War Minister murdered. Enver was now *de facto* ruler of Turkey, although the Sultan continued to exercise nominal power through the Grand Vizier.

The growth of the Prussian state in the latter part of the nineteenth century had brought with it not only a spirit of German nationalism and the creation of a formidable army, but also an awareness that Germany had been left behind in the acquisition of overseas territories. Kaiser Wilhelm II was not content to rest on the laurels gained by his grandfather in a series of successful campaigns against Austria in 1866, and France in 1870–1. He was sensitive to the fact that whilst a strong German empire now existed at the heart of Europe, it had done badly in the 'scramble for Africa'. So Germany began to look to the East.

The decay of the Ottoman Empire was being closely watched from

Berlin and the Kaiser saw here a golden opportunity to set himself up as champion of Islam in a great *jihad*, ostensibly to protect the holy places of Mecca and Medina against the infidel, but in fact to establish an overland route from Berlin, via the Balkans, to the heart of the Arab world by means of the Berlin–Baghdad railway. To achieve this, Germany would have to control the Bosphorus and the Dardanelles, preferably indirectly through the agency of a friendly Sublime Porte – the Ottoman court. In return, Germany would guarantee Turkey's position as the bastion of Islam. This would be the lever for subsequent operations against the British Empire, and a springboard for a swoop on the Suez Canal, seizure of which would throttle the main supply route between Britain and India.

From the early 1890s, help of various kinds was lavished on Turkey by Germany. Increasing numbers of Ottoman officers were sent to Prussian military academies, and Turkish students attended German medical schools. German engineers appeared in Turkey to survey and build the Berlin–Baghdad railway. Huge amounts of financial aid were poured into public works. A German military mission was established at Constantinople in the 1880s, and Kaiser Wilhelm paid royal visits to the Sublime Porte in 1889 and 1898. On each of these occasions, no opportunity was lost to stage ceremonial events designed to display German military and naval prowess, and extravagant gifts were presented to the Sultan for the adornment of the new Dolmabahce palace on the banks of the Bosphorus. The post of German ambassador to the Sublime Porte was considered in Berlin to be of the utmost importance and was filled in succession by men of great talent and presence.

Despite this, however, there remained many strong Anglo-Turkish links. There was a large and respected British business community at Constantinople and in other major cities, and British consulates had long existed all over Asia Minor, especially in eastern Turkey where the incumbents were invariably intelligence experts charged with the job of observing every Russian move on the approaches to north-west India: a continuation of the 'great game' of espionage and deception in which Britain had been involved since the 1840s.

The poor showing of the Turkish army in the wars of 1911 with Italy and against the Balkan League of Greece, Bulgaria, Montenegro and Serbia in 1912–13 was the result of bad leadership, shoddy staff-work, and a defective administrative system rather than the fighting qualities of the troops. It was not hard for the Germans therefore, once invited, to re-introduce a military mission in 1913 to put matters right. The presence of a well-organized and efficient Turkish army astride the Bosphorus and the Dardanelles, equipped from German arsenals, was a useful insurance policy as the Berlin–Baghdad railway began to materialize.

The head of mission was a cavalry general, Otto Liman von Sanders, and his team eventually expanded to over 300 picked officers and NCO instructors. They found an army in terminal decay; its officers, inadequately paid and reliant for advancement on patronage and bribery, had in many cases virtually abdicated their duties. Barracks were filthy and disease-ridden and the turnout of all ranks was slovenly. The new arrivals saw that they had much to do and set about their task with all the energy and efficiency of their race.

In 1913 the Turkish army was recruited through conscription. Every year some 240,000 young men became eligible for the draft, of whom up to 50 per cent were rejected as unfit or exempt. Only about 70,000 actually found their way into the training system. Recruits for the infantry and 'train' (the transportation and supplies service) completed two years with the colours in the *Nizam*, or regular army, followed by no less than twenty-three years on the reserve. All other conscripts, including engineers and artillery, served three years with the *Nizam* followed by seventeen years on the reserve. The bulk of the infantry recruits came from Anatolia and were inured to a hard life and poor rations. There was virtually no effective reserve of regular officers, for their pensions were derisory and they soon vanished into civilian life to take up other careers.

One of Liman's chief staff officers was Major-General Hans Kannengiesser, a Prussian to the core, whose memoirs reveal not only his keen professionalism but also his contempt for the Jewish, Greek and Armenian population of Constantinople. He quickly summed up Enver Pasha:

> In the early thirties, of youthful, vigorous appearance, clever and energetic, with quick powers of appreciation and a first-class memory . . . and yet, as compared with our higher leaders, his whole personality did not appear to be such as to give or receive confidence . . . a true oriental. His immovable features always hid a riddle . . . He gave decisions shortly, clearly and with assurance. Whether they were always correct is another matter . . .

In Kannengiesser's opinion, Enver's rapid promotion had prevented him from mastering his profession in depth and he seldom followed up his orders once they had been given. As the Sultan's son-in-law he had adopted a high lifestyle, resented by all who were aware of his relatively humble origins. One manifestation of his newly acquired status was his penchant for careering through the streets in a powerful open car, surrounded by what he termed his 'ADCs' who were in fact no more than heavily armed personal guards.

Although Liman had initially been posted to command a corps of the Turkish army, the French and Russian governments raised such strong objections that his post was changed to that of Inspector-General with the rank of Field Marshal in the Turkish army. Initially the Germans found it difficult to cope with the sloth and corruption of many of the senior Ottoman officers. However, the desire in the army for another chance to fight the hated Greeks, who had so humiliated them in 1912, enabled the mission to plough ahead with a series of drastic reforms. Progress was remarkably swift and after a ruthless winnowing of incompetents, those Turkish officers who genuinely wished to make a better army collaborated enthusiastically with the Germans.

During the summer of 1914 the German battle cruiser *Goeben* and her escort, the light cruiser *Breslau*, had been showing the flag in the eastern Mediterranean under the command of Admiral Wilhelm Souchon. As part of the Kaiser's policy of wooing the Young Turks, the two ships paid a much-publicized visit to Constantinople where for many days they lay, dressed overall, off the German embassy and in full view of the population. At night they were brilliantly lit, whilst a series of dazzling social events, ashore and afloat, combined to give the visit enormous importance.

At this time, a British naval mission under Rear-Admiral Arthur Limpus was concerned with the modernization of the Ottoman navy and the training of its officers and men on British lines, a task similar to Liman's with the Ottoman army. There was good reason for this despite the presence of the German Military Mission. British shipyards were at this time completing work on two super-dreadnoughts, purchased on the stocks by the Turks for delivery in the autumn of 1914. To lighten the load on the national treasury, the Turkish people had been urged to make their own contributions. There had been a massive response to this appeal. Collecting boxes in the streets of Constantinople had been filled over and over again by patriotic citizens who wished to see the restoration of national pride in concrete terms; the sight of these two great men-of-war, to be named *Sultan Osman I* and *Reshidiye*, was calculated by Enver to give the people exactly the boost to their morale he needed if he was to enjoy their unqualified support.

It was therefore an appalling shock when, on 2 August, the British government announced that it had taken possession of both ships for

impressment into the Royal Navy. As the *Agincourt* and *Erin* they
were to serve with the Grand Fleet for the rest of the war. As *real-
politik* it was justifiable, and several other battleships then building
in British yards for foreign navies were treated in a similar way; but
the delicacy of Anglo-Turkish relations at this stage was of crucial
importance and a more diplomatic method of acquiring the ships
was certainly possible. As it was, the decision played into the hands
of the Germans, who were quick to capitalize on it, thanks to their
formidable ambassador to the Sublime Porte.

Baron von Wangenheim was a man of huge physical presence
whose energetic promotion of German interests had swung many
influential Turkish leaders away from their traditional leanings
towards England. He was given a clear field in the highly charged
months of July and August, for Sir Louis Mallet, the British ambassador, remained away from his post on extended holiday until 18
August, and when he returned the situation had gone completely out
of control. Mallet was a nonentity, appointed by the Liberal government to sustain its historic Gladstonian posture of hostility to the
Ottoman Empire, when a forthright but sympathetic envoy in the
Palmerstonian mould would probably have saved the day by out-
facing the Germans and retaining the Turks' affections.

As Europe slid towards war in July, the two German warships
*Goeben* and *Breslau* had slipped out of Constantinople, heading for
the Aegean and the Adriatic. After paying a visit to the Austro-
Hungarian navy they disappeared from view, reappearing dramat-
ically on 3 August off the coast of French North Africa to bombard
key ports despite the ineffectual attempt of the British Mediterranean
Fleet to shadow them. To make matters worse they now doubled
back, crossed the Mediterranean from west to east, and again gave
the Royal Navy the slip before anchoring off the entrance to the
Dardanelles on 10 August. According to treaties in force at the time
they should have been refused entry into the Sea of Marmara, but
German pressure, and the connivance of Enver Pasha, allowed them
in and then on to Constantinople where they dropped anchor once
more. Shortly after, they were given to the Turkish navy; they served
under the Crescent for the rest of the war, their Germans crews still
aboard (self-consciously wearing the fez when ashore) and Souchon
an admiral in the Ottoman navy. This was a brilliant propaganda
move on the part of the Germans, a consolation for the loss of the
*Sultan Osman I* and the *Reshidiye*.

Prior to the arrival of *Goeben* and *Breslau*, the Turkish fleet consisted
of three ancient battleships, some old cruisers, and nearly twenty

destroyers and torpedo boats. In addition there were seven mine-layers, as well as a number of merchant ships hurriedly converted to that role at the insistence of the German naval advisers who had replaced Admiral Limpus, whose mission was courteously dismissed and withdrawn on 9 September. Limpus' knowledge of Turkish military, as well as naval, dispositions was prodigious and it might have seemed logical to appoint him immediately to command the squadron now guarding the exit from the Sea of Marmara and based on several Greek islands which had been made available by Venizelos, the friendly Greek Premier. The authorities in Whitehall thought differently; Limpus, who held admiral's rank in the Ottoman navy as well as a high Turkish decoration, was popular in Constantinople and had managed to stay on amiable terms with Liman's officers as well as with Admiral Souchon. It was felt that to post him where his unique knowledge would be invaluable was perhaps not quite cricket. Instead, he went off to command the Royal Naval Dockyard at Malta.

The defences of the Dardanelles dated back to the fifteenth century but had been partially modernized. Sultan Mehmed's forts at the entrance to the Narrows were as formidable in the early twentieth century as when they were built, and had now been extended to include various coast defence guns of variable quality. In the nineteenth century the Royal Navy had had two close shaves in the Dardanelles and the Sea of Marmara. In 1807 Admiral Duckworth's squadron anchored off Constantinople but retired somewhat precipitately when it seemed that the Turkish fleet was preparing to do battle. Passing back through the Narrows Duckworth gave orders for a ceremonial gun salute to be fired; mistaking its purpose, the Turks responded with a brisk cannonade which caused a number of casualties aboard the British ships. In 1878 the British fleet was back, to show the flag off Constantinople in the face of a Russian threat. Returning to the Aegean, Admiral Hornby's squadron was allowed to leave the Dardanelles unscathed. In his subsequent report, Hornby drew attention to the problems of taking on shore batteries here with naval gunfire:

An enemy in possession of the peninsula would be sure to put guns on commanding points of those cliffs, all the more if the present batteries were destroyed. Such guns could not fail to stop transports and colliers, and would be more difficult for men-of-war to silence. We should have to fire at them with considerable elevation. Shots which were a trifle low would lodge harmlessly in the sandstone cliffs; those a trifle high would fly into the country without the slightest effect on the gunners, except amusement.

This was the first of a number of reports in modern times on the Dardanelles defences the most significant of which was perhaps a joint services staff appreciation drawn up in 1906 by the director of naval intelligence and the British General Staff. This report maintained that, in any operations undertaken to force the Dardanelles,

> Success must be certain. A mere naval raid into the Sea of Marmara being a dangerous and ineffective operation the work will have to be undertaken by a joint naval and military expedition having for its objective the capture of the Gallipoli peninsula and the destruction of the forts which at present deny entrance to and exit from these waters.

Moreover, the report continued:

> The successful conclusion of a military operation against the Gallipoli peninsula must hinge upon the ability of the fleet . . . to dominate the Turkish defences with gunfire and to crush their field troops during that period of helplessness which exists while an army is in the actual process of disembarkation, but also to cover the advance of the troops once ashore, until they could gain a firm foothold and establish themselves upon the high ground in rear of the coast defences of the Dardanelles . . .

It was doubtful, the General Staff thought, that the fleet could actually do this. The navy, whilst prepared to agree with this, were inclined to think that the soldiers overrated the risk and deliberately underplayed the amount of help they could expect from the fleet. Both were agreed that unaided fleet action 'was to be deprecated'. Success, however, the report concluded, would constitute 'a death-blow to the Sultan even if he were to quit Constantinople'.

The report, surely of crucial value, was duly passed from department to department, initialled, signed, and filed away. Nobody gave a thought to any possible requirement for a joint service command structure as a result of it.

In 1914 the British Military Attaché at Constantinople, Lieutenant-Colonel F. Cunliffe-Owen, had also staked out the ground and sent an unofficial but highly accurate report and assessment of the Turkish defences to the Director of Military Operations at the War Office on 6 September. Its arrival was fortuitous, as Winston Churchill was already calling on the naval staff at the Admiralty for appreciations and assessments of the chances of success were a naval force to try and rush the Narrows and enter the Sea of Marmara.

Cunliffe-Owen's covering letter was of enormous help as a mind-clearing exercise. He pointed out that by the time his report reached London the defences would be appreciably stronger as the result of energetic German activity. Improvements were daily being made to the present defence works and Cunliffe-Owen knew that additional guns were on their way from Germany. He went on to draw attention to the strategic complexity of the situation; if Turkey entered the war on the side of the Central Powers it could be with an emphasis on operations against Bulgaria. Turkey had a score to pay here, as the Bulgarian army had performed well against the Ottomans in 1912 and a revenge match was sought. Cunliffe-Owen added that the more directions in which British power was diverted, the better it would be for the Central Powers. Britain was faced with a number of options, all of which depended on which way the various Balkan nations jumped. Whether such action should be directed against the Dardanelles, however, was doubtful. There were more profitable areas where Turkey could be attacked, where it would be impossible for her to reinforce her garrisons in the face of overwhelming British naval superiority: in the Persian Gulf, along the Red Sea, or in Syria. The overland lines of communication from Constantinople to all of these were difficult and slow.

If, however, continued Cunliffe-Owen, the decision was taken to go for the Dardanelles, the problem would be whether to use naval forces alone or in conjunction with land action. It had to be assumed that in the short term it would be impossible completely to neutral-ize the forts, and that the fleet would have to risk any minefields and steam through at high speed, going for Constantinople in the hope that it would capitulate, enabling the fleet to refuel in safety. There was no threat from the Turkish fleet, but the two modern German warships would have to be eliminated, and the guaranteed destruc-tion of *Goeben* called for a super-dreadnought or at least a battle cruiser, neither of which was on station in the eastern Mediterranean or likely to be so for some months. If, however, it proved impossible to reduce the defences of Constantinople, the fleet would be highly vulnerable once inside the Marmara, for any surviving coastal defences at the Narrows would easily prevent colliers, oilers and supply ships from passing through to victual the fleet.

If the Dardanelles were to be opened permanently, concluded Cunliffe-Owen, military force would have to be applied at or near Besika Bay and at Kilid Bahr. Once a force was securely ashore, the navy would be able to proceed with confidence through the Narrows and on to Constantinople. He pointed out that the Greeks considered themselves capable of bringing this off; but Greek support carried many political qualifications and in the end they were to remain neutral.

Although Cunliffe-Owen's report was circulating in Whitehall in October 1914, neither it nor the joint services report of 1906 was produced in 1915 when the Mediterranean Expeditionary Force was launched; and its commander, Sir Ian Hamilton, was not even aware of their existence when he left London in March 1915 to assume command of the force.

# 4

# Probing the Defence

Arm! Arm! It is – it is – the cannon's opening roar.

Byron, *Childe Harold*

BRITAIN AND TURKEY were not officially at war with each other until November 1914, and events in the eastern Mediterranean and Aegean placed the Royal Navy in an ambiguous position. The British naval mission having been withdrawn in September and the *Goeben* and *Breslau* safely at anchor under the guns of Constantinople, the Narrows were closed to all warships. Merchant shipping of the neutral powers was still passing through the Dardanelles, and a quantity of British and French merchant ships were on the far side of the Bosphorus, engaged in the Black Sea trade. From 15 August the Turks, with German technical assistance, had been laying mines in the Dardanelles. German sailors were sent down from Constantinople to help man the coast defences there, and Liman von Sanders, as the local military commander, pressed successfully for the full closure of the Straits, which was done on 1 October.

Although Turkey and Russia were not yet in a state of war, Admiral Souchon's ships precipitated it, at the instigation of Enver, by sailing into the Black Sea on 24 October. On the 26th, under the Ottoman flag, *Goeben*, *Breslau* and several Turkish warships attacked Russian Black Sea naval bases, achieving total surprise; Russia could not ignore such a blatant act and the two countries were officially at war with each other on 2 November. Twenty-four hours earlier Britain and France had begun hostilities against the Ottoman Empire. Less than a week later the Sultan, as Caliph of all Islam, proclaimed the *Jihad*, or Holy War, against France and Britain; this misfired, for the Islamic leaders in Mecca and Medina declined to join in, thus robbing the act of all its spiritual power.

After mobilization in the autumn of 1914 the Turkish army was deployed to its war stations. Marshal Liman von Sanders, restored to a field command, was in charge of the 1st Army of ten regular divisions, three second-line divisions and three cavalry brigades, all deployed in European Turkey. The 2nd Army was deployed along the Asiatic shores of the Sea of Marmara and down the Aegean coast as far as Smyrna. It comprised four regular and up to three reserve divisions. The 3rd Army, of eleven regular divisions, was assigned to the sensitive Turco-Russian border in the Caucasus; the infantry element there was backed by cavalry and large numbers of Kurdish irregulars whose loyalty was questionable. Turkish Palestine, stretching from Aleppo down to the Egyptian border, was garrisoned by the 4th Army, consisting of seven regular divisions and one reserve, and a horde of Arab irregulars whose fidelity to the Ottoman cause was as suspect as that of the Kurds. Further afield, there were two divisions in the Yemen, poised to attack the vital British coaling and signal station at Aden, two in Mesopotamia, and other garrisons in the Hedjaz.

At various points in the empire were ancient barracks and fortresses, each with its complement of troops; there was also a gendarmerie, found throughout the empire and tasked with peacekeeping duties, recruited from former soldiers of good conduct. Some of these, with one infantry division, comprised the garrison of the Gallipoli peninsula at the outbreak of war.

The sheer size of this cumbersome empire and its lack of modern communications posed an immense problem for the Turkish high command. Sea transport offered the best hope of sustaining the garrisons farthest from Constantinople, but once the Dardanelles had been closed and blockaded by the Allies, all logistic resupply would need to be made overland, using the rickety railway system, now undergoing urgent upgrading by German engineers. The road system was in a deplorable condition as a result of years of neglect. In 1914 the Berlin–Baghdad railway had reached Stamboul on the European side of the Bosphorus and continued from Scutari on the opposite shore down to the south. However, there were several large gaps where the tunnels through the Taurus mountains – requiring formidable engineering resources – were not yet completed, and this required the off-loading of rail wagons on to wholly inadequate road transport for the slow journey over the mountains.

At this stage, and until early in 1915, there were no British land forces within easy reach of the Dardanelles, and when landing parties were required to complete the destruction wrought by naval gunfire, these had to be provided from the fleet. In Egypt, a large British and empire garrison under General Sir John Maxwell was effectively policing a nation which was still theoretically part of the Ottoman Empire but which, since the 1880s, had been firmly under British control. In the face of rising Egyptian nationalist activity, Britain declared Egypt to be a British protectorate early in 1915, appointed a more complaisant Khedive to replace the overtly anti-British Abbas Hilmi, and prepared to meet a Turkish offensive from the Sinai desert against the Suez Canal. Maxwell dealt with this, then with an incursion into western Egypt by the forces of Sayed Ahmed, known as the Senussi, and with rising civil unrest in the Sudan. Maxwell's resources had been depleted by the withdrawal of his regular units – an infantry brigade and a cavalry regiment – to the United Kingdom on the outbreak of war, to be replaced by inexperienced territorial formations, some units of the Indian army, and finally by the Australian and New Zealand Imperial forces, supposedly *en route* to fight in Europe, but now disembarked at Port Said and held in Egypt for possible operational use in the Eastern theatre.

With the outbreak of hostilities between Britain and Turkey naval operations against the Narrows and their defences could begin in earnest. Placed off the Dardanelles to deny the *Goeben* and *Breslau* access to the Aegean and eastern Mediterranean, the Anglo-French fleet under the command of Vice-Admiral Sackville Carden was steadily growing in strength, even though its heavy ships were all obsolete pre-dreadnoughts. On 3 November 1914 Churchill ordered Carden to bombard the outer forts of the Dardanelles. In the course of a ten-minute cannonade, the British battleships, manoeuvring cautiously at extreme range, secured a number of direct hits on the fortifications.

The immediate results of the bombardment were spectacular, mainly because the Turks had failed to keep their ammunition below ground: a direct hit on Sedd-el-Bahr fort detonated not only the ready-use ammunition carelessly stacked in the open but also the main magazine. Severe damage was also caused to the batteries at Kum Kale. However, despite the ostensible success the chief result of the attack, undertaken against the advice of Admiral Limpus who had predicted its effect, was to alert the Turks and their German advisers to the threat on their doorstep, and to cause an immediate acceleration of work in hand on the defences.

Gathered also off the Straits, at its forward base on the Greek island of Tenedos – one of the islands made available by the assent of the Greek premier Venizelos – was a floating submarine depot. The development of the submarine arm in the Royal Navy had owed much to Fisher, whose fascination with the torpedo had driven him naturally to investigate the use of submersible vessels as their means of delivery. Another officer closely involved in submarine development and, as fate would have it, with operations in the Dardanelles, was Captain Roger Keyes. As a Commander on half pay in 1903 Keyes had been sent by Prince Louis of Battenberg as Naval Attaché to Rome, and thereafter to Vienna, Athens and Constantinople. Keyes was an active and energetic officer whose lively and impetuous spirit would have instantly commended him to Nelson. Having success-fully completed his tour and gained promotion to Captain he returned to London to be warmly congratulated by Fisher, then First Sea Lord. He was clearly an officer with a future.

Two years later, attending a court ball at Buckingham Palace, Keyes was painfully snubbed by Fisher, but had no idea why. He asked for and was granted an interview with the Naval Secretary, the arbiter of promotion to higher rank. To his dismay he was told that he had been passed over for further promotion on the instructions of the First Sea Lord because Fisher believed he was a supporter of Lord Charles Beresford and had given confidential information to the *Times* correspondents in Vienna and Rome. This was a mistake; Beresford's Naval Secretary was an officer named Keys and Fisher, when told of this matter, had not bothered to check the spelling. The error was conveyed to Fisher and no more was said. Keyes got his ship, but Fisher, true to his lifelong adage: 'Never explain, never apol-ogize' (which he had adopted from the great Benjamin Jowett, Master of Balliol), made no attempt to do either.

In 1910 a series of naval exercises and war games took place in which the embryonic submarine force was given a role. After these exercises Keyes was given the post of Inspector-General of Sub-marines, though he was not a torpedo specialist. Few senior officers at the Admiralty realized the potential of the submarine. As a result, early British developments in this field had been cautious at a time when the French, Germans and Italians were pressing boldly ahead with larger designs. The British A- and B- (or Holland-) class boats were primarily designed for harbour defence and consequently lacked endurance and speed. They also carried fewer torpedoes than their continental equivalents.

Even though Keyes was no technocrat but a self-proclaimed 'salt horse', he knew how to pick a team and his early officer selections set the tone for what rapidly became an élite branch of the service. Following Fisher's enforced retirement in 1910, Keyes found it difficult to make progress in the face of obscurantism in high places. In 1911, though, matters changed for the better with the arrival of Winston Churchill as First Lord of the Admiralty. Keyes now saw that larger submarines were essential; their future lay far beyond harbour defence and operations in shallow coastal waters, a point already appreciated by the German naval planners.

Up till now, Vickers had monopolized British submarine design and construction, but Keyes had seen the products of French and Italian builders and was impressed. He terminated the Vickers contract and charged Scott's of Greenock with the construction of prototypes based on the Italian Fiat design. He also had some old cruisers converted as submarine depots, with engineering and electrical workshops, magazines, torpedo repair shops and adequate living accommodation for submarine crews when not on patrol. He now had the enthusiastic backing of Churchill, who bombarded him with suggestions, including one on nomenclature; the First Lord thought that 'shoal' was more appropriate than 'flotilla' for a group of submarines. The idea did not appeal to the admirals and was quietly dropped.

In October 1914, during a visit to the submarine depot at Gosport, Fisher railed at Keyes for not building enough submarines. All his vindictiveness was restored and he immediately set about the removal of Keyes from the submarine branch. 'Why can't that fellow Keyes go to sea and fight?' he was heard to shout. Yet within days his mood had swung, and he wrote Keyes a charmingly conciliatory letter ending, 'On no account think I have any designs on you.' Keyes wrote a bluntly phrased reply. He now knew Fisher for what he was – a bully who respected those who stood up to him but despised anyone who flinched in his presence. A few days after this, the two met in a corridor at the Admiralty. Fisher seized Keyes by the lapels and shook him affectionately. 'I got your beautiful letter . . . !' Shortly after this strange encounter, Keyes was posted to the Mediterranean Fleet as chief of staff to Admiral Carden; there he was to play a significant part in the drama yet to unfold.

The first Allied submarine now to take on the defences of the Narrows was the obsolete B11, commanded by Lieutenant Norman Holbrook. Her crew consisted of one further officer and 13 ratings. She had been launched in 1906 and was thus a product of Fisher's electrifying years at the Admiralty in charge of the naval building programme; even by the standards of 1906, however, she compared poorly with the submersibles already in French and Italian service. She was propelled on the surface to a maximum speed of 12 knots by a petrol engine. At this speed she had a range of over 750 miles, and this could be extended by cruising at a more economical speed. Submerged, she was driven by battery-powered electric motors which could give a top speed underwater of 6 knots for three hours, or 4.5 knots for eight hours. Her armament comprised two tubes in the bow for 18-inch torpedoes, and one reload for each tube.

Living conditions aboard these early boats were squalid. When cruising on the surface they rolled abominably, and the fume-laden atmosphere below rapidly induced seasickness in even the most hardened sailor. There was a continual stench of vomit, urine, human excrement (for the plumbing was extremely primitive), petrol fumes, chlorine gas from the batteries stowed under the deck, and unwashed human beings, jammed into a metal tube packed with machinery, whose extreme external length was no more than 142 feet.

Officers lived in such close proximity to the ratings and petty officers that normal conventions of naval life did not obtain. Instead of hierarchical discipline there was that highly developed form which comes when every man, regardless of rank or function, is directly responsible in many ways for the lives of his fellow men. This bond creates an *esprit de corps* dependent on the highest standards of man-management and professionalism. All ranks in the submarine service were volunteers and carefully chosen. In the absence of the elaborate and usually effective psychological tests used in the Second World War for personnel selection, the methods in 1914 were rough and ready, and in the few cases where officers and men failed to live up to the standards demanded, they were returned to the surface fleet.

The training of would-be submarine commanders was a case in point. At that time there was no intensive 'Perisher' course in which candidates could be tested almost to destruction, first in simulators ashore, then under water. Preliminary training until 1914 was carried out in the primitive A-class boats, which had peculiar and often unpredictable buoyancy characteristics. When practising attacks there were no computers for working out the target's speed or course and all had to be done by eye, with brief glimpses through the periscope. All attacks were made from a firing position off the practice target's bow. Lieutenant Oswald Hallifax, an early volunteer for the submarine service, reckoned that if one was a good shot after partridge, and accustomed to allowing subconsciously for the correct

amount of 'lead' when aiming in front of the bird, it should be possible to shine as a submarine commander.

In preparation for *B11*'s first, and highly dramatic mission from
Tenedos – where her depot ships was based – Lieutenant Holbrook
had been carefully briefed on the Dardanelles defences and the latest
known minefield situation, and his boat was fitted with makeshift
guards designed to keep his hydroplanes free of mine cables. The
underwater defences at the entrance to the Narrows consisted of ten
rows of mines. The British naval intelligence estimate was that there
were a total of 373 mines of various sorts, moored at depths from five
to nine metres. In addition, wire nets had been suspended from floats
across the narrowest part of the Straits.

Ashore, eleven forts guarded the Narrows, the largest of these
being at Chanak and Kilid Bahr, on the Asiatic and European sides
respectively. Searchlights played on the waters at night and patrol
boats carrying explosive charges constantly moved back and to,
watching the tell-tale floats which would show if a submarine had
become ensnared in the nets. There was also the danger posed by
mine cables, for if a submarine's conning tower or hydroplanes
tangled with these, the mine to which they were attached could be
dragged down violently on to the superstructure and detonated.

Very early on 4 December, *B11* slipped her moorings at Tenedos
and motored towards the entrance to the Dardanelles. Holbrook and
his crew had all written farewell letters to their families. As dawn
broke, *B11* dived; she was four miles short of the entrance to the
Narrows, and Holbrook had postponed this moment as long as possible, knowing that he had to breast the 3- or 4-knot current which
flows perpetually from the Sea of Marmara into the Aegean, and that
it was essential to conserve his batteries for use in emergency. After
a while, it was clear that something was amiss with one of the
forward hydroplanes, and Holbrook was obliged to surface in order
to examine it. One of the makeshift cable guards had been dislodged,
and had to be jettisoned. This took time, and as daylight broke, the
submarine was spotted and forced to dive. Holbrook then ordered all
hands to breakfast; the two officers devoured a lobster and the
ratings fed off a York ham. Maintaining a depth of 50 feet, the battery
was one-third run down by 8 a.m. and *B11* was abreast of the first
known minefield.

Looking through his periscope, Holbrook now spotted a splendid
target; the ancient Turkish battleship *Messudieh*, moored as a floating
battery in the shallows of Sari Sighlar Bay less than two miles from
Chanak itself. To get into a firing position, *B11* had to pass no less

than five rows of mines. Holbrook closed to within a few hundred yards of his victim. He had already been spotted, as the depth of water under his keel was only a few feet, and the constantly changing density of the waters in Sari Sighlar Bay, due to layers of fresh and salt water, made it impossible to catch a proper trim. This meant that the submarine kept breaking the surface as it approached the target and fire was opened on it from a variety of weapons including every gun on the *Messudieh* and ashore which could be brought to bear. The defences were now fully alerted, and motor launches were converging on the scene from all directions. Both torpedoes hit the battleship and she immediately began to roll over, her staunch gunners continuing to fire at *B11*'s periscope even as their ship turned turtle.

The return to Tenedos was eventful. Holbrook tried to dive but hit bottom at only 30 feet, with his conning tower appearing frequently above the surface. At last he reached deeper water and steered for the open sea. At one point *B11* grounded on a shoal and was under heavy fire again from shore batteries at close range. In all she was submerged for nine hours, four times her designed underwater endurance, and the batteries were almost dead when Holbrook finally brought her to the surface and headed for Tenedos where a hero's welcome awaited him and his crew. He was awarded the Victoria Cross, the first to be given to a submariner; his first-lieutenant gained the DSO, and every rating in the crew received the DSM.

The curtain had now been raised on the Dardanelles; the Turks and their German allies were fully alerted to the Allies' likely intentions and at this stage very conscious of the deficiencies in their defences. All that was lacking was a clearly defined plan of attack which would take advantage of the disarray in the Turkish camp and seize the great opportunity offered to the Anglo-French alliance.

# 5

# *Closing In*

It is a mystery why most people, then and since,
assumed that the fall of Constantinople would lead
to the defeat of Germany.
A. J. P. Taylor, *English History 1914–1945* (1965)

AS THE AUTUMN of 1914 drew on, it had become apparent in Whitehall
that the direction of the war – if indeed it could be said to have any
direction – was proceeding in an eccentric manner. By appointing
Kitchener War Minister, Asquith had made what appeared to be an
exceptionally good choice. The presence, at the very centre of government, of the country's most revered soldier had a calming effect
on the nation. Unfortunately, the power of the Field Marshal's character combined with his idiosyncratic working style soon gave the
impression, confirmed by almost daily events, that Kitchener had
unconsciously revived the defunct post of Commander-in-Chief. The
Chief of the Imperial General Staff, Sir James Wolfe Murray, a
respected and intelligent soldier, was completely overshadowed by
Kitchener and became no more than a cipher, remaining silent at the
meetings of the War Council.

Kitchener, never a man to delegate, was constitutionally incapable
of entrusting his plans to others and equally averse to paperwork.
Very soon, the increasing complexity of the war, and the pressing
demands of theatre commanders in distant parts of the globe, over-
loaded that great intellect, and the War Minister became incapable of
taking a detached view of his many problems; they coalesced into
one great puzzle, with which he struggled manfully, but alone. He
had no team of enthusiastic young officers to help him, as in India a
decade before: Frank Maxwell had gone back to his regiment, then to
command a British infantry battalion, and was to fall at Ypres in 1917
to a sniper's bullet when leading a brigade. Victor Brooke had

returned to the gunners. The best of the army's trained staff officers had gone to France with the BEF, where their professionalism had helped to save French's little army from destruction in the opening weeks; then most of them had returned to fill the gaps in their regiments left by Mons, Le Cateau, the Marne and the First Battle of Ypres; and by Christmas 1914 most of them were dead. The War Office had to make do with officers called out of retirement and whoever else showed any aptitude for the laborious staff work required to keep the BEF in the field, mobilize the reserves, equip and train Kitchener's burgeoning New Armies, and decide on priorities for the many outbreaks of hostilities in places as far apart as West and East Africa, Egypt, Mesopotamia, New Guinea (where the Australians had undertaken to deal with the German colonists and their military) and even Ireland, where nationalist unrest had boiled up early in 1914, and again when the Home Rule Bill was postponed owing to the outbreak of war later that year.

The War Council, set up at the outbreak of war, was the government's executive board for the prosecution of the war against Germany and her allies. Chaired by the Prime Minister, it met at 10 Downing Street in the Cabinet Room. Its composition varied from time to time but invariably included the First Lord of the Admiralty, the Secretary of State for War, the two service chiefs, the Foreign Secretary, and certain politicians, not necessarily from the government benches, empanelled for various reasons. To one side sat the watchful Lieutenant-Colonel Maurice Hankey, Secretary to the Council.

From the start the War Council displayed a fatal weakness: despite its array of political and administrative talents, it lacked firm guidance in the prosecution of the war. In the absence of a central defence staff in Whitehall, with executive power over the combined services, direction of the war effort now lay in the hands of a diverse committee whose members fought incessantly for what they saw as their own service or political interests. Seeing that there was no single leader capable of imposing his will on the War Council or of devising a global strategy, Churchill took it on himself to formulate a comprehensive plan that would unite several political and strategic aims. At a meeting of the War Council on 25 November, he raised the issue of an indirect approach against the Central Powers by means of an attack on Constantinople which would knock their new ally Turkey out of the war, confound German strategic aims in the Near East, and open the passage to and from the Black Sea to Allied shipping. This would in turn permit Russia to export her grain surpluses and thus obtain gold to sustain her war effort. Less easy to implement was the idea that vast supplies of munitions and armaments could then be passed through to the Black Sea ports by the Western Allies. At this stage of the war they were themselves desperately short of artillery, shells, small arms and virtually every sort of warlike stores; furthermore, there were great problems over the lack of standardization of gun and rifle calibres between the Allies.

Although Churchill's case for an immediate naval attempt to force the Dardanelles was rejected, Kitchener was becoming increasingly disenchanted by the prospect of an extended stalemate on the Western Front, for which General Sir John French and the Allied High Command had no solution other than the mounting of successive massed frontal assaults backed by colossal artillery barrages. French, like many of the British cavalry generals, continued to believe that once the luckless infantry had breached the main German defensive lines, the cavalry could be released to pour through into the enemy rear areas, using shock action to sustain their momentum in a relentless pursuit to the banks of the Rhine. This chimera was to guide British strategic doctrine for the next four years.

Churchill continued to push his case for action in the Dardanelles. In doing so he was following a line of strategy which he was to pursue again in 1943 when attacking Sicily and Italy, 'the soft underbelly of the Axis'. This concept of the 'indirect approach' was not new to Churchill, having been pursued triumphantly by his illustrious forebear John Churchill, 1st Duke of Marlborough, in a series of victorious campaigns, most notably that of 1704 which culminated on the field of Blenheim.

Although the subject of Gallipoli had been aired several times during the autumn, no clear evaluation had been reached. There was doubt as to the value of a diversionary attack at the Dardanelles, or anywhere else in the Turkish orbit, until the positions of various other Balkan states had become clear. Such operations would be fraught with hazards, and a purely naval attack, whilst it might temporarily suppress the batteries guarding the Narrows and thus permit warships to break into the Sea of Marmara, gave no guarantee that they could be permanently destroyed. This would certainly entail the use of strong landing parties equipped with sufficient explosives to destroy the defence works as well as any surviving guns in them. Furthermore, the replenishment of a fleet operating at large in the Sea of Marmara would be impossible if even a few guns survived ashore, as they would be able to prevent the fleet's supporting colliers, oilers and supply ships from getting through.

General Sir John French continued to maintain almost daily pressure on Kitchener to send all reinforcements to the Western Front. The most important of these was the 29th Infantry Division – a division which consisted of regular army units brought home from India and elsewhere at the outbreak of war and replaced in their garrison duties by territorials. By Christmas 1914 the necessary redeployments had been made, and the division's units were installed at the very centre of England, around Coventry, Rugby and Leamington Spa, fully equipped and established for action on the Western Front. Sir John French was certain that this division, the last intact regular formation in existence, would shortly be his, and constantly pestered the War Office for information on its progress.

However, early in January 1915 the War Council received an urgent message from the Russian commander-in-chief, Grand Duke Nicholas, via the British ambassador in Petrograd, which redirected attention to Constantinople. The Western Allies were requested to stage a 'demonstration' against the Turks in order to divert their attention from the Caucasus, and permit the Russian war effort to concentrate on the threat posed by the Germans and their Austro-Hungarian allies. In retrospect it is hard to see why the Russian high command had suddenly panicked. Although they had suffered appalling losses in East Prussia in the opening battles of September 1914 the imperial armies were at that moment destroying a large Turkish army under the personal command of Enver Pasha, who had rashly attempted to invade the Caucasus in the depths of winter against the advice of the German military mission who correctly forecast a military calamity. The War Council, however, felt that notice had to be taken if Russia's help as an ally was to be retained.

Although he was silent in the Council, Fisher had plenty to say to his colleagues and friends during the winter of 1914–15. His difficulty lay in reconciling his private views, which were for an operation in the Baltic, with those he had to air in public. On 3 January he sent Churchill a typically fervent memorandum:

> *I consider the attack on Turkey holds the field* but *only* if it's *immediate!* However, it won't be! We shall decide on a futile bombardment of the Dardanelles . . . What good resulted from the last bombardment? Did it move a single Turk from the Caucasus? And so the war goes on!

Fisher now fielded a wilder idea: to send a force of 75,000 experienced troops from the Western Front to the Dardanelles. The expeditionary force would embark at Marseilles with a cover story that it was destined for the garrisoning of Egypt, but would be landed at Besika Bay whilst the Greeks landed at Gallipoli. This would drag Bulgaria into the war: her army would make for Constantinople whilst the Russians, Serbs and Romanians attacked Austria, which would quickly succumb. A force of old battleships would then enter the Narrows. In his habitual style, Fisher ended his dissertation 'as the great Napoleon said: "*Celerity! Without it, failure!*"' Events were to prove him right.

At the War Council meeting on 8 January 1915, Churchill carefully reintroduced the idea of an operation in the Dardanelles. He had been in touch with Admiral Carden, who reported that whilst it was not practicable to rush the Dardanelles it might be possible to reduce the forts progressively by gunfire, using landing parties from the fleet to complete their destruction. Carden's outline plan would require three modern capital ships in addition to a squadron of pre-dreadnoughts, the loss of which would not cripple the fleet. Churchill now proposed that the brand-new super-dreadnought, HMS *Queen Elizabeth*, about to go to sea for gunnery trials off Gibraltar, could carry these out safely as part of the Dardanelles bombardment group, providing that certain safeguards were applied; she was expected to join the Grand Fleet as its flagship and no chances could be taken over her safety. Lloyd George, Chancellor of the Exchequer, approved and Kitchener thought it was worth a try. The bombardment could always be abandoned if results were not obtained.

It is clear that in their acceptance of plans for using naval gunnery against the Dardanelles forts, the War Council were being swayed more by Churchill's eloquence than by practical considerations. Churchill had been greatly impressed by the ease with which the Germans had reduced the strong Belgian frontier fortresses, and those defending Antwerp, in the opening months of the war. Here, the German guns had been large howitzers, whose low muzzle velocity gave them a high trajectory which brought their huge shells almost vertically down on to the target. In most cases, effective fire had been brought to bear on the forts after no more than five ranging rounds, and four or five direct hits had been enough to force the garrisons to surrender.

Naval gunnery was a different matter. Apart from the inherent problems of directing fire off a moving gun platform, the guns of even the pre-dreadnoughts were of relatively high velocity and flat trajectory. Whilst they could wreak spectacular damage against the outside walls of a fortified target, the guns inside stood a good

chance of survival. Naval gunnery, in short, was not the answer to
the Dardanelles forts. The fleet no longer had the equivalent of the
bomb ketch of Nelson's day, with its high-trajectory mortar. The
only way to put the forts out of the way would be by the landing of
troops in considerable numbers. Despite this, however, the War
Council directed the Admiralty to draw up plans for a purely naval
operation, with Constantinople as the ultimate objective. Troops
were to be earmarked, however, in case the naval operation went
wrong.

The land forces immediately available in Egypt consisted of the
42nd (East Lancashire) territorial division and the Australian and
New Zealand expeditionary troops who had been halted there when
it appeared that the Turks were about to launch an offensive against
the Suez Canal. This had duly materialized early in February under
the competent leadership of the German Colonel Baron von
Kressenstein, and some Turks even managed to get across between
Lake Timsah and the Great Bitter Lake. Kressenstein's attack was
flung back, however, with the aid of fire from British and French
warships, and retired back across the Sinai desert. The engagement
on the banks of the Canal provided a baptism of fire for the territorials of the 42nd Division and for some of the Australian and New
Zealand troops. All performed with commendable steadiness in this
action.

Churchill now also made the Royal Naval Division available for
the Dardanelles operation, placing Kitchener under pressure to
release the 29th Division; Sir John French came across from France to
contest this. On 19 February the War Council met again. Kitchener,
having learned that the Turks were in full flight away from the Suez
Canal, released the Australians and New Zealanders in Egypt,
ordered that the 29th Division be transported to the Greek island of
Lemnos within the next ten days, and that the 42nd (East Lancashire)
territorial division also be sent from Egypt.

General Maxwell, the Commander-in-Chief in Egypt, seeing the
gradual erosion of his bloated command, became greatly perturbed.
On 20 February, without reference to any other member of the War
Cabinet, Kitchener had sent him a telegram to say that a force was
being assembled on Lemnos to co-operate with the fleet's operations
in the Dardanelles and to provide garrisons for any forts captured as
the result of naval landings; there were already two battalions'-
worth of marines at Lemnos and these were shortly to be followed
by the rest of the Royal Naval Division. Maxwell was instructed to
warn the Australian and New Zealand force in Egypt to stand by for

land operations in support of the fleet. Further troopships were being sent from England to Alexandria for their move from Egypt to Lemnos.

Maxwell contacted Carden, who sent him a reply on 23 February to the effect that he had been told to plan a landing force of 10,000 men for use if needed, but had received no further instructions from London. At this stage, Carden was considering landing his 10,000 men at Sedd-el-Bahr on the southernmost tip of the Gallipoli peninsula and advancing as far to the east as possible. Estimating that the Turks had up to 40,000 men on Gallipoli, he was not enthusiastic about the project. Carden was a cautious man at the best of times and was already showing symptoms that may have played an important role in his ultimate collapse; with awesome responsibilities thrust upon him when he was not in the best of health, he proved incapable of giving Maxwell a decisive reply.

There was now a scramble for shipping to take the 29th Division and its guns, wagons and horses out to the Aegean. The Admiralty placed somewhat belated orders for special transports and lighters for the conveyance of a force of up to 50,000 men to wherever they might be needed in the eastern Mediterranean, and officers were despatched to Greece and the Levant in order to purchase tugs and other small craft for use in landing operations.

Kitchener now began to waver. He was still under enormous pressure from French to send the 29th Division to the BEF and came back to the War Council to say that he thought that two divisions should suffice for the Dardanelles and that it should not be necessary to send units from the United Kingdom. He professed to be worried about recent German successes against the Russians in East Prussia, which could release huge resources for use against the BEF. Churchill attempted to reassure him by saying that it might not be necessary to land troops, merely to have them 'within hail', but he still pressed for the 29th Division, realizing that the Naval Division, the Lancashire territorials and the untried Australian and New Zealand contingents needed the stiffening of an élite professional formation to ensure victory against the Turks and their German mentors.

The meeting ended without a firm decision; when asked for his opinion as CIGS, Wolfe Murray had no suggestion to make. All that was decided was to send transports to Alexandria for use by the Australians, and that the 29th Division would be sent to the eastern Mediterranean only if required. Maxwell reported back to Kitchener that Carden's signal 'strikes me as being so helpless that I feel unless military authorities take the initiative, no progress is likely to be made'. This telegram was in Kitchener's hand when the War Council met on 24 February.

On this day the debate continued, again without a firm decision despite Kitchener declaring that the army must see the business through if the fleet found its task impossible. The discussion now swung to the forcing of the Bosphorus, assuming that the fleet had got through the Dardanelles. It would be easy, said Kitchener, and the meeting went on. Kitchener asked Churchill if he still considered that land forces would be needed and was told that whilst a full-scale land attack was not comtemplated, a combination of mines and undetected batteries ashore might require the use of strong landing parties. Churchill admitted the presence of strong Turkish forces in Thrace and that an element of risk attended the operations now proposed, but that it was less than that of sending the BEF to France in August 1914.

Kitchener was now less anxious about the situation on the Eastern Front, where better news was coming from the Russians. But there was nothing to alter the case for immediate help for Russia in the form of a strong diversionary operation. Kitchener still refused to make a decision over the 29th Division and revealed his innate cynicism when asked by Asquith if the Australians, New Zealanders and the Royal Naval Division alone were good enough. Kitchener answered that they were 'Quite good enough if a cruise in the Sea of Marmara was all that was contemplated'. The decision over despatching the 29th was postponed yet again; instead, Kitchener agreed to send General Sir William Birdwood – nominated to command the Australian and New Zealand Army Corps following its arrival in Egypt – over to join Carden and the fleet in order to assess the problems facing any attempt to land on the Gallipoli peninsula.

Maxwell grew daily more confused by the telegrams streaming from the War Office. First he was told that the Australians, New Zealanders and marines would have the job of attacking the forts from the rear. Then Kitchener signalled him again; the operation would be carried out mainly by the fleet; its success would probably cause the defenders to withdraw from the peninsula; until the naval part of the operation had met with success it would not be prudent to land a military force of 10,000 against the reputed garrison of 40,000 Turks. In anticipation, the Australians and New Zealanders were to be held ready for embarkation in Egypt, whilst the naval division stood by on Lemnos. On top of this Kitchener further confounded Maxwell, now thoroughly bemused, by telling him that troops would only be used in minor landings; on the same day he

signalled Birdwood telling him to prepare his troops for rapid landings and re-embarkations on hostile shores. Maxwell, exasperated
and baffled, signalled back that he was 'considerably in the dark, as
I have no knowledge of the deep study which must have been made
of the whole question of the forcing of the Dardanelles by the
Imperial General Staff and the Navy for many years, the result of
which must be in the War Office and résumé of which I would much
like'.

At this stage, Birdwood, the ANZAC commander, was under the
clear impression that he was shortly to be confirmed as commander-
in-chief of all the land forces in any campaign to be mounted on
Gallipoli and it was in this belief that he discussed matters with the
now increasingly unsettled Carden. Back in London, another sailor
was getting increasingly uneasy. Fisher had always wanted to mount
a diversionary attack in the Baltic, where the effect on Germany
would be much more direct, and where it would also have the advantage of being within range of the Grand Fleet's massive support
if anything went wrong. The idea of detaching even elderly pre-
dreadnoughts to the eastern Mediterranean was anathema to him, as
it also meant providing a host of escorts, light cruisers, destroyers
and minesweepers, all of which were as gold to Jellicoe, the commander of the Grand Fleet.

The whole central direction of the war was now slithering out of
control as various pressure groups lobbied furiously for their own
interests. On the inhospitable island of Lemnos, Rear-Admiral
Wemyss, the next admiral in seniority after Carden in the Aegean
theatre, had been directed to set up a naval base and launching point
for any military operations against Gallipoli. He and his staff quickly
made two unpalatable discoveries: there was very little water on the
island, and although, in Mudros Bay, it boasted one of the finest
natural harbours in the region, with adequate depth of water and
anchorages for a large fleet, there were no berths at which ships
could load and unload; all transhipment would have to be by lighter
and workboat, and these were non-existent at this stage. Looking
ahead, Wemyss could see many problems piling up. If a large force
was to be set ashore on Gallipoli it would require all the base facilities needed by an army, as Egypt was too distant to sustain a force
which might soon be fighting for its life. Hospitals, reinforcement
and rest camps, safe and abundant water supplies, ammunition
depots, supply dumps, and some sort of road system were all
needed where none existed. Resources for creating these facilities

were nowhere to be found. The seeds of future logistical nightmares were being sown.

In London, political and military interests were in collision. In accordance with hallowed custom, various government departments were attempting to run their own wars: the Colonial Office in several parts of Africa, the India Office in Mesopotamia. Kitchener still had his eyes on the battles in France, having been under non-stop pressure to send troops over so that French could drive the Germans back the fifty miles he considered were needed to end the war, whilst the Admiralty were redoubling their pressure for a campaign to take the Dardanelles. There was no Joint Staff and it did not occur to anyone to appoint a single supreme commander for what was clearly going to be a naval-military operation. Even more dangerously, Fisher was continuing to voice serious doubts as to the feasibility of the entire Dardanelles operation.

Carden resumed the operations against the outer forts which had begun in November 1914, in accordance with his announced policy of nibbling away at the defences until, with the destruction of the inner forts and batteries, it would be possible to take the fleet through the Narrows. The task grew more difficult each day, for the Germans had introduced mobile field gun and howitzer batteries which posed a serious threat to ships by virtue of their plunging trajectories, attacking the relatively thin deck armour. They were to inflict devastating damage on the fleet in the weeks ahead.

On 7 February 1915 Carden had issued his preliminary operational instructions to the fleet under his command. They were worded with great caution, for the admiral was not prepared to commit himself to actions likely to prejudice either his ships or his career:

> My present orders from the Admiralty are that a concentrated force is to be kept off the Dardanelles to prevent egress of the enemy . . . no operations of any importance should be undertaken against shore batteries without direct orders from the Admiralty . . . the submarines have orders that they are not to enter the Dardanelles without permission . . . as mines are now believed to have been laid just inside the entrance.

Full operational orders for the naval campaign were issued a week later. They laid down the sequence of events, which were to be carefully phased in order to achieve a progressive neutralization of the defences. The probability of enemy mines, both moored and drifting, was taken into account. The 'floaters' were to be tackled with rifle fire, or netted and towed away by picket boats. Moored mines were to be dealt with by minesweepers steaming ahead of the bombarding ships. A major problem, not immediately perceived by Carden and his staff, now hove into sight. The minesweepers were almost all hurriedly converted trawlers and drifters. The men who crewed them in peacetime were used to the perils of their job as trawlermen and its alarmingly high mortality rate. But now in strange waters, under fire from shore defences at ranges of less than 5,000 yards – often considerably less – they were called on to sweep the entrance to the Narrows. Their speed up the Straits with sweeps out was no more than two or three knots, making them sitting targets for the Turkish gunners who could see clearly what the little boats were trying to do. It is hardly surprising, therefore, that when they came under heavy fire they abandoned their sweeps and fled for the open sea.

Carden's operational plan consisted of seven stages. The first would see the elimination of the defences guarding the entrance to the Straits in Besika Bay on the Asiatic side, and along the northern coast of the Gallipoli peninsula. This would enable the progressive sweeping of the minefields and destruction of the forts up to, but not including, those at Kilid Bahr and Chanak. Two battleships carrying extra field howitzers were to give close support to the minesweepers, and seaplanes were to be used to direct fire against the elusive mobile batteries ashore.

Once these tasks were achieved, it was the turn of the defences at the Narrows, where the principal forts were to be engaged by the 15-inch guns of the super-dreadnought HMS *Queen Elizabeth*. With the Narrows forts neutralized, the minefields between Chanak and Kilid Bahr were to be swept, allowing the fleet to silence the remaining shore batteries above the Narrows. The fleet could then steam through to commence operations in the Sea of Marmara and establish effective naval patrols to dominate the Dardanelles, the fixed defences having been overwhelmed.

On 25 February the fleet resumed its bombardment and succeeded in silencing the outer forts. A number of the defending guns received direct hits and the damage was compounded by the Turks' laxity in the storage of ready-use ammunition, some of which exploded when hit. From the ships the results appeared successful and some of the batteries were actually abandoned by their crews. It was a promising start and on the following day the next phase began when a small force of three ships went in to engage the intermediate defences. This time, fire from the shore was much more effective and the ships were forced to take evasive action, at the cost of accurate shooting. For the first time, parties of bluejackets and marines from the fleet were put ashore to deal with the guns at Kum Kale and Sedd-el-Bahr damaged by the previous bombardment. They encountered little opposition and set about destroying the guns. The landing parties spent several hours ashore engaged in this work and were safely re-embarked in the afternoon. For a week or so these landings became a daily occurrence, but opposition was to stiffen.

Early in February a special force of Royal Marines had left England for the Aegean; it consisted of a brigade headquarters and the Chatham and Plymouth battalions of the Royal Marine Light Infantry and was designated the Royal Marines Special Service Force. Few of the officers, NCOs or marines in these two battalions had seen action, as most were civilians who had volunteered for service in August 1914. The voyage out through the Mediterranean was an enjoyable and novel experience, as was the shore leave granted at Malta, which Lieutenant Lamplough, with all of six months' commissioned service behind him, remembered as 'good fun, much the best since I left England'. He was in No. 4 Company of the Plymouth battalion and his first taste of action was on 4 March when the company was put ashore at Sedd-el-Bahr to destroy the remains of the batteries there. For him, it was

> the day of my life. We were called at 5 a.m. I had breakfast at 6.15 a.m. and got on to the destroyers at 7 a.m. and sailed off at 18 knots. When we got just off Sedd-el-Bahr the fleet started bombarding like blazes . . . it looked as if we should have no opposition. Well, we got into our cutters and finally got ashore and everything looked in our favour. The patrols got out and went up the cliff. One went to the top through the fort and the others straight up. When they got to the top they got it thick . . . We had quite a nice little scrap . . . we got back about 3.30 p.m. having had nothing to eat since 6.15 a.m. this morning.

Lamplough's company was luckier than the one which went ashore on the Asiatic side at Kum Kale, where it lost 20 killed and 24 wounded, with 3 missing, almost left the commanding officer ashore and was only rescued thanks to accurate close-range shooting by the guns of the venerable battleship *Majestic*. Whilst to some, such as Lamplough, it was all rather like a boisterous game, the venom and vigour of the Turkish resistance on this day gave due warning of things to come.

The Special Service Force was withdrawn to Lemnos where it prac-tised its landing and embarkation drills pending the arrival of the Royal Naval Division on 12 March. Two weeks later, to the enormous relief of Admiral Wemyss, the entire division left for Egypt, as life on Lemnos was intolerable, and facilities for training inadequate.

Seaplanes for gunnery spotting and adjustment of fire were operated by the navy's youngest branch, the Royal Naval Air Service or RNAS, which had its origins in early trials carried out in 1911. In that year a Short seaplane had taken off from a trackway laid on the forecastle of a battleship moored off Sheerness. Trials off moving ships were carried out in the following year, when the Royal Flying Corps was formed to provide aerial observation for both navy and army. In 1913 further trials took place and in that year, with the connivance of Winston Churchill, who had become an enthusiastic aviator, the RNAS broke away from the RFC.

By now it was clear that the need to carry increasing payloads involved longer and longer launching tracks, which precluded the use of the ship's forward turrets. The Admiralty therefore agreed to purchase a merchant ship off the stocks. It was rebuilt *in situ* to emerge as the first seaplane carrier with the name of *Ark Royal*, joining the Fleet in 1914. *Ark Royal*'s covered hangar deck held up to ten seaplanes and workshops; cranes retrieved planes from the water after their missions.

On 1 February 1915 the *Ark Royal* sailed for the eastern Mediterranean, arriving at Tenedos two weeks later. She was not the most elegant of vessels, and the aircraft she carried were disappointing in performance. There were three seaplanes with 200 hp engines, two Sopwith Tabloid single-seaters powered by 80 hp Gnome rotary engines, and three Sopwith two-seaters with 100 hp apiece. Some of these aircraft could barely get airborne when the sea was slightly choppy, and they were equally reluctant to fly in dead calm conditions, for then there was no headwind to augment the lift of their flimsy wings. Only one of the aircraft proved capable of getting aloft with any certainty. However, some preliminary surveys of the Dardanelles and the peninsula were carried out and one of their first discoveries was the unpalatable fact that the earlier naval bombardments had not destroyed all the defences. Another was that their maps were so inaccurate as to be almost useless.

On 17 February, of four flights attempted, only one aircraft managed to get airborne. It spent an adventurous one and a half hours aloft. The pilot and observer reported numerous new batteries which had not hitherto appeared on the maps, dropped a 20-pounder bomb which hit the outer wall of one of the forts, and sustained seven direct hits from rifle fire despite flying at up to 4,000 feet for most of its mission. On 19 February, history was made when an aircraft was used for the first time to adjust naval gunfire. Unfortunately, the primitive wireless telegraphy system failed within minutes and the aircraft's crew became helpless spectators as the fleet blazed away ineffectually. Drastic improvements were clearly indicated to the aircraft and their equipment, if the air arm was to play a significant part in operations against the Dardanelles defences.

# 6

# Muster Parade

Our duty is clear; to gird up our loins and remember
we are Britons.

Andrew Fisher, Australian Prime Minister,
August 1914

IN 1911 LORD Kitchener had visited Australia at the request of the
government, having been asked to advise on an appropriate military
structure for the new dominion. He found a system comprising three
categories of service. Each of the states possessed a small permanent
cadre of technical and instructional officers and NCOs whose job was
to train and administer the militia and volunteers. The militia were
part-time paid soldiers in artillery, engineer, cavalry and infantry
units. The volunteers were all infantry and unpaid. New South Wales
had sent a small contingent of militia and volunteers to the Sudan in
1884 – the first Australian troops to see active service overseas – but
the large Australian mounted force which served in South Africa
from 1899 to 1902 was drawn from all the states. Its performance was
greatly admired by all; life in the great open spaces of the outback
fitted Australians ideally for the mobile mounted operations which
finally brought down the Boers.

Dominion status, attained in 1901, saw the amalgamation of
the state permanent forces under federal direction, the militia and
volunteers remaining under state control. Kitchener was quick to
note that this had not produced a cost-effective military system. He
recommended the federalization of all military forces in the dominion and the creation of a citizen force from the militia and volunteers, which were disbanded. All medically fit males were now
required to undergo training in this force. From the age of 12 they
served in the cadets, who were required to undergo four days of
training a year. At 18, they faced sixteen days a year, of which a

week was spent in camp. The sole function of this force was home defence.

Immediately Britain declared war on Germany on 4 August 1914, Australia, in common with the other dominions, pledged its support in the form of an expeditionary force of 20,000 men for service wherever the home government decided. It was clear that the citizen force would not suffice. Training levels were low and its youthful members constitutionally barred from overseas service. The federal government acted swiftly; a call went out for volunteers for an Australian Imperial Force (the AIF) for foreign service. There was an immediate and enthusiastic response. Many of the volunteers were partly trained members of the old militia and volunteers but the great majority of the AIF came straight from civilian life to offer their service. Enlistment criteria were made as flexible as possible. Age limits were from 18 to 45, but even so, many older men eased their way into the ranks. Fathers and sons enlisted together; many falsified their ages – and in many cases their names – to join. Posters advertised the AIF as 'A Free Tour to Great Britain and Europe'. By the end of August the first intake of 20,000 was fully subscribed and barely six weeks later they were embarked in troopships destined, so they thought, for France and the Western Front. Recruiting for a second contingent now got under way.

In August 1914 the Inspector-General of the young Australian army was Major-General William Thomas Bridges, Scottish-born but brought up in Canada, where he graduated from the military college at Kingston before taking a job with the roads and bridges department of New South Wales in 1885. He soon obtained a posting to the permanent artillery and was placed in charge of Sydney's coastal defences. This gave him time to study his profession. A naturally hard worker, he attended gunnery school, where his contemporaries found him industrious, high-principled, austere and ambitious. His professionalism, though, earned him universal respect. He commanded an artillery detachment with the Australian contingent in South Africa, excelling in the support of a cavalry formation. He had now made a name for himself and subsequent advancement was rapid. As chief of intelligence at army headquarters he played a key role in the reshaping of Australian defence policy, visiting London in 1909 as the Commonwealth representative on the staff of the CIGS.

At this time he was described as having 'a tall, bony, thin, loose-limbed frame and the bent shoulders of a student. Many noted his unsociability and frequent rudeness ... He was ruthless as to the feelings of others; he seemed to make no concessions to humanity; he expected none from it.' His juniors feared him whilst his colleagues found him remote and unapproachable. He was in fact intensely shy and had created a hard carapace to protect himself as he fulfilled his life's work – which was nothing less than the creation of a durable and worthwhile military system suited to Australia's future needs. His greatest memorial is the Royal Military College, Duntroon, where, on the outskirts of the new federal capital at Canberra, he created the institution which gave his country the cadre of a highly professional officer corps.

Historians have frequently commented on the high degree of dedication and patriotism in the ranks of the AIF. Native-bred Australians regarded the rest of the world with a kind of innocence tinged with suspicion. England, with its apparently immovable class barriers, puzzled them. They felt they were members of a far more democratic and meritocratic society, and the way of life on the immense cattle stations of the interior did much to foster this view. Despite this, ties of blood with the old country were strong. More than 30 per cent of those who volunteered in 1914 had been born in Britain, the remainder being almost entirely of British emigrant stock with many relatives still alive in the United Kingdom.

Its high percentage of professional men endowed the AIF with a core of natural leaders to augment the relatively few regular officers who had so far graduated from Duntroon. Many others had been bred to the bush and had grown up sturdily independent and self-sufficient, with plenty of natural initiative. The average AIF man was scornful of authority unless the person giving the orders had already shown ample proof of his mettle. In many ways the Australians compared favourably as material for army training with the townsmen who bravely answered Kitchener's call in Britain. Conditioned to life in the industrial cities, the Britisher tended to move with the herd, awaiting instructions patiently and deferentially, whereas an Australian would set out on his own course of action.

When it was seen that recruiting for the AIF was falling off, various methods were used to revive the flow of volunteers. Patriotic music-hall songs were not long in appearing: 'Britannia is calling', 'Heroes who never turn back', 'Rally round Australia's flag', and perhaps most famous of all, 'Australia will be there', the first verse of which ran:

> There has been a lot of argument going on they say,
> As to whether dear old England should have gone into the fray,
> But right-thinking people all wanted her to fight,
> For when there's shady business, Britannia puts it right.

(*Chorus*)
Rally round the banner of your country,
Take the field with brothers o'er the foam,
On land or sea, wherever you may be,
Keep your eye on Ger-man-y.
But England home and beauty have no cause to fear,
Should auld acquaintance be forgot,
No! No! No! No! Australia will be there,
Australia will be there.

One recruiting poster, addressed to 'The Women of Queensland' depicted a partly disrobed woman standing over the bodies of her children, arms raised heavenwards in a call for vengeance. The accompanying text betrayed a somewhat hazy appreciation of the threat to Australian freedom at that time, reminding its readers 'how the women and children of France and Belgium were treated', and warning the ladies of Queensland that their lot could be even worse, ending with the injunction to 'Send a man today to fight for you'. An even more remarkable effort, privately published in 1915 by one Cecilia Nesbitt and entitled 'A Call from Gallipoli', concludes with the following peroration:

Picture a Hun-invaded Australia. The women and children you love, at the mercy of the Hun soldiery. Remember Belgium! And know that every man who can, but does not, answer the call is a traitor to his dead comrades, to his country and to Humanity. He may crawl in cringing safety between earth and heaven in this fair land, protected by the perfect and mighty sacrifice of our dead and living sons; but we will mark him – we shall know him – Coward and traitor! But that's not *you*. So let your ringing answer, clear and firm, speed on the winds to Gallipoli – 'Coming, mates, coming! Coo-ee! Coo-ee!'

In New Zealand, a different military system had been in operation. The Defence Act of 1909 established the principle of universal military obligation for the able-bodied male population to provide an all-volunteer expeditionary force which would be placed at Britain's disposal in the event of war. Manpower did not present a great problem, for under the 1909 Act a territorial system enabled men to be trained in their own districts, and a first-line force of 30,000, backed by a growing reserve, was already in existence. After his visit to Australia in 1910 Kitchener visited New Zealand, where he made certain recommendations leading to small changes in the 1909 system; these were mainly in staff and administrative arrangements. Major-General Sir Alexander Godley was invited over from the

British army as commandant of the New Zealand military forces and he set about forming the permanent cadre of this mainly volunteer, part-time force.

The Maoris, a warrior race who only sixty years earlier had given so much trouble to the British regulars, were well to the fore in volunteering for service. The first Maori recruits were under training within two months and on 14 February 1915 a Maori contingent of 16 officers and 502 men embarked for the Mediterranean theatre. This unit, the Maori Pioneer battalion, won a glowing reputation in the months ahead on the sports field as well as in battle.

The British military contribution to the Gallipoli campaign comprised a much wider spectrum of units and formations and a greater variation of quality. The formation and content of the Royal Naval Division has already been outlined. The 29th Division set up its divisional headquarters in the Manor House Hotel, Leamington Spa, under Major-General Shaw, who had already commanded a brigade with distinction in the retreat from Mons and was clearly marked for rapid promotion; command of an élite regular formation such as the 29th, now brought up to war establishment by drafts of seasoned reservists, was a highly desirable post, much envied by those of Shaw's seniority who had been doomed to the command of newly formed Kitchener divisions. One of the young officers posted to join the divisional staff early in 1915 was Captain C. A. Milward of the 53rd Sikhs. He was the only Indian Army officer in the headquarters but this signified little as he found himself among old friends with whom he had served in India, as well as from his Sandhurst days.

As soon as the division had assembled and settled into billets, intensive training got under way. It was assumed by all that France was the ultimate destination and all training was dedicated to this end, using lessons already learned at terrible cost during the dreadful winter of 1914–15 in the flooded, then frozen, trenches in which the remnants of the BEF were trying to survive. Milward, who had been about to return to France off leave when his posting order to 29th Division arrived at the end of January 1915, was able to get around and visit units and brigade headquarters and mark progress as the fighting formation took shape around him. The infantry and artillery were all regulars, except for a picked battalion of Royal Scots and the Highland Mountain Battery of the Territorial Force; the engineers and field ambulances were also territorials of very high quality; it seemed to Milward that the best of the country's medical consultants had set aside their lucrative jobs to serve in them. He found General Shaw to be not only an impressively professional soldier, but also 'a most charming and entertaining man'. It was clearly going to be a very happy headquarters.

General Shaw had three brigades under command: the 86th comprised the 2nd Royal Fusiliers, 1st Lancashire Fusiliers, 1st Royal Munster Fusiliers and 1st Royal Dublin Fusiliers and was known within the division as the 'Fusilier Brigade'. The 87th Brigade, with the 2nd South Wales Borderers, 1st King's Own Scottish Borderers, 1st Royal Inniskilling Fusiliers and 1st Border Regiment, was the 'Union Brigade'. The third infantry brigade was the 88th, with the 4th Worcesters, 2nd Hampshires, 1st Essex and the 1/5th Royal Scots (TF). Many of these battalions had served alongside each other in India and in other distant stations. Their officers were old friends and knew each others' abilities; the men were long-service regulars and recently recalled reservists. All the units, including the territorial Royal Scots, were close-knit tribes, jealous of their regimental totems and traditions, eager to prove their superiority over the others in friendly rivalry on sports field and rifle range.

The standard of musketry was unmatched anywhere in Europe. Each soldier was capable of firing fifteen aimed rounds a minute with his Lee-Enfield rifle and the fire power of a good shooting battalion, augmented by its two Maxims, could amount to nearly 15,000 rounds a minute. Fire discipline was immaculate; one territorial officer posted into a regular battalion at Helles was to recall, with awe, how his platoon, confronted with an oncoming horde of Turkish infantry at 300 yards' range, opened the breeches of their almost red-hot rifles and held their fire until the Turks were less than fifty paces away, in order to allow the weapons a chance to cool before resuming rapid fire.

Before long, rumours of a move overseas began to spread through the division. The obvious place was France, but this was changed when the Quartermaster-General's staff (or 'Q' staff), responsible for arranging the supply of clothing, fodder, ammunition, equipment and rations, were required to measure all ranks for sun helmets, and maps of France were withdrawn, to be replaced by maps of Turkey. Milward noted that most of these were taken from surveys made up to fifty years earlier, and doubted if they were still accurate. His reservations proved to be well-founded.

The Turkish maps arrived only forty-eight hours before embarkation; but before this took place there was to be a royal review by King George V. The 29th Division was drawn up at full war strength on

Dunsmore Heath only a few miles from the monument on the village green at Meriden marking the reputed dead centre of England. The line of review extended for one and a half miles along the road from Dunchurch station as the King rode slowly down the ranks, then took the salute as this magnificent formation marched past in quick time to the music of its regimental bands and corps of pipes and drums, the infantry battalions massed in column of eight. Milward was not on parade, having been away on a staff visit, but arrived back in time to be a spectator. 'Never has there been such a division,' he wrote. 'The spectacle was magnificent, guns and horses in beautiful condition and the infantry incomparable. The King was delighted. Getting on his horse, when all were past, he, followed by all of us, galloped off and never drew rein till he reached the station.'

To the mystification of every officer and man in the division, General Shaw was now replaced, two days before embarkation, by Major-General Sir Aylmer Hunter-Weston. Heir to the Laird of Hunterston, Hunter-Weston was aged 51. On his past form (he had been promoted Major-General in the field after the retreat from Mons) he would have seemed worthy of commanding the 29th Division, but it is hard to understand the rationale which displaced the competent and popular Shaw at the very moment when continuity of command was all-important. Hunter-Weston, however, was known to Kitchener, and Shaw was not.

On the evening of 16 March the divisional headquarters packed up and left Leamington for the docks at Avonmouth. Hunter-Weston immediately rejected the ship allotted for the transport of his headquarters as it lacked first-class accommodation, having been recently used for the transport of German prisoners of war. Space for the headquarters was made on board the Cunarder *Andania*, 'a beautiful ship with fine saloons and cabins', Milward wrote. They shared its comforts with two of the infantry battalions and the voyage promised to be convivial.

Hunter-Weston immediately made his presence felt by summoning all members of his staff to give him their ideas as to how landings on the Gallipoli peninsula could be achieved, and the Kilid Bahr plateau taken. At Malta there were scenes of great optimism as the British and French warships lined decks, bands played, and the air resounded with cheers. There was a general mood of high confidence; Turks were poorly regarded as soldiers and the feeling was that the mere sight of the 29th coming ashore would put the enemy to flight.

A day after leaving Malta, when it was clear that an opposed landing might be necessary, came the dreadful realization that all the ships conveying the division had been wrongly laden for such an eventuality, and the order was given to make for Alexandria. Because of the acute shortage of shipping, and the need to take the first waves ashore in warships, all the complex staff and loading tables had to be rewritten. Hunter-Weston was proving to be a hard taskmaster; after one session of briefing him, Milward wrote that 'he leaves one like a bit of chewed string . . . he has a horribly active brain.'

After the interlude at Alexandria, where it was possible to draw up supplies of newer maps and assemble much-needed intelligence on Turkish dispositions at Gallipoli, the convoy of ships set sail for Mudros, where 17 battleships and over 50 transports lay majestically at anchor. Here, some of the crew of the Cunarder *Alaunia*, moored alongside the *Andania*, mutinied in the middle of yet another embarkation drill and refused to lower any more ship's boats, stating that it was 'after trades union hours'. Milward was the delighted spectator of what followed; a party of robust soldiers was put aboard the mutinous ship with orders to arrest the sailors involved, who resisted, and ended in hospital, 'nearly killed'. It may have been unconstitutional but it did wonders for the morale of the hundreds of soldiers who watched, cheering on their regimental boxing team.

The 29th was now poised for action; a final chance to survey the land was given on 18 April when a party of staff officers were taken aboard two of the bombarding battleships, from the foretop of which they had a good view of the Cape Helles area which was to be their destination. They all had no illusions as to the task ahead, for they now realized that the Turk, formerly held in derision, was going to be a formidable opponent. All the same, Milward wrote in his diary that night: 'It will be a great job, and a great feat. The eyes of the world are on us.'

# 7

# The Commander

Who is the happy warrior? Who is he
That every man in arms should wish to be?
William Wordsworth,
'Character of the Happy Warrior'

IN LONDON, THERE was still no firm line of policy regarding the Dardanelles, but there were ominous signs of a widening rift between Churchill and the First Sea Lord. On 20 January Fisher had written one of his famous private notes to Admiral Sir David Beatty commanding the battle cruisers of the Grand Fleet. The letter bore one of Fisher's typical confidentiality markings: 'Burn this letter please.' In it, he launched into a recital of his worries over operations in the eastern Mediterranean, which he felt were likely to deprive the Grand Fleet of modern capital ships.

> Diplomacy and the Cabinet have forced upon us the Dardanelles business, so damnable in taking away *Queen Elizabeth*, *Indefatigable* and *Inflexible*, and a whole lot of destroyers. However, the Grand Duke Nicholas sent an ultimatum and we had to cave in (this is secret and private) or he would have made peace with Germany. He is the Autocrat of the War!

Without Churchill's knowledge, Fisher began to lobby anyone of influence whom he believed might be able to shift the War Council off the idea of an eastern Mediterranean diversion, including Colonel Hankey, its secretary, who, a few days later, advised Churchill of a meeting, to be held on 27 January in Kitchener's office, of a sub-committee of the War Council which had been set up to discuss various options for out-of-theatre operations in the Near East. Churchill was invited to bring any experts he wished; the CIGS and his Director of Military Operations, Major-General Charles Callwell, would also be present. Fisher evaded this meeting, but Churchill wrote to him next day holding him to what he saw as an earlier hint of assent to the Gallipoli expedition. Fisher bridled; he had, he felt, given no such impression, and he wrote at once to Asquith on 28 January:

> My dear Prime Minister:
> I am giving this letter to Colonel Hankey to hand to you to explain my absence from the War Council. I am not in accord with the First Lord and do not think it seemly to say so before the Council.

Storm clouds were gathering.

There was no lack of expert advice from other quarters. Far away in Malta, Vice-Admiral Limpus, lately head of the British naval mission in Constantinople, had written a comprehensive apprecia-tion of the Dardanelles situation, which he sent to Rear-Admiral Phillimore at the Admiralty on 14 March. He was clear on what action was needed:

> I studied the matter from the inside [Turkish] point of view when I was in Constantinople and the Greeks were contemplating the same opera-tion. Landing action was very much more necessary for them, but I still think it necessary for us; the more so since it is not the Turks, but the Germans, who are conducting the defence.

Meanwhile the War Council continued to agonize over the Dardanelles. Kitchener gave his opinion that once the Lines of Bulair at the neck of the peninsula had been outflanked by the fleet's passage through the Narrows, they would be abandoned, together with the rest of the peninsula. Churchill continued to press for the release of the 29th Division, claiming that Constantinople could be won in three weeks if the Allies went in with the strongest possible force. Kitchener still held to his belief that if the fleet got through, Constantinople would fall of its own accord.

Fisher was now profoundly disturbed. As a young officer he had served in the Dardanelles under Admiral Hornby in 1878 and still entertained the strongest doubts as to the wisdom of sending in the fleet without first ensuring the elimination of the forts by landing a substantial body of troops. Indeed, he had studied the problem many times over the years, always coming to the same conclusion. Now, part mesmerized, part repelled by his political master, a man young enough to be his son, the old admiral became daily more agitated. He had been brought up to believe that the Royal Navy held the key to the nation's security and that its function in war was to destroy the enemy's main fleet in battle. Such had been Nelson's creed, which he put into triumphant practice at the Nile, Copenhagen and Trafalgar. To this end, all the best ships had to go to Scapa Flow and Rosyth, the sally-ports from which Jellicoe and Beatty were to charge. Fisher was now 74 and feeling his age. His whole life had been dedicated to the service, and now he was being diverted by schemes which could only weaken the Grand Fleet, yet could not guarantee victory in war.

Churchill knew that he had to handle his irascible colleague with care. In a memorandum dated 15 March he wrote:

> My dear Fisher,
>   I don't think we need a War Council on this. It is after all only asking a lot of ignorant people to meddle in our business. I expect K[itchener] will do what we want about the troops being concentrated on Mudros, if you and I see him together. But if not, there is nothing for it but to wait for Hamilton's report which should reach us on Wednesday. Meanwhile the naval operations are proceeding within safe and sure limits.
>
>                                                             Yrs ever
>                                                               W.
>
> PS I am counting much on Hamilton.

This signifies the entrance on stage of the man selected to be commander-in-chief of the great enterprise now in hand. On 10 March Kitchener had at last decided to commit the 29th Division; it was to be sent to the eastern Mediterranean for use, if needed, in the Gallipoli landings which seemed daily more likely. Although he had earlier given Birdwood to understand that he was to be the commander-in-chief, the force had swollen in size, and Kitchener had a shrewd idea that it would continue to grow as the summer wore on. Already he had his eye on the 42nd Division in Egypt and the 52nd (Lowland) Division, another territorial formation, for the eastern Mediterranean. The Turks had been given plenty of notice and their defences were now in far better order than in the previous autumn when a small force would have had little difficulty in getting ashore and securing the peninsula. A more senior commander was indicated, and Kitchener selected General Sir Ian Hamilton.

Hamilton remains one of the most interesting and complex figures of recent British military history. In 1915 he was 62 and fast approaching retirement after a career of almost incessant action which had made him a national figure. Born in Corfu in 1853 when it was garrisoned by the British army, he was commissioned into the old 92nd

Highlanders. His first real taste of active service came in the second Afghan war. Immediately the campaign was over, he and his fellow subalterns, faced with a return to the home establishment as a new uprising, the first Boer War, began in South Africa, sent a cable to Sir Evelyn Woods, commanding in that station: 'Personal from sub-alterns 92nd Highlanders. Splendid battalion eager service much nearer Natal than England. Do send.' Woods liked the spirit of this and the troopship carrying the 92nd was diverted.

Hamilton and his colleagues envisaged an agreeable little cam-paign against the rebellious Boer farmers, followed by a leisurely voyage home; instead, they were routed. On 26 February 1880 the 92nd were near Majuba Hill, an extinct volcano which the comman-der of their force, General Sir George Colley, intended to occupy in order to dominate the area. After an arduous night ascent they occu-pied the top of the hill but the enemy surrounded them and next morning the Boer marksmen were picking off British troops as they pleased. In the final stages of the Boer attack, as the British broke and fled, Colley was killed and Hamilton was hit in the left forearm by a youthful sniper at 15 yards' range, the bullet shattering his wrist and crippling the arm for life. The mental and physical scars of this dis-graceful episode remained with Hamilton for the rest of his days and played a major part in the moulding of his character as well as his ideas on soldiering.

Despite his almost useless left forearm, Hamilton continued to pursue an extremely active career. In 1882 he became ADC to General Sir Frederick Roberts VC, hero of Kandahar, victor of the Afghan campaign, now commander-in-chief of the Madras army. Hamilton learned much from his master and soon became his apostle. Roberts and he had noted the poor musketry of the British soldiers in Afghanistan and were determined to improve matters by means of a radical new training programme – the genesis of the musketry train-ing which so impressed the Germans at Mons. Roberts perceived the quick brain and literary talent of his ADC and Hamilton was soon writing his speeches as well as preparing his briefing notes and despatches. He had also discovered a talent for writing poetry and had some of it published. He even found time to advise the young journalist, Rudyard Kipling.

When Roberts was sent out to South Africa in 1899 after Buller's disastrous reverses at the start of the second Boer War he asked for Hamilton, who had been in Ladysmith during its siege, to command a mobile column. Hamilton now had the chance to put his tactical theories to the proof and did so brilliantly as the commander of mounted infantry columns, using the horse as an instrument of mobility rather than as a vehicle of shock attack. His spectacular successes, and his disdain for the old theories of mounted warfare, pithily expressed in his writings, made him many enemies in the cavalry, whose defence of obsolete tactics persisted for many more years. His actions caught the attention of the former cavalryman-turned-journalist, Winston Churchill, who was so impressed with the work of the mobile columns that he described them in detail in his book *Ian Hamilton's March*.

Returning to London as a Major-General, Hamilton served briefly as Military Secretary at the War Office, then returned to South Africa as chief of staff to Kitchener. Between the two men there now grew a close, if unspoken, rapport.

On his return to London, Hamilton became Quartermaster-General and in 1904 was sent to Manchuria as official observer of the Japanese army in its victorious campaign against the Russians. His book resulting from this adventure, *A Staff-Officer's Scrapbook*, became a best-seller and in a further volume, *The Fighting of the Future*, he drew attention to a number of important developments in military technology which had been deployed in that savage war: wireless telegraphy, machine-guns, quick-firing field guns, barbed wire, torpedoes and mines. In this book Hamilton again poked fun at the cavalry, an arm which in his view had long outlasted its usefulness on the modern battlefield. In the years leading to the Great War, he was GOC Southern Command, Adjutant-General, then Inspector-General of Overseas Training, a post which took him, early in 1914, to Australia and New Zealand where he met many of the officers who would be serving under him a few months later at Gallipoli.

On 4 August 1914 Hamilton was appointed Commander-in-Chief Home Forces, whilst French, his exact contemporary who had been nominated to succeed him in the Overseas Training post, was assigned to command the BEF. Both men attended the first meeting of the War Cabinet on 5 August. It was a disappointment to him not to get the BEF but Hamilton was philosophic. Kitchener had the highest regard for him but knew his impulsive nature and perhaps wanted a safer if less inspired commander for the country's only professional field force.

On 12 March 1915 Hamilton was summoned to Kitchener's office. He knew that the appointment of commander for the expeditionary force was under review even though no announcement had officially been made. He recorded the experience of the next few minutes in his journal. Kitchener was sitting 'like a graven image' writing at his desk and did not look up for what seemed minutes. When he did, it was to say, in a matter-of-fact voice: 'We are sending a military force to support the fleet now at the Dardanelles, and you are to take command.' Kitchener then outlined the resources available: the Australians and New Zealanders under Hamilton's old friend Birdwood; the 29th Division under Hunter-Weston, appointed only that morning; the Royal Naval Division, 11,000 strong, under Major-General Paris; a French contingent, strength unknown, again commanded by one of Hamilton's old friends from the Manchurian campaign, 'the chivalrous d'Amade'. It was made clear by Kitchener that the 29th were an extra, to be returned to the Western theatre as quickly as possible. He added: 'You may just as well realize at once that GHQ in France do not agree. They think they only have to drive the Germans back fifty miles nearer their base to win the war.' Hamilton was dismissed and told to return next day for a final briefing, with his newly appointed chief of staff, Major-General Braithwaite, who was a proven staff officer rather than a regimental soldier and might have been thought a sound choice.

Hamilton and his chief of staff barely had time to discuss their new task when they were summoned back next day to Kitchener for their final (and only) briefing. Kitchener now summarized Hamilton's operational instructions. The fleet, he pointed out, had undertaken to force the Dardanelles, and the employment of military forces on any large scale for land operations at this juncture was only to be contemplated in the event of the fleet's failure to get through after every effort had been exhausted. Prior to any serious undertaking ashore on the Gallipoli peninsula all the military forces detailed for the expedition must be assembled to ensure that their full weight could be thrown in. Once having entered on the project of forcing the Straits there could be no idea of abandoning the scheme. It would demand time, patience and methodical plans of co-operation between the naval and military commanders. The essential point was to avoid any check which would jeopardize the chances of strategic and political success.

Hamilton was told that the probability of minor operations was not to be precluded. These embraced the clearance of areas ashore from which Turkish mobile artillery was harassing the fleet, and the use of landing parties to destroy guns already silenced and dismounted by naval gunfire. Such operations were, however, to avoid permanent occupation of positions on the Gallipoli peninsula. In the absence of up-to-date intelligence on Turkish troop dispositions it was to be presumed that the peninsula was now held in strength and that the Kilid Bahr plateau had been entrenched for a determined resistance. The remaining instructions were couched in vague terms, dealing with events following the forcing of the Dardanelles and the naval advance on Constantinople.

It is clear that Kitchener had only a hazy idea of what was entailed, and that he was despatching Hamilton in the fervent hope that here was a man who would pick up a multitude of loose ends and come up with a workable plan. The latest reports from Cunliffe-Owen and Limpus had both been ignored and filed away in some Whitehall pigeon-hole. Hamilton's only intelligence consisted of a 1912 manual on the Turkish army, some old (and inaccurate) maps, a tourist guide-book and what little could be gleaned from the Turkish desk at the Foreign Office.

It was time for questions. Neither Hamilton nor Braithwaite had much to ask, if only because neither had yet fully comprehended the enormous scale of what they had been ordered to do, though doubt-less Hamilton thought of a good many questions later. Chief among these concerned command and control. Kitchener had not touched on this, other than to call for 'close co-operation between the service commanders'. Who was to be in supreme command? At that time there was no centralized organization in Whitehall, and the Admiralty and War Office operated in water-tight compartments. Very little time had been given to combined operations planning or training in the years before the war and it was assumed that the navy would follow time-honoured drills for putting cutting-out parties and small expeditions ashore. Opposed landings on hostile beaches, under heavy close-range fire, do not seem to have entered the syllabuses at any of the service colleges.

Braithwaite however summoned up the courage to make one request: he felt that it might be prudent to have an aerial observation capability in the expeditionary force and asked if an up-to-date air contingent of the Royal Flying Corps could be made available. Kitchener, as Hamilton recorded, 'turned on him with flashing spec-tacles and rent him with the words "Not One!"' The two generals made as if to leave; as Hamilton reached the door Kitchener called him back for a few last words. The army was to play second string to the navy; there were to be no major operations until the force was fully assembled. If fighting started 'we are to burn our boats . . . the Government are resolved to see the enterprise through . . . Asia is out of bounds. Even if we force the Narrows no troops are to be landed along the Asian coastline . . .' Hamilton was also told to deal person-ally with Kitchener and not with the CIGS, General Wolfe Murray.

The memory of the Field Marshal's final words was to haunt Hamilton in the months and years ahead: 'If the fleet gets through, Constantinople will fall of itself and you will have won, not a battle, but the war.'

Considering the crucial importance of the operation, this was a hopeless briefing for a newly appointed commander-in-chief. Hamilton was at the outset the victim of gross dereliction of duty on the part of the General Staff. According to the principles laid down in Field Service Regulations, he should have been given an outline plan of operations. This was the clear responsibility of Wolfe Murray, the CIGS, who was even more in the dark about Kitchener's plans than Hamilton. No detailed up-to-date intelligence appreciation was produced by the Director of Military Intelligence despite the availability of recent material. There had been no briefing on the forces available for the expedition, other than in very general terms; Hamilton had no idea at this stage of the provision being made for establishment of a base area, or of the logistic chains of supply and reinforcement. He had no knowledge of the enemy dispositions other than what had been gleaned by the navy operating off the Dardanelles. Above all, he was given no hint as to the relationship between himself and the naval commander in the eastern Mediterranean with whom he was required to work.

At Churchill's insistence, Hamilton prepared to leave London at once with part of his General Staff but without any administrative staff officers, who had not yet been nominated and would have to follow by ship as soon as possible. At the outset, therefore, Hamilton was deprived of the staffs who should have been planning the system of casualty evacuation and hospitalization, and provision of the immense quantities of ammunition, rations, fodder, clothing and other essential stores. He did not know at this stage that Mudros Bay was totally unsuited for a forward base, or that most of the transports sailing out to the eastern Mediterranean had been loaded so hurriedly that the equipment needed immediately by any force deposited on a hostile shore was buried in the ships' holds under tons of less urgently needed stores.

That night, Hamilton and Braithwaite, with a small party of General Staff officers, left London, crossed France by special express train and embarked at Marseilles on the evening of 14 March. Their ship was one of the fastest in the fleet, the new light cruiser HMS *Phaeton*, which took them at 30 knots across the Mediterranean, arriving off Tenedos on the afternoon of the 17th. Hamilton immediately went aboard the flagship, HMS *Queen Elizabeth*. Here he had his first shock, for instead of Vice-Admiral Carden, the bluff figure of Rear-Admiral de Robeck was there to greet him as he stepped on to the immaculate quarterdeck. Carden, finally succumbing to his ills the day before, had broken down completely. The fleet surgeon had examined him and packed him off to hospital in Malta. De Robeck was appointed at once to succeed him, although Wemyss, as the senior rear-admiral, was entitled to be promoted to the post. Wemyss, however, was now wholly committed to establishing the base at Mudros and generously stood back in order that the handover of command should go ahead with minimal disruption.

Hamilton had arrived on the eve of the great naval attempt to destroy the forts and force the Narrows. He was promised a ringside seat aboard *Phaeton*, and it was agreed that he should also use the chance to make a preliminary reconnaissance of the peninsula from the sea.

# 8

# *The Fleet Repulsed*

Stand by to reckon up your battleships:
Ten, twenty, thirty, there they go,
Brag about your cruisers like leviathans,
A thousand men apiece down below.

Sir Henry Newbolt, *Songs of the Fleet*

IT HAD BEEN an anxious week for Vice-Admiral de Robeck, newly promoted to acting rank on the departure of Carden. For some time he had watched his predecessor's health decline to the point where Carden could not eat without discomfort and felt so unwell that on 15 March he had declined to meet his senior captains when they came aboard the flagship for their orders. De Robeck did his best to encourage Carden, and Keyes, now Chief of Staff, begged him to hold on, take a few days' rest, and see a Harley Street specialist aboard the hospital ship *Soudan*. Carden agreed to do so. The specialist gave a gloomy report, predicting a complete breakdown unless Carden was immediately sent to hospital and away from the fleet.

On 17 March de Robeck hoisted his flag in the *Queen Elizabeth* as Carden sailed for Malta and professional oblivion. Hamilton and his staff, together with the French party, came aboard in the afternoon. The new regime had begun with minimal disruption even if it had left de Robeck and Keyes in a state of shock. De Robeck asked to see Hamilton's instructions. These, and the verbal briefing he received, acted like a cold douche, according to Keyes: 'There seemed to be so many reservations, i.e. the employment of military forces on any large scale for land operations at this juncture is only contemplated in the event of the fleet failing to get through after every effort has been exhausted.' Keyes looked down the list. He found it profoundly depressing. Hamilton, when asked to comment, expressed an initial preference for landings at Bulair, thus cutting off the peninsula at the neck, but asked for a reconnaissance by sea before committing himself. This was arranged; he would go back aboard *Phaeton* and would be able to visit Mudros before the attack on the next day.

De Robeck's orders for the great attack were based on Carden's earlier instructions. 'The general idea', he told his subordinates and Hamilton's party, 'is to silence the defences of the Narrows and of the minefields simultaneously, so as to enable sweepers to clear a passage through the Kephez minefield. If this is successful the attack is to be at once continued on the remaining defences until the fleet has passed through the Dardanelles.' The fleet's intention was to enter the Sea of Marmara in strength and destroy the Turco-German navy there as a prerequisite for a general naval advance on Constantinople. Although de Robeck was under strict instructions not to risk the *Queen Elizabeth*, by exposing her to close-range fire from the shore guns, he knew that something better than pre-dreadnoughts was required should the *Goeben* be lying in ambush inside the Narrows. The battle cruiser *Inflexible* was therefore included in the bombardment fleet; fresh from the Falklands she was a match for any German battle cruiser – or so it was hoped. De Robeck, anxious to lead his fleet from the front, prepared to transfer his flag to the battle cruiser for the actual bombardment.

Apart from *Inflexible*, de Robeck had thirteen British and four French battleships. All were pre-dreadnought, some of them very much so. Three of the British ships, however, were relatively modern ones of the *Lord Nelson* class. The battleships were split into two lines. Line A, consisting of the more modern ships, was to open the attack at extreme range. Line B, comprising the French battleships *Suffren*, *Bouvet*, *Charlemagne* and *Gaulois*, was a mile astern of Line A. Its mission was to pass through and engage the forts at shorter range, closing to 8,000 yards if necessary. *Gaulois* and *Suffren* were given the additional task of destroying the torpedo tubes believed to be mounted at the entrance to the Narrows. As the fleet closed in on the entrance, with Line A covering the older ships, *Triumph* and *Prince George*, with *Suffren* and *Gaulois*, were to move on the flanks, close inshore. Minesweepers were to be in action throughout, and after the forts had been silenced they were to sweep a channel 900 yards wide on the Asiatic side, so that the fleet could get close in for the destruction of the guns on that side. As the trawlers had proved almost worthless as sweepers, destroyers fitted with sweeping gear were to precede the battleships up the Straits. Floating mines were to be destroyed by picket boats carrying 3-pounder guns.

The fleet now knew these waters well. The minefields were accurately plotted on charts and de Robeck's staff were confident that with the aid of the minesweeping destroyers it would be relatively easy to clear the channel and get through. Unknown, however, to British naval intelligence, a trap had been carefully laid. Under cover of darkness some nights before the attack was launched, a small Turkish steamer, the *Nusret*, had laid a line of mines down the length of Eren Keui Bay, at right angles to the lines of mines forming the main obstacle in the approach to the Narrows, and well downstream of them. For many days German observers ashore had noted that the bombarding ships had been manoeuvring in this bay whilst re-positioning themselves for further shooting, and in hopes that they would follow this pattern when the main attack came, it was decided to sow the new minefield, which remained undetected by the Allies.

Early on the morning of the 18th, Hamilton visited Mudros, to be confronted with bad news by Major-General Paris, commander of the Royal Naval Division. He had discovered that his transports, loaded hurriedly in England, could not be used for an opposed landing because everything was in chaos in the holds. In the absence of wharfage and cranes at Mudros there was no other course but to sail his division off to Alexandria for complete reloading. Hamilton agreed and signalled Kitchener to this effect. Already, he was sensing that the mounting of this expedition was going to present problems undreamt of in Whitehall. He continued up the western coast of the Gallipoli peninsula where he had a good look at the Bulair positions. They were strongly held and he saw that an opposed landing here would court disaster. Then the cruiser ran back down the peninsula and around Cape Helles. On the way Hamilton was able to see that parts of the coast, especially where there were gaps in the cliffs, bristled with newly dug positions, and that the beaches had been liberally wired. This was clearly going to be a hard-fought operation. After rounding Cape Helles Hamilton became a fascinated spectator of the memorable scene as the Allied fleet made its great bid to force the Narrows.

The fleet, battle ensigns flying, had moved into action at 10 a.m. At first the attack seemed to be going well. Accurate fire secured many hits on the forts and although a brisk cannonade was coming from the shore, little damage was sustained by the ships. Towards 2 p.m. it seemed that the forts had been overcome. Huge clouds of dust and smoke rose aloft and the rate of fire from the shore was dying away. The Turks later confirmed that by this time they were in a parlous state; telephone communications were all but destroyed, many guns had been dismounted by direct hits, others were out of ammunition or buried under tons of masonry. The fleet moved in closer to complete the destruction; so far, only *Gaulois* had sustained serious damage, having been hit by a large shell; she was still in action, however, in the van of the attack.

At this point, disaster struck. Having moved up the Straits, the fleet was able to use Eren Keui Bay for its customary manoeuvre, and in succession the French battleships began to wheel round to position themselves for the next set of targets. Suddenly, observers on all the Allied ships saw huge gouts of yellow and brown smoke, edged with steam, shooting out of the *Bouvet*. Still steaming at full speed, she rolled over on her beam ends and vanished below the water, taking her captain and all but 45 of her crew with her. The fleet continued its bombardment until, at 4 p.m., *Inflexible* signalled that she had been damaged by a mine. Almost at once *Irresistible* hit another mine. Both ships were on the right flank of the attack and had run into more of *Nusret*'s hidden field.

Aboard *Irresistible* Lance-Corporal Powell of the Royal Marine Artillery was serving one of the guns in the secondary battery, which gave him a splendid view of the battle. He had been stirred, early that morning, by the sight of the fleet weighing anchor in succession at Tenedos and steaming off for battle. It was, he thought, truly a sight to remember. The French battleships,

four ships of the line, so different in build to our own yet giving one an impression of their power – very ugly squat ships [Captain Milward said they reminded him of 'giant walnuts'] – yet so very grim and business-like . . . now there remained only the older battleships, the 'old crocks' as we called them; the *Irresistible*, *Albion*, *Ocean*, *Swiftsure*, *Triumph*, and *Majestic* . . . At midday 'Hands to anchor stations' was piped and we were away . . . As we turned the corner we instantly realized what we were in for. A long way up the Straits, spread about all over the place, were the Allied ships . . . the water dotted with white splashes of foam where the Turk shells were falling . . . a sight never to be forgotten . . . the *QE* battering away, her huge 15-inch guns pointing upwards, great clouds of yellow smoke drifting away every time she fired . . . About this time, *Irresistible* sustained her first hit. A shell – I think it must have been a 14-inch – hit us somewhere forward. Fair and square it caught us, for the whole ship shook, actually reeled over a little . . . then, a tremendous shock was felt. Half a dozen of our crew were thrown violently over and when order had been regained there was the old *Irresistible* heeling over to port at an angle of fully 45 degrees and our gun pointing in the air like an AA gun . . . orders came along to clear the casemate, everybody on deck . . . in a very short time all the ship's company, with the exception of a gun's crew still firing, fell in on the afterdeck. Not a sign of panic . . . Our ship had now righted herself

. . . we could see a destroyer speeding towards us, a welcome
sight . . . The Turks must have realized how helpless we were, for
instantly scores of guns were turned upon us . . . At the very moment
when the last batch of men were preparing to leave the quarter deck a
shell landed amongst them. What followed would be too horrible to
describe . . . where before stood a dozen men, nothing remained but a
few mangled scraps . . . [After 600 men had been put aboard, the
destroyer made off at high speed.] The last look we had of the poor old
*Irresistible*. There she lay, the water almost level with her quarter deck,
the shells, now that the batteries had found the range, bursting all over
her; and on the bridge, standing there so calmly . . . Captain Dent who,
with 10 volunteers, remained . . . we heard later that Captain Dent and
the volunteers had been saved. What a cheer we gave when we heard
the glad news.

As soon as de Robeck saw that *Irresistible* was in trouble he ordered
another old battleship, the *Ocean*, to go to her assistance and if possible tow her to safety, as the stricken ship, though down by the stern,
was now on an even keel. The captain of *Ocean* declined to take his
ship into what he believed were shoaling waters and held off while
the destroyer went in to save the other ship's crew. Just after 6 p.m. a
great explosion was seen alongside *Ocean*, and at the same time her
steering was crippled by a shell. Immediately, destroyers rushed to
her aid and took off the crew. As the fleet withdrew from the Straits
and night fell, the two battleships were still afloat, battle ensigns
flying, drifting helpless and silent in the middle of the Dardanelles.
During the night they sank in deep water.

Apart from the three battleships, de Robeck suffered other serious
losses. *Inflexible* had sustained a direct hit on her foretop which had
killed almost all the fire direction team, including the gunnery
officer. She had also been mined, and had to be towed to Malta for
repairs, to Fisher's fury. As she limped out of the Straits on the
evening of the 18th, her crew, except for both steaming watches in the
engine room, were formed up on the after deck. One of her 12-inch
guns had been put out of action; but despite her light armour, she had
been saved by good damage control and the discipline of her crew.
Two of the French battleships had also sustained severe damage and
had to be taken out of service. The *Gaulois* was on the point of sinking
as she crept out of the Straits and was beached on Rabbit Island
whilst emergency repairs were carried out.

Although the Turks now had cause for exultation, they had ended
the day on the verge of despair. Most of the static defences had
received further damage and many of the guns had been perman-

ently destroyed. Had it not been for the mobile howitzers, the defences would certainly have collapsed. Many of the gun crews, demoralized by the weight of fire brought against them, had abandoned their batteries and departed for the open countryside. The Germans, seeing the level of destruction, were certain that the attack would be resumed next day and prepared themselves for the worst.

Before the campaign got under way, Churchill had taken steps to ensure that he had a reliable eyewitness at the Front; his younger brother John (Jack), a major in the Royal Oxfordshire Hussars, the blue-blooded yeomanry regiment in which Winston also held a commission, was given a post on Hamilton's staff as camp commandant. Hamilton was aware of this and trusted Jack to report objectively to his brother as the campaign progressed. There is no evidence to suggest that the younger Churchill abused his privileged position (for his letters were uncensored) and at times Hamilton found him a useful method of unofficial communication.

After the repulse of the 18th, Jack wrote to his brother from the headquarters ship *Franconia*, berthed in Alexandria. He explained why Mudros harbour had been temporarily given up as the expedition's forward base because of lack of water and of facilities for unloading horses and transport, and reported that the French

> are rather a scratch lot. Zouaves, Senegalese and Foreign Legion. They must sort themselves out. The 29th are awaited impatiently – trust they will be quite ready . . . we are up against a very tough proposition. Since the 18th many people have altered their views. The sailors are now inclined to acknowledge that they cannot get through without the co-operation of troops. Long-range fire on forts is no good unless infantry occupy the fort afterwards and maintain themselves there . . . The aeroplane spotting is very bad and does not help very much . . . the ships have the greatest difficulty in locating and firing at the mobile guns . . . De Robeck behaved very well on the 18th. He never showed any anxiety and remained most calm and cheerful until the evening. When it was all over he is reported to have said 'I suppose I am done for' . . . he is very popular in the fleet and there is some fear that he may be superseded. Hamilton considers him a very sound pusher and they are entirely in agreement. Hamilton asked me to write privately to you to say that everyone had confidence in him in spite of the 18th . . . we call this expedition the 'Last Crusade' and shall expect a papal cross for it!

De Robeck signalled London late on the 18th with the results of the day's operations and listed the casualties, but intimated that he intended to resume the attack. The War Council endorsed his view when it met on the 19th, but in the event the fleet did not re-enter the Dardanelles, because the admiral was having second thoughts. A few days later a council of war took place on board the *Queen Elizabeth* at which de Robeck expressed his opinion that it would only be poss-ible to force the Narrows with the aid of Hamilton and his troops. As these had not completed their assembly, and in view of the delays caused by the move of the base from Mudros to Alexandria, opera-tions would now be postponed until April, when the weather would have improved.

Back in London the War Council was still torn by doubts and ham-pered by ignorance of the huge problems involved in setting a force ashore on a hostile coast, far from the launching base, and without any apparent plans for its long-term maintenance. Hamilton had signalled Kitchener after the failure of the naval attack and had received an uncompromising reply:

> You know my views, that the passage of the Dardanelles must be forced and that if large military operations are necessary to clear the way, they must be undertaken, and must be carried through.

# 9

# *Pause for Reflection*

We had to make war as we must, not as we would
like to.

Lord Kitchener, to the War Cabinet, 1916

As FAR AS Hamilton was concerned, Kitchener's latest signal was his
executive word of command, and he immediately initiated the enormous task of planning the operation. He was severely handicapped
by the absence of all his personnel and logistics staff, who had not yet
left England. The administrative implications of an opposed landing
in strength on a heavily defended shore were apparent, and prominent among the requirements was that of medical treatment and
evacuation of casualties. As yet there was no senior medical officer
on the GHQ staff and in his absence the General Staff (or 'G' staff)
responsible for planning operations, using rule-of-thumb methods,
had to estimate numbers of battle casualties, make plans for their
speedy evacuation by sea to Alexandria, and provide local hospitalization for the less seriously wounded and sick. Such planning
should have been carried out by the 'A', or Adjutant-General's, staff,
whose responsibilities embraced all personnel matters.

The officers and supporting staff of Hamilton's General Headquarters now began to arrive from England. Their voyage was not
arduous, for the ships in which they travelled were ocean liners in
which peacetime routines were still sedulously observed. Officers
were accommodated in comfortable first-class cabins and dressed for
dinner, to which they were summoned by Goanese or Chinese
waiters (depending on the shipping line) hammering melodiously on
small dulcimers. Some of the ships were retained in the theatre to act
as temporary headquarters until it was appropriate for the staff to go
ashore.

One officer who found himself on the GHQ staff was the success-ful novelist Compton Mackenzie who, at the age of 32, had volun-teered his services for the Royal Naval Division and made his way from his idyllic home in Capri to enrol. Unfit for front-line service, he found employment on the Intelligence Staff at GHQ and at once sized up his colleagues. Of his immediate superior, he found that

> Colonel Ward's qualifications to be head of the intelligence of an ex-pedition to reduce Constantinople were not immediately obvious. He was a gunner who had spent most of his military career as a specialist on home defence, and the only time he had ever been out of England before this was when he had been sent to France to bring back the body of Lord Roberts. He was a methodical, lethargic, apparently slow-witted man well into middle age, who suffered almost incessantly from haemorrhoids, which made him seem glum and unresponsive when he was really concentrating on a fight with physical pain . . .

There were many other such officers in staff and command appoint-ments, who had been visited upon Hamilton either because the Adjutant-General's and Military Secretary's staffs in Whitehall could not be bothered to find the best possible men, or simply because the best had long since gone over to France. The relentless demands of active service were to remove a lot of dead wood once battle was joined; but in many cases the need for this was not detected until it had been the cause of mortal injury to Hamilton's command.

On 27 March Admiral de Robeck sent a lengthy appreciation to Winston Churchill. It set out his thoughts in the light of the fleet's experiences of 18 March and still contained a strong note of optimism:

> I do not consider check on 18 March was decisive and am still of opinion that a portion of fleet would succeed in entering Sea of Marmara. Nothing has occurred since 21st to alter my intention to press enemy hard until I am in a position to deliver a decisive attack. On 21st I was prepared to go forward irrespective of army as I fully realize that this matter must be carried through to a successful issue regardless of cost . . . On 22nd, having conferred with General Hamilton and heard his proposals I learned that the co-operation of the army and navy was considered by him to be a sound operation of war but that he could not act before the 14th April. The plan discussed . . . will effect in my opinion decisive and overwhelming results. The original approved plan for forcing the Dardanelles by ships was drawn up on the assump-tion that gunfire alone was capable of destroying forts. This assump-tion has conclusively proved wrong when applied to the attacking of

open forts by high velocity guns; for instance, Fort 8 has been frequently bombarded at distant and close ranges; the damage caused is
possibly one gun disabled . . . The utmost that can be expected of ships
is to dominate the forts to such an extent that gun crews cannot fight
the guns . . . To destroy forts therefore it is necessary to land demolition
parties. To cover these parties at the Narrows is a task General
Hamilton is not prepared to undertake and I fully concur in his view.

De Robeck still believed that his fleet might be able to batter its way
into the Sea of Marmara, even without military assistance, and that
its appearance off Constantinople would have a dramatic effect on
the morale of the Turkish people; but he also realized his warships
would need early replenishment and that a fleet of colliers, oilers,
ammunition and supply ships and other auxiliary vessels would fall
easily to any surviving guns ashore at the Narrows. His signal went
to Churchill and Fisher. Churchill replied immediately:

I had hoped that it would have been possible to achieve the result
according to original plan without involving the army but the reasons
you give make it clear that a combined operation is indispensable. Time
also has passed, the troops are available, and the date is not distant. All
your proposals will therefore be approved by Admiralty telegram. I
intend you to retain the command irrespective of Carden's recovery.

Instead of sending his own signal to de Robeck, Fisher, now more
anxious by the day, sent a minute to Churchill on 28 March expressing his unease, citing unconfirmed diplomatic intelligence which
suggested that Holland might shortly be invaded by Germany. This
re-awoke his dreams of operations along the North Sea coast against
the German right flank, but also increased his concern for the Grand
Fleet's ability to overwhelm the High Seas Fleet should the Germans
emerge from Heligoland Bight in support of operations against
Holland. He thus resumed his lobby for the return of what he
regarded as essential ships from the Aegean,

where we have, or shall have, 16 destroyers that are very badly needed
at home; the three monitors have gone; the *Reliance* [a repair ship], so
also the *Adamant* and three subs, besides the Australian new sub [*AE2*]
detained out there; also all sorts of home resources largely drawn on –
e.g. Samson and his aircraft; nets; minesweepers etc etc, and finally the
chief anxiety of all – the large expenditure of big gun ammunition and,
as pointed out by de Robeck, the serious anxiety as to the continuing
efficiency of the big guns in the old ships. They will certainly be worn
out. The *Inflexible* hors de combat and about to be towed to Malta. The

*Elizabeth* with only one engine (and so always a cause for anxiety), the *Ocean* and *Irresistible* sunk, and *Lord Nelson* and *Agamemnon* requiring repair . . . What is Hamilton's report as to probable success? Admiral de Robeck does not look forward to disabling the Turkish guns. Is the capture of the Gallipoli peninsula going to be a siege? We should have the military opinion on this. Is Hamilton assured of the sufficiency of his force? We know Admiral de Robeck to be a brave man, and he talks assuredly but his assurance is really based on military co-operation and especially on the demolition of all the guns, thus assuring him of his safe communication with the sea and the safe passage of his storeships, colliers and ammunition supplies . . .

PS – I am not blind to the political necessity of going forward with the task, but before going further forward let the whole situation be so fully examined that success is assured while safety in the decisive theatre is not compromised.

Seriously worried over the naval balance of power in the North Sea, Fisher started to play for time in the hope that the War Council would have second thoughts about the Dardanelles. At this stage there were 16 British battleships in the Aegean, although only one of these, the *Queen Elizabeth*, was a super-dreadnought. Of the others, most were so obsolete as to have no role in the line of battle of the Grand Fleet but were certainly adequate as floating batteries off Gallipoli. They could even be regarded as expendable; some were in any case due to be paid off and scrapped in 1915.

On 31 March Fisher made it clear to Churchill that no more warships should be sent out to the Dardanelles and that de Robeck's plans should stand or fall on the strength of the naval forces currently at his disposal. His minutes to Churchill were getting more impassioned by the day; on 2 April he wrote again to the First Lord: 'We can't send even another rope-yarn to de Robeck. *We have gone to the very limit! . . . A failure or check in the Dardanelles would be nothing – a failure in the North Sea would be RUIN!*'

This obsession with the North Sea lay behind Fisher's disenchantment with the Dardanelles. He had not been responsible for the decision to go for the Dardanelles in the first place but had uttered a number of oracular warnings in the line of his duty as Churchill's professional naval adviser. In his opinion these had gone unheeded. He had stayed on, however, because, having initiated the greatest naval building programme in history, he wished to see it through. He was also captivated by Churchill even when the two men were diametrically opposed on naval policy.

They were now quarrelling over matters which had little bearing on future events. Fisher grumbled that de Robeck had imperilled *Inflexible* on 18 March by allowing her to enter the Straits where her light armour rendered her more vulnerable than the older pre-dreadnoughts; as a result she had been severely crippled and would be out of action (and therefore not available to the Grand Fleet) for many months. He had also considered sending a signal to de Robeck forbidding him to let the *Queen Elizabeth* into the Straits and authorizing her use only for extreme long-range fire support. He did send him a warning order to the effect that the *Queen Elizabeth, Lord Nelson, Agamemnon* and some of the light cruisers and torpedo boats might be recalled at short notice. All this was done without consulting Churchill. The days of this curious and potent partnership were numbered.

Hamilton had now moved to Egypt where his staff were obliged to set about preparing their plans despite the non-arrival of the 'A' and 'Q' departments, who were not expected to reach Alexandria until 1 April. As the result of the reconnaissance made aboard *Phaeton* on 18 March, Hamilton now had a much better idea of the lie of the land on the peninsula. He had looked at Suvla Bay and noted the flat plain inland, overlooked on three sides by hills on which aerial observers had detected signs of Turkish military activity and positions for artillery batteries. Any landing attempted here would therefore be at severe risk from gunfire accurately directed from the hills. It would also be more difficult to obtain accurate fire support from the fleet, as the distances to the likely targets would place them beyond the range of the secondary armament of ships stationed some distance offshore.

On the western coast of the peninsula south of Suvla Bay the ground rose steeply from the water's edge into an area of tumbled and precipitous country crowned by the high ground of the Sari Bair ridge, on which observers would enjoy panoramic views out over the Suvla Plain and, in the other direction, over the Narrows. This was clearly the vital ground. At the southern end of the peninsula lay Cape Helles. Here was the old fort of Sedd-el-Bahr, now pulverized by the guns of the fleet. Even as early as 18 March it had been possible to see that numerous fieldworks existed and new ones were appearing almost daily.

From the beaches at the southern end of the peninsula the ground sloped gently upwards for perhaps four miles until it reached its highest point on the turtle-back hill of Achi Baba, some 700 feet above sea level. Because of the gradual slope to its summit, however, it could not be described as a prominent feature; yet it was to exercise

a baleful effect on all the Allied troops who strove to take it in the
weeks following the landings.

Where the ground at Helles was not broken by seasonal watercourses, or nullahs, it was predominantly scrubby, with stunted trees
breaking the landscape. The meagre agriculture practised by the
sparse population of the peninsula was confined to grazing sheep
and goats, some poor grain crops, and whatever vegetables could be
coaxed to maturity by the depressed peasantry who scratched a
living there. On the higher ground overlooking the Suvla Plain there
were adequate supplies of water in wells, around which several
villages had grown; on the plain itself the wells were few and far
between, and brackish. Down the western coast there was little
water, but boreholes dug after the landings produced a supply. At
Cape Helles, the water supplies were sufficient for a small fishing
and farming community, but totally inadequate for the support of an
army and its thousands of pack and draught animals. It was here,
though, that Hamilton knew he would have to attempt one of his
landings, for only by going ashore here would he be able to threaten
the forts and batteries at the Narrows; and if this was to be achieved,
the landings must be rapidly exploited with an advance in strength
up towards Maidos, on through Gallipoli town, and up to the neck of
the peninsula at Bulair.

Kitchener's eccentric conduct of the war made little use of the
resources available to him in the form of the General Staff in the
War Office, situated opposite the Horse Guards in an imposing building constructed ten years earlier when the post of Commander-in-
Chief had been abolished and replaced by that of the Chief of the
Imperial General Staff. Under Kitchener's regime neither the CIGS
nor the Director of Military Operations were given the freedom they
should have enjoyed to direct the military machine in conformity
with the political directions received from the Secretary of State for
War. The same applied to all the other branches of the General Staff
and, to a lesser degree, to those of the Adjutant- and Quartermaster-
Generals.

The art of public relations had not, in 1915, reached the stage where
it justified a specialist staff at the War Office, which could vet the
appointments of pressmen to an expeditionary force and, if necessary, methodically censor their offerings before release for publication in London. Hitherto, correspondents had been accredited to the
staffs of generals commanding overseas operations and field forces.
There was no regulatory system, and press representation was not

limited to the presence of professional journalists. Winston Churchill had discovered, early in his career, that there were no obstacles in the way of a serving officer should he wish to offer his services as a correspondent; and Hamilton had himself acted as a military correspondent in India. Kitchener hated and despised the press almost as much as he loathed politicians. After his victory at Omdurman he had brusquely ridden past a crowd of newspapermen desirous of a statement shouting, 'Out of my way, you drunken swabs.' This had not prevented them reporting sympathetically that as he sat on his charger at the subsequent memorial service for General Gordon at the old residency in Khartoum, a tear could be seen making its way down his granite cheek and that he was too emotionally overcome to dismiss the parade, leaving the task to one of his subordinates.

Kitchener had forbidden the presence of special correspondents at the Front in France during the early months of the war, thus giving rise to some highly imaginative reporting of events, drafted in Fleet Street by editorial staff whose ideas of modern warfare bore little resemblance to actuality. After a while the general public began to suspect the authenticity of some of these stories, and that the truth was being suppressed. Photographic coverage of military and naval operations gave rise to numerous imaginative captions and the public was frequently misled by shots of troops supposedly in action but actually photographed during training exercises.

Sir John French, who was aware of the value of good reportage, wanted a press corps in France and to have their despatches published, subject to a degree of censorship which would prevent the release of material likely to be of aid to the enemy. Kitchener was unmoved. Permanently accredited pressmen were not to be allowed to visit operational areas until 1916. Kitchener failed to detect that the damage had already been done, and that the newspaper proprietors and editors in Fleet Street had adopted a potentially hostile view of the War Office which was to have notable repercussions before long in the Dardanelles.

Churchill supported the Newspaper Proprietors' Association in its efforts to get some correspondents attached to the Dardanelles expedition. Reluctant permission was eventually granted for the accreditation of two. These were Ellis Ashmead-Bartlett, representing the London press, and Lester Lawrence of Reuters, representing the provincial papers. Ashmead-Bartlett was no stranger to active service, having represented the *Daily Telegraph* at the Balkan wars. He and Lawrence were told to make their own way out to Malta, where they would be placed under Admiralty authority. Arriving in Rome,

Ashmead-Bartlett was able to call on an old friend in the Turkish embassy there, Prince Djemil Tossoum, who courteously showed him the official Turkish report on the actions of 18 March. The prince, a cosmopolite still strongly sympathetic towards the Anglo-French entente, entertained his guest lavishly before sending him on to Malta, where he called on Admiral Limpus, who was sceptical about the likely outcome of the expedition. In his view, secrecy had been totally lost and the opposition was going to be stronger than was anticipated in London.

Ashmead-Bartlett went on from Malta in the only transport available, a water tanker destined for Mudros harbour, where he arrived on 5 April. The anchorage was filling up again after the departure of many of the transports for reloading at Alexandria and, as the correspondent reported:

> our gaze fell on one of the most magnificent spectacles the world has ever seen – the greatest armada of warships and transports ever assembled together in history . . . the mighty *Queen Elizabeth*, shepherding a long line of pre-dreadnought battleships, beginning with the *Lord Nelson*, *Agamemnon*, *Swiftsure* and *Triumph*, and followed down the tide of times by the *London*, *Prince of Wales*, *Canopus*, *Cornwallis*, *Majestic*, *Goliath* and many others . . .

The two pressmen now had a chance to meet Admiral de Robeck and Commodore Keyes. Ashmead-Bartlett and de Robeck struck up an immediate rapport and it was not long before the correspondent was able to obtain favourable treatment from the naval staff, using picket boats and launches to travel around the fleet and ashore, where he also met some of the GHQ staff. Of these, he was particularly struck by Lieutenant-Colonel Doughty-Wylie, who had spent many years in the Near East and was extremely knowledgeable about Turkey, a country whose people he loved, and where he had served for several years as British Consul at Konya, the home of the whirling dervishes. Ashmead-Bartlett was less impressed by many of the other staff officers he now encountered; his affections lay in any case with the navy, who provided him with comfortable accommodation afloat and accorded him the unstinted hospitality of their wardrooms. He was not attracted by the Spartan living standards ashore, being a man who liked his creature comforts and expected to have ice in his gin as well as good messing.

Although the senior administrative staff expected that at least some of them should accompany the General Staff back across to Mudros in order to co-ordinate a workable operational and administrative plan, Hamilton declined to let them travel, apart from a representative of the Surgeon-General's staff, and they were obliged to start work at Alexandria, 700 miles from the seat of war and 3,000 miles from the home base, accommodated in a building lacking electricity and with uncertain water supplies and drainage, reputedly a brothel until requisitioned for military use.

Brigadier-General Woodward was Adjutant-General of the Mediterranean Expeditionary Force; he had arrived at Alexandria on 1 April to find Hamilton and the General Staff on the verge of departure. Woodward remonstrated angrily with Braithwaite; it was essential, he claimed, that his 'A' staff went with the 'G' staff to Mudros as huge problems of medical treatment and casualty evacuation, to say nothing of reinforcements, loomed ahead. Braithwaite refused point blank to intervene, saying that Sir Ian had already made up his mind. Braithwaite was fond of making statements of this kind and of speaking on Hamilton's behalf even when he had no specific reason to do so. Woodward asked for a personal interview with Hamilton but got nowhere. Braithwaite had briefed his commander-in-chief well before Woodward got to him.

Hamilton, it transpired, had decided to leave the greater part of his administrative staff behind at Alexandria in a typically quixotic gesture of friendship to his old friend General d'Amade, whose own staff was almost non-existent and totally incapable of mounting the French contribution to the expedition without some British help. In the event, Woodward and his staff did not even get a sight of the operational orders for the Gallipoli landings until five days before the attack. The main part of the medical staff under Surgeon-General Birrell had also been left behind at Alexandria, as had the Quartermaster-General's staffs. When Woodward did eventually get to Mudros, it was to find that his staff were virtual prisoners on an anchored liner in the harbour, with no means of communication off the ship and virtually no call on the work-boats that were the only method of transport between the staff branches, split as they were between several ships and almost incommunicado. As no 'A' staff had been sent ahead to Mudros, manpower planning was in total disarray. Such arrangements as had been made for casualty evacuation were seen at once by the medical experts to be hopelessly inadequate, as were arrangements for the supply of reinforcements and transit camps in which they could be held. An administrative disaster was set to take place even before a man had gone ashore at Gallipoli.

Until now, Hamilton had accepted that the navy was the predominant arm in the attempt to break through at the Dardanelles, even though he was considerably senior in rank to de Robeck. Although no provision had been made for a Joint Staff to run the ensuing battle, Hamilton's eyes were fixed on grand strategy, not administration, and he sensed that it was now up to him to bring off what could turn out to be the decisive stroke of the war. Success – and this meant nothing less than getting to Constantinople – would result in the severance of Turkey's links with the Central Powers and her rapid exit from the war. A seaway would be opened through the Bosphorus, enabling military supplies to reach the Russian armies. Wheat and oil from the Ukraine and Caucasus could be exported to the West to earn much-needed currency for the Russian treasury. Finally, a decisive victory over Turkey and the occupation of Constantinople would scotch any likely Balkan alliances against the entente. The responsibility resting on Hamilton was indeed daunting. He had already seen the terrain and although his maps were inadequate, there had been sufficient aerial reconnaissance by the RNAS to give the staff a reasonable idea of the strength of the defences ashore.

On 13 April Hamilton issued Force Order No. 1, in essence an outline operational order. The enemy forces on the peninsula were now estimated as being 34,000 men in three divisions, one of which was astride the neck of the peninsula at Bulair and the others in the area of Anafarta overlooking Suvla Bay, and Kilid Bahr, covering the forts protecting the Narrows. Hamilton planned to keep the Bulair division in its place by staging an elaborate feint attack by the Royal Naval Division in the Gulf of Saros. The main landings were to be on the western coast in the Gaba Tepe area and at Cape Helles on the southern tip. The first of these would be assigned to the newly formed Australian and New Zealand Corps under Birdwood, recovered from his disappointment at not getting the overall command and back in his usual high spirits. Those at Cape Helles, where Hamilton anticipated stiff resistance, would be carried out by the 29th Division. Both landings would take place early in the morning, permitting an approach by the fleet under cover of darkness.

In each case a covering force would go ashore first, with the aim of seizing a beach-head large enough to permit the landing of the main bodies within hours. The fleet was to provide overwhelming covering fire to neutralize the beach defences and prevent enemy troops from rushing forward to repel the landings. Simultaneously there would be a diversionary landing by French troops on the Asiatic shore at Kum Kale, which it was hoped would suppress the fire of the coastal batteries on that side of the Straits. Hamilton was aware of

Kitchener's strictures on operations on the Asiatic shore, and the plan provided for the evacuation of the French and their transfer to Cape Helles after no more than forty-eight hours' fighting. The Royal Naval Division, on completion of the Bulair diversion, would sail round to Cape Helles and come ashore there.

This plan, as Hamilton recognized, suffered from several drawbacks. For a start, there were no reserves worth talking about; more dangerous was the fact that nearly all the landing places selected at Cape Helles were known to be well prepared defensively, with masses of newly laid wire, much of it underwater in the shallows. There were no specialist landing craft, and the navy would therefore have to get the troops as close in to the shore as possible under cover of darkness, then tranship the heavily laden men into 'tows' of cutters and gigs drawn by steam pinnaces. Each cutter would carry between 120 and 150 men. The pinnaces would take them to within a hundred yards of the shore where they would cast off and row the rest of the way. In the last three weeks before the landings, the harbour at Mudros was the scene of a giant regatta as dozens of boats rowed round the harbour and the soldiers, most of whom were non-swimmers, learned the art of watermanship.

It is worth while, at this point, to summarize the difficulties under which Hamilton was labouring at this stage of the enterprise. Some of them were of his own making. For example, he was curiously inhibited when dealing with Kitchener, who still awed him as he had done years before when they had worked as commander and chief of staff in South Africa. Hamilton's second problem was the total absence of a Joint Staff in the Aegean, and the physical separation of the two single-service staffs. Although de Robeck had provided a good naval liaison officer at Hamilton's GHQ, inability to make instant joint decisions at moments of crisis was to dog the enterprise from the start.

All secrecy had been lost before Christmas 1914 with the ineffectual bombardments of the outer forts, and the Turks, with the arrival of the Anglo-French fleet at Tenedos and Mudros, were in no doubt as to the Allies' intentions. As if confirmation were necessary, the intense activity in Egypt early in 1915 was watched with interest by a horde of Turkish and German agents, who were able to deliver a complete Allied order of battle to the head of intelligence in Constantinople by the middle of March. On the other hand, the Allies had little idea of the true strength, or battle-worthiness, of the Turkish forces in the Dardanelles area, even on the eve of the landings.

There was obviously going to be a severe shortage of field artillery in Hamilton's command. The Royal Naval Division could muster only two 12-pounders, one 6-inch howitzer, and three 4.7-inch guns. The three British divisions which would be engaged on the peninsula by June should have had an establishment of at least 300 guns but could muster only 118. The supply of artillery and small arms ammunition was to be critical throughout the campaign, bearing in mind that the Western Front had priority for what supplies were available. The small arms ammunition problem was compounded by the fact that the 29th and Royal Naval Divisions had been issued with different models of the Lee-Enfield rifle, and whilst the 29th's Mark VIIs could fire the Mark VI rounds used in the naval rifles, the reverse was not possible.

Another obstacle to operational efficiency lay in the lack of homogeneity in Hamilton's force. Standards of military proficiency varied alarmingly between the professionals of the 29th and the enthusiastic but generally unfit and ill-trained men in the naval division. The Anzacs were clearly men of superb physical bearing, but militarily raw and inexperienced. The French were an unknown quantity; it was clear that the Foreign Legion element were hardened troops, but the Senegalese gave rise to doubts all too soon to be realized; once their officers had been killed or wounded the Africans frequently broke and ran. There were no standard staff and training doctrines to hold the force together; apart from the regulars, most of the officers were young and inexperienced, albeit courageous. At higher levels there were many senior officers who would prove inadequate for the tests that lay ahead; many had already identified themselves, but the distance from the home base was too great for immediate replacement action to be taken, and some of the formations and battalions which went ashore at Gallipoli would be commanded by men fated to break under the strain.

Communications were of prime importance, as ever, in the running of so complex an operation; yet GHQ arrived in the theatre without its own signals company, held back in England because of an outbreak of measles in its ranks. At short notice, an *ad hoc* GHQ signals unit had to be assembled from Anzac resources. The headquarters was further embarrassed by a lack of lighting generators for its tents when it got ashore on Lemnos. There were no prefabricated piers and jetties for use following an opposed landing; these were essential if the force ashore was to be sustained in the field. Again, the ingenuity of the navy came to the rescue and some were built.

There was a complete lack of trench stores, for use if the initial landings failed to develop into the mobile operations envisaged.

There was no corrugated iron for overhead shelter, scant supplies of timber for revetments, or of sandbags. Barbed wire was in extremely short supply in Egypt, yet it was a necessity if static warfare was enforced. There was certainly no shortage of it on the Turkish side. Undismayed, Hamilton continued to plan. It would have been better for all concerned if he had set aside his innate courtesy and diffidence, and been emphatic in expressing his needs to Whitehall.

# 10

# 'En Avant!'

We were a gallant company,
Riding o'er land, and sailing o'er sea,
Oh! but we went merrily!

Byron, *The Siege of Corinth*

THROUGHOUT THE FIRST three weeks of April, the great armada in the harbour of Mudros Bay continued to grow. As each new ship arrived it was greeted with waves of cheers from those already at anchor. The usual chorus was a concerted shout of 'Are we downhearted?' from the incoming drafts, answered by a resounding 'No!' and the second rhetorical question followed: 'Are we going to win? *Yes!*' – to which the old hands – the troops who had been in harbour for anything up to three or four weeks – would respond with encouraging bellows of 'Get your —— knees brown!' and 'You'll be sorry you joined!' All was good-humoured; morale was never higher. The men who had already spent several weeks at Mudros practising their landing drills had acquired not only a proficiency in handling the cumbrous ships' boats, but were also fitter and more self-confident than they had ever been in their lives, thanks to exercise and plentiful shipboard food. Units went ashore on Lemnos whenever possible for route marches, field training and sports, played on the improvised football and cricket pitches which have long marked the progress of the British army around the world.

Hamilton's plan for the landings, which were to take place early on the morning of 25 April, were now complete. Birdwood's Anzacs (as the Australian and New Zealand Army Corps would henceforth be known) were to land on the west coast in the area of Ari Burnu with the aim of getting inland and seizing the high ground from which it would be possible to advance across to the Narrows. The first troops ashore would be the 3rd Australian Brigade. The selected landing point presented a wide beach just north of the Gaba Tepe headland, from which the ground sloped gently up into the interior of the peninsula. The Turkish coastal battery on the point, it was thought, could be taken quickly at the point of the bayonet, thus making it safe for the transports carrying the main body to approach close into shore.

The Cape Helles landings were to take place on a number of beaches. These, starting from the north, were named 'Y', 'X', 'W', 'V' and 'S'. That at Y was designed as a feint to draw Turkish forces away from the southern tip of the peninsula. At X it was planned to put a force ashore where a cleft in the cliffs, which did not seem to be heavily defended, would allow rapid exploitation and a rapid move inland. W and V beaches were known to be defended, for numerous new entrenchments had been detected by aerial and naval observers. Both were fairly long, overlooked at short range by cliffs and high ground, and strongly wired. Hamilton's reasons for landing here were that there were no other places within striking distance of the Narrows which could accommodate a force of divisional strength. He assigned this difficult task to the 29th Division, confident that their professionalism would see them through.

To help them bring it off, a novel expedient had been adopted. At the suggestion of Commander Unwin, a destroyer captain, the collier *River Clyde* was hurriedly converted into a floating Trojan Horse, to be filled with troops and run aground under the walls of Sedd-el-Bahr fort as the tows approached V beach. To provide covering fire for the landing of the troops in the ship, a detachment of the RNAS armoured car squadron was to go aboard with a number of its Maxim machine-guns, installed in sandbagged redoubts on the forward deck. Unwin volunteered for this desperate enterprise and thus became the temporary captain of the *River Clyde*.

The machine-gun detachment aboard the ship was commanded by Lieutenant-Commander Josiah Wedgwood of the distinguished Staffordshire pottery firm, a close friend of Winston Churchill, to whom he wrote on 24 April, the eve of the great attack:

We are attached to 29th Division under Hunter-Weston . . . this afternoon, 2,400 Munsters and Dublins and the Hampshires come on board and conceal themselves in the holds of the Wooden Horse . . . in the ship's sides great ports are cut. As soon as the crash comes and we grind ashore, these dragon's teeth spring armed from the ports and race along a balcony to the stem of the vessel, then they pass forward along a steam hopper and thence over a drawbridge to dry land . . .

One other landing was included in Hamilton's plan. This was S beach at the far end of Morto Bay where an eighteenth-century defensive work, De Tott's Battery, offered a useful foothold on the right flank of the landing and the chance to divert Turkish attention from the landings at X, W and V beaches. Unfortunately, the navy's resources of ship's boats and pinnaces had all but evaporated once the demands of the Anzac and Helles landings had been met; there were only enough to allow two companies of the South Wales Borderers ashore on S beach (the rest of the battalion being assigned to Y beach) and as no steam pinnaces were left, the men were going to have to row themselves all the way ashore from their ship.

In presenting his plan to his senior commanders, Hamilton had made it clear that he was committing all resources to the attack. There were no reserves, other than the Royal Naval Division which would be available for use at Helles once it had completed its evolutions off Bulair, and the French, who were to be shipped across from Kum Kale as soon as their diversionary landings there had served their purpose. In Hamilton's words it was a case of 'a good run at the Peninsula and jump plump on – both feet together'.

His immediate subordinates, however, were far from confident; he had earlier invited Birdwood, Hunter-Weston and Paris to make independent appreciations of the situation and to give their views on the conduct of operations. He had not been pleased with their pessimistic responses. Hunter-Weston, who had written his appreciation while still at Malta on his way out, favoured a full-scale landing at Bulair, and went so far as to recommend that it would be better to cancel the whole operation than risk a humiliating disaster. Birdwood favoured a landing in strength on the Asiatic shore (as did Maxwell, the GOC in Egypt, whose opinion had not been sought). When Birdwood showed Hamilton's outline plan to his chief of staff, Brigadier-General Walker, the latter was aghast and raised such strong objections that Birdwood almost dismissed him from his post. Paris was also gloomy about the chances of success. He knew better than any that his Royal Naval Division was neither trained nor equipped for sustained combat against a tough enemy.

Hamilton was an even-tempered man but this lukewarm attitude irritated him. He responded to Birdwood by tartly reminding him that he had no mandate to engage in operations on the Asiatic shore. Birdwood and Maxwell were stung by this attitude and tensions began to develop at the highest level. Maxwell continued to be uncooperative, especially when Hamilton, at Kitchener's prompting, asked for more troops to be made available for the MEF from the lavish garrison of Egypt. Hamilton had his eye on an Indian brigade and on the excellent 42nd (East Lancashire) territorial division; but every time he made a hesitant move to obtain these reinforcements, Maxwell signalled London with inflated appreciations of the continuing threat to the Canal from Turkish forces 'reliably reported' to be building up in the Sinai. Kitchener, at last comprehending the enormity of the task he had set Hamilton and aware of the latter's diffidence in asking for additional resources, ordered more United Kingdom formations to prepare for embarkation. The first of these was the 52nd (Lowland) territorial division, destined to play a major, if tragic, role in the forthcoming campaign.

There was not enough room, or water, on Lemnos to cope with the needs of the armada in Mudros Bay, and elements of the expeditionary force were being lodged on other Greek islands of the Aegean. One of these was Skyros, and it was here that Rupert Brooke came to die, a few days before he could fulfil his wish to go into action with the men of his battalion of the Royal Naval Division.

Brooke and his friends had sailed from England on 28 February. He had already written the famous and much-quoted lines beginning 'If I should die . . .' and in all his last elegiac verses, written or merely sketched out in the few weeks left to him, he seems to have had a strong premonition of death. The ship stopped briefly at Lemnos then went on to Egypt, arriving on 27 March at Port Said. Hamilton inspected the division there on 3 April, when he saw Brooke 'looking off-colour' and offered him a post on his staff. His illness was put down to a touch of the sun and he was well enough to embark for the Aegean, where he drafted what were to be his last fragments:

> They say Achilles in the darkness stirred,
> And          Hector his old enemy,
> Moved the great shades that were his limbs. They heard
> More than Olympian thunder on the sea.
>
> I strayed about the deck, an hour, tonight
> Under a cloudy moonless sky; and peeped
> In at the windows, watched my friends at table,
> Or playing cards, or standing in the doorway,
> Or coming out into the darkness. Still
> No one could see me.

I would have thought of them
– Heedless, within a week of battle – in pity,
Pride in their strength and in the weight and firmness
And link'd beauty of bodies, and pity that
This gay machine of splendour 'ld soon be broken,
Thought little of, pashed, scattered . . .

                                   Only, always,
I could but see them – against the lamplight – pass
Like coloured shadows, thinner than filmy glass,
Slight bubbles, fainter than the wave's faint light,
That broke to phosphorus out in the night,
Perishing things and strange ghosts – soon to die
To other ghosts – this one, or that, or I.

On 17 April the ship arrived off Skyros and the young officers eagerly explored the island where Theseus is reputed to be buried. On the 21st Brooke was unwell. An insect bite on his lip had swollen and he was feverish, with pains in his back and head as the blood poisoning overwhelmed his body. He was moved to a French hospital ship, where he died peacefully on the 23rd. That night after sunset his body, followed by close friends, was carried up a hillside by a party of petty officers. Ratings from the battalion stood with flaming torches every twenty paces and the scene was truly Homeric, as he would have wished. A Greek interpreter inscribed his epitaph on the back of the grave cross: 'Here lies the servant of God, sub-lieutenant in the English navy, who died for the deliverance of Constantinople from the Turks.' Of those who stood at the graveside, few were to survive the war.

The news of Rupert Brooke's death came as a blow to some and an evil omen to many. In his diary, Hamilton wrote: 'Rupert Brooke is dead . . . the rest is silence.' In *The Times* of 26 April there appeared a fulsome eulogy by Winston Churchill:

During the last few months of his life, months of preparation in gallant comradeship and open air, the poet-soldier told with all the simple force of genius the sorrow of youth about to die, and the sure triumphant consolation of a sincere and valiant spirit. He expected to die; he was willing to die for the dear England whose beauty and majesty he knew; and he advanced towards the brink in perfect serenity, with absolute conviction of the rightness of his country's cause and a heart devoid of hate for fellow men . . . Joyous, fearless, versatile, deeply instructed, with classic symmetry of mind and body, he was all that one would wish England's noblest sons to be in days when no sacrifice but the most precious is acceptable, and the most precious is that which is most freely proffered.

Not all Hamilton's men were facing the prospect of battle in so exalted a frame of mind. Lance-Corporal Phillips of the 1st Battalion, Lancashire Fusiliers kept a diary in which he chronicled the minutiae of shipboard life. He was not a great admirer of his superior officers.

*14 April.* Sudden activity manifested. Company on parade all day. Musketry. Lecture (by company commander) outlining the task, its difficulties, magnitude etc . . . reminding us that we are regulars . . . wish we were . . . Telling us that we belong to the 1st Battalion of a famous regiment and are destined to be makers of history. Must not think of ourselves but of honour of the regiment. We are pawns in the game and are not to be considered (whilst wading waist deep in the sea under hostile shellfire). Very comforting lecture, summed up as ROT. Hang the regiment, the Army, anything, but look after No. 1 . . . The sentiments above are those generally expressed by all ranks, not by a small minority. True patriotism is dead except in the hearts of those now comfortable and safe in their homes in England. Sensible, every one of them . . . Perhaps it was badly put, but well meant. Our worthy OC No. 9 Company is no orator and could not, even in imagination, be described as popular . . .

*15 April.* Food supplied on *Caledonia* absolutely scandalous; hear talk of best fed army in the world. If that applies to us am truly sorry for the worst fed. Staple diet is bully beef, bread, butter and tea. Condition of butter may be imagined when troops refused to touch it though nothing else was available. Given out by officers on parade that we should use it for boot grease. Exactly like tallow. Quite tasteless. Spuds served up are rotten and when boiled up are black inside and practically uneatable . . . bread burned on top and like dough inside . . . It is almost impossible to obtain a wash on board. True, there is a plentiful supply of salt water but when hundreds of men use the same few gallons of fresh water it is remarkably like washing in rifle oil . . .

At this point the commanding officer was taken ill with a heart attack and removed ashore to hospital. At this news, Lance-Corporal Phillips waxed lyrical:

Colonel Ormond relieved of command; great jubilations. Deck concert organized in honour of event. Everybody most joyful . . . rumoured that he's been invalided home . . . In any case he's gone, for which God be thanked. All his orders reversed. Caps, puttees, boat drill etc. Immediate change in demeanour of men and officers. Perhaps, now, we may lead the life of ordinary soldiers and not be everlastingly pestered by a half-mad, whimsical and pedantic colonel.

The change of command seems to have wrought a transformation in Phillips' hitherto bloody-minded attitude, for on 23 April, as the great fleet weighed anchor and steamed out of Mudros harbour, bound for Tenedos, he was able to describe not only the stirring scenes but also the remarkable change that had come over the battalion.

> Moved out of harbour. Excellent view of battleships lying broadside on, long, lean and powerful looking. Bands on board playing 'Tipperary', 'Rule Britannia' etc. *Implacable, Prince of Wales, Triumph, Euryalus* etc. Rumour is that we move to Tenedos, thence to *Implacable*; to Gallipoli Sunday morning. Hope it's true. Elated at prospect before us. Terrific bombardment is to take place before we land. Have been trying to analyse 'fear'. Have decided it is simply dread of unknown. Have not the slightest fear of future events as it is understood but it is the future which is so mystifying. A peep into the Book of Destiny would satisfy me either way. Anyhow I have great faith in my star and really believe I have to go back and work out my destiny or otherwise.

The eve of battle found Phillips in remarkably high spirits and a different man from the disenchanted grumbler of only a few days before:

> *24 April.* Arrived Tenedos in the morning . . . felt quite ashamed of my previous grumbling now that prospect of action is so near . . . We have been given the hardest task of the campaign and its successful accomplishment will rank with any of the victories in France . . . Anticipate hot stuff holding on to Achi Baba–Krithia line. If we do this, success assured and our part in expedition practically finished. Sat up playing solo whist all night. Expect good day tomorrow and sleepless night in trenches Sunday night. Light from Turkish searchlight at Chanak visible on horizon. Now Sunday morning. 2.30 a.m.

All over the fleet, soldiers and sailors were preparing in different ways for the ordeal ahead. On board the *Queen Elizabeth*, Lieutenant-Colonel Doughty-Wylie was tidying up his personal affairs prior to going aboard the *River Clyde* as GHQ representative on the V beach landing. He had several important letters to write. His thoughts that night were curiously divided between his wife Lily and the celebrated explorer and traveller Gertrude Bell. It is unclear if their relationship was anything more than platonic; they had long been close friends and corresponded for many years, often passionately. He now wrote to her describing what lay ahead:

My dear,

Tonight I pack up all your letters . . . tomorrow, if the weather moderates, I am embarking on a collier, the 'wreckship', or wooden horse of Troy, which we are going to run on the beach and disembark by an ingenious arrangement . . . if I get ashore I can help a good deal in the difficult job of landing enough troops to storm the trenches on the beaches – and to see the most dashing exploit which has been performed for a very long time . . . On the eve of any adventure my spirits have always risen . . . Peace upon you; for you have still the gardens, and the trees to walk under, where there is nothing but peace and understanding . . . Ave valeque.

In the anchorage at Tenedos the staff of 29th Division were busy with last-minute arrangements for the morrow. Checks were made with all units to ensure that the men were fully equipped, with full packs, 200 rounds of ammunition, two days' iron rations of bully beef and hard tack biscuit plus tea and sugar, two empty sandbags, field dressings for wounds, and entrenching tools. Under this weight any man, whether a swimmer or not, would sink to the bottom if he fell into water out of his depth, but such was the general mood of excitement that this was discounted by most. Captain Milward, busy with the routine of 'G' staff work, noted on the 24th that it was

A busy morning – General Hunter-Weston, in his highly-strung way, going through the arrangements for the landing . . . we none of us said what we thought . . . in evening the divisional staff transferred to the *Euryalus* plus the Lancashire Fusiliers. The South Wales Borderers on *Cornwallis*, Royal Fusiliers on *Implacable*, King's Own Scottish Borderers on *Talbot* and *Amethyst*. Munster Fusiliers, Dublin Fusiliers and half the Hampshires on *River Clyde*. At 2200 hrs sailed slowly in dead calm for Gallipoli.

High command brings unspeakable loneliness to those who hold it when all has been prepared, all orders issued, and only the deed remains to be done. Late on the night of 24 April, aboard the *Queen Elizabeth*, Hamilton sat down in his cabin and confided to his journal a prayer: 'Almighty God, Watchman of the Milky Way, Shepherd of the Golden Stars, have mercy on us . . . Thy Will be done. En Avant – at all costs – En avant!'

# PART TWO

## 'Both Feet Together'

# 11

# *Prepare to Engage*

It is said that God is not on the side of the heaviest
battalions but of the best shots.

Voltaire

THE DEFENDERS OF the Dardanelles had been given ample time to
prepare for the Allied landings. At first, following the naval attack,
the Turks, and indeed many of their German advisers, had expected
that the assault would be renewed almost at once and that this time
it would succeed, for the defences had been strained to the limit.
Ammunition was in desperately short supply, many of the forts
had been severely damaged and would require considerable repair
work, and morale was low. At this point, Enver Pasha made a decision which would clinch the outcome of the entire campaign. He
appointed Otto Liman von Sanders, now holding the temporary rank
of Marshal in the Ottoman army, to the command of the 5th Army,
entrusted with the defence of the Dardanelles.

Liman moved at once with a handful of his staff officers and
arrived on 26 March at the town of Gallipoli where he established
his headquarters as the rest of the staff followed overland from
Constantinople. A preliminary inspection showed him that a major
redeployment was necessary. The existing garrison was spread thinly
around the coastline to cover every possible landing place, but there
was no central reserve capable of moving rapidly to meet an unforeseen threat or for use as a counter-attack force. His first action was to
establish such a reserve. The next step would be to improve the land
and sea communications around the Dardanelles so that his forces
could be redeployed speedily to meet any Allied move.

Meanwhile, another formidable old German soldier had arrived in
Constantinople at the end of 1914 to assume Liman's former post as

head of the German mission. Field Marshal Colmar, Freiherr von der Goltz had established himself as a profound military theorist in his book *The Nation in Arms* of 1883, with its prophetic thesis that future wars would be waged as much by whole peoples as by field armies and that vast bodies of conscripts would fight out prolonged battles of stalemate involving great bloodshed. His supportive presence at the heart of the Turkish government, where he had the ear of Enver Pasha, was to be of immeasurable assistance to his compatriot at the Dardanelles.

Within two weeks of Liman's arrival at Gallipoli a defensive force of some 80,000 men – at least twice the highest British estimate – had been concentrated for the defence of the Dardanelles. Of these, about 45,000 constituted 'bayonet strength', the remainder being logistics and labour units unfitted for combat. Initially the main threat was seen as being around Besika Bay on the Asiatic shore. On this side of the Dardanelles lay the principal land defences, for here were not only fixed batteries and forts, but also the majority of the mobile howitzer batteries which had already so troubled the Allied fleet and which, argued the defenders, would be a likely target for neutralization once the Allies moved ashore.

On the peninsula itself, Liman identified three main possible landing places. He still believed that Bulair was the most likely, for its possession by the enemy would throttle the supply routes to the rest of his garrisons further down the peninsula and enable the Allies to pass through the Narrows and into the Sea of Marmara. The next landing place was thought to be the tip of the peninsula, around Cape Helles. This would permit the Allied fleet to close in on both sides in order to give overwhelming fire support to the landings. The Allies, however, would be aware that there were only a few possible landing places here, and that these were not only heavily defended, but could be held by a relatively small force, well dug in and with fire support available from the batteries on the Asiatic shore. The third point of danger seemed to be on the western coast of the peninsula in the area between the headlands of Gaba Tepe and Ari Burnu. A force coming ashore here could be in Maidos within two hours unless repulsed.

For the defence of the peninsula Liman now had six divisions. He decided to redeploy his forces in three main groups whilst assigning all his labour resources to the improvement of the rudimentary road system in his operational area. Two divisions, the 5th and 7th, were held back at Bulair. The 9th Division was deployed in the southern part of the peninsula, from the southern end of Suvla Bay, down the western coast round to the old fort at Sedd-el-Bahr. The 3rd and 11th

Divisions were posted on the Asiatic shore guarding Besika Bay and Kum Kale. In reserve was the 19th Division, held in the Maidos area from where it could move rapidly to any of the threatened points on the European shore.

The officer in command of this last formation was Lieutenant-Colonel Mustafa Kemal. Aged 34 in 1915, he had long been associated with the Young Turk movement; a fact recognized at the military academy, from which he was commissioned in 1904 and promptly banished to the military backwater of Syria where he continued to mix seditious politics with the profession of arms. He actively supported the revolution in 1908 but became disenchanted with the Young Turk movement and in particular with Enver its leader, and concentrated for some years on his military career, slowly ascending the promotion ladder by application and dedication – qualities not widely apparent in the Turkish army of that period. On his own initiative he made his way to Libya to fight against the Italians in 1912. There his ability was recognized, earning him a post as chief of staff of a corps garrisoning the Gallipoli peninsula, where he drew up a detailed plan for its defence, having gained an intimate knowledge of its terrain.

When war broke out in 1914 Mustafa Kemal had been Military Attaché in Sofia. Whilst he believed that Turkey had been too hasty in entering the war, possibly on the wrong side, he made his way quickly home and was given a more active job on the General Staff in Constantinople. This did not suit his restless spirit and he managed to get appointed to the 19th Division, then forming up and mobilizing at Rodosto, on the Marmara coast between Gallipoli and Constantinople. He drove his men hard and the division was fully operational by the end of February 1915 when it moved to Maidos.

Kemal's appreciation, based on his intimate knowledge of the area, was that any Allied landings would take place at Sedd-el-Bahr and Gaba Tepe and he disposed his troops accordingly before Liman's arrival. He watched the naval bombardment of 5 March and was moved by the courage of the coastal defence gunners. It now seemed that an Allied landing was imminent, an impression strengthened by the attack of 18 March. Kemal redoubled his training programme, driving his men to their limits as he practised deployments to meet any conceivable pattern of attack from the sea. As soon as Liman arrived to supervise the defence he recognized the quality of this Turkish colonel, whose division, he noted approvingly, was hard and battle-worthy to an extent he had not seen elsewhere in the Ottoman army. Privately, he decided that Kemal was an officer fit for higher command, who could be relied on to use his initiative without waiting for direction from above and who was ruthless enough to send his men to certain death if needed. As fortune would have it, the 19th Division was out of camp on field exercises on the two days immediately preceding the Anzac landings, and when the moment came, Kemal would know exactly what to do.

The Turkish 9th Division, assigned by Liman to the defence of the southern end of the peninsula, comprised three infantry regiments, each of three battalions, and was commanded by Colonel Sami Bey, an able Arab in the Turkish service. One of the regiments was deployed to cover the Ari Burnu area, one to defend the southern tip of the peninsula around Sedd-el-Bahr, and one, with two batteries of artillery, held in reserve on the Kilid Bahr plateau. Hamilton's chosen landing places were thus defended by relatively few troops, especially as most of the forward regiments were held back within an hour's march of the beaches in case of unforeseen attacks elsewhere. In the southern end of the peninsula, one battalion was deployed on Krithia village, nearly two miles inland, with only one company facing out to the Aegean, covering the entrance of Gully Ravine. The rest of the battalion faced the other way, looking down towards Cape Helles across the slightly inclined bowl of open scrubby ground, punctuated by patches of cultivation, across which any force landing at Cape Helles would have to march. Observation posts on top of Achi Baba commanded an unbroken view of this stretch of country and all likely targets on it had been registered for artillery fire.

From just south of Gully Ravine to Sedd-el-Bahr fort, one battalion held a front of some five miles of coast, supported by a company of engineers who had been given the task of strengthening the fieldworks covering what were to be V and W beaches, a task performed under the expert eyes of their German advisers and carried out with deadly efficiency. One rifle company was positioned at W beach and another, with two elderly Maxim guns, overlooked V beach. Two companies were held back in reserve, about a mile behind Sedd-el-Bahr village, from where they could move rapidly to any point in the battalion area. At De Tott's Battery, overlooking S beach, were two more companies. The defence of X beach was left to an observation party of a dozen men. At Y beach there were no defenders whatsoever. No field artillery had been assigned to the southern end of the peninsula, whose defenders relied to a great extent on fire support from batteries on the Asiatic shore. The 3rd and 11th Divisions were held well back from the lightly defended beaches on the opposite side of the Straits. Liman had deployed a reserve of two regiments (six battalions) in the area of ancient Troy, three miles inland.

Having made these deployments, Liman set about motivating his army. All units were subjected to ferocious route marches to get them fit, intensive training in musketry, tactics, entrenchments and camouflage. Efforts had been made to equip the defenders of the Dardanelles as well as the Turkish system could manage. Most of the infantry were issued with the excellent Mauser rifle, and trained in the use of grenades, of which they had a plentiful supply, as the Allies would find to their cost; they also practised with the bayonet for close-quarter fighting. In the British army bayonet fighting was one of the sacred pillars of infantry training and a War Office pamphlet was devoted to the subject. The theory governing its use was expressed thus:

> The spirit of the bayonet . . . must be inculcated into all ranks so that they may go forward with that aggressive determination and confidence of superiority born of continual practice . . . In an assault the enemy must be killed with the bayonet. Firing should be avoided for in the mix-up a bullet, passing through an opponent's body, may kill a friend who happens to be in the line of fire.

The Turkish artillery was manned by regular soldiers regarded as picked men. Their commonest equipment at Gallipoli was the German Krupp light howitzer, which, boldly handled and capable of rapid redeployment by horse or mechanical transport, gave such trouble to the Allied fleet on 18 March. The static coast defence artillery guarding the Straits was of mixed origin; many of the guns dated back to the 1870s and were of little value against heavily armoured ships, but under the inspired leadership of the German experts, the gunners performed valiantly after the initial demoralization of the earlier bombardments, and there were several occasions when they fought their guns to the end under heavy fire.

Most historians of the Gallipoli campaign have dwelt on the appalling treatment of battle casualties in the early days following the landings of 25 April, and many have laid the blame squarely on the medical staff in GHQ. Examination of the evidence does not entirely support this. Much of the problem actually stems from the decision by Hamilton to leave the Adjutant-General Woodward and his staff, together with the director of medical services, behind at Alexandria when GHQ moved back to Mudros early in April.

Furthermore, the veil of secrecy thrown over the planning of the landings prevented the administrative staff from playing their proper role, which was usurped by the General Staff, whose knowledge of planning for battle casualties on the scale now envisaged was minimal.

From the start an assumption was made which would cost everyone dear, especially those unfortunate enough to become early battle casualties; the plan drawn up by the General Staff for medical treatment and evacuation of casualties envisaged the rapid seizure of the Achi Baba feature at Helles and the majority of the high ground overlooking the landing beaches at Anzac. At this stage, less than a week before the landings, the only medical staff officer with Hamilton at Mudros was Lieutenant-Colonel Keble, the Assistant Director of Medical Services. He was the first officer to express concern over the 'G' medical plan, but Braithwaite would not listen to him. Indeed, both he and Hamilton were remarkably cool towards the administrative staff and studiously avoided taking them into their confidence. At last Hamilton reluctantly agreed to bring the 'A' and 'Q' staff over from Alexandria.

Woodward, the Adjutant-General, was aghast at what he found; arrangements for the supply of reinforcements, and their accommodation on Lemnos, were wholly inadequate. Surgeon-General Birrell, newly appointed as the expedition's Director of Medical Services, was equally shocked when he eventually reached Mudros on 22 April. The 'G' staff at Mudros were expecting up to 3,000 casualties in the opening stages of the operation but Birrell thought that the number could be nearer 10,000. It has to be borne in mind that no attempt had been made for generations to land a substantial British force on a defended shore, and the army medical services were woefully unprepared for such a contingency. Birrell therefore had no guidelines on which to base his estimates, which were ignored by Braithwaite.

The GHQ operational plan, as now outlined to the worried Birrell, provided for the troops going ashore with bearer parties and the tent subdivisions of the field ambulances (one of which was established in each brigade) together with 'as much medical and surgical equipment as can be manhandled by the personnel'. At 2 p.m. on the day of the landing the casualty clearing stations of the 29th Division and of the Australian and New Zealand Corps were to go ashore on their respective beaches, again manhandling as much equipment as the men of the unit could carry. The rest of the medical units were to go ashore 'as soon as they can be disembarked'. It is hard to imagine a more opaque instruction than this, especially as these non-combatant units were expected to go over beaches raked with heavy fire. Two hospital ships were to position themselves off the beaches: *Sicilia*, with accommodation for 400 'serious' casualties, was to anchor off Helles in support of 29 Division, and *Gascon* (300 casualties) off Anzac. The navy were expected to start ferrying casualties out to the ships at about 2 p.m. on the day of the landing and three launches were to be working to each hospital ship.

Having been briefed by Birrell, Woodward could see that these arrangements were hopelessly inadequate and strongly urged the 'G' staff to arrange for the preparation of more ships to receive the heavy casualties he and Birrell foresaw. He estimated that about 1,000 more would need evacuation off each landing point and that the estimated numbers of stretcher cases should be doubled. It was reluctantly agreed that three more stationary (tented) hospitals should be summoned from England and Australia, though these would now be several weeks in arriving. The General Staff gave Woodward to understand that the wounded must be attended to and accommodated, wherever possible, ashore on the peninsula 'in the best way possible', although how this was to be achieved was not made clear. He was also told, somewhat confusingly, that there could be no evacuation off the beaches whilst fighting was still in progress nearby, as all launches, lighters and boats were needed to get fighting men and their equipment ashore. Evacuation by night, it was grudgingly admitted, might be possible. In short, it was doubtful if any serious cases could be evacuated in the first two or three days, despite the provision made in the naval instructions for evacuation after 2 p.m. on the first day.

Woodward's representations achieved something; the 'G' staff agreed to earmark more ships for the evacuation of casualties back to Egypt or Malta. He approached the 'Q' staff and told them that as the two hospital ships would be overwhelmed by the numbers of casualties he had predicted, extra staff from the stationary hospitals already in the theatre should be sent aboard the transports which, when full of wounded, should set off immediately for Egypt and Malta, rather than remain at anchor with the hospital ships.

At the eleventh hour Braithwaite agreed to Birrell's revised medical plan. Whilst it was too late to change the deployments of the forward medical units, some more troop transports were told off to be ready for the transport of casualties and to take aboard additional medical personnel and equipment. These were the *Caledonia*, *Aragon* and *Dongola* for the 29th Division, each capable of carrying 400 stretcher cases and between 1,200 and 1,500 walking wounded. At Anzac, four more transports with a total lift of 600 stretcher cases and 3,200 walking wounded were fitted out so far as possible; but ships which had been used for troop and animal transport for many weeks could not possibly be turned into anything approaching a sterile condition in less than twenty-four hours. On Lemnos, No. 1 Australian Stationary Hospital was earmarked to deal with the sick from ships in Mudros harbour; as it was already bursting with men suffering from a variety of diseases, a hospital ship had to be rushed from Egypt to empty its wards. Other hospital ships from elsewhere in the Mediterranean now began to steam at top speed for the Aegean.

The medical resources available to the units going ashore were reasonably adequate. All the battalions of 29th Division had their regimental medical officers, each with his establishment of orderlies and stretcher bearers and the equipment needed to set up a regimental aid post just behind the firing line for immediate treatment of battle casualties. Each brigade had its own field ambulance from the territorial force, staffed by some of Britain's finest physicians, surgeons and consultants. The Anzacs were also up to establishment in this respect, with a total of six field ambulances, as was the Royal Naval Division. Casualty clearing stations for more elaborate treatment and surgery were due to follow the field ambulances ashore as soon as practical.

Birrell had now made provision for about 10,000 casualties, which was near his original estimate. However, as his planning was made on the assumption that there would be an immediate advance off the beaches, leaving ample room ashore for the deployment of field ambulances and casualty clearing stations, followed rapidly by three stationary hospitals, it was dreadfully flawed. In any case, many of the staffs from the stationary hospitals had now been sent aboard the converted transports – known from their hull colour as the 'Black Ships' – and would not be available to go ashore if needed there. The medical plan was in trouble before a shot had been fired.

# 12

# The Twenty-Fifth of April: I – Anzac

The bravest thing on earth God ever made.
A British officer, speaking of the Australian
infantryman, 1915

THE AUSTRALIAN AND New Zealand Corps was to land on the west coast of the peninsula between the headlands of Gaba Tepe and Ari Burnu. The first battalions ashore, comprising the covering force, were to advance inland with all speed and seize a position on the ridges commanding the country towards Maidos before the defenders could react in strength. The main body of the corps, arriving ashore as soon as possible after the covering force, was to pass through it and advance on Maidos with the aim of capturing it before nightfall.

The covering force was the 2nd Australian Brigade under Acting Colonel Sinclair-MacLagan, a major in the Yorkshire Regiment on secondment to the Australian forces, until recently employed under Major-General Bridges at Duntroon in the quaintly titled appointment of 'Professor of Military Art'. He had been able to look at the coastline from a destroyer some days earlier, and was in possession of the latest information obtained by aerial observers. The maps with which he and all the other commanders of the landing force had been issued were obsolete and, as they did not give the names of most of the principal topographical features, of little use.

The terrain which faced the covering force is formidable. North of the intended landing place, the ground rises to a massif culminating in Koja Chemen Tepe or Point 971. This is the highest of several summits on the Sari Bair ridge which throws off three main spurs running south-west, separated by deep nullahs, down to the beach. The seaward slopes of the first two ridges, known at the time as first, second and third (or Gun) ridge, are extremely steep and in places precipitous, whilst the slopes facing south-east and inland are gentler. At the northern end of the massif the land plunges down to the sea and on to the Suvla Plain in a chaos of cliffs and gullies where the most experienced map reader is quickly baffled and where movement is further hindered by scrub and treacherous footing. The conduct of operations in this tumbled land would have strained the capacity of seasoned troops; it remains a lasting tribute to the inexperienced men of Australia and New Zealand that they accomplished what they did, from the moment they set foot on Turkish soil to their final evacuation some eight months later.

Major-General Bridges, commanding the 1st Australian Division from which the covering force was drawn, ordered Sinclair-MacLagan to get forward on to the third ridge as soon as possible. Had the landings taken place on the intended stretch of beach this objective would have been feasible, for the troops involved were extremely fit and keen to excel in this, their first engagement. Once on to Gun Ridge, the force was to fill out to its left and move higher up until it reached Point 971. The right wing, after forming up on the beach, was to go south and storm the Turkish position at Gaba Tepe. This would ensure a safe landing for the main body, following hard on the heels of the 2nd Brigade. The Indian Mountain Artillery Brigade was to get ashore as soon as possible to provide fire support.

Birdwood had favoured a landing by night in order to gain maximum surprise; he recognized that although the coastline was relatively lightly held, it presented formidable obstacles in the form of the Sari Bair massif, and that early reverses on the beach could lead to disaster if it became impossible to get the main body ashore during the first morning. He had to get the 4,000 men of the covering force on the beach by first light. However, the moon did not set until just before 3 a.m. and until then, the approaching fleet would risk detection by Turkish observation posts. The ships were therefore compelled to heave-to five miles offshore until it became completely dark, after the moon had set in the west. This meant that the first men would not get ashore until 4.30 a.m. when the first tinges of dawn would be lighting the eastern sky. It was going to be a close-run thing, dependent on precise timekeeping and good navigation by the navy.

The covering force was to go ashore in three waves. The first, carried in three battleships, would transfer to twelve 'tows' two miles offshore; the second, close behind, would land from destroyers which, towing ship's boats, were to pass through the line of battleships and cast off the boats only 100 yards from the beach. The third wave was to follow in the same way. Birdwood's main body, in the form of the 1st Australian Division, would start to come ashore off eight transports at 9 a.m., by which time it was expected that the covering force would have attained its initial objectives and that Point 971 could be secured. The rest of the corps was to come ashore as soon as possible. Birdwood placed himself aboard HMS *Queen*, the flagship of Rear-Admiral Thursby, the naval commander in this sector.

On the evening of 24 April a line of battleships carrying the covering force filed out of Mudros harbour and steamed slowly towards the rendezvous at sea off the Gallipoli coast where, five miles off land and invisible from the shore, they hove-to, guided by a masked white light displayed by HMS *Triumph*. Aboard the battleships the Australians prepared themselves for combat. On *London* there had been a church service on the quarterdeck in the early evening. Private Fred Fox would remember the events of the next few hours to the end of his days:

> The departure from Mudros was to the accompaniment of wild cheering from the dozens of British and French ships in the anchorage. The troops were then told to rest; there was no wild excitement, but an air of quiet confidence. Very early on the morning of the 25th the men were roused and given a hearty meal before struggling into their kit. Three empty sandbags, 200 rounds of ammunition, three days' iron rations, full water bottles and packs. Each man carried about 80 pounds, but instructions were to remove packs after landing and stack them in company piles for recovery later. Not a shot was to be fired until broad daylight or until ordered by an officer, and the chambers of all the rifles were empty in order to prevent accidental discharge. Absolute silence was ordered until ashore, when only the bayonet was to be used.

Fox clambered into the boat with his comrades at 2 a.m. and the tows set out into the gloom. The sea was glassy calm; packed closely together, the men sat in total silence as bidden and maintained this rigid discipline all the way in to the beach. The silhouette of the battleship melted away in the dark as the land loomed into view. So far, all was silence ashore.

Unfortunately for Fox, and tragically for the entire force, an unforeseen factor was silently working against them. The current which sets northward along the coast at this point had been underestimated and was steadily bearing the line of tows carrying the first three battalions towards Ari Burnu. Also, in the dark, several of the pinnaces, commanded by youthful midshipmen (many only 15 years old), lost direction and crossed the wake of the neighbouring tow. The order of landing was thus thrown into disarray before anyone had set foot on shore. The flotilla of tows was nearly on shore when the senior naval officer realized a grave error had occurred, and that one of his colleagues had confused Ari Burnu with Gaba Tepe. He made a frantic attempt to alter course but this only compounded the confusion. Already the brigade was one full mile north of its intended landing place when, at 4.25, with dawn now clearly breaking behind the hills ahead, the tows cast off from the pinnaces. They were only 50 yards from the beach, and at this moment the Turks saw them.

Signal lamps flashed, a flare rose into the sky, the sounds of the defenders leaping to arms were heard, and a sporadic fire opened on the packed boats. The covering force's first wave now got ashore, hopelessly intermingled, to find that some boats had landed north of Ari Burnu whilst the rest had arrived, on a very narrow front, just to the south of the headland. Instead of the gentle slope the troops had been led to expect, and the bank behind which they were going to form up and leave their packs, they were confronted by what appeared in the gloom to be a precipitous landscape rising immediately off a very narrow sandy beach. As the Turkish fire steadily increased and men began to fall, the Australians vigorously set about any Turks who were to be seen. A group charged up to what became known as Plugge's Plateau and put its defenders to the bayonet; some of the bluejackets threw down their oars, grabbed rifles from wounded or dead soldiers, and swarmed enthusiastically ashore with the Australians, thus holding up the second lift.

Private Fox leaped out of his boat as it came under fire, to find that barbed wire had been laid under the surface. The noise was tremendous as he and the others threw off their packs, fixed bayonets and rushed up the cliff. No quarter was given or prisoners taken by either side in the deadly brawl which now took place. Turkish shrapnel was raining down and men were falling to snipers concealed in thick scrub. By midday, Fox was fighting his way up towards the high ground ahead; like everyone else he had long since lost contact with his platoon and everywhere he could see little groups of three or four men edging forward under the leadership of whoever asserted himself. He noted that the Indian mountain gunners were ashore and adding their firepower to that of the fleet, whose battleships and cruisers were firing broadside after broadside at targets over the ridge ahead.

He and two others found a small knoll and decided to have a rest, a cigarette and some of their iron rations. Fox was thinking how beautiful it all was – birds singing all round him, the sea spread out below with the great fleet firing steadily, more troops pouring ashore – and wondering how, on 'God's Good Sunday', men could be striving to kill each other, when 'one of my friends dropped; a sniper had got him. He simply sank down and died. Off we rushed again . . . suddenly a shrapnel shell burst right overhead, killing the soldier on my left and hitting me full in the right knee . . . the pain was excruciating.' Fox immediately recharged the magazine of his rifle and began the long journey back to the beach far below, still under heavy fire from invisible snipers. Eventually, weak from loss of blood and with his uniform cut to shreds by bullets, he collapsed unconscious into a trench and was carried to the beach. He had to spent the night lying, with many other wounded, in an open boat as the rain poured down, 'but I knew no more till I was hoisted aboard the transport on Monday morning. I had had a lot of pain but was quite happy. We did what we had to do and I was proud in belonging to the Australian Volunteer contingent.'

As the day wore on, thousands more Australians were undergoing their battle initiation on the precarious beach-head. Some displayed remarkable dash and enterprise. One company of about a hundred men under Major Gordon-Bennett, in civilian life an actuarial clerk and dedicated part-time soldier, wasted no time in leaving the beach; heading south-east they rapidly crossed the first ridge, then the second, and were well across the lower ground and going hard for Gun Ridge when the Turkish resistance stiffened. Gordon-Bennett was badly wounded and despite his protests his stretcher bearers carried him back to the beach – a dangerous venture as the Turks were now fully alerted and hunting down small parties of Australians wherever they found them. Gordon-Bennett's men continued to fight until overwhelmed, very few surviving to be taken prisoner. Among the dead was the company commander's younger brother, serving as a sergeant. The bodies of this gallant band were not to be recovered until 1919 when their remains were found high up on Gun Ridge – the furthest any Australians managed to penetrate on that first day. Elsewhere, Captain Lalor was trying to rally men from various units to stem the gathering force of the Turkish counter-attacks on the feature known as Baby 700. Lalor was Australian to the bone, the grandson of one of the ringleaders of the Eureka Stockade uprising, and went ashore brandishing a family heirloom, a sword which he was still wielding when killed.

The Royal Navy was totally committed to the landing, ferrying troops ashore, providing close fire support, and doing what could be done to get the wounded out to the ships where they could receive urgent surgery. Midshipman Eric Bush, not yet 16, recorded his experiences in his journal in a round schoolboy's hand. He was serving in the elderly armoured cruiser *Bacchante*, detailed as a support ship for the Anzac landing.

With the rest of the fleet, the ship left Mudros late in the afternoon of 24 April and steered a wide course out to sea in order to avoid visual detection. Very early on the morning of the 25th *Bacchante* hove-to and hoisted out her picket boat and pinnace, which went over to the *Prince of Wales* to take on a load of Australians. At 3.50 a.m. they had left the ships behind and were moving towards the shore in total darkness and silence, the faint loom of the land before them. Bush concentrated on keeping his station, a difficult task in the dark with not a glimmer of light showing where the next tow was. At 4.20 a.m. the first shot rang out from ahead followed by a growing fusillade. Within five minutes shrapnel was bursting overhead as the boats neared the shore, taking soundings as they went. At 4.30, shoaling fast, they slipped the tows and the ships' boats, propelled by the oars of the bluejackets, went in towards the shore in an increasing hail of fire.

Bush watched as one boat was hit and the surviving passengers leaped into shoulder-deep water; at last the Australians, who had kept strict silence all the way in to the beach, let out a resounding cheer, shed their packs, fixed bayonets and charged wildly up the hill above the beach. Casualties were already occurring and on his second trip to the shore with more troops, Bush was appalled to see the dead and wounded already heaped on the sand, and several boats drifting away with cargoes of dead and dying: 'three lifeboats and a launch, the crews of all of them apparently killed or wounded . . . some . . . hanging over the sides of their boat, dead, having been killed while climbing out . . . the beach now strewn with soldiers' packs.' By 1 p.m., Bush noted, horses were being landed.

Early in the evening there was a call for more ammunition ashore as almost all had been expended to meet Turkish counter-attacks. Wounded men in their hundreds were now crowded on the beach. Shrapnel bursting overhead was causing yet more casualties but it was only at this point that the first wounded were taken off. Almost at once the hospital ship offshore was filled to capacity and loading of the first 'Black Ship' commenced. This too was full by 7 p.m. By 8 p.m. a jetty had been constructed and this greatly improved matters. Throughout the night, Bush and his fellow midshipmen were carrying wounded out to the transports; ashore, the continual roar of musketry indicated that a fight was going on at the top of the ridge, and a rain of shrapnel and spent bullets fell around the launches and pinnaces as they shuttled back and to from ship to shore. Bush was to get no sleep for seventy-two hours.

As darkness fell on the evening of the 25th the beach-head was in a state of unimaginable confusion. Fighting was going on all along the second ridge and snipers were active in all parts of the landing area. On the narrow strip of beach above the waterline, piles of stores, water containers, ammunition, rations and engineer stores were stacked wherever a space could be found, without regard to their nature. Men were wandering about, apparently looking for their platoon commanders; the wounded lay wherever a space could be found, uncomplaining as men trod on them. Many died unattended in the dark. Any lights shown immediately drew the attentions of snipers, and intermittent shellfire continued to take its toll.

Just above the beach, in a hurriedly dug shelter below Plugge's Plateau, Birdwood, summoned ashore by an urgent signal from his two divisional commanders, Bridges and Godley, conferred with them and Walker of the New Zealand Brigade. At one point Walker personally led Birdwood to the top of Plugge's and showed him where the New Zealand Brigade, fighting its way up the high ground on the left flank of the beach-head, had become isolated on what would soon be known as Walker's Ridge, and that the Turks had already insinuated themselves between them and the Australians on their right. Walker was not addicted to mincing his words and had already earned himself several reprimands from Birdwood and Godley for exceeding the bounds of tact in his dealings with them. A robust Briton who infinitely preferred regimental soldiering to the drudgery of staffwork, Walker thought first and foremost of his men, whose lives he jealously protected and whose personal comfort and safely took priority over all else. He now listened with growing incredulity as his superiors, men for whom he had the highest regard, began to speak of re-embarkation. Birdwood was equally horrified, but Bridges took him aside and told him that if this drastic step was to be taken, it must be taken at once. A warning signal was sent to the fleet immediately.

Admiral Thursby ordered all the transports to hoist out any remaining boats, but made a mental note to resist any attempt to take the Anzacs off. He knew that in their present state of disorganization, any rearward movement could only end in rout as thousands of individuals rushed down the hills for the boats. Bridges had done all that could have been expected during that dreadful day, but was now

exhausted; his honourable nature recoiled from the idea of evacuation but, seen objectively, it seemed to be the only way to save at
least part of his division and the rest of the force. He reluctantly
counselled immediate evacuation. Birdwood replied that he would
sooner stay to fight it out and die on the beach than take to the ships
again. In anguish, he decided to place the responsibility for a decision on Hamilton and drafted a signal to the Commander-in-Chief:

> Both my divisional generals and brigadiers have represented to me
> that they fear their men are thoroughly demoralized by shrapnel fire
> to which they have been subjected all day after exhaustion and gallant
> work in the morning. Numbers have dribbled back from firing line
> and cannot be collected in this difficult country. Even the New Zealand
> Brigade, which has only recently been engaged, lost heavily and is to
> some extent demoralized. If troops are subjected to shellfire again
> tomorrow morning there is likely to be a fiasco, as I have no fresh
> troops with which to replace those in firing line. I know my represen-
> tation is most serious, but if we are to re-embark, it must be at once.

The first person to see this signal on its arrival aboard his flagship,
HMS *Queen*, in the hands of Captain Vyvyan the naval beachmaster,
was Rear-Admiral Thursby. Had he taken the appropriate action he
would have had it passed by wireless to the *Queen Elizabeth* for
Hamilton to see at once. However, in his haste to get the signal off,
Birdwood had omitted to address it to anyone. Thursby knew that it
would be impossible to rescue the force ashore intact. The wind was
rising, it was raining steadily, and the night was extremely dark. He
did, however, issue a precautionary order halting the evacuation of
casualties.

Thursby was on the point of going ashore to remonstrate with
Birdwood and see things for himself, when out of the darkness
loomed the *Queen Elizabeth*, carrying Hamilton, de Robeck, and their
staffs. He immediately went aboard, taking with him two officers of
the Anzac headquarters staff – one of whom was Cunliffe-Owen, the
former Military Attaché in Constantinople, who had secured a post
on the New Zealand staff and was now back on Turkish soil.
Hamilton was asleep but was hastily roused.

A council of war now took place in the admiral's dining-cabin to
study the implications of Birdwood's bombshell. It was the most
crucial decision to face Hamilton in his whole life, for a wrong
appraisal would spell disaster on a huge scale. As it happened, the
decision was made for him. After an inconclusive discussion in
which no new light could be thrown on the confused situation

ashore, Thursby stated emphatically that it would take two days to re-embark the troops, and that they would be better advised to stick it out, as he felt they could if told to. At once, Hamilton drafted a reply to Birdwood which has earned its place in history:

> Your news is indeed serious. But there is nothing for it but to dig your-selves right in and stick it out. It would take at least two days to re-embark you, as Admiral Thursby will explain to you. Meanwhile the Australian submarine [the *AE2*] has got up through the Narrows and has torpedoed a gunboat at Chanak. Hunter-Weston, despite his heavy losses, will be advancing tomorrow which should divert pressure from you. Make a personal appeal to your men and Godley's to make a supreme effort to hold their ground. PS – You have got through the dif-ficult business. Now you have only to dig, dig, dig, until you are safe.

This signal had an immediately invigorating effect on those ashore and the encouragement it gave to Birdwood and his hard-pressed commanders spread rapidly down to the men in the firing line. There would be no more talk of retreat at Anzac.

Liman had been agreeably surprised at the rapid improvement in the quality of the Turkish troops defending the peninsula since his arrival in March. They had responded well to intensive training coupled with the hard labour of improving the existing defences and building new ones, and their morale had greatly improved, as evid-enced by better turnout and a general recognition that they were fighting for the soil of their country. By 24 April, as the Allied fleet weighed anchor and steamed towards the Dardanelles, he was con-fident that his army would give a good account of itself.

News of the landings at Ari Burnu reached Mustafa Kemal's head-quarters at 6.30 a.m., some two hours after they had taken place. As it happened, a training exercise had been ordered for 19 Division that morning, to take place in the country out towards Ari Burnu. A bat-talion set off immediately in that direction and a cavalry patrol was ordered to report on the movements of the invading force. The rest of the division was then called to arms and ordered to march as quickly as possible in the direction of the enemy. Kemal himself, with a small party of staff officers, including his personal medical officer who fol-lowed him everywhere equipped with syringes for the stimulants he had to take, set off on horseback for the high ground overlooking Ari Burnu. Before leaving he sent a report to corps headquarters to say that he had committed 19 Division on his own initiative without waiting for instructions and was off to the fight. In his party was the commander of the 57th Regiment, who received his instructions as they rode along.

On arrival at Point 971 a remarkable sight met their eyes. A great fleet lay anchored below, with myriads of small boats coursing rapidly from ship to shore and back again. Battleships were firing their main and secondary armament as hard as they could and great clouds of smoke were rising from their shellbursts. From the summit it is not possible to see the shoreline, which lies in dead ground; but Kemal realized at once that a major landing was in full swing and that immediate action was required if the enemy were to be kept off the highest ground, with its superb panoramic views out to the Narrows, only four miles distant. The men of the 57th were now beginning to arrive at the summit, blown with their rapid march, and Kemal ordered them to rest. Then he went forward, telling them to follow in ten minutes.

His destination was the top of Chunuk Bair. Leaving their horses behind, Kemal and his party went ahead on foot. As they reached the summit a group of gendarmerie fled towards them, shouting that enemy skirmishers were hot on their heels. Kemal, realizing that the Australians were closer to him than his own units, and that he was in imminent risk of capture, told the gendarmes to stand firm. When they complained that they had run out of ammunition he told them to fix bayonets and lie down. The pursuing Australians were now in full view, but thinking that the Turks had lain down in order to shoot, they also lay down. The two lines of prone men froze, watching each other, as the 57th Regiment now appeared on the scene, immediately went into the attack and swept down the hillside, followed quickly by the 27th Regiment. Kemal remained on the spot, personally directing the fight and drawing up a lucid report of the situation for his corps commander. He had rapidly appreciated that the broken nature of the ground was working against the enemy and that if he maintained the concentration of his troops he could obtain a decisive result; he also saw that the Turkish right flank, where the 57th Regiment was being committed, was the crucial point of the whole battle that morning, as the outcome would decide which side was going to gain possession of the summits of the Sari Bair ridge; and whoever held them, held the key of victory.

Kemal issued terse verbal orders to the men of the 57th Regiment which left no doubt as to what was expected of them: 'I do not expect you to attack. I order you to die. In the time which passes until we die, other troops and commanders can take our place.' As their divisional commander was with them, clearly determined to lead from the front, the men obeyed. The corps commander arrived on the scene at 1 p.m. and Kemal briefed him as the men of the 19th Division flung themselves again and again at the Australians who were struggling to reach the summit against a hail of Turkish fire. Kemal would afterwards refer to the 57th with reverence: 'a famous regiment this, because it was completely wiped out'. They went on attacking the invaders all afternoon and well into the night, when utter exhaustion on both sides forced a lull.

During the night the ever-watchful Kemal went round the firing lines, encouraging what was left of his command and getting them into some form of order to resume the fight on the following morning. He had won his battle, however, for no Allied soldier ever set foot on Point 971. A hitherto obscure Turkish lieutenant-colonel had just won one of the decisive battles of modern history, although he did not know it at the time.

# 13

# The Twenty-Fifth of April:
# II – Helles

The soldier's trade, verily, and essentially, is not
slaying, but being slain.

John Ruskin

THE MOST NORTHERLY of the Helles landing points was that at Y beach, three miles due north of Sedd-el-Bahr. It had been carefully chosen after Hamilton's initial seaborne reconnaissance of 18 March as a possible insertion place for a force which could threaten the Turks' communications down the peninsula to their garrisons at Helles. Although this section of the peninsula's coastline consists in the main of steep cliffs rising to 150 feet, Hamilton had noted a natural fissure in them where seasonal watercourses made their way down to the sea when in spate. From a narrow strip of beach there was a clear way up this which appeared scaleable by infantry, and there appeared to be no fixed defences at this point. He was correct in this assumption; on 25 April the nearest Turkish picket consisted of a half-platoon deployed near the entrance to Gully Ravine over a mile further south, where there was an obvious landing point and path up the cliffs. The Turks, however, perceived no threat from Y beach which was patrolled infrequently.

The troops assigned to the Y beach landing were the 1st Battalion King's Own Scottish Borderers (KOSB) under Lieutenant-Colonel Koe, a company of the 2nd Battalion South Wales Borderers, both from 29 Division, and Lieutenant-Colonel Matthews' Plymouth battalion of Royal Marine Light Infantry from the Royal Naval Division. The marines were mostly men who had volunteered for war service in August and September 1914. The fact that they were raw, semi-trained and had virtually no core of long-service officers or NCOs was not, it appears, appreciated by either GHQ or by Hunter-Weston and

his staff, although Matthews raised the issue at the final verbal briefing for the landing, held four days earlier, when he asked that the
better-trained Scottish and Welsh Borderers be landed first. In this he
was supported by Lieutenant-Commander Adrian Keyes, the commodore's brother, who was responsible for getting the troops ashore.
In contrast to the young marines, the KOSB were an all-regular battalion which had mobilized at Lucknow when war broke out. They
had been in India for eight years, a well-knit and efficient battalion.

Several more misunderstandings were to blight this enterprise. On
21 April, when Hunter-Weston issued his final verbal instructions for
the landings, Colonel Koe was sick and not present; it had been ascer-
tained that Matthews was the senior of the two commanding officers
and he was detailed to be in charge of the troops once they were
ashore. Nothing, however, was committed to paper at this verbal
briefing and no confirmatory orders were written out and distributed
to those present. Also, no one informed GHQ, who thought that Koe
was in charge. Once landed, Koe was also under this impression as
he had not been fully informed of the decisions made at Hunter-
Weston's briefing.

The verbal orders given to Matthews were to explore inland, look
for and capture a Turkish gun thought to be in the area, draw Turkish
reserves towards his sector and away from the main landings further
south, and make contact with the Royal Fusiliers who were going
ashore at X beach, two miles down the coast. It appears that he was
not clear what form this contact was to take – whether by physical
link-up or merely by lamp signal; and he does not seem to have asked
for clarification. He was also told that he was to join in the general
advance of the division towards Krithia and up on to the Achi Baba
feature, a move confidently expected to take place before last light on
the 25th. He was given no instructions for action to be taken if this
victorious advance failed to materialize and the main body became
pinned down on its beaches. Again, he seems not to have raised any
questions.

In accordance with the naval plan for the landing, the force destined for Y beach embarked at Mudros on the two cruisers, *Amethyst*
and *Sapphire*, carrying the King's Own Scottish Borderers and the
company of South Wales Borderers. The Plymouth battalion, less
well versed in their boat drills, went on to a transport. These ships
then put to sea for a rendezvous five miles off the Gallipoli coast
where they waited in the dark for the moon to set; they were accompanied by a flotilla of trawlers, the old battleship *Goliath*, and the
cruiser *Dublin*, whose guns would be available for close support.

At 2.30 a.m. the troops detailed for the first landing were transferred from the warships to their trawlers, each towing a string of six cutters manned by bluejackets who were to carry the men for the last few yards to the beach. The trawlers had been briefed to go in until their keels found bottom before putting the men into the cutters. The battleship and the cruisers closed to 4,000 and 2,000 yards respectively from the coast and cleared for action, whilst the trawlers continued in dead silence. As soon as the cannonade from Cape Helles was heard at 5 a.m., the men got into the cutters which were then rowed the last few yards to the beach. By 5.15 the KOSB were on the clifftops, and the marines were ashore forty-five minutes later. So far the operation had run according to plan; not a shot had been fired from the shore and total surprise had been achieved.

All sense of urgency now seems to have left the two units on the clifftop. A patrol sent inland encountered a small party of surprised Turks who were either killed or captured; some enterprising naval officers strolled inland and made their way across country, round Krithia village and on to the shoulder of Achi Baba, returning to Y beach with the report that they had seen very few Turks and, despite their white naval uniforms, they did not seem to have been detected.

However, a stronger KOSB reconnaissance patrol, moving inland, had immediately come across a significant topographical feature which did not appear on their maps. This was the deep cleft, to be known as Gully Ravine, which runs north-east from a point about a mile south of Y beach and is up to 100 feet deep in places, constituting a notable obstacle to movement from the beach in the direction of Krithia village. Its bottom is dry in summer but can run fiercely with water from the Achi Baba heights in the rainy season. It was to play a fateful role before long in the battles for Krithia. At this point on the morning of 25 April, no move was made by either of the commanding officers to push on across the ravine. More seriously, there was no attempt to dig defensive works to secure the clifftop. Instead, the troops were allowed to ease their packs off and make tea.

Passing Y beach at 8.30 aboard the *Queen Elizabeth*, Hamilton was given a 'success' signal from the troops ashore. Through his binoculars he could see masses of men on the cliffs, strolling around apparently unconcerned by the few 'overs' reaching the area from the naval bombardment at Cape Helles. No firing could be heard and fatigue parties were busily carrying rations, ammunition and water up the steep cliff path, the water containers flashing in the sun. All seemed to be going well despite the fact that there was no sign of urgent exploitation inland. The flagship merely acknowledged the signal and continued on down the coast towards X beach.

Nemesis, however, was about to overtake the force at Y beach. Unknown to Colonel Matthews, the Turks were about to react to his incursion. The commander of the 9th Turkish Division, the Arab colonel Sami Bey, had grasped the situation with commendable speed and saw at once that the force at Y imperilled the entire Turkish force deployed to the south. He already had plenty to concern him, for the 9th Division had a huge area of responsibility, charged with the defence of the coastline from just north of Ari Burnu down to, and including, Sedd-el-Bahr. He now decided that Y beach posed a significant threat and decided to deal with it as soon as possible.

As the morning wore on, Hamilton realized that things were going badly at V and W but remembered that all had appeared calm and under control at Y, and sent a signal to Hunter-Weston, in command of the landings at Cape Helles. Sent at 9.21, it read: 'Would you like to get some more men ashore at Y beach? If so, trawlers are available.' It is unfortunate that the signal did not make it clear why Hamilton thought it would be profitable to capitalize on success. Even more dangerously, the signal was phrased as a suggestion and not as an order. Although Hunter-Weston had been given command of the southern landings and the conduct of operations ashore, Hamilton was the Commander-in-Chief and had every right to override any of his subordinate commanders. It was his unwillingness to do this now, and on subsequent occasions, which spelt ultimate disaster. In his reluctance to intervene he was influenced by Braithwaite who, as chief of staff, insisted that the commanders on the spot should be given a free hand once issued with their operational instructions.

Hunter-Weston ignored Hamilton's message, fixing his gaze on the battles now raging on V and W beaches. At Y, Colonel Matthews had gone forward himself to confirm the reports of patrols which had already crossed the Ravine; with his adjutant he walked on until he was within hailing distance of Krithia village, deserted by its normal garrison who had rushed down towards Sedd-el-Bahr. In his absence, Colonel Koe, under the impression that he was in local command, had sent a heliograph message to the Royal Fusiliers at X beach, in which he reported that his men were ashore unopposed. He went on, rather oddly, to say that he had established a reserve of small arms ammunition on the clifftop and wondered whether he should put a guard on it and march down to X, or sit tight. He received no reply.

Intermittent sounds of action had been heard from the direction of

X during the morning; Matthews had no idea what was happening further south at V and W but could hear heavy fire from that direction, which led him to believe that the main landings had been held by the Turks. He therefore recalled his troops from the edge of the Ravine back to the cliffs and at last gave the order to dig defensive works. It was now mid-afternoon. The line defending Y beach was very thinly held, with the KOSB in the centre and two companies of marines on each flank. It was difficult to dig firing trenches on the rocky clifftops and the men were equipped only with their small entrenching tools. In some places it was impossible to dig any positions and packs were stacked to give some form of protection. Unknown to Matthews or Koe, the Turks were about to launch their counter-attack.

At X beach, which Hamilton passed shortly after his brief inspection of Y, the landing of the 2nd Battalion Royal Fusiliers had gone well. It was backed by the 12-inch guns of the battleship *Implacable*, commanded by the robust Captain Lockyer. He ignored his orders for supporting fire, which were to direct it at the ridges behind the beaches; instead, he decided that he would engage the beach itself with direct fire. He therefore took his ship to within 450 yards of the shore, from which, at point-blank range, its four 12-inch guns were directed at the small garrison of twelve terrified Turks, who fled. A measure of the proximity of the ship to the enemy was given when the ship's surgeon was killed on deck by sniper fire.

At 6.30 the Fusiliers were on top of the cliff and set out immediately in the direction of the main landings. They had not gone far when they ran into heavy opposition and it became clear that the landings further round the cape had run into serious trouble.

At W beach, the next one round from X, the covering force landing was to be undertaken by the 1st Battalion Lancashire Fusiliers. In company with the rest of the fleet, aboard the cruiser *Euryalus*, the battalion moved across from Tenedos after dark on the 24th and stood offshore ready for the final move on to the beaches. Their landing was to be part of the main assault on the southern point of the peninsula and all ranks of the 29th Division were left in no doubt that their formation had been chosen for the primary role because of its superior qualities, and that much was expected of all ranks in the critical hours ahead. The whole of the divisional covering force was to be ashore by 7 a.m. and it was expected that the main body, awaiting the outcome of the landings in its transports four miles off Cape Helles, would begin to come ashore from about 8.30. By then,

Hunter-Weston considered that the covering force would have secured a lodgement sufficient to permit the main force to land with minimal interference from the Turks.

As the Lancashire Fusiliers went on to W beach, the rest of the covering force was to go ashore at V and S beaches. Of these, V was the one for which Hunter-Weston planned to make the principal effort. Apart from the tows carrying the Royal Dublin Fusiliers and other troops, this is where the *River Clyde*, the 'Trojan Horse', was to be run aground in the shadow of the Sedd-el-Bahr fort; inside her holds were nearly 2,000 men of the Royal Munster Fusiliers, the Hampshire Regiment, some of the Dublins, and detachments of signallers and engineers. Also on board were Lieutenant-Colonel Doughty-Wylie, as GHQ representative, and some other staff officers. The landing at S beach, nearly a mile away on the far side of Morto Bay, was restricted in size because of the shortage of ships' boats and consisted of no more than two companies of the South Wales Borderers and an engineer detachment. Their task was to get ashore and seize the old fortification known as De Tott's Battery, having driven any defenders off.

The staffs of both GHQ and HQ 29th Division had seriously overestimated the strength of the Turkish defences in the southern end of the peninsula. At first light on 25 April, south of the line Krithia–Achi Baba, there were only two infantry battalions and an engineer company. At Y beach, as has been seen, there were no defenders at all; at X, the twelve men who fled when *Implacable*'s guns opened up; at V and W, about to be the scenes of desperate carnage, only two platoons in all; and at S, a solitary platoon.

The strength of the defences at V and W lay not in numbers, but in the careful preparation which had been carried out in the month's grace allowed to Liman and his enthusiastic Turkish pupils. Both beaches had been protected below water level with dense entanglements of barbed wire, and electrically detonated mines. On the cliffs overlooking the narrow strips of sand were carefully sited fire trenches, and more wire. Additional trenches and wire belts had been sited on the headland between the two beaches, the defenders having correctly predicted that energetic attempts would be made immediately after the initial landings to link beach-heads in order to create a secure landing place for the main body.

At 5 a.m. the naval bombardment started. On board the *River Clyde* the Royal Munster Fusiliers and Hampshires made their final preparations for landing. As soon as the ship had grounded and the lighters moved into position for use as a floating bridge they were to

emerge from the ports cut in the ship's side, run down the gang-
planks and go ashore; covering fire from the Maxims mounted in the
bows of the ship would keep the opposition's heads down during
this vulnerable part of the operation and it was hoped that casualties
would be relatively light.

As the ships left Mudros on the 23rd, they received the familiar
rousing send-off; bands played and patriotic songs were sung; but on
the Munsters' ship, the *Caledonia*, there was silence, as if every officer
and man sensed the terrible experience that lay ahead. The next day
saw them at Tenedos, transferring to the *River Clyde*. Whilst on board
they were under the command of Lieutenant-Colonel Carrington-
Smith of the 2nd Hampshires, who would be on the bridge next
morning alongside Commander Unwin, Lieutenant-Colonel Tizard
of the Munsters, and Lieutenant-Colonel Doughty-Wylie. Few slept
on the night of the 24th. Doughty-Wylie was writing his final letters
and many others did likewise. The Roman Catholic chaplain of the
Munsters celebrated mass, which for many of his flock would be their
*viaticum*.

As the ships moved closer in to the beaches it seemed that nothing
could withstand the tornado of fire beating down on the land from
the guns of the fleet. There were no signs of life ashore and some
optimists began to think that the Turks had been driven inland. However, the orders for naval gunfire support contained a fatal flaw. It
was thought, after the unsatisfactory results of the March bombardments, that naval high-velocity guns were unsuitable for engaging
entrenched personnel, and the guns were directed at targets inland,
few of which could be seen and most of which were being engaged
in the hope that they were likely to be of importance to the defence.
Only Captain Lockyer of the *Implacable*, off X beach, was prepared to
flout orders and take his ship right in to engage the enemy infantry
over open sights. Elsewhere the captain of the battleship *Cornwallis*,
equally athirst for battle, went ashore with the South Wales Borderers
at S beach in his white uniform, carrying pistol and cutlass, and spent
some time there before a peremptory signal from the flagship
reminded him of his duty afloat. Corporal Phillips of the Lancashire
Fusiliers packed his diary into his breast pocket before going down
into the boat which would carry him to the beach. He was in high
spirits, as was virtually every officer and soldier preparing for battle.

The Lancashire Fusiliers' landing beach was about 400 yards long
and no more than 50 yards deep; from the sand there rose a ridge,
then some sand dunes merging into higher ground inland; at each
end were cliffs on which the Turks had carefully sited their fire

trenches so as to create a killing ground for anyone rash enough to land here. A thick belt of wire ran along the beach a few yards above the waterline. Just below water there was more wire, sown with mines, designed to snare wading men. A machine-gun on either side of the beach commanded excellent fields of fire and could enfilade any troops taking cover behind the wire belt. An interlinking series of fields of fire extended all across the high ground above the beach so that even if men escaped the fire storm at the water's edge they would run into even deadlier fire on the higher ground.

At exactly 6 a.m., as the boats carrying the Dublins headed off towards V beach in company with the *River Clyde*, those carrying the Lancashire Fusiliers approached W. There were six tows, each of four boats, with two more tows coming in from the left, having been launched from *Implacable*. They approached the shore in dead silence, and when 50 yards off, the pinnaces slipped the tows, the signal for the sailors to begin rowing. The Turks were watching intently and their fire discipline was admirable, for not a sound betrayed their presence until, the boats only yards from the shore, a storm of fire broke loose. The only way to escape this was to abandon the boats and go over the side, which the Fusiliers did, to find in many cases that not only were they out of their depth but the water was also laced with tripwires and mines, which began to detonate. The noise was shattering and the shocked survivors of the initial discharge huddled in the lee of the wire on the beach.

The action which now took place lasted only minutes, but secured for the regiment a place in the mythology of the British army, for it won the battalion 'six Victoria Crosses . . . before breakfast'. Their supreme effort was to clamber through the wire and get on to the higher ground above the beach, from which they were able to drive the defenders, allowing the next wave to come ashore. Corporal Phillips did not get very far; he was struck on the chest by a bullet which knocked him over but was stopped by the diary in his pocket – the journal in which he had so gleefully reported the departure of Colonel Ormond only days before and also his extraordinary change of spirit from petulance to exaltation as the prospect of battle came upon him.

The commander of the Fusilier Brigade, Brigadier-General Hare, who had earlier issued a stirring Order enjoining his men to emulate the heroes of Albuhera, the celebrated battle of the Peninsular War in which an earlier Fusilier Brigade had driven the enemy off the field, now showed that he was prepared to follow suit and came ashore from *Euryalus* to assume control of the covering force fighting ashore.

He was soon wounded and taken off to the ships. Command of the brigade now devolved on Lieutenant-Colonel Newenham of the Royal Fusiliers but before he could take over he too was seriously wounded in the mêlée now raging above X beach. Hare's Brigade Major, Frankland of the Royal Dublin Fusiliers, was an inspiration to all, fighting at close quarters with the Turkish defenders and personally despatching several with a rifle taken off a dead Fusilier. Now he too was killed at about 8.30.

By now, British troops were fighting on the high ground overlooking V beach, from where they were witnesses of a terrible sight in the arena below. Here, the *River Clyde* had gone in at the same time as the tows carrying the Dublins. In the final approach to the beach the ship had to take evasive action to avoid running down some of the boats, reducing engine revolutions to avoid getting ashore ahead of them. As a result she did not have enough way on her as she gently ran on to the rocks barely 100 yards below the battered ruins of Sedd-el-Bahr castle. As she did so, the tows, which had been cast 50 yards offshore, were beginning to row in to the beach. As at W, there had been no sign of life on the shore as the boats approached. The stage was now set for a tragedy.

V beach is about 400 yards long and 30 deep. A strip of gritty sand, 10 yards wide, is separated from the grassy slopes above by a low bank which in 1915 was up to four feet high for most of the length of the beach – a factor which ensured the survival of some of those who landed there. The defences had been carefully concealed from view and when the hail of fire hit the boats approaching the shore, few of the victims ever had a glimpse of their tormentors. Troops were going over the sides of the boats in full kit and sinking like stones in the clear water, where their horrified friends could see their upturned faces and gaping mouths as they drowned. Very few of the Dublins got ashore; those that did were pinned down behind the life-saving embankment, or were lucky enough to have landed in the shadow of the fort, under whose walls they were protected from fire and in dead ground.

The bluejackets manning the cutters displayed sublime courage as they tried to bring their passengers to the shore. Whole crews perished at their oars, and one boat captain, Able Seaman Jacobs, was last seen trying to use an oar as a punt-pole in an effort to reach the shore when all but he of the boat's crew had been killed. Flying overhead in his seaplane, Commander Samson of the RNAS was appalled to note that the bullet-lashed water was red with blood for a full fifty yards out to sea and that boats were drifting helplessly off the beach with grisly cargoes of dead and dying.

The terrible scene was also being watched helplessly from the bridge of the *River Clyde*, firmly aground but not nearly far enough up the beach for Unwin's liking. He realized that an immediate attempt must be made to disembark the 2,000 men on board but that this could not be achieved until the lighters had been brought into their proper position below the walkways leading from the exit ports in the ship's bow. The powered barge that was supposed to have moved forward of its own momentum when the *River Clyde* beached, swung perversely out to one side and could not be used as the main component of the bridge of boats.

Unwin acted quickly, and with some of his officers and ratings he went over the side to tie some of the lighters together as a makeshift bridge. Officers and ratings stood waist-deep in the bullet-swept water, trying to hold the lighters in position as Unwin shouted up to the ship for the disembarkation to begin. Several cutters were drifting in the water nearby and some of the naval personnel did their best to drag them under cover of the ship's sides. One eyewitness aboard the *River Clyde* recalled what he thought was the most heart-breaking sight he would ever see; a young sailor, himself wounded, trying to hold a cutter full of dead and wounded in a safe place, whilst the hand of a dying man in the boat continually stroked his in a gesture of gratitude.

Another of Unwin's party was Sub-Lieutenant Arthur Tisdall of the Anson battalion, Royal Naval Division. Seeing the distress of the soldiers caught on the boats down below he joined Unwin in the water. Tisdall, a parson's son, had a brilliant academic and sporting career behind him at Cambridge and everything to live for. He now made repeated attempts to rescue men off the beach, where they were crying out for help, and pushed them to safety in cutters, helped by volunteers from the *River Clyde*'s crew. He survived unscathed, but was doomed to die only weeks later on the peninsula. His post-humous Victoria Cross would not be gazetted for almost another year. The citations which gained Unwin and Tisdall their VCs were unique, for many of the testimonials supporting them were found on bloodstained scraps of paper found later in the boats amongst the dead, having been written on the spot by the dying men they were trying to save.

As soon as Unwin had shouted for the landing to start, the ports in the ship's bow were opened and the first files of Munsters dashed out into a furious hail of fire. Very few got more than a yard or two down the walkways and soon the lighters below were piled high with bodies. The first 49 men out of the portside exit all fell, but the soldiers kept on emerging, to be shot down in droves. The machine-gunners on the ship's bow were still alive and firing but could not identify the places from which the deadly hail was coming. The ship was now under fire from batteries on the Asiatic shore and a near miss killed one of Unwin's ratings, with whom he was trying to secure one of the lighters.

By now, a small body of troops had managed to gain the cover of the fort's walls and were huddled just above the water's edge. Captain Lane of the Munsters rushed down the side of the *River Clyde* as bullets smashed into the steel plates. He got to the first lighter where he found some of his men who had gathered themselves together and were beginning to return the enemy fire.

> I mistrusted the second barge and the track to the shore so I led them over the side. The water came nearly up to our shoulders. However, none of us were hit and we gained the bank. There I found Henderson [his company commander] badly hit, and heaps of wounded. Any man who put up his head for an instant was shot dead. The bank . . . had a small nullah running up towards the barbed wire. I worked my way up under the right hand wall and then tried to cross it, running as fast as I could. A sniper at the top let fly at me; the bullet went through my right ankle and carried on sideways, smashing my left leg to bits. One of my platoon then came out very gallantly and pulled me into safety. I had only been on the beach five minutes and never saw a Turk.

The terrible scene was also observed from further out to sea. On the flagship as it passed W beach, Keyes could see the water lashed into foam by the Turks' fire as the Lancashire Fusiliers struggled ashore, and the beach covered with dead and dying. Some men, up to their shoulders in water, were vainly trying to get under cover behind drifting boats. Others could clearly be seen sheltering under a bank just above water level. Keyes begged de Robeck to intervene and ask for reinforcements to Y beach, where they had just watched the KOSB and the Plymouth marines walking around unopposed. The Admiral declined, saying that this was a military and not a naval matter; but Hamilton's diary notes that the idea, broached by de Robeck, was turned down summarily by Braithwaite, whose view was that it was bad practice to interfere with the conduct of the battle, which was in Hunter-Weston's hands. Hamilton, however, still deemed it proper to send the signal to Hunter-Weston already quoted, offering trawlers for a further landing at Y beach, to which he received no acknowledgement.

At 10 a.m. Hamilton sent a second message. This time, after an hour's delay, a reply came from Hunter-Weston to the effect that he had conferred with Wemyss who, as the naval commander for the actual landing, had given his view that to tamper with the existing transport arrangements in the middle of a hard-fought battle would delay the disembarkation at V and W beaches. Keyes was stunned at Hamilton's readiness to accept this, especially when the C-in-C had seen for himself that troops were ashore at Y and S beaches without opposition, and that the rapid diversion of force to these places, on the flanks of the landings, would have forced the Turks to retire entirely from the southern end of the peninsula. It would have been easy to bring this off, given the fleet's unchallenged supremacy.

By noon it should have been clear to all that it was pointless to continue sending men ashore at V beach until the high ground over-looking it was in British hands. On the *River Clyde*, Colonel Tizard had decided to suspend further landings, having seen half his bat-talion destroyed before his very eyes. In this he was supported by Carrington-Smith, who fell to a sniper's bullet on the ship's bridge in the afternoon. Keyes spent the rest of the day cruising offshore in the flagship. It was, he records, 'quite the unhappiest day of my life'.

Meanwhile, the South Wales Borderers had put two companies ashore at De Tott's Battery – S beach – early in the morning and had stayed there. Their commanding officer made no move forward, not even to reconnoitre possible Turkish defences, and merely continued to await further orders from 29 Division. These did not materialize, despite the fact that the situation above S beach was known to Hunter-Weston's staff. Their attention was riveted on events at V beach to the exclusion of all else. There was no attempt all day on the Turks' part to interfere with the South Wales Borderers other than by desultory exchanges of fire with enemy patrols.

During the day, a number of witnesses had watched the battle as it developed. On the *Euryalus* with the rest of Hunter-Weston's staff, Captain Milward had been on deck before first light. He noted, when closer in to shore, that the Turks had dug trenches and fieldworks all over the tip of the peninsula, and wondered why Hunter-Weston had been persuaded to land at what was clearly the most strongly defended part of the coast. Milward was particularly struck by the theatre-like shape of V beach as the tragedy there unfolded during the morning. He saw the commander of 88 Brigade, Brigadier-General Napier (who was also the designated commander of the main force), go ashore at the height of the slaughter on V beach. Costeker, the Brigade Major, insisted on going with him. He had gained the DSO in South Africa with his regiment, the Royal

Warwickshire, and had already been wounded in France in November 1914. Finding one of the few remaining serviceable boats, and accompanied by the brigade staff and some soldiers of the Hampshires, Napier tried to get ashore; when someone on the *River Clyde* shouted that it was impossible because of the intensity of enemy fire, Napier shouted back that he would 'have a damned good try'. He was almost immediately mortally wounded, as was Costeker. Neither set foot on dry land.

In the evening, when the firing had died down somewhat, Milward went on board the *River Clyde*, where, not surprisingly, he found the survivors sunk in gloom. Colonel Carrington-Smith's body still lay where he had fallen on the bridge and the figures of Napier and Costeker could be seen in their boat below.

Whilst the fighting raged at Anzac and Helles, the diversion in the Gulf of Saros, designed to keep the Turks at Bulair in their positions to repel a landing, had gone ahead according to plan. A force of eleven transports escorted by warships arrived off Bulair just after first light on the 25th; the warships commenced a leisurely bombardment whilst Major-General Paris went closer inshore aboard a destroyer as though reconnoitring possible landing beaches. Later in the morning the transports began ostentatiously to hoist out their boats, and as dusk approached, men swarmed down Jacob's ladders and went through an elaborate pantomime of preparing to go ashore. As darkness fell, boats were seen pulling away from the ships and making for the beaches, to be recalled as soon as it was dark.

The original plan had called for a landing by a small force, which was to make as much noise as possible in order to simulate a major assault. The officer in charge of this party was Lieutenant-Commander Bernard Freyberg. He was a champion swimmer in New Zealand and now produced an alternative plan to what he regarded as a risky landing likely to result in the loss of all his men. He would swim ashore alone, pushing a raft laden with flares and other pyrotechnics, which he would ignite at various points along the shoreline. The raft was towed inshore by a steam pinnace; Freyberg then swam off with an oilskin bag containing some flares. It took him over an hour to reach the shore, where he set his flares at intervals and waited to see if anyone would come along to examine them. He was carrying a revolver and had every intention of using it. Then he walked inland for several hundred yards, found no signs of the enemy, and got back into the water after igniting his last flares. He had to swim for a considerable distance before the pinnace found him, just as he was about to succumb to cramp. For this exploit he was awarded the DSO. Later in the war, on the Western Front, he would gain the VC.

At Kum Kale on the Asiatic shore the French began to land, some hours after the appointed time. They had been given only limited objectives as it was clearly understood that they would be withdrawn to the European side of the Straits as soon as possible. General d'Amade therefore decided to put ashore a regiment of three battalions, supported by a battery of field guns. The infantry comprised one Colonial battalion and two Senegalese who were something of an unknown quantity and whose subsequent performance on the peninsula was inconsistent; they were capable of advancing with great dash when under the control of their European officers and were particularly effective at close-quarter fighting when they used their *coupe-coupes* – machete-like fighting knives – to great effect. When their officers were brought down, however (a relatively easy task for the Turkish snipers who picked them off whenever they appeared) the Senegalese could not be relied on to go forward and frequently abandoned their positions in the face of the enemy. This characteristic was to have dire consequences for their allies at Helles later on.

The Kum Kale beaches were not strongly defended, nor were they wired. However, the Turks had kept strong reserves within easy marching distance of this sector, more in fact than had been waiting at Sedd-el-Bahr for the 29th Division; and these were quick to hasten to the battle. The late arrival of the French had been due to the strong currents round Kum Burnu Point, which had been seriously underestimated; the arrival of the troops on Turkish soil was therefore poorly co-ordinated and all pretence of surprise lost. Turkish reinforcements were now being engaged by the guns of the battleship *Henri IV*. (The British soldiery, with their usual derision for the languages of others, could not pronounce 'Henri Quatre' – or preferred not to do so – and she was known throughout the peninsula as 'The Angry Cat'. In similar vein the five-funnelled Russian cruiser *Askold* was known as 'the packet of Woodbines'.)

An attempt to continue the advance inland was halted by fierce Turkish resistance and at the end of the day the French line had stabilized a mile inland on a frontage of about two miles, the left flank resting on Kum Kale village. After dark, the Turks put in a series of fierce attacks, with the aim of throwing the French back into the sea, but these were bloodily repulsed (the Senegalese, it was noted, fighting with great gallantry) and the French ended the day confident that they could hold their own in the face of any attacks launched against them on the following day.

During the afternoon of the 25th, the situation at Y beach began to deteriorate. Colonel Sami Bey was determined to sweep the British into the sea before they could be reinforced and threaten the Turks fighting in the southern tip of the peninsula. He now decided to commit one battalion of his 25th Regiment against the Y beach landing, supported by a battery of field guns and a section of machine-guns. As Colonel Matthews issued a belated order to dig in, the Turks were already on the move. Their guns were in position by 4 p.m., on ground over which the KOSB and marines had been moving freely only a few hours earlier, between the Ravine and Krithia village; shortly afterwards they began to shell the exposed clifftop positions.

By 6 p.m. the first Turkish infantry probes were being made down the spur of land between the sea and the Ravine; at first, these were beaten off with the help of the ships offshore; as darkness fell, however, naval gunfire became ineffective and the attacks now came in with great determination although the Turks were outnumbered two to one. Towards midnight, when it appeared that his exhausted young marines were in danger of being overrun, Matthews signalled to HQ 29 Division, via HMS *Goliath*: 'For GOC 29 Div. Situation serious. One battalion to reinforce should arrive before dawn.' This was logged in at 29 Division at 15 minutes past midnight but received neither acknowledgement nor reply.

The fighting was now approaching a climax at Y beach, where Colonel Koe lay mortally wounded and his adjutant dead. In desperation Matthews sent another signal, which was received at HQ 29 Division at 6 a.m. on the morning of the 26th; again, no reply was made, nor any action taken. The KOSB had run out of ammunition early in the night and sent a message to HQ 29 Division at 10 p.m., which was received at five minutes past midnight and ignored. The Royal Navy came to the rescue with a load of Mk VII cartridges from HMS *Goliath*. Unfortunately, these were useless for the marines' Mk VI rifles, also running low on ammunition as the Turks kept up their remorseless pressure despite the KOSB's excellent musketry.

The day which had begun before dawn in such high hopes was therefore ending in despair. Birdwood's gloomy signal had met with Hamilton's message of encouragement, and the Australians and New Zealanders were clinging to their toehold, albeit in great confusion. Y beach, which at one stage offered the brightest hopes following the unopposed landing there, had been ignored and marginalized by Hunter-Weston's headquarters. The X beach landings had succeeded because the tiny body of defenders had been frightened off by Captain Lockyer's Nelsonian resolution. At V and W beaches, the best of the British army had been bloodily repulsed and pinned down by a company of resolute Turkish infantry, well led and deployed to exact maximum casualties on their assailants. At S beach, where the landing had gone ashore virtually unchallenged, no effort had been made to exploit success. It was as if Hunter-Weston had been hypnotized by events at Sedd-el-Bahr to the exclusion of any other possibility.

In the battered *River Clyde* hundreds of men still on board prepared for an uneasy night, fully aware of the dreadful fate that had overtaken their colleagues of the Dublins and Munsters, whose bodies could be seen piled high in the lighters and boats and stacked up against the wire on the beach. Others, who had managed to find cover and were still alive, could be dimly seen in the gloom huddled under the walls of the fort. From the shore, and from some of the boats and lighters, came the piteous cries of the wounded and dying.

Despite the evidence of failure all around him, Hamilton displayed all his normal optimism that evening. He had made no further attempt to influence Hunter-Weston's handling of the battle, since offering him the chance to put more men on Y beach earlier in the day, and had contented himself for the rest of the time in being a spectator of the desperate events ashore. When Hunter-Weston came aboard the flagship in the evening to report on the day's fighting he was, Jack Churchill noted, curiously vague as to the actual position and could state that he 'thought that the men at V and W were now in touch with our troops at X but that they had been through some hard fighting to get there', and that as he had heard nothing more from that quarter he assumed that they were all right. 'Anyway', Hamilton wrote in his journal, 'he was cheery, stout-hearted, quite a good tonic and – on the whole – his news is good.' Even as late in the day as this, Hamilton was under the impression that at Y, 'two good battalions are at large and on the warpath some four or five miles in the rear of the enemy and should do something during the next few hours'. From this it seems that Braithwaite and the GHQ staff, whose job it was to keep their commander-in-chief fully apprised of the situation, were either equally ignorant of the true state of affairs or wilfully suppressing the unpalatable truth.

On retiring finally to his bed after sorting out Birdwood's problems, Hamilton wrote in his journal:

One thing is certain. Whatever happens to us here we are bound to win glory. There are no other soldiers quite of the calibre of our chaps in the world; they are volunteers every one of them; they are for it . . . the men are not fighting blindly as in South Africa; they are not fighting against forces with whose motives they half sympathize . . . they understand; their eyes are wide open; they *know* that the war can only be brought to an end by our joining hands quickly with the Russians . . . they *know* the fate of the empire depends on the courage they display. Should the fates so decree, the whole brave army may disappear during the night more dreadfully than that of Sennacherib . . . Where so much is dark, where so many are discouraged, in this knowledge I feel both light and joy.

Hamilton derived great strength from the classics and the Bible. Of his earlier signal that evening to Birdwood, enjoining the Australians to hang on and dig, he later wrote: 'I shall never repent that order. Better to die like heroes on the enemy's ground than be butchered like sheep on the beaches like the runaway Persians at Marathon.' With these thoughts, Hamilton slept soundly in his cabin.

# 14

# *Advance from the Beaches*

In war, there is no substitute for victory.
General Douglas MacArthur

WITH THE DAWN of 26 April came new hope at Anzac. The sound of rifle fire on the heights above the cove had never ceased during the hours of darkness and the Turks had spent the night probing the defences along the ridge lines and launching fierce local attacks, which were beaten off with rifle and bayonet; heavy casualties were sustained by both sides in these small battles, and from the start the Turks and their opponents alike found that they were up against men of determination and courage.

One cause of Birdwood's anxiety during the previous evening had been the large number of soldiers straggling back down to the beach, where they had gathered in noisy groups, some trying to find the units from which they had become separated, others eager to exchange tales of their experiences to date with anyone who cared to listen. The general mood on the beach at the time of Birdwood's crucial conference with his divisional commanders had not in fact been one of defeatism but gregariousness, a characteristic soon noted by all who soldiered alongside the Australians. Having gone ashore and fought all day, they were ready to talk about it as they would after a hard-fought football match.

It proved relatively easy to sort the men out after daybreak on the 26th and lead them back, eager to rejoin their units. During the fight, moreover, a large number of natural leaders had emerged who, before long, would themselves be commanding platoons as the original officers were killed off. Meanwhile, there was much digging to be done, stores and ammunition to be manhandled up to the summits, and wire to be laid, provided the Turks could be held off.

Down at Helles it had also been a restless night. Darkness brought relief and reinforcement for the men pinned down on the beach at Sedd-el-Bahr, and work was already in hand at W to improve the beach exits. Stores were coming ashore regardless of their nature or destination and being stacked anywhere, for the ordnance and supply and transport branches to sort out after day-light. After the traumatic experiences of the landings, officers and men were in a state of shock, compounded by exhaustion. At first light on the 26th it proved almost impossible to get them on their feet to consolidate their positions. Many seemed unwilling to accept the fact that they had come through such an appalling ordeal and could be seen wandering around the beaches in a trance, gazing uncomprehendingly at the hundreds of bodies lying where they had fallen.

For most of the troops it was their first experience of combat and certainly of violent death on such a vast scale. Their generation had been conditioned by images of war presented in the heroic battle paintings of Lady Butler and Caton Woodville; in none of these could they have found anything corresponding to the awful visions now before them. None of the illustrations in the *Boys' Own Paper* depicted men literally torn asunder by machine-gun fire, disembowelled, or beheaded. These were men with whom, like the private of the Buffs in a poem familiar to schoolboys of that age, they 'jested, quaffed and swore' only hours before, lying around them in heaps, stripped of all dignity as they sprawled at the water's edge, on the Turkish wire, or, in the shallows off the beach, glared up through the clear water with the sightless eyes of the drowned.

Although the Turkish garrison above the beach had melted away during the night, there were still plenty of determined enemy snipers in the ruins of Sedd-el-Bahr castle and in the adjoining village when day broke. Aboard the *River Clyde*, Colonel Doughty-Wylie conferred before dawn with the officers around him, and it was agreed that the Turks had to be ejected from the fort, the village, and from Hill 141 immediately overlooking both, before further troops could be landed in daylight. The men who had been sheltering under the walls of the castle since the previous morning were accordingly led to a position where they would be safe when the guns of the fleet opened fire on the castle, from which, as daylight came, a machine-gun and a number of snipers were still firing.

The naval bombardment started but, owing to a misunderstanding, came down on the village instead of the fort, whose garrison stubbornly resisted the first attempt to storm it. Aboard the ship, Doughty-Wylie, realizing that the day's operations were in danger of stalling in the first hour, went ashore again with the other two GHQ staff officers in his party, gathered up a mixed force of Dublins, Munsters and Hampshires, and led them in an attack which cleared the fort and village.

Doughty-Wylie, who had spent a number of years in Turkey as a soldier-diplomat and loved the Turkish people, could not bring himself to bear arms against them and led the attack armed only with his cane, cheering and encouraging the men forward with no regard to his own safety. The troops swept on to the summit of Hill 141, where Doughty-Wylie was killed. He was buried where he fell; after the war, the Turks insisted that their honoured friend should remain alone at the scene of his final victory.

A curious mystery attends this hero's burial; towards the end of 1915, a woman landed from a boat sent ashore from a transport, and laid a wreath on the grave. Speaking to no one, but apparently seen by dozens of British and French troops, she then returned to her boat and departed. It is most likely that it was Mrs Doughty-Wylie, who by then was working for the French Red Cross on the island of Tenedos. She had influence with the authorities and was thus able to arrange for passage to Gallipoli. There is, however, a persistent story that it was his old friend Gertrude Bell, also in the area at the time. She certainly visited the grave in 1919.

At Y beach a most unhappy situation had developed. Throughout the night the Turks had flung their infantry into the attack. Colonel Koe had died of his wounds and the KOSB were short of ammunition. Colonel Matthews, now in undisputed command, put it to the officers of the KOSB that the combined force should attempt to fight its way out of the beach-head and link up with the Royal Fusiliers at X beach. The idea was rejected because of the now exhausted state of the Borderers and their shortage of ammunition. Many wounded were lying on the clifftops and the beach and they could not be left to the uncertain mercy of the Turks; it was therefore decided to stay and fight it out.

At this point, however, Matthews found that his command was melting away. The marines on the flank were already filing off to the beach and stretcher bearers were carrying the wounded down to the shore. There was now no sign of the Turks, who had retired inland with the approach of daylight in order to escape the attentions of the fleet's guns. Had he but known it, Matthews had won his battle and at that moment could have walked into Krithia and on to the top of Achi Baba.

Hamilton was an impotent spectator from the *Queen Elizabeth* as she again cruised offshore. At 9.30 a.m. he could clearly see hundreds of men strolling leisurely down from the clifftops and gathering in knots on the beach as if waiting for boats: 'I disliked and mistrusted the looks of these aimless dawdlers by the sea . . . Hunter-Weston ought to have consulted me first . . . My inclination was to take a hand myself but the Staff are clear against interference when I have no knowledge of the facts – I suppose they are right.'

Hunter-Weston had not bothered to keep Hamilton briefed for the simple reason that he had elected to ignore both Y and S beaches. In addition, those signals parties which did get ashore on the 25th were sucked into the mêlée and suffered heavy casualties. On the 26th, ship-to-shore communication was largely reliant on lamp and semaphore. Matthews' repeated SOS signals had been received by Hunter-Weston, to be brushed aside. Eventually, at 9.30 a.m., Hamilton could bear it no longer and called on d'Amade to land a regiment of French infantry at Y beach. It was too late. By mid-morning the evacuation was well under way, still unopposed by the Turks, who had no idea that their enemy was departing at the moment of victory.

Across the Dardanelles on the Asiatic shore, the French met with mixed fortunes. Throughout the afternoon and evening of the 25th they had been attacked with increasing energy by the Turks. Fortunately they had taken ashore large quantities of barbed wire but no pickets on which to erect it. Instead, they used Turkish corpses, and spent the night behind this grisly barricade. The attacks lasted well into the night and they held their beach-head only with difficulty; but towards dawn the enemy had become disheartened with the loss of most of their officers, and were beginning to surrender in droves. A significant success appeared imminent. Unfortunately, an officer who went out from the French lines to negotiate the surrender of a large number of Turks was cut down by them. The enraged French summarily executed the senior Turkish officer amongst their prisoners and some of his men, and the fighting became savage and pitiless.

As darkness fell on the 26th the French were still in possession of the field, had killed (by the Turks' own admission) about 2,000 of the enemy, and held hundreds of prisoners. D'Amade now asked Hamilton for permission to re-embark and move his troops over to

Helles in accordance with the agreed plan. Braithwaite and de Robeck tried to dissuade him from agreeing, as the French were now clearly in a much better position for exploitation than 29 Division at Helles or the Anzacs further up the peninsula. Hamilton declined; he had his orders from Kitchener and in any case knew that with the limited force available to him, he would be eventually contained and overwhelmed on the mainland of Asia Minor. He therefore agreed to d'Amade's request; the French, unhindered by the badly shaken Turks, evacuated the Asiatic shore and landed at Helles.

At Anzac and to a lesser extent at Helles, the plight of the wounded was terrible. The stretcher-bearer sections of most of the field ambulances had managed to get ashore on the 25th, incurring heavy casualties themselves in the process, and more in the ferocious close-range fighting that followed. One of 29 Division's casualty clearing stations got ashore at W beach towards the end of the first day and set up at the top of the cliffs under a large Red Cross flag, whilst the Australian clearing station was ashore at Anzac, jammed into a cramped site on the beach below the cliffs.

As casualties mounted there was an immediate shortage of bearers and stretchers. At Anzac, this situation produced one of the campaign's great heroes. John Simpson Kirkpatrick, who became a posthumous national figure in Australia, was in fact an Englishman, one of the hundreds serving with the Australian Imperial Force. Aged 23 in 1915, he had enlisted in the Medical Corps under the name of Simpson and landed with the 3rd Australian Field Ambulance near Ari Burnu on the morning of the 25th. Simpson and his squad of four bearers immediately went inland; soon, he was the only survivor. He found a stray donkey, placed his Red Cross brassard on the animal's head and christened it 'Murphy'. The two then started to collect wounded from up the ravines ahead and carried them to the field ambulance for attention. Simpson's officers, seeing the fine work he was doing, allowed him to continue as an independent casualty collection agency.

Later, one of his officers, Lieutenant-Colonel Carrick, recalled that Simpson 'was very game and in fact he laughed at danger. At all times he was cheerful and a great favourite with his mates . . . On one occasion I passed him in Monash Gully and called out to him: "Look out for yourself, Simmy." His laughing reply came: "That bullet hasn't been made for me yet, sir."' Another Australian soldier recalled seeing Simpson carrying his patients carefully down the gully to the beach, then removing the Red Cross from the donkey's head, drawing a revolver, and fighting his way back to the front line against the ubiquitous Turkish snipers. Private Cowtan remembered riding down the gully 'on a donkey not much bigger than a goat. I should have carried the donkey, not the donkey me, as my feet could touch the ground.' In the next three weeks, Simpson lost three donkeys to snipers and shrapnel; then, while carrying a badly wounded man down to the field ambulance, he too was killed, and buried down by the water's edge.

Front line units were admirably supported by their own medical officers and stretcher bearers, but problems started the moment wounded were set down on the beach to await evacuation by sea. For the first twenty-four hours after the landings there were almost no boats available to take them out to the allocated transports and hospital ships. There was no one to take control of their shipment, or to decide which casualties were severe enough to merit immediate surgery on the hospital ships.

Surgeon-General Birrell was a helpless spectator aboard the headquarters ship *Arcadian* where, with no access to wireless communication, he might as well have been on the moon. Many of the medical personnel who had gone ashore in open boats had been killed or wounded in them, and the wounded ones were now coming back on board without having set foot on land. Because of the absence of any system whereby casualties could be assessed at an early stage of the evacuation system, severely wounded men were now being taken to transports – the 'Black Ships' – which were virtually without any sort of medical provision; they had been used for the transport of men and mules, had not been cleaned out for weeks, and were stinking dens of infection. Many of the men going aboard them had received no more than the superficial attention of an orderly ashore and application of shell dressings over uncleaned wounds.

Casualties began to clutter up the beach at Anzac, patient and uncomplaining amidst the turmoil of battle, exposed to constant shrapnel which inflicted further wounds on many and killed yet more. Offshore, the few boats available for their removal went from ship to ship, desperately seeking space for them. To their lasting shame, some ships' masters refused to have them aboard. On one boat, a veterinary officer and two young orderlies tried to succour several hundred casualties, including many with desperately severe wounds; they quickly ran out of dressings and there was no surgical equipment. No other boat was prepared to take the overflow on board. The purser then announced that the ship's food supplies were exhausted. There were still mules and horses on board which could not be disembarked; in this piteous condition the wounded were shipped off to Alexandria, where their condition on arrival at the base hospitals beggared belief. It was, many thought, even worse than the Crimea.

Allied casualties in the first five days were heavy: in 29 Division, 259 officers and 6,334 soldiers killed and wounded; at Anzac, 136 officers and 3,313 men. About one-third of these were killed in action. The French corps lost 246 officers and 12,364 men killed and wounded between 25 April and 12 May out of an original combat strength of 334 and 22,116.

Within a few days, matters began to improve. The hospital ship *Hindoo*, which had been lying off the coast unused, her presence forgotten, was taken into service for the transport of serious cases to Alexandria and Malta. Two hospital ships were anchored off the peninsula, complete with full surgical facilities; by 5 May one of these, the *Alaunia*, was coping with 27 officers, 910 soldiers, and a number of Turkish prisoners. More medical personnel, from stationary hospitals which could not now be landed on the peninsula, were assigned to transports which were used to evacuate less serious cases to Egypt and across to Lemnos, where the first of several Australian stationary hospitals was coping admirably with the workload. Failure to establish large stationary hospitals there earlier despite its lack of water supplies, which could easily be overcome by bringing it in by sea, was to kill hundreds of men who might otherwise have survived. The passage of the 'Black Ships' across to Egypt was marked by continual burials at sea. One soldier noted that his ship stopped briefly for those of Christians, but the bodies of Turkish prisoners were unceremoniously tipped over the side as the ship steamed on.

As darkness fell on the 26th, most of 29 Division was ashore, but still only in a small beach-head. The sounds of firing had died away completely after Doughty-Wylie's success on Hill 141; the Turks had broken off and retired towards the Achi Baba ridgeline and the village of Krithia. Hot pursuit by fresh troops would have clinched the campaign at that point, but Hamilton's resources were not equal even to this task. Instead, the survivors of the landings dazedly dug temporary defensive positions no more than a few hundred yards inland and prepared to receive what they believed would be an almost instantaneous Turkish counter-attack. This view was certainly shared by Hunter-Weston, who let it be known in a General Order that 'There will be no retiring. Every man will die at his post rather than retire.' It is not recorded what his men thought of this exhortation.

On the Turkish side, Liman was hastening to redeploy his troops to meet what he knew would be an attempt to seize Achi Baba hill and to break out of the Anzac beach-head towards Maidos. As soon as he saw that the French had evacuated their men from Kum Kale, he began to switch forces from the Asiatic to the European shore. Although the Turkish divisional commander wanted to dig in along the Achi Baba ridge, Liman ordered him to stay well forward of it.

It was not until the late afternoon of the 27th that Hunter-Weston started to move cautiously forward. Patrols sent out in the morning had failed to make contact with the enemy apart from a few snipers well hidden in the scrub, and there was apparently nothing to stand in the way of a direct advance to the top of Achi Baba. As the troops advanced in files of platoons across the plain towards the high ground ahead they knew they were under observation and that the Turkish artillery was to be feared; they also realized that their own artillery was still extremely thin on the ground; so far only a few field guns had come ashore and almost no pack or draught animals. The first animal transport unit to land was the Zion Mule Corps, raised in Palestine and manned mostly by émigré Jews from eastern Europe. (A peninsular joke had it that its motto was 'No advance without security.') On the beaches, harassed ordnance and commissariat officers were trying to put stores in some sort of order. The entire length of the peninsula below Achi Baba was within easy range of enemy field artillery which kept up a desultory harassing fire, and larger projectiles came across from the other side of the Straits, fired from a gun which soon became known as 'Asiatic Annie'.

By last light on the 27th the British had gained a line whose left flank rested on the sea about a mile north of X beach. On the extreme right the line ran down to the water less than half a mile from S beach. This sector was allotted to the French, who established themselves on V beach and in the battered fort at Sedd-el-Bahr. Late that night, Hunter-Weston issued orders for what became known as the First Battle of Krithia.

Only sixteen 18-pounders, four 4.5-inch howitzers and four ancient mountain guns had been landed, with little ammunition. Few of the guns had been joined by their teams of horses and were thus limited to providing fire support from down by the beach, which effectively prevented them from engaging the Turkish field batteries on the far side of Achi Baba. Much reliance had therefore to be placed on the navy, whose remarkable gunnery had been demonstrated only that morning by the *Queen Elizabeth*. Controlled by a spotter balloon, she had engaged a Turkish troop transport crossing the Narrows with her 15-inch guns, firing clean over the top of the Gallipoli peninsula from a position off Anzac. The troopship, laden with reinforcements from the Asiatic shore, had been hit at a range of nearly ten miles with the third round fired, an event which had a salutary effect on the Turks and did much to raise British morale.

The 29th Division had been terribly cut up in the landings, losing many experienced officers. All the original brigade commanders had been killed or wounded and their successors, hurriedly promoted, had only been in post for twenty-four hours when ordered to resume the offensive. The 86th Brigade had been so badly mauled on the 25th that one of its battalions, the 1st Dublins, had only four surviving officers and, having lost 550 of its men on V beach, was no more than a token unit. The 87th Brigade was obliged to go into action without the 1st KOSB, who had not rejoined from the abortive landing at Y beach and were themselves now only at half strength. All ranks in the division had reached the limits of endurance, having been without sleep for ninety-six hours, and the supply of rations and water was spasmodic owing to the shortage of mules.

Hunter-Weston's plan for the capture of Achi Baba visualized an advance on the left flank, after which the line of attack would wheel due east on to a line running along the road which leaves Krithia village and runs north. On the extreme right flank, north of S beach, the French would stay where they were as a pivot, but their left flank troops were to move forward to conform with the right of 29 Division.

Orders did not reach most of the battalions in 29 Division until after dark on the 27th. They now had to face up to that most difficult of manoeuvres, a change of front in face of the enemy; it required meticulous timing in addition to familiarity with the ground, and these were not forthcoming. Bleary-eyed staff and regimental officers toiled through the night to get intelligible orders out, and the gunners did their best to manhandle as many guns forward as they could. The commanding officers of the infantry battalions were not finally briefed until first light on the 28th, by which time it was far too late to observe the proper battle drills and ensure that every man in the battalion knew what was required of him. 'Nevertheless', as the official historian writes, 'in the case of all the battalions engaged, company officers and the rank and file appear to have been too dead with fatigue to understand their orders or to have much idea of what was required of them when the time to advance had arrived.'

The Turks, reinforced to a strength of nine battalions thanks to the energy of Liman and his Turkish subordinates, waited for the attack in hurriedly dug trenches guarding the approaches to Krithia village. Their positions extended right across the peninsula to the Allied right flank. Additional reinforcements, fresh and athirst for battle, were hastening to the fight. When the advance started, it looked as if it would not be too hard a task; resistance appeared to be almost non-existent as the troops moved forward across scrub and patches of sparse cultivation, interspersed with clumps of dwarf trees.

Soon, however, lack of reconnaissance and preparation made themselves felt. Companies began to veer off their lines of advance and merged with each other or even crossed paths. The few maps were useless and the advance became an ill-directed shambles. Snipers found no difficulty in picking off the officers, conspicuous in service dress and Sam Browne belts, rank badges prominently displayed on the slashed cuffs of their jackets. By noon, all order had been lost as the troops blundered ahead against growing resistance. Some even got into Krithia village but had no idea of the whereabouts of units on their flanks, and withdrew under the impression that Hunter-Weston had ordered a general retirement.

On the right, the French who were trying to conform to the movement of 29 Division ran into a well-prepared (and hitherto undetected) Turkish position along the Kereves Dere, a deep gully running down from the Achi Baba ridge. On the extreme left of the British line the 1st Border Regiment had advanced on to the spur separating Gully Ravine from the sea and were doing well until, at 11 a.m., they were stopped in their tracks by resolute Turkish resistance. By midday the attack was flagging and the reserve brigade, the 86th, was committed to the fight. As its officers had little or no idea of what was going on ahead of them, or of the positions of the units in the other two brigades already embroiled, their entry contributed little of value, merely compounding the growing atmosphere of frustration and bewilderment.

By mid-afternoon the Borders had been driven back in confusion, watched impotently by Hamilton from the *Queen Elizabeth*, whose guns were now trained on dense masses of advancing Turks. Led by an officer who could clearly be seen from the flagship as he waved his sword, they received one round of 15-inch airburst. When the smoke cleared, awestruck observers could see that of the leading Turkish company, not one officer or man remained on his feet. For the moment the situation was restored; the Borders rallied and the line held.

All along the front, Turkish reinforcements were joining the battle, and by late afternoon it was apparent that no further progress was going to be made. Hunter-Weston decided to discontinue his attack and dig in. Nightfall saw almost all the battalions back where they had started in the morning. Once more the officers and men of 29 Division had no sleep, as battalions were now thoroughly intermixed and had to be sorted out as quickly as possible. Few managed to get a square meal and had to make do with whatever they had saved of their iron rations; it was a cold night, endured in the open without blankets or fires. The morale of a lesser formation would have been broken by the cumulative experiences of the past four days, but that of the 29th remained high and their professionalism saw to it that by dawn on the 29th, they had regained much of their good order.

Up at Anzac, following the chaos of the first twenty-four hours, it had been extremely difficult to sort out the intermixed units and form them into a strong front line. By the 28th this ran up what had become known as Second Ridge from the beach two thousand yards south of Anzac Cove, then north-east to within 500 yards of Baby 700, now firmly in Turkish hands, which had been furiously contested on the day of the landings. From there the line was not continuous, because of the broken terrain, enabling Turkish snipers for a time to move in with impunity amongst the Australian positions. A continuous line of defence was possible from Russell's Top, starting at a point 400 yards short of the Nek, and running along Walker's Ridge. For the time being this marked the proper left flank of the Anzac position. Beyond it, in the tumbled landscape leading down towards the coast at Fisherman's Hut, was an area in which the New Zealanders were able to show their aptitude for patrolling; here they set up strongpoints from which they were able, in the weeks ahead, to dominate the country around the northern shoulder of the Sari Bair uplands and even out on to the Suvla Plain.

No reorganization of the Anzac perimeter would have been possible without the remarkable performance of Lieutenant-Colonel Braund's 2nd Australian Battalion – or what now remained of it – which had clung to Russell's Top for seventy-two hours in the face of increasingly violent Turkish attacks, losing 450 men in the process. It was one of Gallipoli's many tragedies that only a few nights after his magnificent battalion had been relieved, Braund, who was somewhat deaf, failed to hear the challenge of one of his own sentries in the dark and was shot dead.

The Anzacs were now as exhausted as the men of 29 Division, and in order to give them respite, four fresh battalions of the Royal Naval

Division were sent to relieve the most hard-pressed sections of the line. The initial Anzac reaction to the arrival of the youthful marines and sailors was anything but favourable. Their physique seemed puny in comparison with the Diggers, and matters were not helped at one front line post when a newly arrived sub-lieutenant asked a bronzed, half-naked soldier where he could find the officers' mess. It was not long, however, before the Australians were ready to concede that the new arrivals were up to standard.

One of them was Lieutenant Douglas Hallam, a Canadian in the Royal Naval Volunteer Reserve who landed at Anzac on the 29th. He had been in uniform just five months and had no military experience whatsoever. Now he was on a strange shore, under fire, and with no idea of what he was supposed to do with the thirty men and six machine-guns under his command. Following a guide from a New Zealand unit he and his men carried their guns up Shrapnel Gully. All the time they could hear bullets passing overhead; to Hallam they sounded like the rushing of a high wind. Aloft, against the duck-egg blue sky, could be seen dozens of shrapnel canisters tumbling through the air after they had burst above the front line trenches along the ridge. Snipers' bullets cracked around him and his men as they toiled up the narrowing valley. A friendly Australian soldier advised him to take off the cap, tunic and Sam Browne belt of which he was extremely proud; the snipers, he was told, made a point of aiming at officers.

Almost at once the machine-guns were in action, repelling a series of Turkish attacks in the form of dense masses of infantry, shoulder to shoulder and shouting the name of God. Hallam manned a gun and wrought great execution on the Turks as they came on to the attack. On one occasion he was talking to his own commanding officer, when 'there was the ear-splitting crack of a sniper's bullet and Commander Boothby fell dead, shot through the head . . . as I was considering the situation a message was brought to me that my sub-lieutenant, Lord Loughborough, had been shot through the left shoulder. I was now the only officer left in the unit.'

Almost at once he was summoned up to Courtney's Post where another Turkish attack was imminent. He had not been told all, for 'I did not know that Courtney's Post and Quinn's Post, side by side, were the hot spot of Anzac. They were nothing less than the keys to the entire position.' If they fell, everything else would go. Around them, for weeks to come, great deeds of heroism were to be performed. It was during his sojourn here that Hallam saw Simpson the donkey man at work. One of the naval gunners was shot through both legs, but 'a small quiet man turned up with a donkey across whose forehead was a white bandage and on it a red cross. He was a bearer from an Anzac field ambulance and we were glad to have him take charge.'

The final stages of the steep ascent to Courtney's were a nightmare. Snipers were claiming victims all round the sweating gunners as they struggled up a slope as steep as the roof of a house, bent under the weight of Maxim guns, tripods and ammunition. From below the summit the party watched in amazement as the Australians above emerged from tunnels cut into the rear face of the slope to repel another Turkish attack. Led by a huge officer, they charged over and out of sight, and the sounds of hand-to-hand combat could clearly be heard, punctuated by cheers.

The machine-guns were taken to the top after dark, when the snipers could no longer see their targets; as the sailors went up the last slope, a dreadful procession of wounded men slid, shuffled and crawled down past them. In the trenches were masses of Australian dead. When Hallam asked to see the Australian machine-gun officer he was told laconically that he had just crawled over him on his way into the trench, and that 'this is a hell of a place for machine-gunners'. Advised that his predecessor and his men had succumbed to snipers' bullets from the side and rear, he spent the rest of the night constructing a redoubt with overhead cover, stopping work from time to time to repel Turkish attacks.

The men were asleep on their feet long before dawn, slithering down to the bottom of the trench and waking only when Hallam beat the soles of their boots with a pickaxe. He, and they, knew that their sole chance of surviving the coming day was to dig for their lives. One of the men, trying to deepen the trench, struck something soft; lighting a match to see what it was, he went mad and had to be tied down. The trench floor had been used as a temporary mass grave. Later, the man, still raving, broke his restraining ropes and fled, never to be seen again.

The beach-head secured at Anzac in the first ten days was to undergo little change in terms of its size until the end of the campaign. The front line held by the Australians and New Zealanders was at no point more than a thousand yards from the sea, sustained across a beach less than one and a half miles long exposed to the full force of north-easterly and westerly gales as well as observation by Turkish posts on each flank. Although the actual shoreline was hidden from enemy view it was vulnerable to the effects of shrapnel, a commodity with which the enemy gunners were well provided.

The offshore anchorage was in full view of the enemy and frequently under fire during daylight. As at Helles, generals were just as much at risk from routine hazards as the soldier in the firing trench.

Almost immediately a unique spirit developed amongst the men who served and fought in this tiny enclave. As a viable defensive position it would fail all criteria in a staff college pamphlet, for it was overlooked by a powerful and determined enemy occupying the dominant ground and possessing interior lines of communication endowing him with freedom of movement. For the Anzacs defeat could be expected at any moment following yet another massed attack by the dogged and brave Turkish infantry, and this meant nothing less than bloody annihilation on the beaches. This thought was never far from the mind of any officer or soldier with more than a grain of imagination, and it stamped itself on the personalities of all who withstood the remarkable siege which now took place.

# 15

# *Reinforcing Defeat*

In strategy the longest way round is apt to be the
shortest way home.

Sir Basil Liddell Hart

HAMILTON'S BOLD CONCEPT of 'a running jump and both feet together'
had seemed reasonable enough when it was thought that the Turkish
defence would fade rapidly away. Now, following the bloody scenes
of the initial landings and failure to take the first night's objectives of
Krithia and Achi Baba, the Allies knew that they were confronted by
formidable opponents, effectively stranded on an extremely hostile
shore with virtually no reserves or reinforcements at hand. Hamilton
was not to blame for this; as early as the beginning of April he had
anxiously signalled the War Office for first reinforcements – the
portion of each unit in the order of battle held back for contingencies
such as this – to be despatched from the United Kingdom.

Those reinforcements for the 29th Division should have amounted
to 17 officers and 1,692 men. When their release was finally sanc-
tioned at the end of April, nearly a week after the landings at Helles,
they totalled one officer and 46 men for each battalion, a derisory
figure given the casualties sustained to date. In the Fusilier Brigade
only 35 officers and 1,824 soldiers were now fit for combat; the ration
strength of the 1st Royal Dublin Fusiliers on 1 May was one officer
and 344 men, and for the time being the remnants of this battalion
were merged with the 1st Royal Munster Fusiliers to form what was
known on the peninsula as 'The Dubsters' until such time as reinforcements arrived. The 29th Division had taken severe punishment
in those terrible first five days and its effective strength was now
down to 149 officers and 6,746 men.

Hamilton's awe of Kitchener inhibited him when asking for

reinforcements, whether of men or *matériel*. The matter was resolved, however, on 27 April when Kitchener was visited in his office by a worried Churchill, accompanied by the First Sea Lord. Fisher had just received a report from de Robeck which left him in no doubt as to the parlous state of the troops on Gallipoli as Hunter-Weston prepared to launch the first attack on Krithia. Kitchener immediately signalled Maxwell in Egypt, ordering him to despatch the 42nd (East Lancashire) Division of the Territorial Force.

The idea of sending any reinforcements from England to the eastern Mediterranean was now under heavy fire in Whitehall. In the same week as the Gallipoli landings, the Second Battle of Ypres had started, bringing a new dimension to the war with the Germans' use of poison gas against the British lines. The gas was not as effective as the Germans had hoped, but it lent muscle to the case of the 'Westerners' for absolute priority to be given to General French's command. Maxwell, equally aware of the impact on the Islamic world if the infidel expeditionary force at Gallipoli were to be driven into the sea by the despised Turks, now changed tack, and from his previously guarded reluctance to part with a single man from the Egyptian garrison, was making energetic arrangements to ship reinforcements over to Hamilton and Birdwood. He even made a suggestion of his own: that the Australian and New Zealand Light Horse brigades be sent dismounted to Gallipoli as infantry.

As reinforcements were being scraped belatedly together for Hamilton, the Turks were pouring men into the peninsula. Liman drew formations across from the Asiatic shores and new divisions were sent down from Constantinople; their journey, however, would not be without incident, thanks to the outstanding performance of the Allied submarines now lying in wait for the troopships in the Sea of Marmara.

By the first week in May the reinforcement situation was clearer. The 29th Indian Infantry Brigade – minus its Muslim personnel, barred by a crass political decision from fighting the Turks – was about to arrive from Egypt. The 42nd (East Lancashire) Division was expected on the 9th, and one more French division, together with the dismounted Australian Light Horse brigades, would arrive by the 15th. For the time being the only course open at Helles was to hold the ground gained in the first few days after the landings, fight off any Turkish attacks, and await reinforcements before attempting further offensive action on any scale. It was important, Hamilton felt, not to adopt a purely defensive posture and to this end he directed that every opportunity be taken to harass the Turks. He therefore planned a limited and local advance as soon as the Indian brigade was in the line, and decided that the best place for this was on the left flank at Helles.

At Anzac on 2 May a determined attempt was made by Birdwood to get his troops on to Baby 700, but despite meticulous preparation and desperate courage on the part of the assaulting troops it failed. Initially the dash of the New Zealanders in the Otago battalion took them forward and General Godley called for two battalions of Royal Marine Light Infantry, who had been moved round from Helles to buttress the Anzac garrison, to exploit the New Zealanders' success. When the order to advance reached them, the marines were bivouacked in Shrapnel Gully; night was falling, and the move forward was over difficult and strange country which had not been reconnoitred beforehand. The advance was painfully slow and the tired men struggled in the dark to climb up towards the top of the ridge where the Otagos were holding on grimly. As daylight broke the toiling marines were confronted with the demoralizing sight of masses of wounded men, Australians and New Zealanders, attempting to get back down to the beach. A salvo of friendly artillery fire then hit the Anzac positions on the ridgeline and the Australian 16th Battalion fell back in the resultant confusion, carrying the marines with them; the intermingled mass of British and Anzacs streamed back down to Shrapnel Gully and it was some time before order was restored; by this time it was too late to consolidate the gains made by the Otago battalion and although the Turks failed to follow up, the top of Baby 700 remained firmly in their hands.

Birdwood was as keen to inculcate the offensive spirit as Hamilton, and whilst the fight for Baby 700 raged, he had resolved to launch raids against two troublesome observation posts held by the Turks, from which they were able to observe every movement of shipping off the beach and direct artillery fire accordingly, making daylight replenishment extremely dangerous. One of these was to the north, at Nibrunesi Point overlooking the plain of Suvla as well as the Anzac beaches; the other was a short distance to the south of the Anzac right flank, on the headland of Gaba Tepe.

At last light on 30 April a landing party had gone ashore at Nibrunesi, climbed the nearby hill known as Lala Baba, and driven off the Turkish observers posted there. The raid was repeated on 2 May with similar results. The attempt on Gaba Tepe was less successful, however; early on 4 May the Turks spotted the boats carrying an Australian raiding party ashore from destroyers and a fierce fight ensued, in which the destroyers came close inshore to give covering fire for the re-embarkation. It was during this that the Australians found that the previously despised and hated Turks were clean fighters, for they scrupulously withheld their fire when they saw stretcher parties going ashore to rescue the Australian wounded. It was the beginning of a curious and lasting relationship between friend and foe which was to survive even the savagery of the later battles.

As Hamilton had predicted, the Turks lost no time in mounting the first of many counter-attacks at Helles. Liman was given a succession of orders by Enver Pasha to drive the infidels into the sea and he accordingly ordered von Sodenstern, commanding at Helles, to launch a heavy attack on the night of 1/2 May. The Turks were able to deploy 21 battalions for this, supported by 56 guns. After a brief but intensive cannonade the troops were ordered to advance with empty rifles and fixed bayonets. Shortly after 10 p.m. the massed Turkish infantry left their trenches and poured across the narrow strip of no man's land; as luck would have it, they fell upon the 'Dubsters', still in the process of re-forming.

The Turks were on the verge of breaking through when the situation was saved by the British reserve battalion, the 1/5th Royal Scots, the sole territorial infantry unit in the 29th Division. It had been selected to join a regular formation because of its high reputation in Edinburgh, where it recruited; like the other local Royal Scots territorial units it was justifiably proud of its roots in the volunteer movement and had an enviable reputation for its musketry. The volunteers had placed great emphasis on range work and the officers' mess of the 5th Royal Scots was full of handsome trophies testifying to the unit's skill-at-arms. The Turks broke and fled in the face of the Scotsmen's deliberate fire.

The main thrust of the Turkish attack had been directed at the sector of the line held by the French, on the Allied right flank. Here, a Senegalese battalion, displaying what came to be all too familiar form, fought tenaciously until its European officers became casualties, then broke and ran. The rest of the French corps fought stoutly, and its artillery, mainly the outstanding 75-mm field gun, came to the rescue of the British at Helles time and time again.

The gap in the Allied line following the abrupt departure of the Senegalese was plugged on this occasion by British gunners, fighting desperately as infantry alongside a company of the Worcesters. All night the battle raged, as wave after wave of stolid Turkish infantry came in to the attack chanting 'Allah, Allah', having been told by their imams that death in battle was a glorious way to a Paradise of incomparable carnal pleasures and, to most of them, a far better lot than that to which they had been bred. In the light of dawn the British and French stared in amazement at the heaps of dead in front of their positions where the Turks had fallen rank by rank. Similar sights greeted the Anzacs as they held grimly on to their gains on the spines of the hills and ridges overlooking Ari Burnu.

Far away from the peninsula the strained relationship between Churchill and Fisher was about to dissolve in bitter recrimination. Fisher, never enthusiastic over the Dardanelles expedition, had been growing increasingly uneasy since the failure of the naval attack of 18 March. The catalyst for final rupture was an appreciation sent to him by de Robeck on 10 May, in which the admiral gave his assessment of the current situation:

> General Hamilton informs me that the army is checked. The help which the navy has been able to give the army in its advance has not been as great as anticipated. Though effective in keeping down the fire of the enemy's batteries, when it is a question of trenches and machine-guns the navy is of small assistance; it is these latter that have checked the army. From the vigour of the enemy's resistance it is improbable that the passage of the fleet into the Marmara will be decisive and therefore it is equally probable that the Straits will be closed behind the fleet. This will be of slight importance if the resistance of the enemy could be overcome in time to prevent the enforced withdrawal of the fleet owing to lack of supplies.

On receipt of this, Fisher wrote his own appreciation of the situation and sent it to Churchill as a refutation of the latter's suggestion that the fleet could make another attempt to force the Narrows, using the more effective minesweeping equipment now available. Fisher was not one to mince his words:

> I therefore feel impelled to warn you definitely and formally of my conviction that such an attack by the fleet on the Dardanelles forts, in repetition of the operations which failed on 18 March, or any attempt by the fleet to rush the Narrows, is fraught with possibilities of disaster utterly incommensurate to any advantage that could be obtained therefrom . . .
>    In my opinion we cannot afford to expose any more ships to the risk of loss in the Dardanelles, since the ships there . . . are the reserve on which we depend for supremacy in the event of any unforeseen disaster.

Fisher was haunted by the vision of Turkish gunners hiding during the bombardment, then emerging to serve their guns as the ships passed at unmissable 'hulling' range. He also believed that even by using powerful destroyers as minesweepers it would not be possible entirely to clear the minefields. In his view, the naval operation was impossible until the army ashore had secured the land on both sides of the Narrows. He was also worried by thoughts of the logistic back-up required for a fleet cruising in the Sea of Marmara, and even more by the growing threat of German submarines operating against the easy targets offered by the warships and transports clustered around the entrance to the Straits and off the beaches. His letter to Churchill ended on a thoroughly pessimistic note:

> For the above reasons I cannot under any circumstances be a party to any order to Admiral de Robeck to make an attempt to pass the Dardanelles until the shores have been effectively occupied. I consider that purely naval action, unsupported by the army, would merely lead to heavy loss of ships and invaluable men, without any prospect of a success in any proportion to the losses or to the possible further consequences of those losses. I therefore wish it to be clearly understood that I dissociate myself from any such project.

Churchill read this with dismay. He responded at once with a dramatic letter:

> My dear Fisher,
>     You will never receive from me any proposition to 'rush' the Dardanelles and I agree with the views you express so forcibly on that subject. It may be that the Admiral will have to engage the forts and sweep the Kephez minefield as an aid to the military operations and we have always agreed in the desirability of forcing them to fire off their scanty stocks of ammunition. But in view of Hamilton's latest telegram this is clearly not required now . . . We are now in a very difficult position. Whether it is my fault for trying or my misfortune for not having the power to carry it through is immaterial. We are now committed to one of the greatest amphibious enterprises in history. You are absolutely committed. Comradeship, resource, firmness, patience, all in the highest degree will be needed to carry this matter through to victory. A great army hanging on by its eyelids to a rocky beach and confronted with the armed power of the Turkish Empire under German military guidance. The *whole surplus fleet of Britain – every scrap that can be spared – bound to that army and its fortunes as long as the struggle may drag out!* I beg you to lend me your whole aid and good will; and ultimately their success is certain.

> Yours ever,
> W.

Fisher, however, was determined to clear himself. He was also fully aware of the devastating ability of his colleague to charm him back to his own line of thought. He was old and knew it, and could no longer stand the strain of incessant argument, certainly not with Churchill. He therefore wrote, on 12 May, to Asquith:

My dear Prime Minister,
  It will be to your recollection that you saw me and the First Lord of the Admiralty in your private room prior to a meeting of the War Council to consider my protest against the Dardanelles undertaking when it was first mooted. With extreme reluctance, and largely due to earnest words spoken to me by Kitchener, I, by not resigning (*as I see now I should have done*) remained a most unwilling beholder (and indeed a participator) of the gradual draining of our naval resources from the decisive theatre of the War. The absence especially at this moment of the destroyers, submarines and minesweepers in the Dardanelles most materially lessens our powers of dealing with the submarine menace in home waters – a menace daily becoming greater, as foreshadowed in the print I submitted to you six months ago.
  I have sent the enclosed memorandum to the First Lord and I ask for it to be circulated to the War Council.

There were good grounds for Fisher's worries about the submarine threat in the eastern Mediterranean as well as in home waters; that same afternoon, as the result of highly classified intelligence reports, Churchill sent a Most Secret telegram to de Robeck. German submarines had now been positively identified in the eastern Mediterranean and the Admiralty could not accept the risk of the *Queen Elizabeth* falling victim to a torpedo. De Robeck was therefore ordered to send her home forthwith; she would be replaced by two old ships, the *Exmouth* and *Venerable*. More French ships were also on their way to join the Allied fleet off the Dardanelles.

Late in the evening of 12 May the Prime Minister answered Fisher's letter, expressing his pleasure that Fisher and Churchill had apparently declared a truce and were now back in harmony. This was true, but not for long, as was to be seen from Fisher's note to Asquith on the 13th. After thanking the Prime Minister, he had to report that the truce had been short-lived: 'I regret to say within four hours of the pact being concluded the First Lord said to Kitchener "that in the event of the army's failure the fleet would endeavour to force its way through" or words to that effect.' After assuring Asquith that he will continue to help him 'in the very biggest task any Prime Minister ever had', he continued: 'Still, I desire to convey to you that I honestly feel I cannot remain where I am much longer, as there is an inevitable and never-ending drain daily (almost hourly) *of our resources in the decisive theatre of the War*.' After complaining of the unceasing activities of Churchill, as he sought to control the operations of the fleet, Fisher concluded: 'this purely private and personal letter, intended for your own eyes alone and not to be quoted, as there is no use threatening without acting, is to mention to the one person I feel *ought* to know, *that I feel my time is short!*'

If Fisher needed confirmation of his increased anxieties, it occurred on the night of 12 May off Helles. Hamilton's journal for the following day tersely reports, with a tinge of admiration for a remarkable feat, that 'Last night a Turkish gunboat sneaked down the Straits and torpedoed the *Goliath*. David and his sling on the grand scale. The enemy deserve decorations, confound them.' The Turkish torpedo boat *Muavenet-i-Millet*, under the supervision of a German officer, Lieutenant-Commander Rudolf Firle, had come through the Narrows undetected and gently run with the current until off Morto Bay, unseen by the patrolling destroyers. She was finally challenged by the sleepy anchor watch aboard the old battleship at a range from which her three torpedoes could not miss. All were direct hits; the battleship immediately lurched over on its side and went down in minutes. Firle left the scene at high speed under heavy fire from both British and Turkish guns ashore. There had been no time for the stricken battleship to launch any boats and only 183 officers and men were saved from the *Goliath*'s crew of over 800. Captain Shelford went down with his ship.

Firle reached Constantinople to be greeted as a hero. Sheep were slaughtered on the deck of the *Muavenet* and their blood splashed on the torpedo tubes. Firle was awarded the Iron Cross, 1st Class, and the Austrian Iron Cross as well as the highest Turkish gallantry award and all his crew were presented with gold watches by the Sultan in person.

On the evening of 14 May Churchill passed Fisher the draft of a plan calling for the allocation of further naval resources from home establishment to the Dardanelles. These included some monitors, 70 more aircraft, including seaplanes capable of carrying a 500-lb bomb load, four elderly pre-dreadnoughts fitted with anti-torpedo and mine bulges, and various other naval stores. This was too much. Fisher immediately sent a memorandum to Asquith stating his inability to continue as First Sea Lord. Early the next morning he minuted Churchill:

After serious reflection I have come to the regretted conclusion I am unable to remain any longer as your colleague. It is undesirable in the public interest to go into details . . . but I find it increasingly difficult to adjust myself to the increasingly daily requirements of the Dardanelles to meet your views. As you truly said yesterday, I am in the position of continually vetoing your proposals. This is not fair to you, besides being extremely distasteful to me. I am off to Scotland at once, so as to avoid all questionings.

Yours truly,
Fisher

The old admiral also sent a formal notice of resignation to Asquith, while Churchill sat down to write to Fisher in a last desperate bid to retain his services:

The only thing to think of now is what is best for the country and for the brave men who are fighting. Anything which does injury to those interests will be very harshly judged by history on whose stage we now are.

I do not understand what is the specific cause which led you to resign. If I did I might cure it. When we parted last night I thought we were in agreement. The proposals I made to you by minute were I thought in general accord with your views; and in any case were for discussion between us. Our personal friendship is and I trust will remain unimpaired.

It is true the moment is anxious and our difficulties grave. But I am sure that with loyalty and courage we shall come through safely and successfully. You could not let it be said that you had thrown me over because things were for the time being going badly at the Dardanelles.

In every way I have tried to work in the closest sympathy with you. The men you wanted in the place you wanted them – the ships you designed – every proposal you have formally made for naval action – I have agreed to.

My own responsibilities are great also. I am the one who gets the blame for anything that goes wrong. But I have scrupulously adhered to our original agreement that we should do nothing important without consulting each other. If you think it is not so, surely you should tell me in what respect.

In order to bring you back to the Admiralty I took my political life in my hands with the King and the PM – as you know well. You then promised to stand by me and see me through. If you now go at this bad moment and thereby let loose upon me the spite . . . of those who are also your enemies more than they are mine, it will be a melancholy ending to our six months of successful war and administration. The discussions which will arise will strike a cruel blow at the fortunes of the army now struggling in the Gallipoli peninsula and cannot fail to invest with an air of disaster a mighty enterprise which with patience can and will certainly be carried to success . . .

I hope you will come to see me tomorrow afternoon. I have a pro- position to make to you with the assent of the PM which may resolve some of the anxieties and difficulties which you feel about the measures necessary to support the army at the Dardanelles.

Though I shall stand to my post until relieved, it will be a very great grief to me to part from you, and our rupture will be profoundly injurious to every public interest.

Yours ever,<br>
W.

There was a final flurry of hasty notes, going over the same ground, Fisher freely acknowledging the debt he owed to Churchill but stressing his determination to go. In reply, Churchill emphasized that the fleet should not be rushed into any attempt to force the Narrows. It was to no avail, for Fisher's last scrawled memorandum came back at once:

Dear Winston,

As usual your letter is most persuasive but I really have considered everything and I have definitely told the PM that I leave town Monday. Please don't wish to see me. I could say nothing as I am determined not to. *I know I am doing right.*

He did stay at his post until after the weekend, hiding in the Charing Cross Hotel to avoid the press and Churchill's attentions. Asquith tried to hold him back by telling him that a major reshuffle of the Cabinet was in hand. He even went so far as to charge him to remain at his post in the King's name. But by 19 May, Fisher had gone north, to Dungavel Castle in Lanarkshire, from where he sent a curious ultimatum to the Prime Minister, containing a savage attack on his erstwhile colleagues at the Board of Admiralty and his suc- cessor as First Sea Lord, as well as a string of conditions for his return to Whitehall. Since these would have created another warlord with even greater powers than Kitchener's they were rejected out of hand by Asquith, who did not bother to reply. Fisher was placed in a relat- ively obscure job for the rest of the war, handling new inventions for prosecuting naval warfare, and departed from the scene as far as the Dardanelles were concerned. It was an ignominious end to a long and influential career.

# 16

# Fresh to the Fight

Damn the Dardanelles; they will be our grave!
Lord Fisher, 1915

AFTER THE REPULSE of the Turkish night attack of 1/2 May at Helles, Hamilton wished to advance immediately in order to capitalize on it. But the Turks were ready, and within an hour all the attacking troops, French and British, were back in their original trenches, having suffered yet more casualties. These were particularly heavy in the French sector, where over 2,000 fell. In the 29th Division they were lower, but five battalion commanders had been killed or seriously wounded, together with four adjutants. Having failed in this botched surprise attack while the enemy was supposedly off balance, Hamilton decided to launch a set-piece divisional assault as soon as further reinforcements had been landed.

Meanwhile, the resilient Turks attacked again with eight battalions, which had only just arrived after a 20-mile forced march from the fishing port up the coast where they had landed a few hours before. Without preparation of any sort they were hurled into the attack on the night of 3/4 May against the French sector. The Senegalese broke and ran for the beach at Morto Bay and the line would have fallen apart had it not been for the determined fight put up by every staff officer, cook, clerk, bandsman and orderly in the French corps capable of holding a rifle.

At dawn the Turks were still charging repeatedly against the French line, but as soon as the French could see to fire, their field guns – the lethal '75s' – caught the attackers in the open and slaughtered them. The '75' was capable of a phenomenal rate of fire – a good gun crew could get off twenty rounds a minute, and the effect of this at close range was devastating. After this great effort, however, the French were prostrate. Their best troops, the Foreign Legion and Zouave battalions, were drained by heavy losses and near breaking point; the Senegalese, in d'Amade's opinion, were unfit to go back into the line until stiffened with new European officers. Hamilton therefore agreed to place the 2nd Naval Brigade of the Royal Naval Division under French command for the time being.

Kitchener, frustrated by the lack of progress to date, now sent Hamilton a signal urging rapid action and warning of the danger attending any delay, which would 'allow Turks to bring up reinforcements and to make unpleasant preparations for your reception'. There was very little time to prepare for the Second Battle of Krithia. To make up for the lack of field artillery, the fleet closed in and did its best to suppress resistance and delay Turkish defensive preparation. Every night, after dark, one or two British battleships stole into Morto Bay and anchored there as floating batteries, thus sealing the fate of one of them, the *Goliath*, as already described. Intelligence of Turkish dispositions at Helles was scanty, despite a certain amount of aerial reconnaissance. The enemy trench system appeared still to be in an early stage of development and there was optimism at GHQ; provided the attack was launched decisively, it might be possible to secure a break-in at low cost.

Because of the heavy Allied casualties already incurred, Hamilton had to reorganize his forces. The 86th Brigade was broken up and its remaining units shared out to other brigades. A composite division was formed under Major-General Paris of the Royal Naval Division, and a brigade apiece of Australians and New Zealanders was shipped round from Anzac. The forces available for 2nd Krithia were thus:

*29th Division* (*Hunter-Weston*)

87th Brigade – 2nd South Wales Borderers, 1st King's Own Scottish Borderers, 1st Royal Inniskilling Fusiliers, 1st Border, and the 'Dubsters' (the temporarily combined survivors of the Dublins and Munsters)

88th Brigade – 4th Worcester, 2nd Hampshire, 1st Essex, 2nd Royal Fusiliers, 1/5th Royal Scots (TF), 1st Lancashire Fusiliers

125th Brigade (42nd Division TF) – 5th, 6th, 7th and 8th Lancashire Fusiliers

29th Indian Infantry Brigade – 14th Sikhs, 1/6th Gurkha Rifles, 69th and 89th Punjabis (less their Musulman companies, who were relegated to work on the beaches)

*French Expeditionary Force (d'Amade)*
1st French Division – Colonial Brigade of 6 battalions, Metropolitan
 Brigade of 6 battalions
2nd Naval Brigade – Hood, Howe and Anson battalions

*Composite Division (Paris)*
2nd Australian Brigade – 5th, 6th, 7th and 8th battalions (2,300 men)
New Zealand Brigade – Auckland, Canterbury, Otago and Wellington
 battalions (2,700 men)
Composite Naval Brigade – Plymouth and Drake battalions

The entire force amounted to a bayonet strength of 25,000 and the
supporting artillery consisted of 95 guns, ranging from a few antique
mountain guns to four large naval guns brought ashore by the
French. Some Australian guns, for which there was no room ashore
at Anzac, were added to the artillery for the attack on Krithia.
Artillery ammunition was in desperately short supply; the 56 British
18-pounders only had shrapnel shell, useless against well-
entrenched infantry or for cutting barbed wire entanglements, and
all other types of shell were rationed.

It had been Hamilton's wish to launch the attack on 6 May an hour
before dawn so as to surprise the Turks and get in amongst their positions with the minimum number of casualties. He was dissuaded
from this by Hunter-Weston, who put it to Hamilton that the severe
casualties to senior officers in the first ten days ashore had reduced
the chance of accurate marching in the dark; this was hardly a valid
argument, as all regular officers and NCOs were capable of using
prismatic compasses and marching to a given bearing. Hamilton
yielded and the hour of attack was selected as 10 a.m.

The ground over which the attack was to be launched was much
more complex than could be surmised from the inadequate maps
issued to units taking part. These only gave vague indications of con-
tours and the presence of principal deres, or watercourses, now dried
up for the summer, which punctuated the southern end of the peninsula. The main thrust line ran south-west to north-east, parallel with
the dried-up stream beds and the spurs of higher ground separating
them from each other. Going from the Allied left flank, resting on the
shore of the Aegean, the first nullah was Gully Ravine; then came the
Kirte Dere, Kanli and Kereves Deres. The spines, again running from
left to right flanks, were known as Gully, Fir Tree, Krithia, Central
and Kereves Spurs.

On 1 May the first elements of the 29th Indian Infantry Brigade
had landed on V beach alongside the *River Clyde*. Second-Lieutenant

Reginald Savory, the junior subaltern of the 14th (King George's Own) Sikhs, gazed around in amazement as the battalion marched to its bivouac area at the top of the cliffs nearby. In all directions lay great stacks of rations, ammunition, and warlike stores of every description. Shells were falling haphazardly all over the area, ignored by the more experienced dwellers in the beach-head, but lethal to some. Savory saw a shell land in the middle of an impromptu football game. The wounded were quickly removed to a nearby dressing station and the game was resumed, with depleted teams. The Zion Mule Corps was hard at work, its animals, beautifully groomed and fed, carrying stores from the beach depots to the forward troops only two miles ahead. Once the battalion had been placed in its tent lines and low walls of sandbags erected as a protection against shell splinters, the officers went forward to visit the unit holding the section of line they were due to take over, near Gully Ravine.

They found the outgoing unit dog-tired, edgy, angry and baffled. Snipers were constantly taking their toll and this had had a bad effect on morale; it was the officers, they were told, who were the prime targets – and the commanding officers of many British units made their task easy by insisting that officers wore Sam Browne belts and service dress hats. In an Indian battalion, Savory reckoned, the snipers would have an even easier time of it. The Turkish barbed wire, it was said, was so tough that it resisted all types of issue wire-cutters. Savory noted with surprise that the French officers of the Metropolitan units were still wearing their red trousers, kepis and dark blue coats. He now understood why their officer casualties had been so high. The 14th Sikhs now moved up into the line, on the extreme left, astride Gully Spur. They were to hold this position whilst the Australians, brought round from Anzac, advanced through them and on up the spur in a later phase of the operation.

The 42nd (East Lancashire) Division was the first territorial formation to land at Gallipoli. It had been sent out to Egypt in September 1914 to relieve regular units and had spent some months training intensively for war; some of its units had actually seen action along the Canal during the abortive Turkish attack from the Sinai; as a result, the division was fit and ready for operations. After inspecting it in March 1915, before he ever thought of asking for it as reinforcement for Gallipoli, Hamilton wrote in his diary:

*28 March*. Inspected East Lancs Division and a Yeomanry Brigade . . . how I envied Maxwell those lovely lads. No chance to use them here with summer coming up and the desert getting as dry as a bone. What wouldn't I give to carry them off with me *now*. These Lancashire men especially are eye-openers. How on earth have they managed to pick up the swank and devil-may-care of crack regulars? They *are* regulars, only they are bigger, more effective specimens than Manchester mills or East Lancs mines can spare for the regular service in peacetime. Anyway, no soldier need wish to see a finer lot.

The Second Battle of Krithia began somewhat half-heartedly on the morning of 6 May. Most of the troops, with the exception of the untried territorials on the extreme left, were still exhausted by their previous exertions. In the words of the official historian: 'In the centre, the 88th Brigade, made up of five very weak battalions, was but a skeleton of its former self; it had lost all but one of its battalion commanders and the majority of its company, platoon and section leaders; and not a man in the brigade had had a real night's rest for a fortnight.' The French were in a similar state, further depleted by the unreliability of their African troops, who could not be entrusted with any role in the attack.

The advance was hesitant. Preceded by a thin screen of scouts, the 88th Brigade moved up Fir Tree Spur; artillery support was so sparse that Turkish officers later stated that they thought the attack was being conducted without it. Under increasingly heavy shrapnel fire the advance slowed, then came to a halt. Elsewhere the British advance was delayed by the French, who were forty minutes late out of their trenches. After advancing no more than half a mile the 88th Brigade began to dig in on Fir Tree Spur without engaging the Turkish main defences. On the extreme left the newly landed territorials of the Lancashire Fusiliers ran into strong opposition and suffered heavily. They had been given the task of outflanking the Turks and turning their position, being the only fresh troops available; but by the end of the first day they had lost 300 officers and men with nothing to show for it.

If Brigadier-General Breeks, the artillery commander of the 29th Division, had started the day with forebodings over the ammunition shortage and its certain effect on the scale of support his gunners might be able to give, the news which now came from GHQ must have appalled him. Hamilton had signalled urgently to Kitchener two days earlier, noting the artillery ammunition shortage on the peninsula and indicating that he was almost out of 18-pounder high explosive shell. He received a curt reply from the War Office, pointing out that his artillery ammunition scales had been worked out on the basis of a short-term operation and that he should now press on and conclude the campaign. This intelligence was imparted to Breeks, who was already showing signs of imminent physical and mental breakdown; it can hardly have helped his condition.

By the end of the day, the French were clearly in distress. The commander of their best formation, the Metropolitan Brigade, reported that the morale of the Zouaves was failing, and that the effects of heavy enemy fire and fatigue were affecting all ranks. As a large gap opened between the French left flank and the right of the Composite Brigade, the commander of the 2nd Naval Brigade, Commodore Backhouse, ordered the Hood and Anson battalions forward to close it. Unfortunately, the Hood battalion found that the French were unable to advance at all, and soon had their right flank open to Turkish enfilading fire which killed the commanding officer, Lieutenant-Colonel Quilter of the Grenadier Guards, and many of his men.

It had been a calamitous start to what Hamilton had hoped would be the deciding battle on the peninsula. At no point had Hunter-Weston's attack grappled the main Turkish position and it was clear that the assault on this would have to take place next day, with reduced artillery support, and greatly reduced numbers of exhausted soldiers, because of the heavy casualties suffered on the 6th. If the GHQ staff had been privy that evening to the deliberations of the Turkish staff, they might have been heartened, for great uncertainty prevailed in the enemy camp. Von Sodenstern had been removed from his command by Liman after the failure of his two costly night attacks and replaced by another German officer, Weber Pasha, who took one look at the battlefield and immediately counselled a withdrawal behind Achi Baba. This was not accepted by Liman who ordered that no further ground was to be given up, and that attack was Weber's best method of defence.

Hunter-Weston's plan for 7 May was for a general advance after fifteen minutes of artillery preparation – all that could be spared. The attack was to begin at 10 a.m. Divisional orders were issued at 10 p.m. on the previous evening. Hunter-Weston attempted to instil some aggression into his wilting force by means of individual telephone briefings of all the brigade commanders, and he sent a special order of the day to the territorials of 125 Brigade, who were expected to advance up Gully Spur almost three miles to take Hill 472, which lies over a mile due north of Krithia village: 'The eyes of Lancashire and the world are on you, and the honour of your country and the welfare of your own folk at home depend on your deeds today. The Major-

General knows that no fire and no losses will stop you, and that you will win through to a glorious victory.'

In the event, the attack of 7 May was another disastrous failure. In order to permit the rapid advance of the 125th Brigade the navy had undertaken to bombard the concealed machine-gun nests on top of Gully Spur and above the former Y beach, which had caused many casualties and held up the advance on the previous day. These were so well camouflaged, however, that even observers in balloons towed by the ships could not detect them. The ammunition shortage meant an even weaker artillery fire plan, further enfeebled by the almost total lack of information on enemy positions. When the Lancashire Fusiliers left their trenches to begin the assault, they were immediately engaged by a number of hidden machine-guns which could not be pin-pointed, and the advance died away. To the right, the 88th Brigade did its best but as its flank was unsupported, every step forward meant going further into enfilading fire, and casualties mounted steadily. After two hours of this attrition the forward move came to a halt. Nowhere had more than 300 yards been gained, and these at terrible cost. On the right, the French had made no progress. The Turks appear barely to have noticed that a full-scale set-piece attack had been launched against them, as their main defences were not seriously threatened.

As the British position worsened and artillery ammunition began to run out, the defenders were steadily reinforcing their position and strengthening their defences. Hamilton nevertheless decided to make one more attempt to break through. For the third successive day, the attack would commence in mid-morning, this time with virtually no artillery support. Orders for the morrow were given by GHQ at 10.25 p.m. and passed down the weary chain of command until they reached the dazed infantry at 9 a.m. the next day. The New Zealand Brigade was to capture Krithia village. A more subtle approach was to be made in the Gully Ravine area; instead of a direct assault, the troops were to infiltrate themselves along the line of the ravine and cover the left flank of the New Zealanders as they worked their way forward into Krithia. No one appears to have realized that this plan of attack was pitting four depleted battalions of New Zealanders in an advance across open ground against more than nine battalions of entrenched Turks supported by an unknown number of masked machine-gun positions and covered by artillery which had registered its targets carefully.

Hamilton came ashore to watch the battle from the high ground above the Helles beaches. His command post looked out over an apparently calm and sleeping landscape, sloping gently up towards Achi Baba nearly six miles away. At 10.15 a brief cannonade started, and then the infantry began to move forward. On the right, the French did not stir from their trenches. On the left, men could be seen attempting to edge up Gully Spur in the face of relentless machine-gun fire, which soon stopped the advance. In the centre, the New Zealanders bravely moved forward from the fire trenches of the 88th Brigade, but fared no better. All this was visible to Hamilton who, though he shrank from interfering in the conduct of operations over the head of Hunter-Weston, decided to throw in his reserves late in the afternoon, ordering the entire line, now reinforced by the Australian brigade, to 'fix bayonets, slope arms, and advance on Krithia village' at 5.30 p.m. after a fifteen-minute artillery bombard-ment. The French at last joined in. On this battlefield, the passage of orders was no faster than it might have been in the eighteenth century. Consequently, the Australian brigade commander, Colonel M'Cay, was told of Hamilton's order only thirty minutes before the attack. His brigade was nearly a mile to the rear of the British front line but within minutes all his battalions were hurrying eagerly forward to join the battle.

Unsurprisingly, the sparse preliminary bombardment did little to the Turks apart from alerting them, and everywhere the advancing Allies were cut down. The Australians had the furthest to go, and well before they reached the British front line they came under heavy and accurate artillery fire. When they got further forward, they were mown down in a gallant but futile charge. Over on the right, the French had gone forward to be greeted, as had all the other advances, by the terrible execution of the hidden machine-guns. That night, it was apparent that apart from some ground taken by stealth after dark without loss – the very ground where 2,000 Australians had fallen in vain earlier in the day – nothing had resulted from the Second Battle of Krithia. Nearly a third of all the Allied troops committed had been killed or wounded.

The 29th Indian Brigade played little part in the battle and had stayed under cover in its trenches. Savory had watched his first battle, appalled and fascinated. He noted the gallantry of the territ-orials as they went unflinchingly up Gully Spur to their deaths, straight off the ship from Egypt, given no clear objective or artillery support – just launched in lines 'into the blue'. It had been imposs-ible for junior leaders, he thought, to maintain any control as the men scattered under fire and the officers went down. One of the Australian battalions had attacked through the Sikhs' lines, leaping clear over the trenches in full fighting order with shouts of 'Come on, Australia!' One of the Australians was hit and fell into Savory's trench. Out of his pocket fell a collection of pornographic postcards picked up in Egypt, which caused the Sikhs much mirth as they bound his wounds and gave him a mug of hot sweet tea; he departed for the field ambulance voicing his thanks for the return of the post-cards as well as the first aid. Savory was greatly impressed by the Australians and by the vigour of their attack: 'It had been another wasted effort; another frontal attack by strange troops, in long un-controllable lines, against an unreconnoitred position and with an invisible objective.'

So ended the Second Battle of Krithia.

## 17

# Hanging On

War means risks, and you cannot always play the
game and win.

Lord Kitchener, 1900

WITH NO MORE than the gain of 500 yards of worthless ground, the
Second Battle of Krithia had been as dismal a venture as the first.
Hamilton, always ready to shoulder the blame, signalled London
candidly that night, admitting failure. Whilst praising the gallantry
of his troops he knew that for the time being they were played out
and disheartened. He had thrown his entire bayonet strength at the
Turkish positions but their cunningly sited machine-guns had won
the day. All hopes of quick resolution and victory on the peninsula
had evaporated. Hamilton told Kitchener that he now felt that the
only way to victory was through attrition, by 'hammering away', as
he put it. It was impossible to disengage and a reappraisal was
urgently needed. Hamilton had fallen, in fact, into the same sort of
military quagmire as French and the BEF; lacking the resources to
sustain open warfare, French's army had now dug and wired itself in
to await massive reinforcements of men and *matériel*. In any case, the
constricted spaces of Helles and Anzac gave little scope for a war of
manoeuvre. The only solution at Gallipoli, as in Flanders, was to ask
for more troops, guns and ammunition, and Hamilton requested two
more infantry divisions, organized as a corps, so that he could break
through to the summit of Achi Baba and resolve the deadlock at
Anzac.

Kitchener responded immediately; he would send another territorial division, the 52nd (Lowland), currently employed on home
defence duties around Edinburgh. Preparations for its embarkation
were immediately put in hand. Although it would not have time to

acclimatize in Egypt, as the 42nd Division had done, or to practise tactical methods which would be of use on the peninsula, it represented the very best of the territorial tradition and was highly regarded in military circles. Hamilton, nurtured in the ethos of the Scottish regiments, was pleased at the choice of the Lowland Division, in which many of his lifelong friends were serving.

The 42nd Division was now complete on the peninsula and settling down well. Hamilton might have regretted using only a single brigade of this high-grade formation in the second attack on Krithia when he could have waited for the whole division to come ashore. It was, after all, the territorial division with the best chance of success, given its extended and rigorous training in Egypt; to have held back until its brigades and full command structure were in place would have certainly produced better results than those obtained by pitching the luckless Lancashire Fusilier brigade into battle. But at that stage Hamilton had very little good intelligence information to go on; he believed that the Turks were rapidly building up semi-permanent defences and that it was imperative despite his very limited resources to attack them as soon as possible. He was wrong, for at this time the Turkish defences were far from complete and their trench system was not continuous.

In the days following Second Krithia there was time to examine the reasons for the disaster. The whole operation had been hastily planned and executed, with little time for the passage of orders down from GHQ through Hunter-Weston's headquarters and on down to brigades and battalions. A well-practised regular formation, accustomed to working together as a single entity, should have been able to use staff drills to cut corners and relay the commander's intentions speedily down to the soldier in the fire trench; in front of Krithia, however, this was asking too much of a force completely lacking homogeneity, where units barely knew those on their immediate flanks, and often had no contact with them. All staffs and most of the troops went into the battle prostrate with exhaustion. The territorial Fusiliers came fresh to the fight but were straight off the ship, with no chance to get their bearings or learn what was asked of them. The paucity of artillery support has already been mentioned. Above all, Hamilton erred fatally in not insisting on a pre-dawn attack, which would have offered at least a sportsman's chance of success through surprise. To attempt three successive frontal attacks by tired troops in broad daylight, with virtually no fire support apart from a lot of misdirected fire from the fleet, was perhaps the real cause of the débâcle.

Hamilton had begun to realize the difficulty of his task as early as 18 March, when he had watched the fleet being driven off by the shore batteries and viewed the hostile shores from HMS *Phaeton*. The Turks were later to admit freely that Gallipoli lay at the mercy of the Allies until the end of February, but after that, the two months' period of grace enabled them to get their defences in order. There was in fact no time after the end of April when a force of the strength at Hamilton's disposal could have secured the aim hoped for in Whitehall.

Now that the army was ashore, however, a host of problems had to be faced. The Mediterranean Expeditionary Force depended on absurdly long lines of communication, whilst the Turks enjoyed all the advantages conferred by interior lines, which had only to extend 150 miles back to Constantinople. Initially these were largely dependent on sea transport, but with the entry of Allied submarines to the Sea of Marmara, overland routes had to be used. Even so, this was easy compared with the Allies' 600-mile sea crossing to Egypt, vulnerable to German submarine attack and costly in terms of the shipping requirement. It was another 3,000 miles to the United Kingdom, 7,000 to Australia and 10,000 to New Zealand. These vast distances imposed a great burden on shipping, particularly as Britain's maritime lifelines were falling increasingly prey to the U-boat threat throughout 1915, with ships being sunk close in to the western approaches and particularly in the Bristol Channel. The nearest railhead from which ammunition and other supplies could be shipped to the Dardanelles was Marseilles, 1,400 miles away.

On the peninsula, all supplies had to come over dangerously exposed beaches, which were vulnerable to the prevailing westerly winds, especially in winter; the flimsy piers and breakwaters which had been built at Helles and Anzac were continually being destroyed by high seas and had to be rebuilt immediately if the troops ashore were to be sustained. As the beaches were all within enemy artillery range, every ship coming inshore was at risk, and the steady fire of the guns on the Asiatic shore was felt particularly by the French at their main depot on V beach and in Sedd-el-Bahr castle.

The fleet was now totally committed to the role of supporting the army on the peninsula. There was to be no naval breakthrough on the lines of that which had failed so disastrously on 18 March. Even Churchill was losing his appetite for such an attempt. He had called on the Admiralty for an estimate of likely losses in capital ships if the fleet was to 'charge' the Narrows. He was told that if sixteen battleships, in two columns, tried to force their way through, half might succeed but would arrive in the Marmara severely battered and with their magazines almost empty. There was no chance of any unprotected supply ships getting through to replenish them. Of the eight battleships which might get through, only four could expect to return, and these would be very severely damaged. Kitchener accepted the Admiralty's report and no more was said about an assault on the Narrows.

In mid-May the War Council met to review the situation on all fronts. The problem of Gallipoli was discussed at length; Hamilton was all but marooned ashore and the fleet was incapable of forcing the Narrows without incurring unacceptable losses. The Russians, on whose behalf the whole expedition had been launched, appeared to be on the verge of military collapse as their armies fell back in Galicia. The last hope of intervention by a Russian army corps in the area of Constantinople had evaporated. In France there was deadlock and General French was pressing insistently for priority in men and supplies. Kitchener was obsessed with the threat of a German invasion of England; the German high command, he believed, was planning to knock the Russians out of the war and then apply the full force of its armies to a gigantic offensive in the West which would drain forces from the home establishment and lay England open to invasion. For this reason he placed an embargo on further reinforcement of the Western Front with divisions of his New Armies.

As far as Gallipoli was concerned, Kitchener considered that three options were open: first, Hamilton's force could be pulled out at once; this carried with it the risk of terrible slaughter on the beaches and humiliation in the Muslim world, with far-reaching consequences in India, the Suez Canal and the oilfields of Mesopotamia and Persia, as well as a wholly unpredictable effect on the as yet unaligned Balkan states. Secondly, immediate reinforcements could be despatched to Hamilton, permitting a major resumption of the offensive in the peninsula; this rested on the supposition that suitable troops were available. Thirdly, an attempt could be made to hold on to the ground already taken at Gallipoli with the aid of the extra territorial division now about to embark in the United Kingdom (the 52nd Lowland); this was certainly feasible, although it would continue to place a heavy strain on merchant shipping as well as on the navy.

The War Council examined these options but could not arrive at a decision. To Kitchener's discomfiture the majority view seemed to favour the second option despite inevitable dilution of

effort and weakening of resources for home defence and the
Western Front. Kitchener therefore shifted the burden of making the
decision to Hamilton and sent him a signal which could be read in
several different ways: 'The War Council would like to know what
force you consider would be necessary to carry through the operations upon which you are engaged. You should base this estimate
on the supposition that I have adequate forces to be placed at your
disposal.'

Hamilton pondered for three days, before replying that he would
now need three more infantry divisions in addition to the 52nd. He
did not presume to specify what sort of divisions these should be, but
knew that no more regular formations were available, so presumably
hoped that he would get some more territorials. Little did he know
that when the extra divisions did come, they would be the first-fruits
of Kitchener's appeal to the nation for New Armies. He had to wait
a further three weeks for a reply to his signal, for at long last
Asquith's Liberal government was on the verge of falling. At Helles
and Anzac, the time was usefully spent in consolidating the meagre
gains that had been made at such fearful cost in the first three weeks
of the campaign.

If the military situation at Gallipoli was in crisis by the middle of May
it was nothing to the political problems now afflicting those
entrusted with the conduct of the entire war effort. Fisher had gone,
determined to resign no matter what his personal loss. Churchill
could not bring himself to accept the fact that so important a servant
of the state could desert his post at such a time. But the old sailor was
not to be induced to return.

In the face of growing national impatience with the conduct of
the war, especially the inadequacies of ammunition production
revealed in the *Daily Mail*, the government seemed about to fall.
To add to Asquith's political discomfiture, his confidante Venetia
Stanley now announced her engagement to Edwin Montagu,
Asquith's private secretary. She had long been the Prime Minister's
soul-mate and, no longer able to confide his most intimate thoughts
to her, he felt lost. Unwilling to resign the premiership, he decided
to form a National Coalition government on 25 May; the new
Cabinet comprised 13 Liberals, 8 Conservatives and one Labour
minister; the energetic Lloyd George was given a new portfolio as
Minister of Munitions in an attempt to resolve the shell shortage.
Churchill lost his cherished post at the Admiralty as his enemies on
the Tory benches gathered round for the kill, eager to chastise him

1. On mobilization day, 11 August 1914, D Squadron of the Berkshire Yeomanry forms up in Wantage marketplace. According to contemporary local press reports, Captain C.C. Stone was in command. The regiment served in an infantry role at Gallipoli as part of the 2nd Mounted Division

2. Lieutenant Holbrook and the crew of the submarine *B11* pose on the forward casing of their boat after sinking the Turkish battleship *Messudieh* off Chanak in December 1914

3. The destroyer HMS *Racoon*, hit by Turkish gunfire whilst minesweeping in the Straits, blows off steam in the foreground as another destroyer manoeuvres to take her in tow. A battleship of the *Lord Nelson* class – the last of the pre-Dreadnoughts – stands by to give covering fire.
Cape Helles can be seen on the extreme left

4. Men of the Australian and New Zealand Army Corps aboard a transport, the former German *Lutzow*, from which they were taken ashore at Ari Burnu on 25 April 1915

5. The *River Clyde* beached below the walls of Sedd-el-Bahr fort. This photograph, taken a few days after the landing of 25 April, shows some of the Turkish wire in the foreground and the stretch of V beach on which the luckless Dublin Fusiliers were pinned down

6. In the front line at Anzac, an Australian uses a trench periscope to 'spot' for a marksman who is using a sniperscope attached to a clamped rifle. This scene is typical of the extraordinary conditions in which the garrisons of the forward posts – Quinn's, Courtney's and Steele's – served for weeks on end, only a few yards from the Turkish firing trenches

7. The elderly pre-Dreadnought battleship HMS *Albion*, having run aground off Gaba Tepe whilst supporting the Anzacs, fires a series of broadsides to free herself while under heavy fire from Turkish batteries ashore

8. A party of naval ratings on shore leave at Lemnos. In the background a mass of transports and warships fills Mudros harbour. The sailors are wearing wide-brimmed straw hats of a pattern adopted in Nelson's day

9. The view north from Walker's Ridge, showing part of the chaotic landscape which the 'left hook' attacks of August 1915 had to negotiate. In the distance, North Beach sweeps round to Nibrunesi Point, where the low mound of Lala Baba can just be seen. To its right is Suvla Plain and beyond, hidden in the haze, the Kiretch Tepe Ridge

10. A 60-pounder gun in action near Cape Helles. It is positioned near the cliff-top, behind the rising ground on which now stands the main Helles war memorial. There were never more than eight of these useful heavy pieces in support of VIII Corps and by early August, due to lack of spares, only one was still fit for action

11. British infantry of the 42nd (East Lancs) Division coming out of the line down Gully Ravine, probably in July 1915. Note the numerous dugouts cut into the walls of the ravine; these housed medical and administrative units as well as brigade and battalion headquarters

12. The dramatic scene following the torpedoing of the battleship HMS *Majestic* off W beach on 27 May by *UB21*. Within minutes, every ship in the vicinity slipped anchor and made for open waters, as small boats hurried to pick up survivors. The merchantman in the foreground is already under way

13. A Short floatplane of the RNAS preparing for take-off in Mudros harbour

14. On Sunday, 8 August 1915, the survivors of the 2nd Battalion, Hampshire Regiment, at church parade on Gully Beach, following two days of ferocious fighting as part of the attack launched at Helles to draw Turkish attention away from the Sari Bair offensive further north. The battalion had gone into action nearly a thousand strong. The senior Hampshires officer on this parade was 2nd Lieutenant G.R.D. Moor VC

15. Australians in the firing trenches near Hill 60, baiting the Turks by displaying home-made targets to draw the fire of enemy snipers

16. Officers of the 6th Battalion, Highland Light Infantry, in the firing trench at Helles, facing Krithia. The officer on the left is the regimental medical officer. Their service dress, Sam Browne belts and conspicuous rank badges made it easy for Turkish snipers to pick off British officers, whose casualties were extremely high as a result

17. Australian gunners with an 18-pounder, probably on top of Plugge's Plateau, which was one of the few places in the beach-head where field artillery could be deployed

18. Terrified mules brace themselves, and an Indian muleteer tries to calm them as a Turkish shell lands in the transport lines at Suvla, August 1915. In the background is part of the Kiretch Tepe Ridge

19. Infantry coming ashore at Suvla, aboard one of the newly arrived armoured landing craft known as 'beetles'. Each of these was capable of carrying up to 500 men

20. On the morning of 7 August, troops form up at Suvla and await orders. Already, many are suffering from a shortage of water. In the distance can be seen the heights of the Sari Bair Ridge, the main objective of the 'left hook' attacks from Anzac. It was scenes of inactivity such as this, clearly visible to the embattled Australians on the heights, which led them to believe, with justification, that Stopford's IX Corps was failing to play an active part in the operation

21. Private William Begbie, who enlisted in the 7th Royal Scots (Leith Rifles) in 1914 at the age of 15½, photographed during convalescence from the wound sustained at Helles; he returned to Gallipoli and was later evacuated sick when, his true age discovered, he was packed off back to England. In 1918 he was back in action, this time in France, where he was gassed, but survived

22. Private Campion of the Warwickshire Yeomanry (note his bear and ragged staff cap badge). After undergoing an enlistment procedure worthy of description in Shakespeare's *Henry IV Part 2*, he served with the 2nd Mounted Division at Suvla, taking part in the celebrated march under fire across the Salt Lake

23. Captain and Quartermaster W.J. Saunders MC of the 10th Battalion, Hampshire Regiment. At Hill 60, in August 1915, he rallied the survivors of the battalion – consisting entirely of Kitchener volunteers – after all the officers had been killed or wounded, and acted as adjutant thereafter

24. A horse-drawn ambulance of the 42nd (East Lancs) Division struggles up Gully Ravine after a rainstorm. Every watercourse on the peninsula was vulnerable to flash flooding, greatly increasing the problems of moving supplies up to the firing trenches. During the November storm a six-foot torrent swept down the ravine, carrying living and dead alike away to the open sea

25. A chronic shortage of grenades forced the British and Anzac troops to improvise by using precariously fuzed jam tins filled with scrap metal and an explosive charge. 'Grenade factories' such as this one at Anzac were set up. In this case the manufacturers, with cheerful disregard for any evident safety precautions, are using a metal punch and anvil to prepare the tins for filling, whilst a mule train passes close by, oblivious to the risk of spontaneous detonation

26. Lieutenant-Colonel Parker (centre, wearing woollen cap comforter) of the 1st (East Lancs) Field Ambulance tending the wounds of Turkish prisoners at the third battle of Krithia

27. At Suvla, in the aftermath of the great storm of November 1915, men suffering from deep shock, exhaustion, frostbite and hypothermia recuperate as best they can in a shelter made from ration biscuit cases bearing the manufacturer's name – 'Huntley and Palmer, Reading'

28. Old comrades: Generals Sir Ian Hamilton and Sir Aylmer Hunter-Weston at a reunion parade of 'The Incomparable 29th' Division in 1926

for his defection to the Liberals in 1904. He was succeeded at the Admiralty by Arthur Balfour who, although an adept politician with one of the finest minds in Parliament, had never immersed himself like Churchill in the professional interests of the armed forces. A downcast Churchill, in the grip of one of his periodic bouts of acute depression, was given the sinecure Cabinet post of Chancellor of the Duchy of Lancaster, which deprived him of any say in the control of the navy. After a brief tenure, Fisher's successor as First Sea Lord, Admiral Sir Arthur Wilson, handed over to Admiral Sir Henry Jackson, a man virtually unknown even in his own service.

Though now shorn of executive power, Churchill still sat in his customary place in the War Council at Kitchener's left hand, and no one seemed disposed to challenge him. Because of the turmoil attending the collapse of Asquith's government in late May it was only on 7 June that Kitchener took up the reins once more and attended to Hamilton's request for more divisions. He emphasized the need to persevere at Gallipoli, confirmed the identity of the reinforcing divisions to go to Hamilton, and persuaded the Council to agree to further attacks at Gallipoli in the second week of July and the despatch of a number of light cruisers fitted with bulges as well as shallow-draught monitors, whose heavy guns would stiffen the amount of naval support without risking battleships and their large crews.

The choice of New Army divisions as Gallipoli reinforcements reflected Kitchener's prejudice against the territorial force. He had called for volunteers in 1914, when he might have built the New Armies around the existing territorial structure. This was because he felt that an organization which had sprung from the unashamedly dilettante if acutely patriotic volunteer movement was unsuited to general, continental warfare of the type he had accurately forecast; a war in which, no matter how it was presented, there would be a national requirement for thousands of infantry in battles of attrition on the Western Front. Kitchener believed that his New Army troops were superior in every way to the territorials, a view shared at the time by many senior army officers.

The delay of three weeks in reaching this decision proved fatal to the whole enterprise, although this was not readily apparent at the time in Whitehall. It bought invaluable time for the defence, and ten new Turkish divisions were even now heading towards the peninsula. Churchill was to write in later years:

A week lost was about the same as a division. Three divisions in February could have occupied the Gallipoli peninsula with little fighting. Five could have captured it after 18 March. Seven were insufficient at the end of April, but nine might just have done it. Eleven might have sufficed at the beginning of July. Fourteen were to prove insufficient in August.

Hamilton, buoyed by the prospect of reinforcement, began to plan a major offensive. The timing of this was governed not only by the likely arrival dates of the reinforcing formations, but by the phases of the moon. If any further landings were contemplated, Hamilton argued, they would need to be carried out in pitch darkness, and this pointed to the end of the first week in August. Birdwood believed that a landing at a new location was required if the deadlocks at Anzac and Helles were to be broken. The logical place was in Suvla Bay, to the north of Ari Burnu. Since the original landings this area had frequently been reconnoitred by the enterprising New Zealanders. From Fisherman's Hut on the extreme left flank of Anzac, a sandy beach swept along the shores of a wide bay. Inland, across the Salt Lake, could be seen the Anafarta ridgeline, possession of which granted wide fields of view and considerable tactical advantages, for this high ground also held the key to the northern approaches of the Sari Bair feature, the vital ground of the whole southern part of the peninsula. A landing at Suvla Bay, followed by rapid exploitation inland on to the Anafarta ridge, offered the hope of tactical advantage which had so far eluded Hamilton.

The staffs of the Anzac corps and GHQ therefore began to work on a plan, based on the landing of a new corps, comprising New Army and territorial divisions and stiffened by the addition of the long-suffering 29th, in an operation which would be launched by night in Suvla Bay, link up with the Anzac left flank, sweep forward on to Anafarta, and seize the saddle between this and Sari Bair in order to turn the Turkish right flank. Hamilton was much encouraged by reconnaissance reports from both the New Zealanders and the Royal Naval Air Service to the effect that the Suvla Bay area continued to be only lightly held, with few continuous lines of trenches, and very little artillery.

The new corps was to be numbered the IXth. At home, a headquarters staff for it was being assembled by the beginning of July; Hamilton wanted above all else for it to be commanded by an experienced and dynamic general, such as Byng or Rawlinson, who had made his name in France and had plenty of recent combat experience.

His pleas fell on deaf ears, and when the officer to command IX Corps was finally chosen, it was to be on the basis of seniority rather than military competence.

Whilst the 29th and Royal Naval Divisions, with their French allies, licked their wounds at Helles following the Second Battle of Krithia, the line at Anzac was gradually stabilizing. A week after the landings of 25 April the situation had been desperate and it had been necessary to feed in four battalions of the Royal Naval Division who, despite earning the early derision of the Australians on account of their obvious youth, the poor physique of many of their men and apparently condescending attitudes of many of their officers, eventually earned unqualified Australian praise for sheer doggedness in defence, as well as courage in attack.

Once a lodgement had been secured at Anzac, Birdwood was ordered by Hamilton to hold on and not to attempt major offensive operations apart from such action as would facilitate any later move to break out of the Anzac beach-head as part of a major offensive, and to keep as many Turks pinned down in that sector as possible in order to relieve pressure on Helles.

Along much of the Anzac perimeter there was no continuous front line; but up on the ridge-line the opposing sides faced each other at extremely close range, often less than ten yards separating the firing trenches. The Anzac garrison was at one time down to around 10,000 men whilst two brigades were detached at Helles, and under continual pressure from the Turks. Behind the firing trenches a vast system of dugouts, shelters, dumps and mule tracks was constructed within weeks; visitors marvelled at the industry and ingenuity displayed by the inhabitants of this teeming troglodyte community, compressed as it was into an area measured by hundreds of acres rather than miles. Supplies of all sorts could only reach the front line – itself barely a thousand yards from the beach – by mule, then man-packing for the last near-vertical ascent to the posts of danger along the crest. There was a constant air of strain and stress, and the sickness rate began to rise alarmingly.

Early in May the northern or left sector of the Anzac position was held by the New Zealand and Australian Division under Major-General Godley. Here there was no continuous line, owing to the tumbled and chaotic nature of the terrain. On Bolton's Ridge and on the 400 Plateau it had been possible to dig deep trenches, dugouts and galleries, but at the apex of the triangle which constituted the Anzac stronghold, the line consisted of the desperately contested forward posts, named after early heroes of the expedition: Quinn's, Courtney's and Steele's being the most dangerous. The Turks still overlooked parts of Monash Gully from the high ground and movement here was lethal if attempted by day, owing to the persistent sniping which took a steady toll. Eventually, a deep communication trench was dug down the steep slope from Russell's Top, permitting safe movement by day; but by then, the Turks had claimed their most distinguished victim.

On 15 May, Major-General Bridges was mortally wounded by a sniper while ascending the Gully from his divisional headquarters. A medical officer was able to stem the blood gushing from a huge exit wound in the general's thigh, but it was clear that with the main nerves, veins and arteries severed, his chance of survival was low. Bridges was taken aboard a hospital ship in deep shock and visited that evening by Hamilton, who found him composed but pale. The only hope lay in amputation before infection and gangrene set in, for the leg, deprived of its blood supply, was cold and dead; the surgeons shrank from the operation, maintaining that Bridges would not survive the trauma. Within twenty-four hours blood poisoning had set in and the only chance of saving his life had gone. He died less than three days after being wounded, and the Australian army had lost the man who could claim to be its founding father. His body was taken home to Canberra and buried at Duntroon, his enduring memorial.

After two weeks of continuous fighting the ground in front of the Australian positions was covered with Turkish dead. The weather was hot and there was an appalling stench of rotting corpses, accompanied by a plague of flies. The risk of disease steadily increased, exacerbated by the problems of sanitation in such a confined space, and after a few weeks had reached the stage described in unappetizing detail by the official historian of the Australian Medical Services:

> Gastro-intestinal disease dominated the situation and by the end of July was quite out of control. The latrine poles were continually thronged with men, so that attempts at covering or disinfecting excreta became a farce. Black swarms of flies carried infection warm from the very bowel to the food as it passed the lips; they contaminated the unwashed messtins . . .

Even at GHQ, Compton Mackenzie had problems with flies:

> Tea was the most squalid meal, because at tea the flies reached their maximum of numbers and offensiveness. One was lucky to get a sip

that only included a couple of flies, and for those who did not like sugar in their tea the foul sweetness of biting a fly was not enjoyable . . . the sunbeams lit up the stains and spills on the long trestle table, every one of which was the centre of attraction for a quarrelsome mob of these flies which merely used our table for a light dessert after the solid filth they had been gorging all day. They used to alight in threes and fours on one's lips and sometimes had to be actually pulled away, so greedy were they of the moisture; they were loathsome, too, when they clung sizzling to the rim of one's cup.

Despite growing health problems and the constant drain of battle casualties the Anzacs used abundant initiative to improve their positions. They dug saps forward from their front in order to bring themselves closer to the enemy and gain ground just over the crest line. Then they started to mine under the Turks, who responded in kind, thus setting off a never-ending battle of wits in the darkness of the mine galleries.

On 9 May the Australian 15th Battalion under Lieutenant-Colonel Cannan had carried out a raid aimed at deterring the enemy who were believed to have begun an extensive mining operation under the Australian position. A hundred men, divided into three groups, went over the parapet at 10.45 p.m., followed by a large trench digging party with orders to extend the Australian front line into the raided Turkish position. Total surprise was achieved in the initial assault and the Australians leaped into the Turkish trenches with the bayonet. Unfortunately, a large part of the assaulting group enthusiastically over-ran the objective and advanced well into the enemy position where they were subjected to a ferocious counter-attack. Cannan's men were driven back to their original position with nearly 200 casualties, including no less than ten officers killed.

On 18 May there were signs that the Turks were preparing for a full-scale attack at Anzac. Aircraft of the RNAS spotted large numbers of reinforcements marching down the peninsula and at last light the entire Anzac garrison stood to with fixed bayonets, at a fighting strength of some 12,000 men. Nothing happened, but there were unmistakable signs of activity in the Turkish trenches, especially at a point where they were about 200 yards distant across a dead flat stretch of ground. A further stand-to was called at 3 a.m.; after twenty minutes of tense waiting the Australians were amazed to see a dense mass of infantry charging at them in the gloom with fixed bayonets. The Turks were met by a storm of fire and went down rank by rank but kept on coming, heads down, chanting as they advanced.

In order to gain better fields of fire the defenders got out of their trenches and set up their machine-guns on the forward edge of the parapets, standing in the open to fire. Only briefly, at Courtney's Post, did the Turks break into the Australian position, and they were ejected from there by a party of men of the 14th Battalion, of whom only Lance-Corporal Jacka, their leader, survived. He was awarded the VC, the first Australian to gain this distinction, fighting with rifle, bayonet and bare hands until the enemy fled.

At dawn the Australians looked out over no man's land to see a dreadful sight; the Turks later admitted to suffering 10,000 casualties in this attack, and over 3,000 of their dead lay where they had fallen, hundreds of desperately wounded men amongst them. Birdwood, fearing a repetition of the attack once the Turks had reorganized, called for the return of his two brigades from Helles. His instinct was to launch an immediate counter-attack before the Turks were in a position to offer resistance, but GHQ declined to make a quick decision and by the time they did, a golden opportunity had passed. After dark, on the first night following the Turkish attack, enterprising Australians crept out into the field of the dead to see what could be found and came back with a number of excellent up-to-date maps, which were quickly copied by the GHQ map section and issued wholesale; similar maps had recently been taken from dead Turkish officers at Helles.

By the afternoon of 20 May the rapidly decomposing bodies of the Turks killed on the night of 18/19 May posed a grave health risk to both sides. Already the smell of shattered and disembowelled corpses pervaded the air for up to a mile away, and the problem was made worse by the distress of hundreds of wounded Turks, still out in the open without water or medical attention.

The Australians put up a Red Cross flag towards dusk as an overture to arranging a mutual truce for burial of the dead; it was shot down, but almost at once a Turkish soldier came across under a white flag with a courteous message apologizing for the breach of etiquette. A Red Crescent flag was now hoisted over the Turkish trenches and both sides began to leave their positions to succour the wounded. When news of this unofficial truce reached Birdwood's headquarters he was torn between instincts of common sense, decency, and the delicate inferences which he judged might be drawn from his consent to an armistice; he felt that the request should come from the Turks, and they, conscious of the need to avoid any loss of face, were keen that the request should come from the British commander.

At this point, an unusual truce-broker came to the fore in the shape of a GHQ Intelligence staff officer, the Hon. Aubrey Herbert, son of the Earl of Carnarvon. Using his command of the Turkish language, he persuaded both Birdwood and the Turks that the other side had called for the truce, and honour was satisfied. Birdwood invited the Turks to send an officer under a white flag to negotiate a formal truce on the following day. The officer came across, was blindfolded and taken to the Anzac headquarters. An armistice was arranged for 7.30 a.m. to 4.30 p.m. on 24 May. Conditions for this were duly agreed between the two sides and the armistice went off without incident. Some 3,000 Turks were buried in front of the Australian positions.

One fascinated observer of the truce was Compton Mackenzie, sent from GHQ up to Quinn's Post to see that the truce conditions were being observed. Here, the opposing trenches were only twenty yards apart and packed with the dead of both sides – the gruesome relics of a month's close-quarter fighting in which it had been impossible to move or bury the fallen, many of whom, in varying stages of decomposition, had been built into trench walls and parapets. Beyond the Turkish front line the country stretched away into the distance as far as Mackenzie could see. Along the narrow strip of scrub which constituted no man's land, flags had been stuck at intervals marking the demarcation line beyond which none of the participants was to go. Cameras were forbidden under the terms of the truce, but numerous surreptitious snapshots were taken by officers on both sides; there was also a considerable amount of friendly conversation. Each side had posted a line of sentries who stood at ease with rifles and bayonets, facing each other without hostility. Mackenzie noted that

> Staff officers of both sides were standing around in little groups, and there was an atmosphere about the scene of local magnates at the annual sports making suggestions about the start of the obstacle race . . . Everywhere, Turks digging graves for some four thousand of their countrymen who had been putrefying in heaps along this narrow front for nearly a month of warm May air . . . looking down I saw squelching up from the ground on either side of my boot, like a rotten mangold, the deliquescent green and black flesh of a Turk's head . . . I cannot recall a single incident on the way back down the valley. I only know that nothing could cleanse the smell of death from the nostrils for a fortnight afterwards.

When the time approached for the armistice to end, Aubrey Herbert found himself chatting affably with some Albanians in the Turkish service. As they smoked a final cigarette, he pointed out that they would be trying to kill each other the next morning. 'God forbid!' they cried. 'We will never shoot you!' Some Australians joined the group, shaking hands with their opponents before returning to the trenches. Herbert finally received a deep salaam from the Turkish positions. The last words he heard from the enemy were 'Smiling may you go, and smiling come again.'

# 18

# New Dimensions of War

The instruments of battle are valuable only if one
knows how to use them.

Ardant du Picq, *Battle Studies* (1870)

LACK OF SOUND intelligence on the Turkish positions, especially on
the location of their gun batteries and concealed machine-gun nests,
has been cited as one of the causes of failure at Krithia. The only way
of obtaining such information was by aerial reconnaissance, which
was clearly inadequate at Gallipoli, and would be for most of the
campaign. Kitchener had refused point-blank to allow any Royal
Flying Corps aircraft to go to the Dardanelles, and Hamilton was
totally reliant on the Royal Naval Air Service for his aerial reconnaissance. The RNAS, however, existed for an altogether different
role from that of the RFC. The latter was specially trained in army
observation and had already developed high levels of skills in this
field when it took some seventy frail aircraft over to France with the
BEF in August 1914. The RNAS, on the other hand, was seen as an
aerial extension of the fleet, capable of delivering bombs on to
targets which were considered part of the naval struggle, even
though many miles inland.

The advance party of No. 3 Aeroplane Squadron RNAS had
arrived on Tenedos on 24 March under Wing-Commander C. R.
Samson, a pioneer naval aviator already famed for his attack on the
German airship sheds at Düsseldorf, where a Zeppelin had been
destroyed, as well as for a number of daring exploits on the Belgian
coast. Immediately, a landing ground measuring 300 by 600 yards
was cleared for the squadron's eighteen assorted aircraft; Henri
Farmans, BE2cs, BE2s, Sopwith Tabloids, a Breguet and three
Maurice Farmans. All were seriously underpowered, hideously slow

and cumbrous, and very demanding in terms of maintenance. Soon, only three Maurice Farmans and two BE2s were operational.

Samson was a colourful character with fierce ginger beard and whiskers, and he quickly stamped his personality on the squadron. His standing orders reflect not only this but also the hazards of early operational flying:

> Pilots are always to be armed with a revolver or pistol . . . binoculars, some safety device, either waistcoat, patent lifebelt, or petrol can . . . At all times the pilot should carry out independent observations and note down what he sees (noting the times). Nail a pad of paper to the instrument panel for this purpose . . . Pilots and observers are to familiarize themselves with the photographs of Turkish men-of-war described in *The World's Fighting Ships*. This book is in the office . . . Don't make wild statements; a small accurate report is worth pages of rhetoric giving no useful information. If an enemy aeroplane is sighted, attack it, reporting you are doing so, if spotting. Don't try to do what is termed by some people as 'Stunt flying'. This is not wanted for war and is not conduct required of an officer.

The first attempts at using cameras from aircraft were made early in April and the prints developed were of great use; however, a proper photographic section did not arrive at Tenedos until August, after which progress was rapid, giving the troops on the ground excellent service within twenty-four hours of a request being originated. Samson was more interested in offensive operations; on 18 April, as the result of earlier reconnaissance, a successful bombing attack was made on the aerodrome at Chanak, where a German Taube aircraft had been identified. Six 100-pounder bombs were dropped on to its hangar and the Taube was destroyed, keeping the Turco-German aviators out of the sky for two months. In the same month two unusual aircraft joined Samson's squadron; these were the Sopwith biplanes which had been part of the 1914 British Schneider trophy team, and for which no use could be found elsewhere. Samson used them as fast single-seated scouts.

Balloons were used as well as aircraft. In March the fleet had been joined by the balloon ship HMS *Manica*, a converted merchant vessel with a somewhat unromantic pedigree, for her previous role had been the conveyance of Manchester's nightsoil and horse manure down the Ship Canal to the sea. Her effectiveness was quickly recognized by the Turks, who opened fire on her balloons with shrapnel every time they appeared in the sky above the fleet. The balloon observer enjoyed numerous advantages over his colleague in a rickety seaplane, as he had no controls to distract him and could stay aloft indefinitely. The first successful shoot directed from a balloon was on 19 April when the guns of the *Bacchante* were used against a large Turkish tented camp well to the rear of their lines. Total surprise was achieved. As the balloon commander's report puts it: 'No reveille ever blown commanded so instant a response. Every tent burst into life and the ground was soon swarming with running specks . . . a scene of indescribable confusion followed . . . of the once orderly camp nothing remained but torn earth and twisted canvas . . . The trial was simple but convincing.'

One RNAS bombing attack, carried out on 23 April with great success on Maidos town, one of the principal landing places for troop reinforcements from Constantinople, had an unforeseen and potentially disastrous effect on the landings at Ari Burnu two days later. Two of the Turkish battalions in the garrison were moved away from the town and redeployed seven miles nearer the beaches, and thus readily available for use in the counter-attacks launched against Birdwood's troops on the afternoon and evening of the first landings.

Churchill's last day at the Admiralty on 25 May had brought depressing news. The old battleship *Triumph*, anchored off Gaba Tepe, had been torpedoed in full view of the army ashore, on whose morale the event had a devastating impact. The German U-boat *UB-21*, commanded by Kapitän-Leutnant Hersing, had made an epic voyage to the eastern Mediterranean from Germany, leaving Wilhelmshaven on 25 April and steering a course round the north of Scotland. On 3 May she was off Cape Finisterre for a rendezvous with a supply ship. The new fuel taken on turned out to be contaminated, but Hersing decided to push on and on 6 May passed undetected through the Straits of Gibraltar on the surface, close in to the African shore, at *UB-21*'s top speed of 16 knots. A few days later, *UB-21* was spotted at sea and a general alarm was passed to de Robeck. Nets were placed around the battleships anchored off the peninsula and a high degree of alert ordered. On the 11th, the U-boat was sighted and shelled ineffectually off Sicily by French warships. Two days later she made contact with the Austro-Hungarian fleet, by which time only one and a half tons of usable fuel remained of the 56 tons taken on at Wilhelmshaven.

As he approached the Dardanelles Hersing saw many tempting targets but exercised great self-control and let them pass, preferring to achieve total and dramatic success by opening his score with the destruction of a capital ship. On the morning of 25 May he began his attack on *Triumph*, which lay behind torpedo nets protected by destroyer patrols. The first attack failed and Hersing was detected. The troops ashore were treated to a novel spectacle as every warship in sight, other than those lying behind the illusory protection of their nets, began to manoeuvre wildly in an attempt to dodge any torpedoes fired at them. The impression was one of extreme nervousness on the part of the fleet. At 11.25 a.m. Hersing began his second attack as a destroyer located him and forced him to go deep. He fired a bow torpedo as he dived, at a range of little more than 300 yards. Fitted with an ingenious net-cutting device, the torpedo scored a direct hit, clearly heard by the crew of *UB-21* as they went deep. Hersing was worried that even at 70 feet he would be seen in the clear waters of the Aegean, but at 2.20 p.m. he came up to periscope depth and could see no trace of his target.

The occupants of a Turkish observation post high up on the Sari Bair ridge had been fascinated spectators, with thousands of others, of the remarkable scene. A German artillery officer recorded the event in his daily journal:

> Towards noon I heard a dull explosion, upon which destroyers, fishing boats, etc rushed . . . to render assistance. On the other hand, all the capital ships at once steamed off under full speed. The sinking ship still fired a few rounds . . . hitting, however, only one of the vessels nearby. Confusion reigned on board. I could clearly hear bugle signals, also loud commands. Boats were lowered and a good many things jettisoned. After a few minutes, the mighty ship capsized, coming to rest with her keel upside down. Twenty-one minutes later she disappeared in the sea bow first, leaving behind a tell-tale collection of debris.

Another witness of the loss of the *Triumph* was the newspaper correspondent Ellis Ashmead-Bartlett, who was in the wardroom on board the flagship HMS *Swiftsure* when the explosion was clearly heard. All rushed on deck in time to see the stricken ship heel over and capsize. Rear-Admiral Stewart Nicholson, his officers and *Swiftsure*'s crew stood to attention, bareheaded, as the *Triumph* went down. In the last few seconds engines and machinery broke loose; she vanished to the accompaniment of a great growling roar – like an old dog dying, many thought – amidst clouds of smoke and steam. As if to conclude the rite of passage the admiral snapped his telescope shut, turned to his staff, and remarked, 'Gentlemen, the *Triumph* is gone.' He then gave orders for his flag to be transferred to the *Majestic*, the oldest ship in the fleet, renowned more for her comfort than her residual fighting power. The admiral, accompanied by his staff, well-stocked wine cellar, large quantities of luxury tinned foods and the fascinated Ashmead-Bartlett, went over to her that afternoon.

Early on the morning of 27 May, Ashmead-Bartlett was roused on deck, where like many others he had prudently gone to bed, by a mess steward who politely informed him that a torpedo had been seen approaching the ship. This was followed immediately by a great explosion; the ship jerked violently and began to list at once. It was soon clear that she was doomed. Many elderly reservists who had gone over the side could not swim and were crying piteously for help. A great surge of men carried Ashmead-Bartlett on to the torpedo net shelf where hundreds of officers and men were gathering. He jumped into the sea and was dragged aboard a boat from which he watched the battleship going down. There were 94 men in a boat designed to hold 30 and it was down to its gunwhales. The ship was on its beam-ends in minutes, with men still clinging to her as hundreds more swam frantically away to avoid being sucked down. The admiral and his flag captain, Talbot, still wearing his monocle, were among the survivors. This was Hersing's second capital ship in forty-eight hours and the discomfiture of the fleet was complete.

As with the highly public sinking of the *Triumph*, the end of the *Majestic* was watched by thousands of dismayed troops on shore. Able Seaman Joseph Murray, aged 17, was serving in the Hood battalion of the Royal Naval Division. On the morning of the 27th, with a number of his friends, he was swimming out to the *Majestic* to ask for some freshly baked bread – at that time not available on the peninsula. The swimmers were halfway to the ship when they felt a concussion in the water and saw that the battleship was heeling over. Everyone aboard seemed to be very calm and men were walking deliberately to where they could slip into the water and get clear. Soon she lay inverted, with a solitary figure walking up the keel, clutching a bundle. It turned out to be the ship's writer, who had rescued the purser's ledgers and was determined to keep them dry. As the keel slowly slipped below, he moved to the inverted bow and sat there awaiting rescue.

The old but faithful *Majestic* [wrote Murray] . . . built in the 90s and considered obsolete when the war broke out, now lay upside down on the bottom of the Aegean . . . We shall miss her protection. She was an inspiration to us all; how we cheered when her shells landed on Achi Baba . . . a few days ago there were ships everywhere; now the *Majestic* has gone, we feel as though the navy has deserted us.

In London, Churchill found it necessary to impress on Balfour the absolute necessity of persisting with naval operations in the Dardanelles, reinforcing the anti-submarine measures already in hand but temporarily dispersing the fleet to Mudros and even the Suez Canal. For the time being, argued Churchill, a much lower degree of naval gunfire support would have to be accepted by the army ashore, until the arrival of yet more elderly battleships and cruisers fitted with torpedo bulges, which could operate with merchant ships tied alongside to take the force of torpedo attacks. At least a hundred trawlers were now required, Churchill told Balfour, in order to lay a hundred miles of detector netting around the offshore anchorages. Floatplanes would be needed to maintain constant aerial watch over the clear waters of the Aegean. Above all, the former First Lord wrote, 'Punishment must be doggedly borne.'

Although *UB-21*'s successes had been spectacular, they were brief. Meanwhile, British submarine exploits in the Sea of Marmara soon became legendary. Following the sinking of the *Messudieh* by Holbrook's *B11* in December 1914 there had been a pause in British submarine activity pending the arrival of larger and more powerful boats from England. These were the E class, a distinct advance on the older 'Holland'-based classes. With a much larger crew, more torpedoes, diesel propulsion for surface cruising, and vastly increased all-round performance and endurance, they offered a chance to penetrate the Narrows and operate in the Sea of Marmara which was seized with gusto by the resolute officers who commanded them.

The first attempt to pass a submarine into the Sea of Marmara ended tragically. On 17 April *E15* entered the Dardanelles, after the captain had been flown over the Narrows in a seaplane to work out his best course through the minefields and barrier nets. Running into the shallows, she went aground off Kephez Point in full view of the Dardanos battery. Whilst she was manoeuvring to get into deeper water a shell hit the conning tower and killed the captain as he was going on to the bridge. Several more shells hit the boat, one entering the engine space and bursting several oil pipes. As thick smoke poured into the main compartments the crew abandoned ship and took to the water. *E15* was about three-quarters of a mile from shore but most of the crew managed to struggle to the beach, where they were taken prisoner.

The first submarine to get clean through the defences and into the Marmara was the Australian-manned *AE2*. Early on 25 April, as the great armada of warships and transports edged in towards the peninsula for the landings, she negotiated ten rows of mines and detector nets. Once through, *AE2* wasted no time and within hours had torpedoed a Turkish gunboat off Nagara. Unfortunately, she was forced to the surface by another gunboat a few days later and had to be scuttled by her crew.

Meanwhile, the Australian submarine had been followed through the Narrows on 27 April by *E14* under Lieutenant-Commander Boyle. In a sensational cruise lasting over three weeks he sank two Turkish patrol boats as well as numerous smaller craft carrying supplies down the inshore waters to Liman's troops at Gallipoli. His greatest triumph, however, was the sinking of two large troopships. One of these, the *Guj Djemal*, had 6,000 luckless Turkish troops on board when she sank in deep water, taking most of them with her. For this feat, curiously enough, Boyle was granted more than £30,000 in prize money, which was shared out amongst the crew in the prescribed manner, according to rank and seniority. Boyle also received the VC for his outstanding performance, and went on to even more sensational forays in the Marmara.

At one point, when trying to attack a gunboat off Chanak, he was hindered by a party of men in a motor boat, who kept trying to put a rope around his periscope. Despite their exertions, the gunboat went to the bottom. Whilst operating in the Marmara Boyle found that some of his torpedoes failed to detonate, and instituted a practice taken up by his fellow commanders: the torpedoes were recovered and repaired for future use. During the day, the submarines, emboldened by the absence of Turkish gunboats, would haul off out of sight of land, and the crew would sunbathe, swim and fish. When a vessel was sighted by the lookout it would be approached on the surface, stopped and boarded. If it carried warlike cargo the crew would be put over the side in a ship's boat and the vessel burnt. At other times the captured vessel was lashed to the submarine on the landward side to fool any coastwatchers.

On 18 May the *E11* under Lieutenant-Commander Dunbar-Nasmith passed through the Narrows and embarked on a three-week cruise which effectively put paid to further Turkish attempts to sustain their Gallipoli army by sea, apart from the use of dozens of small craft dodging down the coast from fishing port to fishing port. Signalman Harry Plowman kept a detailed diary which gives a vivid picture of life aboard. On 22 May he recorded that *E11* sighted a sailing ship: 'boarded her and took 2 hens and 80 eggs. Much sport. Tied up to her for rest of day.' On the 24 May, 'Being Sunday we made a glorious start at 0800 hrs by sinking a gunboat . . . she was not done in at first when she spotted our periscope; she fired 2 rounds, hitting our periscope with the second; good shooting, captain earns his smoke and his bottle of beer . . . came to surface and worked on periscope remainder of day.'

On the following day Plowman was able to record an even more exciting adventure. *E11* spotted a large transport making its way down the coast and stopped it with a few rounds of rifle fire.

> Got alongside of her when a panic ensued. Her crew got away under the supervision of a Yank who caused much sport, his name being Mr Swing of Chicago, war correspondent. We boarded her and found one 6-inch gun and mounting for same . . . after which we sank ship with 16 pounds of guncotton. We then dived to attack another store ship on the same route. We had to rise and chase her as she made for harbour after she saw the first ship sink, until fired on, then dived, firing our second torpedo at her as she was tying up alongside the pier at Rodosto, making a grand splash by blowing ship and pier skywards.

After this *E11* went out to sea and surfaced for swimming parade, during which another ship was sighted and stopped with rifle fire. She turned out to be 'not so green as the others . . . as we went along-side she tried to ram us but failed; she started for the beach and we still carried on firing, smashing all windows aboard her. She went very slowly on the shore.' As a boarding party started in pursuit in the *E11*'s folding boat a squadron of cavalry trotted into sight and a most unusual exchange of fire continued for another hour until *E11* pulled out of rifle range, having put a torpedo into the beached ship.

The climax of *E11*'s cruise came with her arrival off Constantinople on 26 May. The boat's log describes the hectic events of that morning; after scoring a hit on a steamer lying alongside the Arsenal quay, another torpedo was fired towards the Golden Horn, but as no explosion was heard, a second one was launched. It hit and sank a gunboat. At that moment the apparently faulty torpedo came to life and was seen through the periscope to be heading for the Galata Bridge. It passed clean through and sank a merchant ship moored nearly a mile up the Golden Horn. Wild confusion broke out ashore as Nasmith extricated his boat. Thousands ran into the streets, under the impression that the Allied fleet had arrived and was bombarding the city. *E11* was now just off the entrance to the Golden Horn, close to the Leander Tower, barely under control and bumping along the bottom, carried along with the perpetual current which runs out from the Black Sea and down through the Bosphorus.

Dunbar-Nasmith had kept two torpedoes for the return trip, to fire at two Turkish battleships reported at anchor off Chanak, but as they had moved away he returned to a large transport seen earlier; this was torpedoed and sunk before *E11* started the hazardous journey back through the Narrows. During this highly dangerous phase she was caught in a net below Kilid Bahr; then the crew heard the sinister sound of what could only be a mine cable scraping against the hull. It had snagged the hydroplanes and was being dragged alongside the submarine, bumping against the outer casing. For over five miles, moving dead slow through the depths, *E11* carried the mine with it, surfacing as soon as Dunbar-Nasmith reckoned that it was safe to do so, in the midst of a surprised flotilla of British destroyers. *E11* then continued on its way, to receive the thunderous cheers of all the ships in the Mudros anchorage. Dunbar-Nasmith duly became the third submarine commander to win the VC for this outstanding exploit. Plowman noted with evident relish that the whole crew had been awarded the DSM 'which we will have to wet up'.

Despite the hideous dangers involved in forcing the Narrows, boats continued to pass through. In June *E7*, under Lieutenant-Commander Cochrane, went through for what proved to be another eventful cruise. The First-Lieutenant was Oswald Hallifax, last heard of as a submariner under training in 1914. He was now serving under a captain with whom he got on well and it was a happy and efficient boat. On the evening of 30 June *E7* approached the Narrows on the surface; the sky over the peninsula was lit with lightning as well as gunfire, and off Cape Helles a hospital ship lay at anchor, brilliantly lit and displaying her illuminated Red Cross.

In the small hours the submarine began its dive under the defences, which had been greatly strengthened since April. Once through these, Hallifax noted that some of the men, who were suffering already from dysentery, were behaving oddly. In the absence of a doctor or even a sick bay attendant, unusual remedies were tried out; one man, thought to be at death's door, was revived by doses of the oil from sardine tins. By day the submarine remained on the surface, enabling the crew to swim and wash. From time to time the captain ordered a dive to 'catch', or adjust, the boat's trim – essential when cruising in the Sea of Marmara where the mix of fresh and salt waters can give rise to serious fluctuations of buoyancy.

On 15 July *E7* was nearing Constantinople. Hallifax noted:

There is a devil of a tide in the entrance to the Bosphorus and we were first carried across to Seraglio Point where we grounded at 30 feet and ran along the bottom for some time; then we got clear of that and ran around several times at 30 feet off Scutari; once to my horror we touched and ran along the bottom when at 22 feet . . . the water was so greasy and thick that after the periscope had been up for a few seconds a film dried across the glass . . . We fired . . . from close to Leander's tower at 1529 hrs being at that moment aground at 22 feet . . . At the arsenal there was no steamer alongside but plenty of dhows and lighters . . . One minute and 35 seconds after firing, while we were turning ourselves, on the shingle, the explosion took place; it was a mighty big one and not a crack like the other TNT head had made . . . but a more prolonged explosion . . . We got off the bottom and retired at 40 feet.

Throughout this attack, which yet again threw the city into panic, Hallifax was in agony from severe burns sustained a few days earlier when he had boarded a small ship and rashly tried to set it on fire with gasoline. For the next two weeks he had to watch as his skin sloughed off and the burns became infected, preventing him from wearing shoes; in addition he was suffering, like most of the crew, from acute diarrhoea and dysentery. His burns began to heal but as the skin contracted he was in great pain, to the point where he could not place his feet on the deck and had to swing from pipe to pipe as he struggled to get around the cramped boat.

The return passage was fraught with danger. Advised by another submarine, which had just passed through, that extra nets had been slung across the Narrows off Nagara, *E7* negotiated these by hugging the shore around the Point, moving dead slow so as not to cause spray when the periscope was raised. Suddenly Hallifax saw through the periscope a new line of net marker buoys only 100 yards ahead and took *E7* deep: 'must have gone through the bally thing for we started to come up again instead of going down and had to let a lot of water into Y tank. Then got really caught in the nets. Flooded and blew to get a trim and avoid coming to surface.' At 11.50 a.m. they believed they were clear and gave the coxswain a celebratory bottle of beer, but then became entangled with a mine, which took twenty-five minutes of frantic manoeuvring to dislodge.

The batteries were now running low and the lights burned dimly. By 2 p.m. they were no more than red glims and the compartments were in darkness. Fortunately they were now off Achi Baba. Ninety minutes later they surfaced to let the foul air escape through the conning tower hatch, which it did as a nauseous brown cloud. When the diesels were turned on, every light failed. It had been a narrow escape from oblivion, and the crew relished the cheers which greeted them as they entered harbour at Mudros.

The submarines went from strength to strength. Following *E14*'s return after a 24-day cruise in the Marmara in June, the Turks continued to improve the net defences at the Narrows. By mid-July the net extended from shore to shore and down to the deepest part of the channel at over 200 feet, then considered to be near the limits for submarines. Tell-tale floats indicated if a submarine was attempting to break in, and motor launches with explosive charges patrolled incessantly, aided at night by searchlights. These measures failed to deter the submarine captains.

In the first week of August two submarines, Boyle's *E14* and Dunbar-Nasmith's *E11*, were running riot in the Sea of Marmara. It was Boyle's second extended patrol and, like Nasmith, he now carried a gun on the foredeck of his boat, giving both of them a vastly increased potential for harassing Turkish shipping. On the 7th, as Stopford's IXth Corps was landing at Suvla, Boyle sank a 5,000-ton steamer and on the following day Nasmith torpedoed the old Turkish battleship *Heiruddin Barbarossa* as well as several small transports.

In general the smaller British boats fared better when attempting to get through the Narrows than the larger French submarines, bravely as these were crewed and handled. It was an act of negligence on the part of the commander of the French boat *Turquoise*, forced aground and abandoned by her crew on 30 October, which led to the loss with all hands of the *E20*. A Turkish boarding party found that the captain of the French submarine had failed to destroy his secret books; amongst these was a signal giving details of a planned rendezvous out at sea. When *E20* arrived there on 6 November a German U-boat was lying in wait and a torpedo sent her to the bottom.

Nasmith could not resist the lure of Constantinople and returned to its harbour early in December, taking a series of photographs of defence installations through his periscope and sinking a gunboat in the harbour for good measure. This was in the course of a record-breaking cruise of forty-eight days in which *E11* sank over forty ships of various sizes and virtually brought maritime activity in the Marmara to a standstill.

On 9 December *E2* was the last British submarine to enter the Narrows and she continued to sink any ship she saw until recalled on 2 January. By now, half the Turks' merchant fleet had been sent to the bottom by the submarines and their army on Gallipoli was subsisting almost entirely on the laborious and inefficient overland line of communication from Constantinople. Of the thirteen British and French submarines which successfully got through into the Marmara eight were lost, several with all hands, and the two-way transit had been made no less than twenty-seven times. For a new branch of the service it had been an outstanding achievement, doing much to restore the *amour-propre* of the fleet.

Meanwhile, the naval aviators, re-equipping with more powerful aircraft, began to look for new roles. Commander Samson was willing to undertake any sort of mission. When one of his scout pilots reported seeing a hostile submarine stalking a French cruiser off Rabbit Island at the entrance to the Straits, he immediately took off with a 100-pound bomb and dropped it directly above where he could see the outline of the submarine in the clear Aegean waters. The bomb detonated in a great plume of water but he was chagrined to see the target carry on and slip right underneath the cruiser as it made its escape. Later that day Samson saw the submarine on the surface, safely inside the barriers near Chanak, and could not resist flying over and blazing away at it with his carbine.

The first victorious air-to-air combat took place over Helles on 22 June when an RNAS aircraft encountered a rare German aerial scout over the battlefield; after twenty minutes' manoeuvring the British observer hit the German's engine and forced his plane down behind Turkish lines, where it was later destroyed by French artillery.

Encouraged by the success of their first aircraft carrier the *Ark Royal*, the Admiralty now sent another one out to the Dardanelles. She was a converted Isle of Man ferry, the *Ben-my-Chree*, and an improvement in every respect on her predecessor. With a top speed of 22 knots and greatly increased facilities for hangarage and maintenance, she was able to move rapidly around the expanding theatre of operations after Bulgaria's entry into the war in mid-October had added to the might of the Central Powers.

In June, at the request of the Admiralty, Colonel Frederick Sykes, a pioneer of military flying, paid a visit to the Dardanelles to advise on the use of aviation. On his recommendation, the RNAS concentrated all its resources on Imbros, leaving the French flyers in sole occupation of Tenedos. Sykes was not impressed by the large number of aircraft types in use, many of them virtually useless for military purposes, and advised greater standardization. Machine-guns were fitted for use by aircraft observers and improved signalling equipment installed. Sykes also recommended the use of non-rigid airships, or 'blimps', for anti-submarine patrolling, and greater use of kite balloons for artillery observation.

On 12 August another pioneering flight was made with a successful torpedo attack on a Turkish ship. She was spotted close inshore and a 14-inch torpedo was dropped from a Short floatplane which came down to 15 feet above the water and within 300 yards of the target. A satisfying explosion was observed and the ship started to sink by the stern. The fact that it was already beached, having been hit by one of *E14*'s torpedoes a few days earlier, did little to quench the naval pilots' elation. Five days later another steamer was hit by an aerially launched torpedo and burned out to the waterline. Then a torpedo bomber was forced down to the water with a faulty engine, landing close alongside a Turkish hospital ship whose understandably nervous crew and passengers were reassured by a cheerful wave as pilot and observer tried to repair the machine. They got the engine going fitfully, then spotted a large tugboat some distance away. There was insufficient power for take-off so they taxied into a firing position and duly sank their victim. Even without the torpedo's weight the seaplane required a three-mile run before it could be coaxed back into the air.

Bulgaria's entry on the side of the Central Powers gave the RNAS the chance to make some long-distance attacks on the strategic railway from Berlin and Sofia to Constantinople and Salonika. The key target was the rail bridge over the River Maritza. To get there and back from Imbros involved a hazardous round trip of 180 miles and extra fuel tanks had to be fitted to the three aircraft taking part, of which two were seaplanes, the other a landplane flown by Samson. Each machine carried two 112-pounder bombs. Samson obtained two near misses on the bridge which weakened the piers, and the other bombs all missed, but much damage was caused to the permanent way, and to enemy morale. The attacks were repeated several times and although the bridge remained intact, traffic was seriously disrupted.

During one such attack on 19 November, an aircraft flown by Flight Sub-Lieutenant Smylie was hit by rifle fire and forced down after he had dropped one bomb. With the other still slung under his machine he carried out a forced landing within rifle shot of the target; enemy infantry at once began to run towards the aircraft, so Smylie set it on fire, hoping that this would detonate the bomb and scare off the infantry. As the flames roared up, he saw that his commanding officer, Squadron Commander Bell-Davies, was about to land alongside, so he detonated the bomb by firing at it with his revolver. Bell-Davies landed, Smylie scrambled on to the centre section of his CO's Nieuport single-seater, and they got away. Bell-Davies' subsequent report is a masterpiece of brevity: 'Saw H5 burning in marshes. Picked up pilot.' It earned him a VC.

Throughout the long summer, RNAS pilots continued to render invaluable service as spotters for naval gunfire support. On 30 August the redoubtable Samson enjoyed a sensational success when controlling the 9.2-inch gun of the monitor *M15*, which was moored to a buoy off Ari Burnu, firing clean over the peninsula at extreme range of 18,000 yards. Samson directed the monitor's fire on to a concentration of steamers and sailing boats which, having run the gauntlet of the submarines, were unloading supplies at a small fishing village up the coast from Maidos. The first ranging round was 800 yards short, and as it landed behind a hill, was not immediately perceived as such by the hordes of stevedores and soldiers busily unloading the ships. The second round landed on the beach, killing a number of soldiers, and the third established the desired 'bracket' so beloved of naval gunnery officers. Panic now set in as the huge shells rained down. The eighth and ninth rounds were direct hits on the steamers, moored alongside each other, producing resounding secondary explosions. At the end of the shoot, there was total disorder at the target end. After this, any attempts by the Turks to replenish by sea were made at night, and even so, the RNAS managed to conduct a number of highly effective shoots.

It was in September that mere chance prevented Samson from altering the course of history. Whilst on combat patrol over the Anzac and Suvla sectors he noted a staff car travelling at high speed on a road to the rear of the Anafarta ridge; he attacked it at once, scoring a near miss with his first bomb, and was gratified to see driver and passengers rushing for cover in the ditch. He stood off until the car resumed its progress, then attacked from behind; this time his bomb was so close that the car was peppered with fragments as its occupants once more took to the ditch. After the war it transpired that one of the passengers in the car had been Colonel Mustafa Kemal.

# 19

# High Summer at Helles

Freely they stood who stood, and fell who fell.

Milton, *Paradise Lost*

THE BURIAL TRUCE of 24 May at Anzac, by disposing of several thousand putrefying corpses and greatly reducing the numbers of flies, led to an immediate improvement in health and morale, even though ferocious close-range fighting broke out again almost immediately. But although the Turks were only yards away, the Australians at Quinn's and Courtney's, and elsewhere along their precarious front line, continued to display enormous spirit. Hamilton was encouraged by the visit he made to the Anzac forward positions on 30 May. On the previous day the Turks had detonated a large mine under Quinn's Post, following it up by charging a section of the defence isolated by the explosion. The fighting took place before dawn and at close quarters; at first light the Australians had counter-attacked with the bayonet and recaptured the lost ground after a brutal fight. Coming ashore on Anzac beach, Hamilton was met by Birdwood and the two generals made their way up the gully known as the 'Valley of Death', to the headquarters of the 4th Australian Infantry Brigade. From there it was possible to see the fighting around Quinn's.

It was still extremely dangerous to move around the beach-head by day and Hamilton noted the precautions taken to avoid a repetition of Bridges' death only days earlier.

Along the path at the bottom of the valley warning notices were stuck up. The wayfarer has to be [as] punctilious about each footstep as Christian in the *Pilgrim's Progress*. Should he disregard the placards directing him to keep to the right or to the left of the track, he is almost certainly shot . . . yet I never saw a more jovial crew. Men staggering under huge sides of frozen beef; men struggling up cliffs with kerosene cans full of water . . . digging . . . cooking . . . card-playing in small dens scooped out from the banks of yellow clay . . . All the time, overhead, the shell and rifle bullets groaned and whined . . . to understand the awful din, raise the eyes 25 degrees to the top of the cliff which closes in the tail end of the valley and you can see the Turkish hand grenades bursting along the crest, just where an occasional bayonet flashes, and figures . . . crouch in an irregular line. Or else they rise to fire and are silhouetted a moment against the sky, and then you recognize the naked athletes from the Antipodes and your heart goes into your mouth as a whole bunch of them dart forward suddenly, and as suddenly disappear . . . all the time, there comes a slow constant trickle of wounded – some dragging themselves painfully along; others being carried along on stretchers . . .

It was soon time to plan the next assault on Krithia and Achi Baba. Hamilton would have preferred to await the arrival of the 52nd (Lowland) Division but this would have meant another three weeks' delay. Hunter-Weston and Gouraud, the Allied corps commanders, were for attacking as soon as possible, before the Turks made their positions impregnable.

But before the set-piece was mounted, the killing went on. In civilian life, Sergeant Carr of the 8th Lancashire Fusiliers had been a shorthand writer, and during his sojourn on the peninsula as machine-gun NCO he kept a detailed record of his experiences which he afterwards transcribed into longhand. His battalion landed at Helles on 5 May and was soon in action. He and his Maxim gun crews were forced to urinate into the cooling jackets surrounding the red-hot barrels, owing to the acute water shortage. Dead and wounded lay thick on the ground all round the gun position and one in particular earned Carr's sympathy: 'a poor Turk lies a dozen yards ahead of us wrapped in his blue overcoat. His moans sound pitiful but it looks as if his time is limited.'

The first taste of war had left a profound impression on the Fusiliers. Nothing had prepared them for the carnage all round them.

The pitiful sights we witnessed will go with us to our graves . . . we encountered any amount of wounded – one young-looking lad with his arm smashed was wild-eyed and open-mouthed and shouting 'Mother! Oh Mother!' Another fellow amongst the next batch – they seemed to be coming in their dozens – was beseeching us, 'Don't go, lads, it's bloody murder down there – don't go!', and the blood trickling down his face made him look more hideous and his words are ringing in my ears yet . . . the medical chaps are working like Trojans – stemming the blood from the wounded with bandages that looked already to have reached the limit of their use.

All ranks were soon lousy. Carr found 'about 20 of the best. Little black things – I've no idea what they were but they felt like elephants the way they walked around last night.' Within days the battalion was losing officers and men at an alarming rate: 'Captain Radford of A company was shot in the neck last night and now lies dead at the bottom of the trench. Any amount of dead lying in front and behind us. Our breakfast bacon which the Australians kindly left us has been lying alongside a dead Turk for a few days but went down with gusto for all that.' The burial of the dead absorbed much time and effort, for if attempted too near the front line it invariably drew fire. Carr describes the last resting place of one of his men: 'What a grave – a foot down – we cannot expose ourselves sufficiently long to dig too deeply. Buried just as he fell – minus equipment and helmet. The only reverence we could display was to put a sack over his head – perhaps a tender feeling that the earth would not hurt his face!'

As rumours of another attack spread round the unit, Carr and his men were taken to see a demonstration of the new Vickers machine-gun on the RNAS aerodrome at the tip of the peninsula. They were impressed and agreed that it was a great advance on their old Maxims. When the battalion was in reserve, or 'resting', Carr noted that

> just in the rear of our trenches one of those fellows caught sleeping on sentry duty is doing his No. 1 Field Punishment – young Rix – Private Symes Rix – looks quite pathetic – he is fastened to the wheel of our battalion water cart chained with both hands behind his back. The crucifixion we call it. Looks quite barbaristic on the poor devil – but I suppose it will teach the rest of us the necessary lesson; he has 2 hours daily, like that.

In the middle of May, in one of the few actions carried out with a dash of imagination, the Gurkhas of 29th Indian Brigade had secured a position astride Gully Spur by means of a daring attack after scaling the cliffs south of Y beach and taking the Turks by surprise. Despite fierce counter-attacks they had held on, and it was hoped that any further advance on the extreme left of the line would spring from this startline. The Allied line now ran from around Y beach, across Gully Ravine, then south-east to Fir Tree Wood and on down to the Kereves Dere, which was the boundary with the French Corps, who held the extreme right flank resting on the Dardanelles shoreline a mile north-east of S beach. The front line had moved steadily forward, thanks to industrious nocturnal sapping since the Second Battle of Krithia, both sides trying to undermine the opposing defences. On Gully Spur, where the Gurkhas had made themselves secure on what was now known as Gurkha Bluff, the ground was particularly suited to mining and counter-mining.

The British front line was in a position known as 'KOSB Trench', dug during its brief occupation by that regiment after the landing at Y beach on 25 April. Now greatly strengthened, it was held on 20 May by the Royal Inniskilling Fusiliers; from here a series of mines was begun with the aim of blowing up the Turkish trenches only 20 yards distant.

In charge of the digging was one of the eccentrics who somehow found their way to Gallipoli. Frank Sutton was born in 1884; from infancy he displayed considerable strength of character, described while still in the nursery as 'angelic in appearance, diabolic in disposition'. From Eton he went on to University College, London, gaining a diploma in engineering before deciding that academic life was not for him. He wandered for some years in South America where he failed in an engineering business but continued to seek his fortune; in August 1914 he was in Argentina but came home to enlist and, at the age of 30, was granted a commission in the Royal Engineers. Athirst for action, he volunteered for service in the Near East but found himself commanding a searchlight detachment at Malta. From there he contrived a posting to Egypt and thence to Helles, where he arrived in command of a party of thirty sappers and a bag of golf-clubs, carefully wrapped in hessian and prominently labelled 'Theodolite, Legs of'. When the ruse was detected the news quickly travelled round and greatly delighted the Anzacs, always readier to appreciate an unconventional Englishman than the stereotype.

Sutton and his men, reinforced by volunteers from all over the peninsula who had been miners, were on the point of exploding a large mine at Gurkha Bluff when the Turks, alert to the danger, launched a vigorous attack on the afternoon of 22 May. The Inniskillings were driven back but the Gurkhas, with Sutton at their head, re-entered KOSB Trench, killing every Turk in sight. Sutton's party were now pinned down by a Turkish grenade attack. With none of his own, Sutton was reduced to catching the Turkish bombs and throwing them back until one exploded in his hand, blowing it off. The grenade was followed immediately by a huge Turk with whom the disabled Sutton fought, killing his man. A counter-attack by Inniskillings and Gurkhas retook the trench and Sutton was carried down to the beach, where his golf-clubs were found and restored to him after the shredded remains of his hand had been cut away. As he lay on his stretcher awaiting evacuation, General Hunter-Weston visited him and awarded him an immediate MC, which he duly received from the King's hands some months later. He was soon playing single-handed golf again with the clubs he had taken to Gurkha Bluff.

From 24 May the Royal Naval Division, 29th and 42nd Divisions, with the 29th Indian Brigade, had been formed into a new corps, the VIIIth, under the newly promoted Lieutenant-General Hunter-Weston, in order to provide tighter operational control over these formations. As Kitchener was now pressing for an early attack, Hamilton reluctantly gave his assent on 31 May and on 2 June GHQ issued its operational instructions for the Third Battle of Krithia, which was to take place two days later, thus giving time for orders to percolate down to unit level.

Since the second attempt to take Krithia the tactical situation had turned to static trench warfare, and the plan for the attack of 4 June was that of a set-piece daylight frontal assault. Two continuous trench lines confronted each other from shore to shore of the peninsula; some (but not all) of the enemy positions were protected by wire and the Turkish line was punctuated by strongpoints, or redoubts, facing in all directions and lavishly equipped with machine-guns, firing on fixed lines as part of a well co-ordinated fire plan. These guns, moreover, were skilfully concealed and sited so as to provide mutually supporting, enfilading fire against the flanks of any attacker. A number were manned by German sailors from the *Goeben* and *Breslau*.

The plan adopted by Hunter-Weston and Gouraud required careful study when it had been issued as operational orders. Shortly before the assault began, all troops in the firing trenches were to brandish their fixed bayonets above the parapet in the hope that this would draw the Turkish reserves into their forward trenches, on to which the artillery barrage would then be resumed. The actual attack would be in two waves: the first to advance and occupy the Turkish first line; the second, following up fifteen minutes later, would pass through and take the enemy second line. Large parties of pioneers and sappers were to follow hard on the heels of the first wave in order to prepare the captured Turkish trenches for defence against the

inevitable counter-attacks; they were then to construct communication trenches from the original British lines into the newly won
positions to permit resupply once the objectives had been secured.
Special parties of marksmen were detailed as sniper-hunters. As was
the accepted practice on the Western Front, enemy trenches were to
be cleared by grenadiers. However, the supply of hand grenades
at Helles was minimal, apart from uncertain home-made jam-tin
bombs; the allocation of proper grenades to 42 Division was a mere
eight per platoon. As a novelty, it was decided to involve the
armoured car squadron of the RNAS, whose machine-gun sections
had done so well on 25 April aboard the *River Clyde*. The only place
for their deployment was on the meagre track from Cape Helles up
to Krithia, but it was felt that their presence, and the firepower
offered by their Maxim guns, would be of moral value if nothing else.

An advance of 800 yards was confidently predicted by Hunter-
Weston. Apart from the seventy-eight British artillery pieces available, VIII Corps could rely on fire support from the French on their
right and a certain amount from the greatly reduced fleet: two battleships would be cruising up and down the coast at 12 knots, zigzag-
ging as a precaution against submarine attack, and some destroyers
would lie close in for immediate support if needed.

The bayonet strength of the Anglo-French assaulting force was
about 30,000, of whom 20,000 were in the first wave. GHQ had only
a hazy idea of Turkish strength; it was in fact about 28,000. As a planning yardstick, staff colleges teach that the assailant should outnum-
ber the defender by three to one; on that basis, Third Krithia was
unlikely to be the dazzling success for which Hamilton prayed.
Despite this, there was an air of cheerful optimism at all levels as the
troops were carefully briefed on their roles.

The Manchester Brigade of 42 Division had now been on the peninsula for nearly a month and was acclimatized to trench life. Its initiation to active service had been handled well, unlike later arrivals at
Helles or the luckless Lancashire Fusilier brigade, pitched into
Second Krithia virtually straight off the boat. The first spell in the line
for the Manchesters was almost without incident. The troops stared
up from their trenches as the Turks fired vainly at a British aeroplane
high above, and watched the splinters from the bursting shells flying
down through the clear sky. As they had come ashore they had been
greeted by 'Asiatic Annie' but suffered no casualties. Their initial
bivouac had lacked tentage, camp kettles and blankets but, as
Colonel Darlington of the 5th Manchesters reported, they were very
well fed: 'A lovely climate, absolutely perfect, the flowers and the

birds are lovely . . . the food is good of a sort. We live on tinned stew which we heat up and we sometimes buy bread and eggs, but we have plenty of jam and bacon and tobacco and make out with bully beef and biscuits.'

The 5th Manchesters had gone into the fire trenches for the first time on 16 May. Every morning, at 3 a.m., the entire battalion stood-to, bayonets fixed, to guard against any surprise attack. The worst thing about the front line, Darlington felt, was the stench of hundreds of dead Turks and Australians who had been killed in the earlier battle for Krithia, still lying out in the open; although the corpses were only yards away, it was death to try to bury them; the Turkish snipers never relaxed and took a steady toll of unwary newcomers. At first, the young territorials were inclined to fire nervously at shadows during stand-to; Darlington cured that by threatening to send the culprits out to bury the Turks they had shot. All the officers now dressed identically to their men because of the sniping; the battalion, recruited as it was from mining communities, soon became renowned for the extent and quality of its digging.

Darlington continued to write reassuring letters home: 'You will be glad to hear that in case of an attack the authorities do not allow commanding officers to lead their men . . . so don't imagine me charging at the head of the battalion.'

Elsewhere in the Manchester Brigade, Private John Morten arrived on the peninsula on 6 May. He had enlisted into the 7th Manchesters on the outbreak of war, together with several other members of the Heaton Mersey Lacrosse Club. At the end of May, in pouring rain, the battalion moved into the line, the men forcing their way up a gully against a torrent of muddy water which carried off Morten's rifle and spade; he took another rifle from a wounded man and pressed on. The battalion arrived just in time to be thrown into a local advance at night, designed to push the front line forward, 'a day which I shall never forget if I live to be a centenarian'. He gave an account of the action:

> At dusk we marched out in partners; one carrying a pick, the other a spade; each carried his rifle, entrenching tool and 200 rounds of ammo, and a sandbag half full. We doubled across the open to the first line of trenches. We now doubled in open formation (a long line of us) for over a hundred yards further on and had to dig ourselves in; however, the moon was full and before we had dug a single spadeful the enemy discovered us and opened fire. It was most awful; we were lying flat on the ground with no cover except a bag half full of sand which has been proved to be not bullet proof . . . I can't describe my feelings as I

lay there, especially when four men on either side were wounded, crying out for help and we could do nothing to relieve them except to put field dressings on their wounds.

By first light the Manchesters had managed to dig shoulder deep, and then linked the individual slits to form a trench of sorts. This drastic baptism of fire had brought it home to the territorials that they were embroiled in something beyond the experience of recruiting sergeants back home. Morten lost one old friend on that first night: 'I expect you will have heard about Harold Grainger, poor chap; he was shot in the head and lingered for 24 hours. He didn't suffer much as he was unconscious the whole time. If he had lived he would have been blind for life, so he is better where he is.'

On 4 June the barrage started early in the morning and appeared to be much more effective than hitherto. In particular, the French '75s', firing obliquely across the British front, seemed to be wreaking havoc on the Turkish positions. A great cloud of smoke and dust rose into the clear blue sky and blew slowly back on to the Allied trenches, now packed with men preparing to go over the parapet in the first wave. At 11.20, in accordance with the plan, the barrage lifted, and every man put his bayonet over the parapet to lure the Turkish reserves into the artillery trap prepared for them. Whether this ruse succeeded or not could not be determined, as visibility was deteriorating all along the line.

At noon the troops went over the top along the entire front. On the extreme right, the French were immediately confronted with difficult terrain in which the Turks had cunningly sited a number of machine-gun nests protected by dense barbed wire entanglements. These halted the advancing infantry in their tracks, to be mown down in their hundreds. Very soon the survivors had crawled back to their original positions; the French attack had failed completely, with great slaughter, within the first fifteen minutes. On their left, the Royal Naval Division, at full strength for the first time since arriving on the peninsula, left their trenches and advanced, noting uneasily as they did so that the French on their right were already recoiling into their own trenches, led as usual by the nimble Senegalese.

The first objective was reached and taken despite mounting casualties, but when the newly arrived Collingwood battalion, which constituted the second wave, moved forward in immaculate extended order, as though on parade, a dreadful massacre took place. Hidden machine-guns, which should have been dealt with by the French, opened up; the well-regulated lines of sailors went down, as one eyewitness put it, 'as a field of corn under the reaper'. Another likened it to 'a ship sinking, with all hands'. The battalions of the first wave then rose again from the Turkish front line and continued towards the second objective, supported by the handful of Collingwoods who had survived. Having reached the Turkish second line the sailors took up defensive positions; they had done all and more than was asked of them, and the men who had so recently earned the jeers and scorn of the Australians for their youthful and puny appearance had fought like veterans.

Now, they found that their new trenches were commanded by the enemy machine-guns which, firing along the trench line from defiladed positions, inflicted yet more casualties. The position, which had depended for its security on a safe right flank, was a death trap. By 1 p.m. the survivors of four battalions had been driven back to their original startline. The 2nd Naval Brigade had lost, in the space of one hour, 60 out of 70 officers and 1,000 men out of the 1,700 who had left their trenches at the beginning of the attack. The Collingwood battalion had literally ceased to exist in its first action and the handful of survivors were dispersed to other battalions.

Further to the left, the attack of the 42nd Division, led by the Manchester Brigade, got off to an inspiring start. All accounts testify to the steadiness of the Lancashire territorials as they moved forward despite suffering very heavy casualties. On this day alone the 6th Manchesters lost 11 officers killed and 10 wounded, and the 8th Battalion 10 killed and a similar number wounded. The Manchester Brigade's most grievous loss was that of Brigadier-General Noel Lee, its commander. Lee was one of the few territorial officers to have attained general rank in peacetime: he had been a volunteer soldier for over thirty years. His enthusiasm for soldiering went back to his days at Eton in the early 1880s, when he had played in the cadet corps band. Although aged 48 he had insisted on going to war with the battalions he had commanded, especially his old unit the 6th Manchesters, of which he was the honorary colonel.

Captain Farrow, the medical officer of the 6th Battalion, had set up his aid post just behind the trenches and was attending to the first of the wounded to reach him when a runner came to tell him that the Brigadier had been hit. He found Lee lying at the bottom of a trench in the support line. Against the urgent advice of his staff, he had been looking over the parapet with his binoculars, refusing to use a trench periscope as he watched his men going forward, when a sniper's bullet hit him in the throat. As Farrow was dressing the wound, he also was hit, by a shell fragment, but continued to attend to Lee, who was placed on a stretcher for removal to the field ambulance.

Shortly afterwards, Farrow was himself on the way to the dressing station to have his own wounds dressed when to his astonishment he saw Lee walking unsteadily to the rear, having dismissed his bearers so that they could deal with more serious cases. When Farrow remonstrated, Lee, who could not speak, wrote on a scrap of paper that 'he was not going to leave the field on a stretcher and preferred to walk to hospital down at the beach'. Loss of blood, however, compelled him to revert to a stretcher. On arrival at the dressing station an emergency operation was carried out; the surgeons held out high hopes of recovery, but Lee insisted on getting up and visiting the men of his brigade lying around the area. He died two weeks later aboard a hospital ship *en route* to Malta.

The 42nd Division was magnificently served by its medical staffs. The East Lancashire Field Ambulance had some of the most distinguished doctors and consultants in the Manchester area. On its arrival at Gallipoli the unit immediately found work to do, as many wounded were lying unattended on the beach, having been carried down from their units after receiving only the most rudimentary first aid. Part of the field ambulance was sent aboard one of the notorious 'Black Ships', packed with wounded awaiting evacuation to Alexandria. The ship carried no trained medical staff and the wounded had been faced with a nightmare voyage. The main body of the ambulance went inland, hoisted a huge Red Cross flag and got to work. Although the Turks scrupulously respected this flag, congestion at Helles was such that the doctors were treating casualties within 150 yards of artillery batteries, and it was inevitable that some enemy shells landed close alongside.

Within days of its arrival the unit suffered a severe loss when its commanding officer, Colonel Pritchard, was mortally wounded during a tour of inspection of his forward detachments. He had opened several advanced dressing stations behind the front line in anticipation of heavy casualties and over 2,000 of these were treated by the ambulance on 4 June alone. Pritchard had just visited the main dressing station, commanded by his brother, and promised to return later. At this point in the battle the Manchesters were being relieved by the Lancashire Fusiliers of the second wave, and the open ground was covered with hurrying men. Colonel Pritchard was hit in the head by a shell splinter and carried back to the field ambulance. On the operating table, he recognized his brother and asked him about the other wounded who were now flooding in. Almost his last words were 'I'm all right – attend to those patients.' A huge shell fragment was taken from his head and he was put aboard a hospital ship, dying at sea off Malta on the 29th.

Throughout this battle, the quality of leadership displayed by the territorial officers was outstanding, as testified by many letters and diary entries. One Lancashire Fusilier was to write home: 'Our officers are a credit to England, especially Lord Rochdale, Captain Scott and the adjutant. There was Lord Rochdale giving his orders and saying, "Give it 'em, lads!" and we were doing it for all we were worth.' Major Heywood of the 6th Manchesters wrote that

> we are proud that the Sixth were the first battalion to get to the firing line, and I think it is a tribute to the men that, taken as they were from peace conditions in Cairo and thrown straight into the firing line, they behaved so splendidly. They never hesitated to advance in the face of the machine-guns and the shrapnel. In the first day's fighting the officers were splendid. Lord Rochdale and Major Lees and Captain Spafford the adjutant bore charmed lives. They walked about as though on a parade ground.

The Manchesters had done better than they had dared to hope. The violence of their assault carried them clean through the Turkish first and second lines and one company of the 6th Manchesters was up on to the lower slopes of Achi Baba and amongst the Turkish fourth line when the advance, which had far outreached its prescribed limits, began to lose momentum. Casualties were mounting, especially among the officers, and the men were exhausted. The effect of this attack on the Turks was electrifying; many of their officers and some of the German advisers believed that the British were on the verge of a great victory. In the Turkish gun lines behind Achi Baba, field batteries were limbering up preparatory to driving the guns to the rear, and only the resolution of a few determined officers saved the day.

Hamilton, who had come ashore for the day to watch – but not to direct – the battle, was visibly excited as the Manchesters could be seen amidst the smoke of battle, apparently breaking through the Turkish defences. He was, however, unable to understand the reasons for the eventual halt in the forward movement and wrote, somewhat testily, in his diary that 'the Manchester Brigade took two lines of trenches and carried on to the lower slopes of Achi Baba – then *lay down*, when they had a clear run at the summit.' He was too far away, it seems, to recognize that the men 'lying down' had been mortally hit and would never rise again.

Now was the time to call up the reserves and exploit this success before the fire went out of the advance. Eighteen battalions of VIII Corps were still in reserve, but the nearest was over a mile to the rear of the morning's front line, whilst the rest were even further back. Hamilton felt, as he had done on 25 April, that he must on no account interfere with Hunter-Weston's handling of the battle. Once more, his reticence was a significant factor in the failure which now took place.

To the left of 42 Division was the 88th Brigade, or rather its pale shadow, for its losses since 25 April had compelled its further reorganization as a composite formation of six weak battalions, augmented by territorials from 42 Division. Few of the officers who had come ashore on 25 April were still on their feet and with their battalions. When the remnants of the KOSB, the Hampshires and the Royal Fusiliers went forward on 4 June they ran almost immediately into the German machine-gunners, who had escaped the preliminary artillery bombardment and were full of fight. But the 88th Brigade pushed ahead and by 1 p.m. was well into the enemy defences. At this stage all communication appears to have broken down, so that it was impossible to push further troops through the gap created by the Worcesters, who had broken into the Turkish main position. Inevitably, increasing Turkish pressure forced them to retire: another golden opportunity, and hundreds of lives, had been squandered for no gains.

On the extreme left the 14th Sikhs attacked astride Gully Ravine whilst the Gurkhas advanced along the line of the clifftops. The Sikhs were virtually annihilated by machine-gun fire; only 2 British officers, 2 Indian officers and 71 men answered the roll call at the end of that terrible day. The commanding officer was one survivor and Second-Lieutenant Savory the other; he now found himself, formerly the junior subaltern, elevated to the appointment of adjutant. The battalion's Parsee medical officer, Captain Cowasjee, particularly distinguished himself, tending the wounded under heavy fire. No further progress was possible in Gully Ravine in the face of the machine-guns, few of which could be located. They had been carefully positioned so as to be out of reach of naval gunfire support and would have to be winkled out one at a time.

The armoured cars barely played any part in the battle. Although the engineers had done their best to improve the track to allow them forward in support of the infantry, they quickly became bogged down or slipped off the narrow road. They did not appear on the battlefield again at Gallipoli.

By 1 p.m. the battle had all but died out. Apart from the outstanding performance of the Manchester Brigade, now well into the

Turkish position but endangered from both flanks, no penetration of the enemy position had been achieved. Hunter-Weston was confronted with two courses of action. He could either push his eighteen reserve battalions forward through the rapidly closing gap made by 42 Division, or launch them at the positions on which no impression had been made in the first attack. He consulted with General Gouraud and they agreed to reinforce defeat with an attack that evening against the unbroken Turkish lines on each flank. Whilst the reserves were being called up, 42 Division was left with flanks exposed and under increasing pressure. It was agreed that the second attack would be launched at 4 p.m., but Gouraud reneged at 5 p.m. before a single French soldier had gone forward, telling Hunter-Weston that his men would not be attacking that night.

At 5.30 Hunter-Weston ordered VIII Corps to stand fast and dig in to repel the inevitable Turkish counter-attacks. He had hoped that 42 Division would be able to hold on to the ground it had taken but this was a fond delusion. The troops, left without reinforcement or replenishment, were tired, thirsty, short of ammunition and devastated by their fearsome casualties. Slowly and resentfully they drew back on to their original positions and braced themselves for an eventful night. The shaken Turks also took stock. Later they admitted to having suffered 9,000 casualties on that terrible day.

# 20

# *The Battle of Gully Ravine*

Life, to be sure, is nothing much to lose;
But young men think it is, and we were young.
A. E. Housman, 'Here Dead We Lie',
*Last Poems* (1922)

IT HAD NOT been an auspicious day for the change of command of the 29th Division. With Hunter-Weston's promotion to the command of VIII Corps, his successor at 29 Division was Major-General Sir Beauvoir de Lisle. Aged 51, de Lisle had been commissioned into the Durham Light Infantry in 1883. A fine horseman, he captained his regimental polo team to many victories before commanding a mounted infantry unit in South Africa, then transferring to the Royal Dragoons in 1903. Since then he had followed the conventional career of a cavalry officer, endlessly practising the outdated tactics of shock action for which the heavy cavalry existed, and the mounted sports at which he excelled. He now came fresh from the Western Front, having won promotion in the field. The staff of the 29th awaited his arrival with the curiosity invariably attending the advent of a new commander. Captain Milward had already noted that 'De Lisle is coming to command the Division. I wonder what he will be like'; a few days later, he knew.

De Lisle came ashore at V beach after dark on 4 June accompanied by his ADC, 'Hardcross Lloyd the polo player', noted Milward somewhat disdainfully. The new commander cannot have been reassured by what he saw and heard. Shells were falling all over the beach area, some from the direction of Achi Baba, some from the Asiatic shore. Hundreds of wounded were arriving at the shore-line and harassed embarkation officers were desperately trying to find spaces on boats to take them off to the hospital ships. Few had any time to spare for a newly arrived general amidst that tumult.

News of the Third Battle of Krithia evoked mixed reactions in London, where the newly formed Dardanelles Committee was settling to its task. There was now a better understanding of the problems facing Hamilton as the result of earlier, ill-considered decisions in Whitehall, and a growing consensus that something needed to be done if the Dardanelles expedition was not to wind down in stagnation and defeat.

Until now, the insistent demands of the Western Front had absorbed every priority for weapons, manpower and supplies. Winston Churchill kept the Dardanelles at the forefront of the Cabinet's agenda by badgering all in sight for reinforcements to go to Hamilton rather than to Sir John French. On 11 June he penned a forceful memorandum in which he urged the immediate despatch of two more divisions to Gallipoli, stressing the debilitated state of the troops already there, based on information received in letters from his brother Jack, now on the island of Imbros with the newly arrived GHQ which, having come reluctantly ashore at Hamilton's bidding from its luxurious ship, was miserably encamped amidst the flies and dust. It now seemed to the Cabinet that with stalemate on the Western Front showing little sign of resolution until adequate artillery was available, the only theatre of war in which a strategic result might be obtained was the Dardanelles.

Churchill, sensing a change of mood at Cabinet level, wrote yet again to Asquith summarizing the case for reinforcing Hamilton at once. From April to mid-May, he pointed out, the Allies had lost more than 300,000 men on the Western Front with nothing to show except the gain of eight square miles of worthless ground. Even if all the troops currently ashore at Gallipoli had been used in France, the results obtained there would not have been different, and the men would still have died. Every week of delay saw Turkey revitalized, the Central Powers increasing their armies and the progressive failure of the Russian war machine as its armies reeled under the battering of the Germans and their markedly less effective Austro-Hungarian allies. If Russia was to be saved, it was imperative to force the Dardanelles and then the Bosphorus, knock Turkey out of the war, and get relief convoys through to the Black Sea. However, given the munitions shortages at home it is difficult to see how worthwhile supplies of guns and ammunition could have been sent through to Odessa, even if the shaky Russian railroad system was capable of transporting them to the hinterland.

Sir John French had attacked at Givenchy in response to an urgent appeal from General Joffre, to be bloodily repulsed with the loss of

3,000 men, most of them from two brigades. This strengthened Churchill's case and he redoubled his efforts. He sought permission to make a fact-finding visit to the Dardanelles; preparations for it were well advanced and he was actually making his farewells in Downing Street when the Conservatives heard of the proposed trip and threatened to make a major political issue of it; so much so that Asquith, sensing the imminent collapse of Liberal influence and impending Conservative triumph, caved in and withdrew permission.

In fact it was now agreed that more troops were urgently needed on the peninsula in order to reopen the offensive there in August. The 53rd (Welsh) and 54th (East Anglian) territorial divisions were already earmarked; now there were three Kitchener 'New Army' divisions: the 10th (Irish), 11th (Northern) and 13th (Western). Three giant liners, the Cunarders *Aquitania* and *Mauretania*, and the White Star Line's *Olympic*, were chartered and hastily converted to the trooping role. Each was capable of carrying up to 4,000 men. For a few weeks, Hamilton found that his theatre had acquired favour in London. Kitchener was signalling him almost daily, asking him to state his requirements for men and *matériel* and even directed Maxwell, in Egypt, to make available, if required by Hamilton, up to 15,000 British and Indian troops.

This was the limit of help that Kitchener could now give without denuding Britain of its home defence forces or setting off another political crisis over reinforcement of the Western Front. Joffre was continually nagging Sir John French for more British efforts in support of projected French offensives, and although the BEF had been planning to postpone its offensive action until the spring of 1916, French reluctantly agreed to stage a limited offensive in August. The alarming reality behind Joffre's requests was the spectre of mutiny, now beginning to stalk the French high command. Ever since the appalling casualties of the 'Battles of the Frontiers' in August and September 1914 there had been numerous incidents where French infantry had refused to leave their trenches to advance, and their generals believed that only a sacrificial example set by the BEF would keep them in the field for another year.

With remarkable efficiency, the British war machine assembled the reinforcements for Gallipoli and shipped them off. Less successful was the search for equipment, particularly artillery, and the new arrivals were conspicuously short of this vital arm, to say nothing of gun ammunition. The home base, barely nine months after the out-break of war, was now maintaining twenty-four British divisions in

France, with another twenty-five being raised and shortly to go to join the BEF. Four British and two Australian/New Zealand divisions were ashore on the peninsula and five were under orders or *en route* to join them by the middle of June.

Conditions for the troops on Gallipoli were steadily worsening with the onset of hot weather, and the impact of heavy casualties suffered in the three battles for Krithia. Colonel Darlington's battalion of Manchesters had been hard hit and his letters home were beginning to lose their early optimism. On 5 June he wrote after the battalion's first big battle: 'we had a big scrap yesterday . . . Our casualties were heavy and most of all poor old Archie Brook, Sydney James and G. Leech were killed . . . I can't mention casualties but they were: officers, the last numeral in the year we were married. Men, about four-fifths of my Wigan telephone number.' In this roundabout way, and weeks before the official figures were released, the families of the territorials were given the first dark hints of the tragedy in which their men were involved.

Two days later, Darlington was writing again to his wife:

> still in the fire trench . . . Our men are played out for want of sleep but are splendidly game . . . Don't think I am downhearted; one could not be with my battalion, what is left of them. They simply loved going in with the bayonet on the 4th. Our men did not fire a single shot as they charged . . . They jumped out of their trench, legged it splendidly across the 200 yards of open and bayoneted every Turk in the trench.

According to Darlington his battalion was left with its right flank exposed after the successive retirements of the French, the Royal Naval Division, and finally the 7th Manchesters,

> leaving B company with their flank 800 yards in the air. They hung on . . . for about three hours, then gradually fell back as the Turks were then around them. This left A company's flank in the air . . . they hung on till 7 p.m. when I ordered them back on my own . . . quite calm, only *very* angry . . . We have no transport and all our pack horses and mules have been killed . . . The 6th Manchesters have been nearly wiped out. It is sickening.

By 14 June Darlington had time to take further stock as the battalion rested on the island of Imbros. He and all the other surviving - officers now realized the full extent of the brigade's losses: 'There are not 30 officers left in the brigade and only about 40 per cent of the men . . .' Two days later: 'still on this island . . . but am afraid that we shall have to go back soon to the peninsula . . . I wonder what Manchester and Wigan will think of our losses. 80 officers killed and wounded out of 128 is a bit thick . . . we get chits here every day telling us that Turkish morale is gone. We haven't noticed it in the trenches.'

Early in June the 52nd (Lowland) Division began to arrive on the peninsula, warmly welcomed by the exhausted units of the 29th Division who had been continually within range of the Turkish artillery since 25 April and were long overdue for a rest.

The 52nd (Lowland) Division comprised territorial units from the Edinburgh, Borders and Clyde Valley areas. It was commanded by Major-General Granville Egerton, who was aged 56 in 1915. He had been commissioned into the old 72nd Highlanders and had served, as had Hamilton, in the Afghan war of 1879–80. After further active service as adjutant of the Seaforths in the Egyptian war of 1882 and in Kitchener's expedition to recapture Khartoum in 1898, he transferred to command the Yorkshire Regiment in 1903 and followed this with a tour as commandant of the School of Musketry at Hythe. From time to time his career had coincided with Hamilton's and the two men knew each other well.

Egerton, like Hamilton, was a musketry expert and believed that he and his Hythe instructors, especially Major Norman McMahon of the Royal Fusiliers, had been responsible for the sensational improvement of the army's shooting in the years between the Boer War and 1914. This contention was to be at the centre of the vendetta he pursued against Hamilton after the war. Egerton was a confirmed bachelor and had few interests outside his profession other than the conventional sporting pursuits of his class. He firmly believed in the paramount value of close order foot drill as the very foundation of discipline (he would describe himself in private letters as 'an old Drill') and as soon as he assumed command of the 52nd (Lowland) Division in 1914 he made it very clear that the way to military proficiency, as far as he was concerned, lay on rifle range and drill square. The territorials soon realized that they were in the hands of a dedicated professional who was also something of a martinet.

Once the various battalions of the 52nd Division arrived at Helles the troops were marched inland towards the firing line. At once they began to realize one of the problems of life on the peninsula; the 4th Royal Scots, despite every effort to navigate in the dark as taught back in Scotland, found themselves blundering on to W beach, cursing the guides from the 7th Battalion who were supposed to be leading them forward. Eventually they found the area assigned to them and started to dig shelters against the intermittent shelling which came from two directions: 'Asiatic Annie' and her larger shells were soon recognized from the lighter but more frequent projectiles coming over the shoulder of Achi Baba. The 4th Royal Scots were sent into the line for a taste of what awaited them, and they found the veterans of the 5th Battalion, which had arrived much earlier as part of the 29th Division, to be useful tutors.

The 5th Royal Scots, familiarly known by their old volunteer title, the Queen's Edinburgh Rifles, were typical of the best type of Scottish territorial unit. Officers and men knew each other from years of association in kirk, school, college, the Boys' Brigade and the Boy Scouts. The 5th were conscious of the honour of being the sole territorial infantry battalion in the 29th Division and were initially somewhat in awe of the regulars. Major Muir, who served at Helles with the battalion, recorded that 'the 1st Essex were magnificent men, tall, well built and trained to the moment. We looked like pygmies in comparison . . . the greatest compliment I was ever paid was when their adjutant came up to me one day, shook hands, and said "Muir, I should be damned proud to lead your men anywhere."' Muir also noted that the Australians, famously slack over most aspects of military punctilio, invariably saluted officers of the 29th Division: 'It was a sort of Masonic hallmark given by them to a division whose conduct they had witnessed and approved.'

One of the 52nd Division's battalions, the 7th (Leith Rifles) Royal Scots, had already undergone the terrible experience of the Quintinshill disaster, arriving at Helles at barely half strength. In their ranks was Private William Begbie who had enlisted early in 1914 at Leith when only fifteen and a half by giving a false age. Travelling in the second of the two troop trains carrying the 7th Battalion to Liverpool, Begbie was spared the horrors of the crash, news of which had been announced on the dockside to the stunned half-battalion. Deep and heartfelt grief spread over the port of Leith and the city of Edinburgh, and the drill halls were besieged by relatives seeking news of their men. The survivors embarked on the Canadian Pacific liner *Empress of Britain*, hastily converted to a troopship for the duration, and sailed in sombre mood for the Mediterranean. Captain Rutherford of 'C' Company 4th Royal Scots noted in his diary that over 4,000 men had been packed into a ship designed to carry 1,500 passengers and crew. A troopdeck collection by 'C' Company for the Quintinshill disaster fund raised the respectable sum of £12 5s. and all ranks soon slipped into the routine of the ship. By the time they reached Helles, the survivors were in good shape and determined to maintain the fighting traditions of the regiment which, as the 1st of Foot, was the senior unit of the British infantry of the line.

Of the companies of the 4th Royal Scots now joining them two arrived a day late, having been involved in a near disaster at sea when the naval transport HMS *Reindeer* on which they were travelling came into collision in pitch darkness with the empty transport *Immingham*, which quickly sank. On the decks of the *Reindeer*, whose bows were stove in, the territorials fell in quietly as on the parade ground and stood steadily as their ship limped back to Mudros and safety. Comparisons were immediately drawn with the troops who had gone down standing in their ranks on the *Birkenhead* off the African coast in 1852 and the reputation of the 4th Royal Scots, publicly praised in a General Order, stood high on the peninsula even before they saw action.

Although there was no plan for a major offensive, Hunter-Weston and Gouraud were mindful of the need to maintain pressure on the Turks and agreed to a series of limited attacks aimed at securing the Allied flanks on either side of the Helles peninsula. The French, conscious of their earlier failures and galvanized by their energetic commander, were keen to capture the Turkish strongpoints that had given so much trouble in the previous battle; they now planned to attack on 21 June. Their objectives were the Haricot and Quadrilateral redoubts, both formidably defended by machine-guns and wire. Gouraud assembled all his artillery until he had one gun for each ten yards of front, backed by all available naval gunfire, which was also tasked to swamp the Turkish batteries on the Asiatic shore during the attack.

The assault was due to start at 6 a.m. after forty-five minutes of intense gunfire. The assaulting troops were given a hearty hot meal beforehand and primed with an extra wine ration; a generous measure of brandy was added to every man's water bottle shortly before they went over the top in an elated condition. The Haricot redoubt was rushed and taken in great style within minutes, but on the right, the defenders of the Quadrilateral hurled the colonial regiments back. Gouraud ordered another attack at 6 p.m. The Colonials were not fit for this but the Régiment de Marche Afrique went forward with great spirit and, although it failed to take the entire Quadrilateral, seized a foothold in the Turkish defences and hung on. The French had thus greatly improved their position and, more importantly, regained the confidence of their allies.

Following the success of the French operation, Hunter-Weston decided to mount an attack on the Gully Ravine area. The operation had to wait until the French artillery was ready to participate, owing to the parlous state of the British ammunition supply as well as the shortage of guns. By mid-June there were no high explosive shells for the British 18-pounders, and what shrapnel there was had been rationed, except in dire emergency, to what one cynical artillery officer described as 'Two rounds per day, per gun, perhaps.' The strain of providing artillery support had told quickly on the 29th Division's first artillery commander, Brigadier-General Breeks, who was sent before a hastily convened medical board and shipped off on the sick list, the first of many senior officers to succumb to the strain of the campaign.

The Battle of Gully Ravine, as it became known, was set to begin on 28 June. The objectives were the Turkish positions dominating Gully Spur and Ravine, and Fir Tree Spur to the right. On information available it seemed that the Turkish trenches were not continuous or heavily wired. In the Gully Spur and Ravine area there was scope for tactical ingenuity because of the broken nature of the ground; this called for well-trained troops who could be relied on to use initiative if out of contact with their company and platoon officers. Hunter-Weston therefore assigned this side of the attack to the regulars. One of 52nd Division's brigades, the 156th, had now landed at Helles and its four battalions were ordered to attack the Turks on Fir Tree Spur where, they were told, the Turkish trenches had been easily taken in the previous attack and had then been abandoned only because enfilading fire had made them untenable. If this was meant to hearten these untried troops it was unwise, for they went into battle bolstered with misplaced confidence.

The attack was entrusted to Major-General de Lisle whose staff issued voluminous orders. The artillery resources scraped together for the attack on a frontage of 700 yards seemed impressive, even if most came from the French, whose 155-mm howitzers offered a good chance of breaking up the machine-gun nests known to lurk in the Gully area. Some 12,000 rounds of ammunition had been allotted, compared with the 10,000 spread over a frontage right across the peninsula for the last attack. The heavier guns were to open up at 9 a.m. on 28 June, concentrating on a search of the Turkish positions on Gully Spur and in the Ravine. After 10.20 they would be joined by field guns which would endeavour to cut the Turkish wire. For this the British guns were useless, as their shrapnel was only effective against troops in the open. At 10.45 the guns would lift the range and the infantry were to rush the Boomerang Redoubt, a Turkish stronghold on the eastern side of the Ravine which had effectively delayed earlier British advances in this sector. Fifteen minutes later there was to be a general attack up Gully Spur and Ravine whilst the 29th Indian Brigade moved carefully along the line of the clifftops to secure the extreme left flank.

De Lisle, clearly believing that the task of the 156th Brigade on the right at Fir Tree Spur would be a light one, had allotted virtually all the artillery support to the centre and left of his attack, a decision which would cost the Lowlanders dear. They had spent a miserable sleepless night under intermittent artillery fire which had already caused casualties as they moved up from their reserve position on the previous evening. Young Private Begbie in the 7th Royal Scots noted the Turkish guns scoring direct hits on the British lines, packed as they were with men waiting for the order to attack. The 4th Royal Scots had been in the trenches for two weeks, picking up the necessary skills. On 24 June the battalion had gone out of the line to prepare for the attack of the 28th and all ranks had swum in the Aegean and sunbathed when not carrying out fatigues.

On 26 June Captain Rutherford, possibly with a premonition of what was about to befall his company, handed its diary over to Second-Lieutenant Grant, who recorded the wearisome trudge back into the line, each man carrying up to 90 pounds of kit and ammunition. The men, still wearing their heavy serge uniforms, were desperate with thirst when they reached the fire trench and relieved the Manchesters at 5 p.m. There was no food either until well after dark. Only now did most of the Royal Scots realize that they were to attack next day, and the night was spent preparing for the ordeal. Orders were passed down from brigade to battalion, from battalion to company and then on to the assaulting platoons as they waited tensely in the fire trench. Grant summarized these in the diary:

> Every man to be ready for assault at 0800 hrs. To have as much rest as possible. Steps to be cut in parapet by every man. All to carry entrenching tool, 220 rounds of ammo, 2 sandbags, iron rations, full waterbottle. At least every third man to carry artillery disc on back [made from jam tins, and designed to flash in sun to identify friendly units to artillery observers]. Packs to be stacked out of way in trench by 7 a.m. Picks and shovels to be left at rear of trench. At 10.30 every man to go to front of trench to allow A Company to file in. At 10.57, bayonets fixed. No man will fire before reaching second trench. At 11, company commanders with give word '*Attack*' and every officer and NCO will repeat this and swarm over parapet.

All 29 Division's machine-guns had been massed together in the Royal Scots trenches, rendering movement in them almost imposs-ible. Two men stood to every yard of trench; sentries peered over the parapet in the dark; an occasional flare rose to illuminate the open ground ahead, over which the battalion was to attack next morning.

When the bombardment started at 9 a.m. the Royal Scots were at first surprised, then increasingly apprehensive, at its lack of intensity. They had been told that over 300 guns were trained on the Turkish positions ahead and were not to know that their attack was going to be virtually without any fire support. Grant watched the men 'lying about in the trenches, smoking or reading or laughing and chatting . . . in great spirits'. As zero hour approached, however, the strain began to tell and 'the odd man was led to the rear, broken down, his hands manacled, a raving maniac for the time being'. At 10.45 the sound of the Border Regiment storming the Boomerang redoubt could be heard and ten minutes later the company were standing by with fixed bayonets.

> Excitement ran high and a certain tense nervousness. It was the supreme test of our months of training. Would we stand the test? . . . and with a yell that thrilled the very marrow in one's bones the men hurled themselves over the parapet and dashed forward into the inferno of flame and smoke, bursting shells and zipping bullets. Over the remainder of that day it is perhaps as well to draw a veil, suffice it to say that we gained and held our objective but at great cost. Out of the 6 officers of C Company 3 were killed: Captain Rutherford, Lt Mackie and 2nd Lt Johnstone. One is missing – Lt Allen – and two were wounded, 2nd Lts Riddell and Grant. Of the men, more than half fell or are missing.

In Private Begbie's unit, 7th Royal Scots, many men became casu-alties even before the battalion went over the top, owing to the accur-ate work of the Turkish guns on the crowded trenches, where it was impossible to dodge the hail of shrapnel. He would never forget the next few minutes:

> At last the hour came and at the words 'Over you go, lads', the troops gave vent to one resounding cheer and swarmed over the parapets into the perils of the open ground . . . rifle at the ready, and ran like hell into the enemy trench. Before I reached it I could see some Turks retreating to the next lines . . . after a short halt during which the sup-porting waves closed up, the advance on the final objective was begun. By this time the Turks, having recovered from their panic, delivered such a terrific fire that our company fell in bundles. Halfway across

Major Sanderson dropped and Captain Dawson and Lt Thompson were killed as they neared their goal. By now, men were falling on my left and right.

Begbie now found himself running forward apparently alone, as he could only see a few yards in the dust and smoke; he had no time to reflect that it was barely a year since he had 'fraudulently enlisted' under age at Leith, and was even now some months short of his seventeenth birthday. He pushed on single-handed, wondering what had happened to the men on either side, when

> I then felt as if a horse had kicked my right thigh. I fell, and when I got up I had no feeling in my right leg as I fell again. When I felt where the pain was I saw my hand was covered in blood. When I started to move I heard bullets striking the ground. I lay still. I did not feel much pain but the sun high in the sky threw down intense heat on the sand which was crawling with insects of every shape and size. The worst thing was the craving for water – mouths were so parched by heat and sand that tongues swelled . . .

Begbie crawled back towards the trench from which he had charged, passing crowds of his friends, some dead, others with appalling wounds. Two stretcher bearers found him and bound his wound so that he was able to hobble back towards the dressing station. Eventually he was loaded on to a wagon drawn by four mules which galloped to the beach under continual shellfire. He heard later that his battalion ended the day with only 3 officers and 80 soldiers unscathed. After arriving at a hospital on the island of Lemnos he was evacuated to Egypt, temporarily out of the battle. He was given a golden opportunity to leave Gallipoli for ever when asked his age in the base hospital. If the truth had emerged he would have been returned home at once; but he could not bear the thought of escaping and deserting his few surviving friends in this way. Soon, he would be returning to the peninsula and to what remained of his unit.

Considering the adverse conditions under which they had been thrown into battle, the territorials had done remarkably well, charging into the enemy position with tremendous dash and inflicting many casualties on the Turks. 156th Brigade had attacked with three battalions leading and the 7th Scottish Rifles (Cameronians) in reserve. All suffered terrible losses as the morning wore on. The 4th and 7th Royal Scots got into the Turkish line, but on the right, where there was virtually no artillery support to keep the Turks' heads down, the 8th Scottish Rifles were massacred. In the first five minutes of the attack they had lost 25 out of 26 officers killed or wounded, and more than 400 men. In the words of the divisional history: 'All ranks were slaughtered, literally by platoons . . . in a few minutes nothing was left of the battalion but one officer and a few men who dribbled back to their own front line . . .'

The stretch of ground in front of their trenches was now heaped with corpses and grievously wounded men trying to crawl out of the fire of the Turkish machine-guns. At 11.40, seeing that the Scottish Rifles had not reached their objective, and unaware of the extent of their casualties, General de Lisle sent an order to Brigadier-General Scott-Moncrieff to resume the attack immediately, directing that the Turkish position had to be taken 'at all costs' and ordering him to send in his reserve battalion, the 7th Scottish Rifles, if they were required.

Scott-Moncrieff was 57 years old. He had been commissioned in 1878 and saw his first active service in the Zulu war of 1879. After transferring to the Cameronians he served in South Africa and was seriously lamed by a wound incurred at Spion Kop in 1899. For the rest of his days he had to use a stick, but this did not deter him from an active life and he was proud to command the brigade in which two territorial battalions of his old regiment, the Scottish Rifles, were serving. He now knew where his duty lay. Summoning up the reserve battalion, he and its commanding officer, Lieutenant-Colonel John Boyd Wilson, led it in two successive waves unflinchingly over the parapet just after 1 p.m., to certain death. Neither of these two officers had advanced more than a few yards before they were killed, and the battalion, still facing the enemy lines, disintegrated around their bodies. The first brigade of the 52nd Lowland Division to see action had virtually ceased to exist. As the divisional historian records, of Scott-Moncrieff's death: 'So died the Laird of Fessaway . . . most fearless and true-hearted of gentlemen, determined at all costs to do his duty.'

Major-General Granville Egerton, the commander of the 52nd Division, was powerless to intervene in the conduct of this battle, for the 156th Brigade had been detached under command of de Lisle. He was heartbroken at the fate of his men and furious with GHQ for letting these untried but enthusiastic beginners in for such a terrible baptism of fire. He was even more distressed to hear of Hunter-Weston's comment that he was 'delighted to hear that the pups had been so well blooded'. The performance of the Turks had also amazed him; on arrival at GHQ he had been shown a copy of a document purporting to show that the enemy's morale was on the verge of collapse; parts of it read as follows:

> All prisoners taken recently tell the same story, that the Turks are getting more and more depressed – the peninsula is now known amongst them as 'The Slaughter House' as all their finest regiments have been brought against us, one after another, and have had to go back with heavy losses. The other day 20 Turkish officers refused to go forward. They were arrested and sent to Constantinople, where they were paraded through the streets in handcuffs – one of them shouted out to some soldiers 'Don't go – it's Hell'. They put a muzzle on him and led him on – to be shot . . . A large number of Turks in the trenches are villagers and refugees who have had about a month's training.

This crude propaganda had actually been concocted by Compton Mackenzie as part of his duties in what would now be called 'psychological operations'. Egerton duly noted this on the margin of his copy of the piece, which is dated 27 June 1915, adding a sour comment: 'The following day, 28 June, my 156th Brigade found the Turkish villagers anything but depressed, and lost nearly 1,400 men of whom over 800 were killed.'

There had been better news from Gully Spur, where some progress was made, but in the afternoon the Turks began a series of fierce counter-attacks, using lavish supplies of grenades, of which the attackers had none. Despite this, the Border Regiment grimly defended their gains in the ravine and placed a barricade across it, which was held successfully. The net result of the attack had been an advance on the left of near three-quarters of a mile and the capture of some very useful ground, enabling further guns to be brought ashore. Two days later, the French finally succeeded in taking the hotly contested Quadrilateral; at the height of the battle, however, the dashing Gouraud was hit by splinters from a shell fired off the Asiatic shore and lost an arm. His departure from the peninsula was greatly deplored by his own troops and his Allies, for he had succeeded in reinvigorating the French corps after its earlier reverses. His acutely personal style of leadership, from the front of the battle, was not often to be seen at Gallipoli.

On the afternoon of 29 June, Major-General de Lisle, as commander of 29 Division, in whose support 156 Brigade had been sacrificed, sent a message to Egerton:

> General de Lisle wishes to express how much he valued the help given to the 29th Division in yesterday's attack by the 156th Brigade. [It] . . .

was almost entirely successful. The 4th and 7th Royal Scots succeeded in every detail in the tasks imposed on them. The 8th Scottish Rifles met with enormous resistance owing to the fact that our artillery had not prepared the Turkish position in front of them quite as successfully as in other places. The 8th Scottish Rifles were very gallantly led . . . General de Lisle does not blame the 8th Scottish Rifles at all for their failure. He much regrets the death of Brigadier-General Scott-Moncrieff.

In his official despatch of 29 June, however, de Lisle barely mentioned Scott-Moncrieff's brigade. Part of this curious document reads: 'East of Ravine, two battalions of Royal Scots made a fine attack, capturing the two lines of trenches assigned as their objective. But the remainder of 156 Brigade on their right met severe opposition and were unable to get forward.' It now appears that the artillery commander of 29 Division was not even made aware of the attack by 156 Brigade, which accounts for the almost complete lack of artillery support given to it. The brigade had no guns of its own, having left them behind in Scotland.

On 1 July the 7th and 8th Scottish Rifles, or what remained of them, were formed into a composite battalion, and the 4th and 7th Royal Scots were also amalgamated. The other two brigades of the 52nd Division, the 155th and 157th, now came ashore, to be met, when they went into the line, with the gruesome sight of the dead of 156th Brigade still lying unburied where they had fallen. It was not the happiest of reunions.

**21**

# The Destruction of the 52nd Division

The Flowers of the Forest, that foucht aye the
    foremost,
The Prime o' our land – are cauld in the clae.

Scottish ballad

IN ACCORDANCE WITH Hamilton's instructions, Hunter-Weston had to maintain an aggressive posture at Helles in order to convince the Turks that a major offensive was likely to be launched there in the near future. However, the divisions under his command in VIII Corps were now exhausted, heavily depleted by battle casualties and sickness, and in urgent need of rest. This could not be secured on the peninsula, where all the so-called 'rest areas' were well within range of enemy artillery, most of them in full view of the Turkish and German observers on Achi Baba or the Asiatic shore. The mishap to General Gouraud had emphasized the perils from the latter, and the French corps was suffering heavily from guns deployed in the Kum Kale area. Many of the victims had been French officers and soldiers who had discovered archaeological sites in their sector, and spent much of their time out of the line in 'digs' searching for treasure. Unprotected in the open as they happily scraped away, they fell easily to shrapnel.

Hunter-Weston's first thoughts were for another attack, east of the Sedd-el-Bahr–Krithia road, to be carried out by the Royal Naval Division, but this formation was now in no state to embark on any such operation. Its officers and men were displaying alarming signs of impending collapse, with a high rate of disease and mental illness. The 29th Division, near breaking point following its appalling losses in the earlier stages of the operation, and 42 Division, after its sudden and bloody introduction to battle, were both now considered neither suitable nor, for the time being, even reliable enough for an immediate attack. The only troops available were the 52nd Lowland Division, one of whose brigades, the 156th, had been so badly cut up in the battle of Gully Ravine. Plans for an attack on 7 July were therefore put back to the 12th, by which time the French agreed that they would also be ready to resume the attack, having replenished their artillery ammunition.

In order to give some respite to the longest-serving units at Helles, it was decided to use some of the battalions of the 13th New Army Division, about to arrive in the theatre and earmarked for the August offensive. It was felt that some trench duty, albeit in a strictly defensive role, would accustom them to life on the peninsula as well as provide useful training. Plans went ahead for 29 and 42 Divisions and the Royal Naval Division to go across in relays to Lemnos and Imbros, out of range of the guns, for much-needed rest and recuperation, and to receive reinforcements.

Meanwhile, disease took its toll, aided by ceaseless artillery harassment. Most vulnerable were the wretched sufferers from diarrhoea and dysentery, obliged to hover in their hundreds close to the reeking latrines where they perched miserably on long poles over insanitary pits, into which many of them fell when hit by shell splinters or shrapnel. Others, too weak even to get to the latrines, lay bleeding nearby as the foul disease racked their bowels. Standards of sanitary discipline on the peninsula, even allowing for the appalling conditions, were generally deplorable other than in the 29th Division. As a regular formation whose units were used to soldiering in hot climates, this had well-trained unit sanitary personnel who did their best to maintain hygiene. For the first few weeks, Anzac was by far the unhealthiest, where space was extremely limited and insufficient attention paid to the disposal of human and animal waste. At Helles, the experimental incineration of several tons of horse manure quickly drew enemy fire and had to be abandoned in favour of burial or disposal out to sea.

There was no specialist sanitation staff officer at GHQ until August, by which time the deadly combination of flies, dirt, ignorance and poor sanitary discipline had raised the sick lists to alarming levels. Throughout the campaign there was a grave shortage of materials necessary for construction of flyproof kitchens, waste disposal sites and latrines; such supplies of timber and wood that did come ashore were immediately diverted for the construction of dugouts. The thousands of corpses which continued to lie unburied all over the battlefield, apart from those interred on 23 May during the Anzac burial truce, were a primary source of infection. At this time, one observer wrote that Helles 'looked like a midden and stank like an open grave'. There were, however, no recorded cases of either cholera or typhus on the peninsula throughout the campaign. This was attributed to the policy of inoculating all ranks *en route* to Gallipoli.

Helles was not a pleasant place, even when a set-piece was not raging, for the so-called 'rest camps' were continually under shellfire. As no provision had been made for canteen facilities, which were readily available on the Western Front, it was virtually impossible to buy the small luxuries that mean so much to the soldier on active service; some enterprising Greek merchants opened up stalls on the beaches, from which a few items could be purchased; but letters home reveal a universal hunger for sweets, chocolates, tinned delicacies (ox tongue, sardines, salmon, ham, biscuits, cakes and chicken being the favourites), waterproof clothing for the approaching wet season, and articles such as writing paper, razors and toiletries.

Despite the heroic efforts of the Army Service Corps – known to all as 'Ally Sloper's Cavalry' (after a well-known comic figure of the day) or 'The Murdering Thieves' (in the old army, the more pejorative a nickname, the greater the affection in which its bearer was held) – the food eaten by all ranks was monotonous and generally unpleasant. Chilled fresh meat and bacon shipped from Australia and New Zealand deteriorated rapidly once brought ashore at Gallipoli, where there were no facilities for keeping food cool or, more importantly, from the hordes of 'corpse flies', as the sluggish, bloated greenish insects were known. Maggots appeared on fresh meat within twenty-four hours and fly-borne gastric infections spread like wildfire from unit cookhouses where the cooks were unable to practise even the most elementary hygiene. The staple meat dish was therefore bully beef; not the modern, lean and palatable product but inferior gristly meat purchased in bulk in the Argentine or Australia, canned with a high fat and salt content, preserved with chemicals no longer permitted for the treatment of foodstuffs. In the furnace heat of the peninsula, this low quality product turned into an unappetizing greasy soup which could be poured out of the can. Its many names testify to the lack of enthusiasm with which its appearance was greeted by the soldiers: Horse-and-Water, Working Mule, Corned Dog, and worse. Other tinned rations included a meat and vegetable stew bearing the name of the maker: Maconochie's. It was notable for the paucity of its meat content and the near impossibility of identifying the accompanying vegetables.

Tea, sugar and condensed milk were available in quantity, for their absence would have induced mutiny. The tinned jam made by the firm of Tickler was the butt of universal jokes, as it appeared to contain no recognizable fruit, emerging from the can as a luridly coloured sweet mess with the consistency of glue. Tinned butter, again from Australia, liquefied in the heat and had to be spooned on to the plate. Fresh vegetables and fruit were seldom seen ashore. Until the Army Service Corps opened a field bakery on the beach at Helles, hard tack biscuit was the only accompaniment to meal after monotonous meal. There was no specialist catering corps and soldiers who had either volunteered for kitchen duty as a means of escape from the firing trench, or been pressed into it after failing at every other job in the unit, did their best or worst with the ingredients supplied. The French, mindful as ever of the importance of feeding an army as well as possible, were the envy of the British and dominion troops if only because of the daily ration of coarse red wine, brought ashore on lighters stacked high with huge barrels, sufficient to ensure cheerful oblivion or rouse soldiers to the frenzied fighting pitch exhibited in the storming of the Haricot Redoubt.

The aim of the attack planned for Helles on 12 July was to capture a Turkish trench system to the east of the Sedd-el-Bahr–Krithia road whilst the French consolidated their earlier gains on the extreme right flank. Hunter-Weston had only the 52nd Division at his disposal and planned to attack with two brigades up: the 157th on the left and the 155th on the right. The remains of the 156th were to be the divisional reserve. The 52nd Division's frontage was 1,000 yards and that of the French on their right, about 700. The Turkish trench system was confusingly laid out, having been developed haphazardly during the previous fighting. Some of it little more than shell-scrapes, other positions were deep and well built, and some had been abandoned. There was no way of ascertaining this, however, in the limited time available for planning the battle.

Egerton decided to launch two separate brigade attacks, one on the right at 7.35 a.m. and the other on the left at 4.50 p.m., thus denying his inexperienced troops any chance of success through surprise and concentration of effort. The reason for this apparently eccentric scheme was to ensure maximum concentration of artillery support, and it received Hunter-Weston's unqualified approval. Egerton had studied the Western Front, where the doctrine of heavy and prolonged artillery preparation had the status of Holy Writ, and where the art of the silent night attack had never yet been practised. Another factor which doomed the operation before it started was the adverse psychological effect on tense young soldiers of standing by for nine hours to launch the second attack as they watched the other brigade going into the assault.

Because of the high casualties suffered by the 156th Brigade in its recent engagement, Egerton ordered that the assaulting units on 12 July should send 10 per cent of their men and all officers above three per company to the rear beforehand, to form a first reserve. This further weakened the attacking force, cutting 52 Division's bayonet strength down to just over 200 officers and 7,500 soldiers. The Turks had one division – the 7th – deployed across the trench systems to be attacked by the 52nd, with another division, the 6th, in reserve just south of Krithia village. As on the previous occasion, GHQ intelligence assessments proclaimed that the Turks' morale was low and that their will to resist had been sapped by recent losses, bad food, and brutal treatment by their officers. There was to be little evidence of this when the 52nd, heavily outnumbered by the defence, went forward on the 12th.

As the result of new aerial photographs of the Turkish lines, a last-minute change of plan was issued late on the evening of 11 July, together with revised trench maps; unfortunately for the men of 157th Brigade, these never reached them and the trench which was their objective, far from being strong, deep and readily capable of conversion against Turkish counter-attacks, turned out to be no more than a shallow scrape offering little or no protection. Even if the correct trench maps had arrived, they would have been useless in the light of a divisional order that no maps or plans of any sort were to be taken into the attack; officers leading this enterprise were presumably meant to memorize the complex plans and act on them.

It was going to be another extremely hot day. In their assault trenches the men of the two leading brigades sweltered in their heavy serge uniforms. At 7.35 a.m. the bombardment lifted and 155th Brigade went over the top as though on parade, spurred on by the pipes. As on earlier occasions the French artillery support was of a very high order and the Turkish front line had been severely battered. The first wave entered the enemy position and all seemed to be going well; amidst the ruin of the Turkish defences the enemy lay in heaps and the 4th Royal Scots Fusiliers pressed on into a maze of badly damaged trenches. Here they ran into determined resistance from previously unlocated machine-gun posts and within an hour all the battalion's officers bar one had been hit. To the left the 4th KOSB went forward with the same dedication, but they too ran into devastating fire. Those units which had gone forward now found themselves with almost no officers, no maps or trench plans, and no idea of the divisional commander's intention. Garbled messages were flooding back to brigade and divisional headquarters but were so contradictory that staff officers made their way forward to find out what was happening. Drawn into the confused fighting, most were killed and few returned.

Early in the afternoon the situation was so confused that General Egerton was in the grip of terrible doubts as to the wisdom of launching the second attack. All he knew, from the sights and sounds ahead, was that 155th Brigade was fighting for its life deep inside the Turkish position but no coherent information was coming from its battalions. Egerton had by now committed his reserves, the sorely tried survivors of 156th Brigade, and they too had been sucked into the maelstrom, lost in huge clouds of smoke and dust. In due course, Egerton's mind was made up for him by an order from Hunter-Weston to proceed with the second attack. A message was sent to the embattled 155th Brigade telling them that the attack would take place, and to take every advantage of it to improve their own position.

One of the few staff officers from GHQ present on the battlefield was Captain Milward, and his account of the initial attack of the KOSB gives an indication of why the operation dissolved so quickly into chaos. He had been getting increasingly uneasy over the conduct of operations. As early as 8 May he noted that the campaign 'is really a badly-planned and ill-conceived expedition. Winston's Own – a bad dissipation of strength, political and doing no harm to Germany at all.' His days with the 29th Division were numbered, however, for on 18 June he was posted to the staff of GHQ on Imbros. 'Very sorry to leave the 29th, the finest division in the army. *Not* sorry to leave de Lisle.' According to his brutally frank account of the initial assault of the KOSB on the 12th, the battalion attacked

> in great style, in fact so much that they didn't wait to examine the communication trenches, left them full of Turks, ran over their objectives, on and over another, up and over a rise and disappeared – far beyond the wildest hopes – above 500 yards ahead. They saw Red. This was really bad work – the work of ill-trained men and bad officers. An advance like this, uncontrolled, far beyond the objective and out of touch with troops on right and left and behind must lead to trouble. And so it proved.

Some of the Scottish territorial officers were also worried by certain aspects of the training and discipline of their units. A month earlier, Second-Lieutenant Sinclair of the 5th Royal Scots in 29th Division had started a diary, like so many others at Helles, 'out of sheer boredom' whilst lying in a 'comparatively safe dugout two miles from our front line trenches'. As he wrote, shrapnel was bursting overhead and it was prudent, as ever on the peninsula, to remain below ground whenever possible. There were no books to read. Sinclair did not enjoy cards, nor could he sleep. He confided to his diary all the frustrations and misery of training back in Scotland, and felt that it had been inadequate for the battalion's task on the peninsula. In particular he envied the regulars:

> What makes the difference between the regulars and the territorials is the Barrack Square. If all the territorials in the country had six weeks of Barrack Square drill without arms, starting 4th August, the territorials would now be the finest fighting force existing. The training of the territorial lacks foundation and that foundation is Discipline.

Egerton, his divisional commander, would have certainly agreed with every word as he tried to bring the 52nd under control on the afternoon of 12 July. Somewhere out in front his division was being destroyed. In the clouds of smoke and dust great acts of heroism were taking place unnoticed. Lieutenant-Colonel M'Neile of the 4th KOSB cheered on his men until he was killed; Lieutenant Innes asked his cousin, also a subaltern in the same battalion, to cut off the remains of his shattered arm, lit a cigarette, and shouted encouragement to his men until he too was dead.

It is clear from the war diaries and battle narratives of this confused and terrible day that the battalion seen by Milward and criticized for its lack of discipline was in fact the 4th KOSB. Its officers, forbidden to carry trench maps, cannot therefore be blamed for losing their bearings; their sublime courage, and that of their men, deserves enduring respect. They had pressed on under the mistaken impression that there was yet another Turkish trench line ahead, and many actually gained the lower slopes of Achi Baba. They were now so far forward that the tin plates on their backs, designed to identify them to forward artillery observers, were no longer visible, and they inevitably came under friendly fire as Colonel M'Neile, in the last minutes of his life, ordered them to fall back to the main body. M'Neile, his adjutant, and 262 men of the battalion were never seen again.

As Egerton was now most unhappy about the situation he asked for the corps reserve, the Royal Marine Brigade of the Royal Naval Division, to move forward and stand by in case the 52nd Division collapsed. It was now time for the 157th Brigade to carry out its attack.

Its men had been standing by in their fire trenches since early in the morning, tortured by appalling thirst. In 155th Brigade, no water reached the forward troops until late in the day, when one company of the Cameronians managed to acquire a biscuit tin of it, which was dished out, a tablespoon per man.

The battalions of the 157th went forward as ordered. The first two Turkish lines were rapidly overwhelmed but trouble began when the 7th Highland Light Infantry reached what was supposed to be their final objective. Instead of a deep, well-protected trench, it was no more than a shallow depression, useless for defensive purposes. This had been revealed in the belated air photographs, but these had not been issued in time. An immediate Turkish counter-attack was beaten off and the troops, or those who survived, wearily prepared to defend themselves during the coming night. On the front attacked by the 157th Brigade, all objectives had been taken and held; but the casualties incurred had virtually put the formation out of action and later that evening the marines of the Plymouth battalion relieved them in the line.

As night fell on the 12th, the 52nd Division was all but broken, despite the remarkable heroism of its officers and men. The survivors were either manning trenches whose position they did not know, or wandering around the area searching fruitlessly for their officers and comrades; some were straggling to the rear, accompanied by a horde of Turkish prisoners equally anxious to get away from that dreadful place, picking up others as they went, until the trickle became dangerously like a torrent and was arrested only by the intervention of a few officers, who gently led the exhausted men back into the line.

Hunter-Weston was no more in the picture than most of his command and had, in fact, lost control of the battle. His reaction to the situation on the morning of 13 July was to call forward the remaining brigade of the Royal Naval Division, a formation he himself had considered unfit for combat only a few days earlier. He knew that the objectives of 157th Brigade had been taken on the 12th and were held, whilst those of 155th Brigade were still mainly in Turkish hands. He therefore ordered what was left of the Royal Naval Division to pass through the line held by the survivors of 155th Brigade and take the trenches still in Turkish hands. Three battalions – the Chatham and Portsmouth marines and the sailors of the Nelson – were to attack at 4.30 p.m. As had been the case with 52 Division, the naval divisional staff had no idea of the updated trench plans, and thus only a vague idea of what was required of their men. The units of 155th Brigade were told to expect the naval division's attack and to lie low while it passed through their positions. Although a short impromptu artillery bombardment was arranged, various delays resulted in the attack going over the top twenty minutes late, long after the guns had stopped firing.

The Turkish guns were ready with shrapnel and the Chatham battalion was stopped in its tracks as it crossed the startline. The Portsmouth marines went forward to find, as had the Scotsmen on the previous day, that their objective was no more than the trace of an unfinished trench, and although they courageously tried to consolidate in what was virtually open ground, they were forced to retire with very heavy loss. When the Nelson battalion, after a costly advance, jumped with relief into what it thought was the objective, it was to find the trench packed with men of the 52nd Division. The sacrifice of the Portsmouth, Chatham and Nelson battalions, amounting to 24 officers and over 500 men, including the deaths of two commanding officers, had been totally unnecessary.

There now took place a most extraordinary development. Hunter-Weston called Egerton to his headquarters and formally relieved him of his command. A surprised Major-General Shaw of the 13th Division, whose troops were still arriving at the Dardanelles and who was present that day solely as an observer, was placed in temporary command of the 52nd Division. That evening, Hunter-Weston, realizing that an explanation would be called for, wrote to Hamilton; he had visited Egerton, and 'found him very much exhausted after two days' fighting. He had not been able to sleep . . . I put General Shaw in command of 52nd Division.' Egerton was sent on board a hospital ship, sedated in order to get a good night's rest, and returned to his command on the 14th, by which time the battle had ended. When Hamilton heard of this he was displeased and wrote a note to Hunter-Weston admonishing him for taking such action, ending: 'Will you please at once send in an official account of the matter to the Deputy Adjutant-General. There is no way out of it.' Hunter-Weston sent a suitably abject reply but followed it on 16 July with a fuller explanation; he was alarmed by the 52nd's state of morale following the tremendous casualties it had endured so soon after its arrival on the peninsula:

> I have got the 52nd Division back out of the trenches . . . [and] recommend a complimentary message to them on their gallantry in capturing two lines of trenches . . . will do them a lot of good and buck them up for their next operation . . . I am sorry to say that in most points of the line they ran away back for very inadequate cause . . . panic and

rabble retirement . . . many are immature and weak and not really fit
for continual hard exertion.

Hunter-Weston went on to draw comparisons with the 13th Division,
of which he had in fact seen very little, and none of whose troops had
yet been in action; the 13th, he claimed, were 'very good stuff, well
trained and will serve you well'. Hunter-Weston ended this remarkable epistle with his opinion that 'from the Naval Division, from the
52nd Division and from half the 42nd Division we cannot expect
much.' After reading this, one is left with the impression that Hunter-
Weston had little knowledge of the ordeals through which the men
under his command had passed.

Only the previous day, the 15th, Egerton had taken issue with
Hunter-Weston over the corps commander's allegation that 4th
KOSB was 'in an unsatisfactory state of moral [sic] and not fit to go
into action'. Egerton further undermined his own position when
showing Hamilton around the division as the battalions were at rest,
persisting in introducing Hamilton to the troops with the words
'These are the remnants of the 4th KOSB'; he had repeated this at each
unit Hamilton visited, until at last the irritated commander-in-chief
had told him to stop using these words. Although Egerton remained
precariously in command of his shattered division, it was only a
matter of time before Hamilton would have to remove him. As early
as May, he had expressed his doubts over Egerton, whom he had
known for many years. In a signal to Kitchener, thanking him for the
news that the 52nd Division was on its way to Gallipoli, he had asked
him to think twice about the commander: 'Please take stock of
Egerton. In peacetime an excellent commander and strict disciplin-
arian, but at Malta I found him to be highly strung and apt to be
excitable under distress.' Despite this, Kitchener had insisted that the
52nd should go to war under Egerton.

Major-General Shaw was confronted with an unpalatable situation
on assuming temporary command of 52nd Division on 13 July. He
did not know any of the staff, who could be forgiven their resentment
at the sudden change of command and the need to brief a new commander in the middle of a hopelessly confused tactical situation. He
therefore sent forward staff officers, who reported back on the following morning, the 14th, that the line held was nowhere continuous, that units were intermixed, casualties far heavier than had been
thought, and that all the troops were on the verge of physical and
mental collapse.

By degrees, over the next twenty-four hours, the equally weary

Royal Naval Division relieved the 52nd in the line. Fortunately, the Turks were so spent that for the time bing they too were incapable of action. Out of the 7,500 men of the Lowland Division who had gone into the attack on the 12th, 2,500 had fallen; the naval division had lost 600, most of them in two battalions as they relieved the 52nd and tried to resume the attack; the French had also lost heavily. Such was the faulty state of the intelligence available to Hunter-Weston that he did not realize that despite the eccentricity of the operational plans and poor staffwork, the sheer gallantry of the division in whom he clearly had no confidence had won him a battle; but there were now no reserves capable of exploiting it.

At this point, with VIII Corps in a debilitated condition, the Turkish 2nd Army was arriving in the Krithia area. Achi Baba would never fall to the Allies now. It was perhaps appropriate that Hunter-Weston now collapsed, with physical and nervous prostration and sunstroke, and was carried off the peninsula for ever.

# PART THREE

## *The Final Act*

# 22

# Planning for the August Offensive

The most total heresy in war is the heresy that
battles can be won without heavy loss.

Sir Ian Hamilton, Diary, 1915

BIRDWOOD'S ORIGINAL PLAN for an August offensive, hatched in May
and accepted in principle by Hamilton in mid-June, was largely the
work of Colonel Skeen of the Anzac General Staff; this brilliant staff
officer, an instructor at the Indian Army's Staff College at Quetta
before the war, had been personally selected by Birdwood for his
present job. Following the appalling results of daylight attacks at
Helles earlier in the summer, Skeen and Birdwood both agreed that
the best hope of success against the Turks lay in a combination of surprise and darkness. Skeen's original plan, conceived without knowledge of further reinforcements being available to Hamilton (other
than those already expected), envisaged a left hook out of the northern flank of the Anzac beach-head, with the aim of scaling the heights
behind the main Turkish positions, rendering them untenable. The
way would then be clear for a general advance across the peninsula
to Maidos and the Narrows.

Everything hinged on being able to get on to the high ground. As
no landing at Suvla was anticipated at the earlier stages of planning,
space had to be found for the attacking force to be launched from
Anzac; the additional forces necessary would have to be accommodated in absolute secrecy for the brief duration of their transit
through the beach-head, fed in over a period of several nights and
hidden away in newly dug galleries and shelters. This imposed an
exceptionally heavy load on the resources of the Australians and
New Zealanders already ashore, but there was no other way of
getting the job done and they set to, accomplishing their huge task

rapidly and efficiently without giving the great secret away to the Turks.

Skeen selected the left, or northern, flank for the break-out in preference to the southern, or Gaba Tepe, end of the Anzac front because careful and daring reconnaissance by the New Zealanders over a period of several weeks had shown the northern approaches to the Sari Bair feature to be relatively lightly defended, whereas earlier attempts to probe the Turkish defences in the south had revealed strong positions at Gaba Tepe. Any attempt to break out here would certainly risk unacceptably heavy casualties.

In the northern sector, the New Zealand Mounted Rifles under Major Overton had made it their business to dominate the rugged country by aggressive patrolling. The Turks had reacted by recapturing what was known as No. 3 Post on one of the spurs leading down to Fisherman's Hut; this was an inconvenience and the post had to be retaken if a night march around the Turkish right flank was to stand any chance of success. A simple but ingenious scheme was devised. For three weeks before the attack a destroyer would approach the coast every evening at the same time and floodlight the Turks in No. 3 Post with its searchlight, then shell it for exactly thirty minutes before switching off and standing out to sea. On the actual night of the attack the same procedure was to be observed, except that an assault group of New Zealanders would be lying up close in to the Turkish post, ready to rush it with the bayonet the moment the light went out.

Once it was clear that Hamilton would receive three more infantry divisions, formed into a new corps, for the express purpose of renewing the offensive, Birdwood was obliged to postpone the left flank attack until all the new formations arrived. One of them, the 13th Division, was assigned to Anzac, as it had been the first to arrive and had already seen some trench service down at Helles, albeit in a strictly defensive and static role. The other two divisions, the 10th (Irish) and the 11th (Northern) were to be landed in Suvla Bay. The date of the offensive was put back to early August and Skeen set to work on a revised version, taking the Suvla landings into account.

Throughout the month of June, the New Zealanders had mounted numerous bold and skilful expeditions by night across the Suvla Plain and now knew a great deal about it. One patrol of the Canterbury Mounted Rifles made a useful discovery on the night of 20/21 June after landing from a warship on the northern side of the Kiretch Tepe ridge, which runs north-east from Suvla Point and constitutes the northern edge of the Suvla operational area. Unseen by the enemy, they moved south to the foothills of the Anafarta ridge and right on to the W Hills, where lay the Turkish gun lines commanding Hill 971. They observed numerous Turkish patrols but returned to the ship confident that the enemy was not holding the Suvla Plain in any strength. This was borne out by aerial photographs which pin-pointed gun positions – some of them dummies – and confirmed that there were few entrenched positions other than on Lala Baba and a few on top of the Anafarta ridge. Most importantly, there were no continuous lines of trenches and very little wire. In fact the garrison defending the Suvla area amounted to no more than two or three scattered battalions and a force of gendarmerie. Confidence grew at GHQ when these facts were reported.

What the staff did not know was that these scanty enemy forces were under the command of an exceptionally able German officer, Major Willmer. He knew the area like the back of his hand and frequently rode around the Plain noting, as the summer wore on, that the Salt Lake in its middle was rapidly drying up and no longer a barrier to infantry. A force put ashore at Suvla – which he regarded as inevitable – would be able to march straight across it and get on to what he correctly identified as the initial British objectives: the Chocolate and Green Hills; once on these, the British would have a useful springboard from which to attack the Anafarta feature and move up on to the Sari Bair range. Willmer therefore decided to offer battle to any landing force as early as possible, placing detachments on Lala Baba and Hill 10, wired in and supported by artillery fire. Late in July, Willmer's suspicions were confirmed when a British destroyer cruising in the bay fired a single round into the dried-up Salt Lake; he now felt sure an attack was imminent and that this shell had been fired to gain knowledge of the 'going' on the lake's surface.

From Suvla Point in the north to Nibrunesi Point is almost exactly two miles; the two points embrace Suvla Bay and afford a good sheltered anchorage. However, in 1915 the bay was only sketchily charted and de Robeck's staff were dubious about inserting the main landing force there until it had been checked. In this they were correct, for the bay is shallow and contains a number of unmarked reefs. It was on naval advice, therefore, that the initial landings were decreed south of Nibrunesi, where there are good beaches and shoal-free approaches.

The arena inland is flanked to the north by the Kiretch Tepe ridge, 650 feet high at its summit, running along the coast some four miles until it meets, at right angles, the Anafarta ridge which runs almost due south until it merges with the much higher Sari Bair massif. At its southern end the Anafarta ridge slopes away to a low saddle in the area of Biyuk Anafarta village before climbing up again into the main mass of high ground below Point 971. One look at this country reveals that whoever is in tactical control of the Anafarta ridge and the saddle around Biyuk Anafarta can dominate the plain below. Unless they wanted to be dominated throughout by Turkish guns on the higher ground, early possession of the Anafarta ridge was essential to the attacking force.

By the end of July, the Salt Lake was completely dry, a condition seldom encountered since, and rare enough before. However, 1915 was an exceptionally dry year on the peninsula, and by August only the barest trickle of brackish water was leaving the lake and draining into Suvla Bay through the narrow channel known as the Cut. The ground on the plain itself looked deceptively open from a distance; on closer inspection it turned out to be covered with patches of dense tinder-dry scrub, punctuated by a few miserable patches of cultivation and peasant farmers' huts. Agricultural activity was at a standstill in midsummer and the plain shimmered day after day under the oven-like heat. Although water was readily available on the Anafarta ridge, the plain boasted only a few near-dry wells producing unpalatably salty water which many of the animals would not touch.

As soon as he had received firm news of the additional three divisions on their way to join him, Hamilton was emboldened to ask for yet more, and on 28 June he telegraphed Lord Kitchener expressing his hopes of attaining success with the use of the three divisions but adding 'with four the risks of miscalculation would be minimized; and with five, even if the fifth had little or no gun ammunition . . . success could be generally assured.' Pending a reply, Hamilton went ahead with his plans.

Command of the IXth Corps had been given to Lieutenant-General the Hon. Sir Frederick Stopford. In 1915 he was 61 years old and had been retired for five years when war broke out. Commissioned into the Grenadier Guards in 1871, he had made his steady if unspectacular way up the ladder of promotion barely seeing active service, and had never commanded troops in battle. He had been an ADC in the Sudan campaign of 1884–5 and, ten years later, on the Ashanti expedition in West Africa. In 1899 he accompanied the ill-fated General Sir Redvers Buller to South Africa as his Military Secretary, returning to London with his master when the latter was dismissed after the disasters of 'Black Week' in December 1899, when the Boers inflicted resounding defeats on the British at the Modder River, Stormberg and Magersfontein. He had then become Director of Military

Training at the War Office and rounded off his career as GOC London District from 1906 to 1909. He was universally liked, a military historian of scholarly repute, the august officer commanding the Household Troops and an expert in ceremonial duties:

> ... the bemedalled Commander, beloved of the throne,
> Riding cock-horse to parade when the bugles are blown.

His amiable disposition and readiness to learn as much as possible about his new and frighteningly unfamiliar duties gained the respect of those who met him. However, Compton Mackenzie sat next to Stopford shortly after his arrival at GHQ and found him

> a man of great kindness and personal charm [but] whose conversation at lunch left me at the end of the meal completely without hope of victory at Suvla. The reason ... was his inability to squash the new general opposite, who ... was holding forth truculently about the plan of operation drawn up by the General Staff, while Sir Frederick ... appeared to be trying to reassure him in a fatherly way ... I longed for Sir Frederick to rebuke his disagreeable and discouraging junior; but he was deprecating, courteous, fatherly, anything except the commander of an Army Corps which had been entrusted with a major operation that might change the whole course of the war in twenty-four hours.

Although Mackenzie does not name this truculent officer, it seems to have been none other than Stopford's own chief of staff, Brigadier-General Reed VC, who had come straight from the Western Front where he had planned many set-piece frontal assaults against well-established trench systems, and considered lavish artillery preparation an essential part of any attack. Colonel Aspinall, another General Staff officer serving in GHQ, had the task of briefing Reed and found him obsessed with the need for overwhelming gun support, displaying incredulity when apprised of the IX Corps plan for the Suvla landings. According to Aspinall, 'he had the whole air of a man who does not think he is going to perform his task.' In vain did Aspinall show Reed the air photographs confirming the limited nature of Turkish prepared positions on and around the Suvla Plain. There appeared to be no more than three battalions of Turkish infantry, a few guns, a squadron of cavalry and a battalion of gendarmes in the area; Reed was disinclined to believe this, and communicated his doubts to Stopford, whose mind became infected by them to an extent that crippled the enterprise from the beginning.

Hamilton had not greeted the news of Stopford's selection with enthusiasm. He had wanted a far more lively commander for IX Corps such as Byng or Rawlinson, both of whom had made reputations for themselves on the Western Front as dynamic and thoughtful leaders. It seemed, however, that they lacked the required seniority. There were several lieutenant-generals apart from Stopford with prior claims for the next corps vacancy. One of these was Sir Bryan Mahon, who had insisted on retaining command of the 10th (Irish) Division, having raised it in the first place. In any case, Hamilton had already made it clear that he did not regard Mahon as fit to command a corps in battle. Kitchener seemed to agree, noting that Mahon, 'without being methodical, is a fine leader and has the confidence of his men. He knows his division thoroughly and has trained them well. He will shine more in a tight place or in a hard fight than in ordinary daily work.'

Mahon's division was held up as the first truly 'Irish' division to be raised in modern times. Although there were regular infantry regiments bearing illustrious 'Southern' Irish names – Connaught Rangers, Royal Dublin Fusiliers, Royal Munster Fusiliers and the Leinsters among them – there was no Territorial Force in Ireland, nor was there an ethnically Irish officer class. The regular Irish regiments recruited their overwhelmingly Roman Catholic soldiers in the south but their officers were drawn from amongst the Anglo-Irish gentry, predominantly Anglican, a class with an exceptionally strong martial tradition. When Kitchener's call for volunteers went out in August 1914 it was decided to create New Army battalions bearing the names of the Irish regular regiments; but the provision of officers immediately raised difficulties as each battalion required twenty-nine of them. But the problem was not just at officer level; the public's response to Kitchener's call in Ireland was nowhere near as enthusiastic as in mainland Britain or in Ulster, where virtually the whole of the previously illegal Ulster Volunteer Force, Sir Edward Carson's private militia, rushed to enlist, to form the basis of the magnificent 36th (Ulster) Division which went to France and suffered appallingly on the Somme.

To fill out the ranks of the 10th Division recourse was made to drafts from many quarters. A number of old soldiers, many well into their forties, were allowed to enlist in the Irish Kitchener battalions. There were more men from England in the two Munster battalions than Irish, although some of these were from immigrant families long settled in the Liverpool area. Recruits surplus to the needs of English regiments were then injected into the 'Irish' Kitchener battalions. The

6th Munsters received a draft from the Wiltshires and the 7th from the King's Own Yorkshire Light Infantry and the York and Lancaster, who made up half the battalion's strength. They were shipped over to The Curragh and soon became absorbed in their 'alien' units. In April 1915 the division was moved across to England for its final training at Basingstoke. By then it had acquired its own particular character, regardless of ethnic composition.

General Mahon worked hard throughout this period to create a good fighting division. He was constantly to be seen riding around its units as they trained, cigarette in long holder always in evidence. The troops took to him, liking his direct and friendly manner, and he gained the respect of his officers; he was clearly a good soldier with a style of his own, which he succeeded in imparting to the formation under his command. At Basingstoke, emphasis was placed on weapon training and musketry. Early in July Kitchener came to review the 10th at Basingstoke; as they marched past, the battalions saw a statuesque figure on a great black horse, expressionless as he acknowledged their salutes. Then they entrained for war and sailed to Mudros on the *Mauretania*. Arriving there on 19 July the division marched into filthy transit camps, where disease soon began to take its toll. When the 7th Royal Munsters embarked for Gallipoli three weeks later their strength had fallen from 1,000 to 700.

Planning went ahead for the great Anzac break-out. Birdwood had extended the scope of the attack to include the seizure of the highest point on the Sari Bair ridgeline, Point 971, as well as the Turkish gun positions in the areas of Chocolate and Green Hills. The ground to be traversed by the troops assigned to the 'left hook' was the most difficult on the whole peninsula. Birdwood required this force to advance in two columns; one to ascend the spur running up from the old No. 3 Outpost to Table Top and then on to Chunuk Bair, the other to go further out into no man's land off the Anzac left flank and turn right into the deep re-entrant known as the Aghyl Dere, where it was to split into two sub-columns. One of these was to march straight ahead and up on to Hill Q, the other to branch left and make for Point 971 along the Abdul Rahman Spur, attacking the objective from the north, in the rear of the Turks – if any happened to be deployed there. All this was to be undertaken by night, relying on dubious local guides and showing no lights, at best with a little assistance from the moon. The terrain was extremely rough, hard to negotiate even with good maps by daylight. This was asking the impossible of troops who, whilst eager for the fight, lacked training in night operations.

Only the lower reaches of the deres had been fully reconnoitred by the New Zealanders, for fear of arousing Turkish suspicions, and Birdwood had forbidden any form of preliminary exploration for this very reason. The plan provided for covering forces to occupy the lower ends of the spurs as firm bases from which the assaulting columns would begin their hazardous ascent.

Three other factors militated against success even at the planning stage; no one seems to have allowed for the tumbled nature of the ground, which reduced progress by even lightly equipped men to a crawl. Secondly, scant attention had been paid to the physical state of the units who were expected to bring off this daring operation. This particularly applied to the formation allotted to the capture of Point 971, the 4th Australian Brigade. Those of its veterans who survived were pitiful shadows of the magnificent men of the April landings; battle casualties and sickness had ravaged the ranks, now filled with inexperienced reinforcements lacking battle knowledge and stamina. The more experienced men were by now understandably sceptical and their old fire had largely dissipated.

Thirdly, initial landings would have to be conducted entirely without animal or wheeled transport. Everything needed for the immediate exploitation of the landings would have to be carried on men's backs: signals stores, engineer equipment, ammunition and, above all, water. The men would already be carrying heavy loads, for although they were not to be festooned with large packs or great-coats and blankets, they would have to carry 200 rounds of small arms ammunition and two days' iron rations. As each machine-gun section would have to go ashore with an extra 3,500 rounds in addition to guns, tripods and a generous supply of cooling water, the load would have to be shared out amongst the marching infantry. It would not be possible to send even the artillery's gun-team animals ashore before first light on the 7th, and thus any guns landed during the night would have to be manhandled into position.

In the next twenty-four hours a total of 1,267 animals would be brought ashore, together with 36 assorted guns and 650 carts and wagons; by this time it was expected that the front line would be well up on the high ground across the plain. The staff tables even provided for the landing, on the 7th, of 164 bicycles for the two divisional cyclist companies, whose roles were close protection for headquarters and message-carrying. For the first twenty-four hours at least, there would be no water carts ashore and the only method of carrying the precious commodity forward would be 8-gallon containers strapped to pack animals. Later on the 7th, the navy were expected to bring water lighters up to the beaches, where their contents would be pumped into collapsible containers on shore. Each soldier was to carry a full water-bottle, and all were enjoined to conserve this carefully. The inadequacy of these measures was soon to be most drastically exposed.

By the end of July the plan was almost complete. The main thrust, from Anzac, was placed under the command of Major-General Sir Alexander Godley, commander of the Australian and New Zealand division. Like many of the senior Anzac officers on loan from the British army, he was already cordially detested by his troops. In Egypt, prior to embarking for Gallipoli, Lady Godley is alleged to have shouted out to him at a review of the troops, 'Make 'em run, Alex!' and was also supposed to have insisted that soldiers in hospitals she graciously visited should lie to attention when she entered the wards. Godley was thereafter known to all ranks at Anzac as 'Make 'em run Alex', and now commanded little loyalty or respect from his men.

The day selected for the start of the great attack was 6 August. In an attempt to divert Turkish attention, the troops at Helles were to mount a 'demonstration' in the centre of the Allied line. Meanwhile, Birdwood called for a full-scale divisional attack at Lone Pine by the Australian 1st Division. Its commander, Major-General Walker, had started the campaign as Birdwood's chief of staff. Another British regular officer, he was a true 'soldiers' general' who jealously husbanded the lives of his men and feared no one. On the first night of the initial landings he had had a blazing row with Bridges and Birdwood when the idea of re-embarkation was mooted, and he now objected violently to flinging his splendid division against strong Turkish positions in the middle of the afternoon. He managed to gain a postponement until later in the day but still feared the worst. His men had been sapping steadily towards the Turkish line for weeks to create an ingeniously concealed front line only yards from the enemy position. A complete complex of fire trenches, firing bays and communications trenches had been prepared, all with full overhead cover. When the order to advance was received, the cover would be thrown aside and the assaulting troops would burst into the open and dash the remaining few yards into the Turkish trenches. Birdwood's idea in launching Walker's division at Lone Pine was to draw Turkish reserves off from the higher ground, thus enabling it to be taken more easily.

Meanwhile, during the three preceding nights, the 13th Division was to come ashore at Anzac and lie up in the newly prepared dugouts and galleries. The 29th Indian Infantry Brigade was also to be brought secretly ashore and hidden. After last light on the 6th, the New Zealanders would edge forward on the extreme left, clearing the Turkish outposts in order to provide a clear line of march for the left hook, culminating in the seizure of old No. 3 Outpost. Meanwhile the troops for the two 'left hook' columns were to be marching to the flank via the Great Sap – the huge thoroughfare of a trench which now extended right across the lower reaches of the Anzac positions, enabling troops to march three abreast. After dark, as the right column made its way up towards Chunuk Bair, the left column, which had much further to march, would move up the Aghyl Dere towards Hill Q and Point 971. If all went well, both columns would be on top by first light on 7 August; at this point the Australian Light Horse were to attack uphill from their trenches at the Nek and other attacks were to be made from Quinn's and Pope's. All this assumed that the 1st Division's attack at Lone Pine would have succeeded and that the Turks, penetrated and outflanked – and at Battleship Hill under attack front and rear – would be broken and in full flight.

At Suvla, the 11th Division was to start coming ashore immediately south of Nibrunesi Point at about 9 p.m. on 6 August with the aim of seizing Lala Baba as a launching base for further advances towards Chocolate Hill, which was to be taken by first light on the 7th, and across the Cut to Hill 10. Early on the 7th, the 10th Irish Division was to come ashore north of the Cut, to be directed along the crest line of the Kiretch Tepe ridge, advancing as fast as possible towards the Anafarta hills. By midday on the 7th at the latest, it was expected by GHQ that IX Corps would be well ashore and on to these hills, ready to support the main attack on Point 971. The front line at Suvla would be established with its left flank, guarded by destroyers, resting on the sea at Ejelmer Bay, and its right in touch with Birdwood's advance on the Sari Bair feature.

In addition to the three divisions of IX Corps, Hamilton had persuaded Kitchener to let him have two more divisions of the Territorial Force, the 53rd and 54th. They would be coming without their organic artillery, because of the scandalous shortages of ammunition at home. Undeterred, Hamilton abandoned his normal diffidence when dealing with the War Minister and made what he archly described as 'a temporary preferential claim' for extra gun ammunition to compensate for his lack of guns. His bid was for 15,500 rounds for the howitzers and for 400,000 rounds of all natures a month for two months. Casting caution to the winds he also asked for a battery of 4.5-inch howitzers apiece for 10 and 11 Divisions and eight extra medium and heavy howitzers; even these modest demands, however, could not be met. IX Corps was destined to go into battle with woefully inadequate artillery support. Those artillery pieces that were available were a mix of ancient mountain guns and worn-out 5-inch howitzers.

Hamilton's Director of Medical Services, Surgeon-General Birrell, was determined to avoid a repetition of the casualty evacuation scheme prepared largely by the General Staff which had failed so disastrously in April. He accordingly drew up a new medical plan for Suvla and Anzac envisaging 30,000 casualties in the first three days. Hamilton thought Birrell was unduly pessimistic and revised the figure down to 20,000. Birrell, in fact, was much nearer the mark, and another medical shambles was in the making.

The situation was further compounded by an absurd medical chain of responsibility. Following adverse comments on the April arrangements, a new functionary had been introduced. This was Surgeon-Admiral Sir James Porter, dragged out of retirement to be 'Principal Hospital Transport Officer', in charge of all the hospital ships and the misemployed transports known as the 'Black Ships'. His remit was to direct all movement of casualties, sick and wounded, naval and military, by sea in the Mediterranean. A Principal Director of Medical Services, Surgeon-General Babtie, had also been introduced into the system. Like Porter, his sphere of interest embraced the whole Mediterranean theatre. Porter's sphere of control was defined as extending 'from high water mark' (in a virtually tideless sea) and Hamilton had no control over his activities. The three senior medical officers were thus placed in an impossible position, none really knowing where his responsibilities began and ended.

Stopford had arrived in the theatre on 11 July. He was not in the best of health and at Victoria station, boarding the boat train, was so enfeebled that his ADC had to carry his briefcase. Before leaving London he had been personally briefed by Kitchener, who had made it very clear that once ashore at Suvla, IX Corps had to be handled with despatch if it was to secure the objectives assigned to it. Unfortunately, at this stage neither Stopford, nor indeed Kitchener, could have had more than the faintest idea of what was in store.

When he reached Hamilton, Stopford asked for some details of his corps' task but was told that it was all so secret that nothing could be vouchsafed at that stage. Instead he was sent over to Helles to gain some experience and it was there, on 22 July, that he received his initial operational instructions. These, Braithwaite emphasized, were to be treated with utmost secrecy and never allowed out of an officer's possession. This obsession with secrecy stemmed from the fact that the Greek islands, as well as Cairo and Alexandria, teemed with enemy agents searching for crumbs of information. Unfortunately, the 'need-to-know' rule meant that insufficient information percolated down to the combat units in time for them to brief their troops properly. The launching of the Suvla offensive was to be as much of a surprise to them as to the enemy.

From what happened thereafter it is clear that the instructions given to Stopford were insufficiently specific. The role of IX Corps, as Stopford afterwards claimed to understand it, was to secure Suvla Bay as the main logistic base for further operations to clear the Gallipoli peninsula and permit the unopposed entry of the battle fleet into the Sea of Marmara.

## 23

# The Grand Assault

The lines of wounded are creeping up to the
cemetery like a tide, and the cemetery is coming to
meet the wounded.

The Hon. Aubrey Herbert, Diary, 12 August 1915

AFTER SOME AGONIZING, Hamilton decided to direct the August offensive from his GHQ on the island of Imbros rather than go ashore to a forward command post at Anzac. Imbros was a logical choice, being more or less equidistant from Helles, Anzac and Suvla Bay, and underwater telegraph cables, laid by the Eastern Telegraph Company, now linked all three.

It had been decided that only a limited 'demonstration' would be possible at Helles; apart from the 29th Division, which had been made up to strength with a series of drafts from England, all the other VIII Corps divisions were at their last gasp; between them the 29th, 42nd, 52nd and Royal Naval Divisions could now only muster a bayonet strength of 26,000 against war establishments of 46,000. The two French divisions were even weaker at 7,500 apiece. The Turks, on the other hand, were well entrenched and in much greater strength. GHQ therefore gave VIII Corps a modest objective as its contribution to the great design; a limited attack on a frontage of no more than a mile to straighten out a Turkish salient. Artillery support was still at a premium, so the corps plan was for another two-phase attack, dangerously similar to that which had failed so miserably on 12 July. The first 'bite' would be taken on the afternoon of 6 August, and the second early the next day. Both would be launched in broad daylight.

The Suvla plan contained several anomalies, which Stopford does not seem to have questioned. He was directed to seize Chocolate Hill, not by a direct thrust across from Lala Baba – a distance of no more than two and a half miles even if the southern edge of the Salt Lake had to be skirted and only one and three-quarter miles if the troops marched across its dry surface – but by marching clockwise round the lake, a distance in excess of three miles, involving the crossing of the Cut and negotiating trackless scrubland in the dark. It was asking a lot of inexperienced officers, few of whom had enough training to lead a night march, and for their overburdened men with limited water the journey would prove too much. The success of IX Corps' landing and deployment ashore depended on meticulous adherence to a tight timetable; it was inevitable that it would fall victim to what Clausewitz termed 'friction' – the cumulative factors of delay, misunderstanding and sheer chance which conspire to bring down every military plan, however well considered, and however good the troops invòlved.

Hamilton was now under pressure from his French allies to divert at least two divisions across the water to the Asiatic side of the Narrows, from where at least eight batteries of Turkish guns were harassing the French rear in the Morto Bay–Sedd-el-Bahr area from less than 8,000 yards' range. Casualties were becoming so heavy that morale was seriously affected, never more so than when a chance shell destroyed the corps' reserve of *vin ordinaire* as it lay, ready for issue, on V beach.

Gouraud, who had lost an arm to these guns, wrote personally from his hospital bed to the French government, and the phlegmatic Bailloud, his successor, appealed to the French War Minister for action to be taken. When Kitchener was approached by his French opposite number, he sent an anxious signal to Hamilton who, mindful of his instructions to leave Asia Minor well alone, must have enjoyed drafting the tart reply: 'I am sure you will agree that a diversion, if and when necessary, must be made at my own time and not Bailloud's.' Kitchener, relieved, told the French that he could not impose on Hamilton to meet their request, and the matter lapsed.

The Helles demonstration got under way on time on the afternoon of 6 August. The objective was the tip of the strongly held Turkish salient astride the Krithia spurs. The 88th Brigade of 29 Division was to attack that afternoon and the 127th Brigade of 42 Division on the following morning. Each of these attacks was to receive the support of every available gun at the artillery commander's disposal, backed by the massed machine-guns of VIII Corps and the guns of the fleet.

Although Major-General Douglas of 42 Division had been in nominal command of VIII Corps since the departure of Hunter-Weston, *de facto* command reposed with the chief of staff, Brigadier-General Street. Thoroughly imbued with the spirit of his former chief,

Street was a born optimist who firmly believed in his own ability to devise a plan which would be far more than a mere demonstration and, given a fair wind, could propel the Turks out of Krithia and off the top of Achi Baba. The 88th Brigade now consisted of the 4th Worcesters, 2nd Hampshires and 1st Essex, with the 5th Royal Scots in brigade reserve. The assaulting troops had 300 yards of open ground to cross before reaching the Turkish trenches, exposed to heavy enfilading fire from both flanks. It was hoped that the massed machine-guns would suppress this for long enough to give the attackers a fair chance as they charged. The Turks waited for them in two lines of trenches, supported by a strong redoubt.

The fireplan supporting the attack started at 2.20 p.m. with an hour's steady bombardment by medium and heavy guns. At 3.20 the field artillery joined in. It was a calm, airless afternoon and the sun struck down pitilessly on the men crowded in the trenches. Great clouds of dust hung motionless over the battlefield, making conditions difficult for the artillery observers. At 3.50 the infantry went over the top and disappeared into the murk. All ranks were reported as being rested and confident, well briefed and cheered by the knowledge that for once they had not been set an apparently impossible task. When the Allied artillery started their bombardment, however, there was an immediate reply from over 60 Turkish guns of various calibres. Casualties mounted as the men went across the open, even though they could not see their enemy in the smoke and dust. To the rear, the corps commander designate, Lieutenant-General Davies, watched incredulously; he had come straight from the Western Front where gigantic artillery barrages were considered essential for the support of any attack; here, in front of his eyes, a set-piece attack was going in with less support than that given to a trench raid in France.

Within minutes, the 88th Brigade had been destroyed. Cayley, the brigade commander, could see nothing through the dust and smoke which had swallowed up his troops, two-thirds of whom were casualties within ten minutes. No information was coming back to him; most of the officers were already dead or wounded. Well to the rear, on the hill above W beach, the staff of VIII Corps were observing the distant battle through binoculars and sent an excited message to de Lisle at HQ 29th Division: the Turkish trenches had been taken – they could see the tin plates fastened to the backs of the infantry flashing in the sun on the enemy parapet and beyond. They were much too far away to realize that these plates were being worn by corpses.

Fortified by this false intelligence, de Lisle now sent in his divisional reserve, the 1st Munsters, to reinforce what he vainly believed was success. The commanding officer of this battalion, Lieutenant-Colonel Geddes, was already well forward and could see what had happened. At 9.10 p.m., preparing to comply with orders for a further attack, he sent a message to the brigade major of 86th Brigade asking if, given the confused situation around him, he should carry on. The reply he received was in the best tradition of bone-headed brutality to which the 29th Division was now well accustomed: 'The attack will take place as stated . . . The fact of another regiment being unable to take the enemy's trenches is no reason for the Royal Munster Fusiliers being unable to take them.'

Geddes, a strong-minded officer, would not stand for this. He sent another message, reporting the 'indescribable chaos' all around. He now had only 50 men of his battalion with him, he went on, all under very heavy and accurate fire. On his own initiative he told the 1st Royal Dublin Fusiliers not to proceed with the attack until the Munsters were in a fit state to do so. The brigade major now realized the true situation and postponed the attack in a signal which ended by exhorting the forward troops 'to get as much sleep as possible'. Geddes must have relished this. De Lisle was now getting news of the extent of his failure; by midnight it was clear that the Turks were still in full possession of almost all their trenches, and he called the attack off. Further bad news filtered back to HQ 29th Division during the night, confirming that 88th Brigade's part of the operation had failed.

Despite the dreadful reverse of the previous day, the 42nd Division was sent over the top on time at 9.40 a.m. on the 7th after a perfunctory artillery preparation. As on the previous day, all ranks were confident in their task and had been scrupulously briefed in detail. Despite this, the Manchester and Fusilier Brigades were immediately hurled back into their trenches. Within two hours the Manchester Brigade was the equivalent of a weak battalion. The net gain of the attacks of 6/7 August was the retention of part of the feature known as the Vineyard, which remained in the stout hands of the 6th and 7th Lancashire Fusiliers. The price paid for this minuscule gain was 3,500 casualties; the ability of VIII Corps to hold the line was now in question and Hamilton ordered a standfast.

After the battle, Lance-Corporal Morten of the 7th Manchesters wrote home to say that

> The last trip up in the trenches lasted three weeks and we have now come to the dugouts for a rest. I'm hoping to God that we shall not go back. I expect you will see in the papers that our brigade has made

another charge . . . came back early next morning after suffering heavy casualties. From the military point of view it was very successful but very costly in lads. The 6th fairly caught it, even worse than us.

At Anzac, Walker's battle plan for Lone Pine was for four battalions of Australian infantry to storm the Turkish trenches at 5.30 p.m. on 6 August, followed at midnight by another forward move into the next line of Turkish trenches and on to Gun Ridge. As zero hour approached, the Australians moved into their assault trenches. Two battalions were to emerge from the concealed underground trenches and dash for the enemy line whilst a further two battalions would charge from the main Australian position. The artillery preparation lasted for exactly an hour, then the infantry sprang into the attack.

Total surprise was achieved, but on arrival in the Turkish front line the troops were dismayed to find that the enemy had roofed his trenches with pine logs; although excellent air photographs had been used to prepare accurate trench maps and to brief the assaulting units, a lack of photo-interpretative experience had failed to note the overhead cover. Anxious watchers in the Australian main positions saw the attackers desperately wrenching at the logs covering the Turkish trenches, firing down through the weapon slits and embrasures, then disappearing into the darkness below, where a fight of frenzied violence took place. Fists, knives, bayonets, bombs and teeth were all employed as the foul-smelling underground stronghold was taken. The Turks fought as stubbornly as their attackers and for forty-eight hours the issue was in doubt. When sheer exhaustion compelled both sides to rest, the Turkish position had been taken, but at dreadful cost.

In the next line of Turkish trenches the garrison watched as their old front line began to bristle with Australian trench periscopes, silhouetted against the skyline, and they nervously prepared to withstand another Australian onslaught. As the battle raged, Australian soldiers from all parts of the beach-head swarmed towards Lone Pine to join in, many offering a month's pay to reliefs going up to the line for a place in the mêlée; regimental police had to be posted, most unusually, to stop unauthorized men going forward to join the attack. Seven VCs were awarded for this battle, in which 1,700 Australians fell. It was the apotheosis of all that the AIF stood for and the pinnacle of the Australian effort at Gallipoli. The Turks admitted to more than 5,000 dead. The attack served its purpose well, unlike the 'diversion' at Helles, for Essad Pasha, commanding the Turkish troops in this sector, now moved reinforcements to the scene.

Unfortunately, they arrived in the area in time to thwart the New Zealanders' drive for the summit of Point 971 and Chunuk Bair.

As the sounds of battle floated up from distant Helles and the Australians went magnificently into the attack at Lone Pine, the two columns detailed for the 'left hook' were silently marching to the flank of the beach-head. In addition to his own New Zealand-Australian Division, Godley had a mixed force under command: the 3rd Australian Light Horse Brigade, 39th and 40th Brigades of the newly arrived 13th Division and two extra British battalions, the 6th South Lancashires and the 8th Welsh. There was also the 29th Indian Infantry Brigade, still without its thoroughly disgruntled Mussulmans. The timing for the secret landing of these troops had been extremely tight and part of 29th Indian Brigade had only managed to get into the Anzac beach-head late on the previous night. The Gurkhas, habitually poor sailors, were still suffering badly from seasickness. Close fire support for the columns was provided by the mule-packed screw-guns of an Indian mountain artillery brigade. In addition to this force, Godley could call on the corps reserve, comprising seven new Kitchener battalions drawn from 10th Irish and 13th Divisions.

The two covering forces, charged with securing the lower slopes and spurs to guard the initial advance of the main columns, had set off immediately after a splendid sunset behind the distant island of Samothrace. Godley's staff were optimistic that the main columns would be clear on the summits by first light on the 7th, when the Australian Light Horse were to attack up Russell's Top from their trenches at the Nek, and other diversionary attacks were to be launched from Quinn's Post and Pope's further along the ridge line. After the capture of Baby 700 and Battleship Hill a general triumphant advance to Gun Ridge was planned.

Successful execution of this intricate plan called for precise time-keeping. Unfortunately for all concerned, this condition was not observed. Inadequate account had been taken of the appalling difficulty of the unreconnoitred terrain which the columns – particularly the left-hand one – had to traverse, heavily laden and at night. Also, Godley's staff appeared not to have noted the marked decline in the health and battleworthiness of Monash's 4th Australian Infantry Brigade. Of Monash himself, now past his 50th birthday, it was said that he could command a brigade better than a battalion, a division better than a brigade, and an army better than a corps; a brilliant Jewish immigrant engineer with a thirst for the profession of arms, he had mastered it as a non-regular citizen soldier and was to go on to command a corps in France. But on the night of 6 August he was exhausted and long overdue for a rest.

The men ascending the heights of Sari Bair were heavily laden with ammunition, tools, rations and water-bottles. They had been warned that once their iron ration was consumed, it could be forty-eight hours before more food reached them, and eighteen hours before their water-bottles might be refilled. Another matter which did not receive close attention was the reliability or otherwise of the locally recruited guides, Greek villagers who claimed intimate knowledge of the terrain.

Godley set up his tactical headquarters at the New Zealanders' No. 2 Outpost, a good choice for the opening phase of the operation but hopelessly out of touch – and sight – for subsequent operations planned for the morning of the 7th. The command post was further crowded by the presence of Major-General Shaw of the 13th Division and his staff. Initially all went well; the New Zealanders, in a brilliant attack, captured the Turkish No. 3 Post as planned, with the assistance of the nightly destroyer and its dazzling searchlight. The left column's covering force, under Lieutenant-Colonel Gillespie of the 4th South Wales Borderers, with his own battalion and the 5th Wiltshires, also did well, and the main left column pressed on and upwards.

The right column had possibly the easier task, for it had less far to go. It was commanded by Brigadier-General Johnston and consisted of his New Zealand Infantry Brigade supported by some mountain guns and sappers. The column was required to be on top of Chunuk Bair at least an hour before first light on the 7th and as no Turks were believed to be entrenched there it seemed that Johnston's task was straightforward. Unfortunately for all concerned, he proved a disastrous commander in this enterprise. For some time he had not enjoyed the confidence of his officers and men and was known to be drinking heavily to allay the strain of the campaign. He delayed his start on hearing the sounds of battle from the covering force ahead. The main column did not begin its march, therefore, until 11.30 p.m. Few Turks were encountered on the ascent, but the guides proved useless and the column, with frequent halts, steadily lost time. One battalion became hopelessly lost after going up the wrong re-entrant – an easy mistake to make even in broad daylight in that country – and went right back to its start point. Units were now hopelessly intermingled in the steep gullies, some countermarching and giving misleading instructions to others. As the first trace of dawn appeared in the eastern sky, Johnston's men were still far from their objective.

As the right column groped and cursed in the dark, the left column attempted to meet its demanding timetable; it had much further to go, over much worse ground. In view of this, Overton appointed himself as guide at the head of the column. Behind him came Monash's 4th Brigade, the 29th Indian Infantry Brigade under Major-General Cox (whose seniority over Monash made him column commander), a mountain battery, and a company of New Zealand engineers, 5,000 bayonets in all. Cox had only been at Anzac for two days and had absolutely no knowledge of the terrain to be negotiated by his men, and he hardly knew the units of his own brigade. With Overton as guide, the column initially made better progress than Johnston's and climbed steadily, if slowly, up the Aghyl Dere, then along the Abdul Rahman Spur, at the top of which a firm base was to be established from where the main assault was to be launched. Meanwhile the 1/5th and 2/10th Gurkha Rifles steered directly for Hill Q.

The Australians soon began to lag, as a result of lack of fitness and their heavy loads. It was clear that the head of Abdul Rahman Spur would not be attained by the appointed time of 2 a.m. as the column edged its way up the ever steeper slopes, slipping and falling in the dark and quickly losing cohesion. Nerves were overwrought and sudden waves of panic ran down the ranks, causing several rushes to the rear. Lack of experience in the 13th Division as well as in the Australian brigade was now apparent. At first light Monash found himself still down in the depths of the Aghyl Dere, almost alone except for the now wounded Cox and his Gurkha orderly. The Indian brigade had completely disappeared and was presumably seeking out the Turks on the upper slopes. The 4th Australian Brigade was exhausted, its men dropping in their tracks. Once down it was almost impossible to move them and the despairing order to dig in was given, to be obeyed by those who still had the strength or will to use an entrenching tool.

The Indians had in fact gone well ahead, still led by the inexhaustible Overton; but even he had to admit himself hopelessly lost on unknown ground. Undeterred, the 1/6th Gurkhas under Major Cecil Allanson had continued to push on and by 9 a.m. were only 1,000 yards short of Hill Q. The 14th Sikhs were still well to the rear, entangled with the right flank of the 4th Australian Brigade. A pause was now indicated for reorganization; sniping was continuous, and it was to a sniper's bullet that the gallant Overton now fell. Some of the troops began to prepare breakfast from their iron rations and to brew tea; others were unconscious with fatigue and could barely be roused. Momentum had been lost, and every minute that passed was time in which the Turks could rush reinforcements to the threatened heights.

At the Nek, dawn found the Australian Light Horse making final preparations for their attack. They lay astride the only direct route up to the immensely strong enemy position atop Baby 700, from which Turkish snipers had long dominated Monash Gully far below, claiming many lives including that of Major-General Bridges. The Nek is a very narrow humpbacked ridge and where the opposing lines faced each other at a distance of 60 yards, little more than 30 yards wide, with steep slopes down to each flank. The flanks of the substantial Turkish trenches here were further protected by machine-guns firing in enfilade from neighbouring spurs.

Birdwood's orders recognized the problems faced by the Light Horsemen and had provided for diversionary attacks to take place further down the main ridge to the right, against the Turkish trench system known as the Chessboard, and from Quinn's Post. Zero hour was set at 4.30 a.m., half an hour after first light. Waiting in their trenches, the attackers could hear the sounds of furious fighting from the direction of Lone Pine, and from the depths of the ravines below to their left could be heard bursts of firing as the 'left hook' columns struggled belatedly up the hills. Far away to the left, beyond the grand sweep of North Beach, lay Suvla Bay, where a great armada of warships, transports and landing barges was disgorging what seemed to be a considerable army; curiously, however, there seemed to be very little noise from that quarter.

The attacking force at the Nek was drawn from Hughes' 3rd Light Horse Brigade, with 300 men apiece from the 8th and 10th Light Horse regiments. Space permitted only 150 men to attack at the same time and the assaulting group was therefore divided into four waves. Their aim, after taking the Turkish trenches immediately up the slope to the front, was to advance and capture the Baby 700 position, then exploit to the summit beyond. After the first three waves had gone over, the fourth was to back them up and, carrying entrenching tools, to make good a strong defensive position on Baby 700, assisted by the 8th Cheshires.

The attack was to be preceded by a short but intensive artillery barrage; when this stopped at 4.30, the first wave was immediately to rush the Turkish trenches, carrying small red and yellow flags to mark progress. Morale and expectation ran high. The Light Horse represented the flower of Australia's manhood; drawn almost entirely from the agricultural and cattle-rearing communities of the countryside and outback, the men were supremely fit and active. This was their first real attack and they were determined to perform every bit as well as the infantry who had come ashore on 25 April. With fixed bayonets they waited impatiently in their trenches for the artillery preparation to end. Then, at 4.23, seven minutes early, the guns fell silent. In the eerie silence, the Turks could be seen manning their fire trenches and rigging machine-guns on the parapet, ready to fight off the inevitable charge. Something had clearly gone dreadfully wrong, most probably an error of synchronization between the gunners and the Light Horse. All hope of surprise had been thrown to the winds. Colonel White knew full well what was about to happen. No orders came for cancellation of the attack; shaking his adjutant's hand he led his regiment over the parapet and, with all the officers and most of the men who charged with him, was dead in seconds.

Major T. H. Redford of B Squadron, 8th Light Horse, had kept his diary faithfully since volunteering for the Australian Imperial Force in September 1914 in Victoria. Arriving at Anzac on 21 May, he had witnessed the armistice of the 24th when both sides buried their dead. On 25 May he had a grandstand view of the sinking of HMS *Triumph* and then served with his squadron in trenches on Walker's Ridge, facing the Nek. In early July he wrote of a Turkish attack:

> After an evening's rifle fire, Turks charged us at midnight after crawling to within a few yards of the 8th Light Horse positions. Held on strongly. Official estimate is of 300 Turks killed and captured. For next three nights, we dragged in Turk bodies and collected their rifles . . . 80 bodies, 113 rifles . . .

Not all the perils were confined to the front line. Redford reported on 14 July that 'One of the finest men in the brigade, Capt. Campbell, had both his legs blown off above the knees while undressing to go in for a swim; he died a few hours later. He was loved by all who knew him.'

Shortly before going over the top with the first wave of his regiment at the Nek on the morning of the 7th, Redford made some personal notes in the back of his diary and left it in the trench. The diary continues in another hand:

> B Squadron manned trenches on 5th August all day and all night. Relieved for meals, one troop at a time. Major Redford and Mr Henty were more serious than the other officers and seemed to realize the gravity of the situation . . . each man either took all his valuables or

packed them in his kit . . . a double issue of rum was given to each troop and as the night was very cold was found most acceptable. At 4 a.m. on 7 August a short bombardment by howitzers and warships, which did no damage, was succeeded by the word being passed round for the attack. Every man sprung out of the trench eagerly and crawled carefully for a few yards. Suddenly as they stood up . . . a terrific fire from machine-guns, at a range of ten yards, swept everything down. Men were shot down in wonderful fashion and never before have I heard such a terrific volume of fire . . . our gallant major, whilst lying facing the enemy trench, ten yards away, in the front of his men, received a bullet through his brain as he raised his head to observe. He died with a soft sigh and laid his head gently on his hands as if tired. A braver and more honourable man never donned uniform . . . the second line had jumped out of the trenches by this time . . . they were in the act of going past the first line when the awful hail of metal struck them. Not a man got a yard further and the same fate overtook the third line except in a good many instances the men were climbing out of our trenches . . . Colonel Miall of the 8th Light Horse was shot observing over the trench. As it was madness to press the attack further the order was given to the remnants to gather on the cliffs while the 9th manned the trenches supported by the 8th Cheshires . . . on going round the cliff face I could see only 14 unwounded men. Most in such a state of shock that it was impossible to get coherency . . .

Another survivor wrote of his troop commander's death:

Mr Wilson was foremost of the crowd and was crying 'Now then, Boys' when he got hit. However, he struggled bravely forward when a bomb seemed to strike him and he fell forward . . . beloved by all, a true and brave gentleman. He can never be replaced . . .

Ten minutes after the first wave went over, an area less than the size of two tennis courts lay piled high with hundreds of dead and dying Light Horsemen. A few managed to struggle back to friendly hands, but most were still lying where they fell when the War Graves Commission arrived at that dreadful spot in 1918 to clear the battle-fields of the unburied dead.

The Turks defending the Nek were in much the same position as had been the Australians in the Turkish attack of 19 May, when the defenders stood up on their parapets to get a better aim at an unmiss-able target. A few men managed to get into the Turkish trenches where they were immediately overwhelmed and put to death. The commanding officer of the 10th Light Horse had agreed with Major Todd, commanding the third wave, that it was futile to persist in the attack and ran to brigade headquarters, in a trench close at hand, to make this point. Hughes, the Brigade Major, told him that a flag had been seen on the Turkish trench, and that the third wave had to go. Todd and his men therefore went unquestioning to their deaths, and owing to a further misunderstanding, half the fourth wave had gone before the attack was halted. The Turks suffered no casualties at all.

The diversionary attacks at Pope's Hill by the 1st Light Horse and at Quinn's also failed with heavy loss, but at the latter, having seen the first wave of 50 men cut down, the officer in charge ordered the remainder to stay in their trench, undoubtedly saving their lives. In a matter of a few minutes, 650 officers and men had fallen – over half those committed to the attack. No useful purpose whatsoever was served by their sacrifice, for the New Zealanders in whose support they went to their deaths were still halted, under Johnston's inept leadership, a long way down below on Rhododendron Spur. The plan, with its grand aim of taking Point 971 by dawn on the 7th, had proved far too ambitious. The experienced troops who took part were too exhausted to give of their best, and the newly arrived drafts, British and Australian alike, were simply not up to the task required of them. The Turks were still in possession of the vital ground, and Liman, awake to the danger, was already redeploying his reserves to meet the threat.

The preliminary movements of the covering forces out on the flank of Anzac had been detected by the Turks late on the evening of the 6th, but not the approach from the sea of IX Corps, which did not close with the shores of Suvla Bay until well after dark. Liman realized, however, that the crisis of the campaign was at hand and sent a warning order to General Feizi Bey, commanding at Bulair, that his men should watch for any sign of a landing in the Gulf of Saros. Another order was sent to Major Willmer at Anafarta, directing him to shift one of his battalions across to watch the northern foothills of the Sari Bair range.

As the night wore on and messages reached him telling of the landings at Nibrunesi Point, Liman divined the Allies' intention; at 1.30 a.m. on the 7th he ordered Feizi Bey to release three battalions from the army reserves at Bulair and despatch them by a forced march towards the Suvla landings, in order to pre-empt any British move to picket the Anafarta ridge. Another message went to Wehib Pasha, commanding at Helles, ordering him to send his reserve division to the aid of Essad Pasha, which he did, albeit with much grumbling.

At this point, Colonel Mustafa Kemal Pasha realized that although Birdwood's attacks had been stemmed at all points, the summit of the

Sari Bair ridge was empty of Turkish troops and highly vulnerable to attack, and that if the Allies gained possession of this ground, the entire Turkish position overlooking Anzac would be hopelessly compromised. On his own initiative he immediately despatched his sole reserve of two rifle companies to the ridge and reported his action to higher headquarters. As daylight came he too was able to see the fleet of ships in Suvla Bay, and he knew that his moment had come.

# 24

# *Fiasco at Suvla – I*

Every commander who orders a night operation
which is not preceded by a complete reconnaissance
increases the risk of failure and incurs a heavy
responsibility. Reconnaissance from a distance is
insufficient.

Field Service Regulations, 1914

ON 24 JUNE Hamilton had viewed the Suvla Bay area from a
destroyer, cruising discreetly offshore. 'No sign of life, not even a
trickle of smoke . . . looks peaceful and deserted. God grant that it
may remain so until we come along and make it the other thing,' he
wrote in his diary. He was still optimistic as to the outcome of the
expedition. Even after watching the abortive and costly attack at
Helles a few days later, he could write that 'this is probably our last
onslaught before the new troops and new supplies of shell come to
hand in about a month from now . . . The Turks are beat. Five lines
of their best trenches carried . . . we have advanced 1,000 yards – a
wonderful show!'

Hamilton had been led to expect much from the Kitchener Army
divisions on their way to join him. According to a War Office letter
sent to him they were

well trained with fine personnel. From the training point of view there
is not much to choose between them but they might be phased in the
following order: 11th, 13th, 10th. The infantry is excellent and their
shooting . . . The artillery have fired well – the Royal Engineers, RAMC
and ASC are above the average. You will understand that the new
officers' knowledge is not yet instinctive, and allowances should be
made for this by the staff. If so, in a short time there will be no finer
troops in Europe.

What this letter did not point out was that the three divisions had
been trained up for the Western Front. They had no experience of

night work in open country or of amphibious warfare. They were also totally unacclimatized to the savage heat of the parched Gallipoli landscape in high summer, and highly vulnerable to the pathogenic organisms that would immediately assail their guts.

The first of the new divisions to arrive was the 13th, which was put into the line at Helles to gain experience in a strictly passive defensive role. Hamilton crossed over to Gully Beach on 17 July to inspect them: 'The men are very fit and cheery . . . De Lisle told me that one week had made the most astonishing difference to the savvy of these first arrivals of the New Army. At first, confusion, loss of energy and time; by the end of the first week they had picked up the wrinkles of the veterans.' As ever, Hamilton was ready to see the best in everything and everyone. Had he spoken to the officers and men of battalions in 29 Division who had handed their trenches over to the new arrivals he would have heard a very different tale; the veterans were aghast at the low standards of training and discipline prevalent in 13 Division, due almost entirely to the lack of experienced junior leaders. The troops themselves were pathetically keen to do their stuff, noted one regular officer. Major Hore-Ruthven, a staff officer in GHQ, believed that Stopford's headquarters, who knew the shortcomings of the Kitchener troops, deliberately suppressed any reports to GHQ which might have indicated substandard performance.

The next Kitchener division to arrive in the theatre was the 11th, commanded by Major-General F. Hammersley CB, who had raised it from scratch in August 1914. For nearly a year the division had been training for the Western Front and, as it turned out, their instinct whenever held up by enemy fire or under shrapnel bombardment would be to halt and dig. Hammersley's mental health was known to be frail. In a subsequent letter to Hamilton, de Lisle stated that he did not think he was fit to command a division:

> I thought it was a wicked thing ever to have sent him out there. It is well known that he had been in a lunatic asylum and he had recovered from that, and they sent him out there in command of a division of new troops, in a most important operation . . . here are absolutely new troops, and one of the three commanders I considered quite incapable of command.

Hammersley had been commanding a brigade at Aldershot in 1911 but then 'disappeared' for a time. He subsequently claimed to have suffered no more than a severe nervous breakdown; but his contemporaries, including de Lisle, all knew that he had been so disturbed that he had required physical restraint when undergoing treatment.

As Hammersley's troops sat in their unsavoury camps on Imbros they were severely affected by gastric disorders and dysentery, as well as by the effects of cholera inoculations; when finally marched to embark, all units were under their fighting strengh and well below combat fitness.

A final aerial reconnaissance of Suvla on 6 August confirmed that there were very few Turkish troops in the area, that apart from the strongpoints on Lala Baba and Hill 10 there were no continuous trench lines, and only a few pieces of artillery were in a position to threaten the landings. In view of this it is difficult to see why Hamilton refused to use the 29th Division to spearhead the Suvla landings and make the dash for the Anafarta ridge, a task well within the grasp of this formation; instead, it was left at Helles where its 88th Brigade was allowed to suffer unacceptably high casualties in the 'demonstration' of 6/7 August. The true reason for Hamilton's reluctance is apparent in a revealing letter he wrote in 1917 to one of the former Suvla naval beachmasters:

> The fact is that I am not a big enough commander altogether to suppress feelings of fair play and humanity. The 29th had carried out the most terrifying landing recorded in the annals of war and had been practically wiped out since then. If my General Staff had miscalculated the enemy forces, or, if our plan had come to the enemy's ears . . . the troops landing on the night of the 6th of August might have been met by the fire of a couple of Turkish divisions and a hundred field guns. These are the sort of risks a commander must take and expect to be judged by results, but to subject the 29th Division a second time to this particular type of ordeal was, I felt, just a bit too hard.

Whilst Stopford was temporarily commanding VIII Corps at Helles in order to gain some experience of operational conditions on the peninsula, he had been visited by Lieutenant-Colonel Aspinall, of Hamilton's General Staff. Aspinall gave him a briefing on the outline plan of operations for IX Corps and Stopford, according to Aspinall, expressed his satisfaction. It was, he said, exactly what, in broad outline, he had hoped would be decided on, that 'it was a good plan, and ought to succeed.'

Returning from Helles, Stopford opened his corps headquarters on Imbros. Here he fell firmly under the influence of his chief of staff, Brigadier-General Reed, who was appalled by the scanty artillery available to IX Corps and brushed aside Aspinall's assurances that there were few Turks in the Suvla area and only a handful of guns. Speed was the essence of the plan; once the high ground on the far side of the Suvla Plain had been seized, the Turks would have been outplayed. Success in this was essential by first light on the morning following the landings in order to give maximum support to Birdwood's left flank.

On the afternoon of 6 August, as the troops on Imbros and Mitylene were preparing to embark for their first operation, Aspinall visited HQ IX Corps to wish them well. He found Stopford in his tent, lying on a camp bed. He had, it was explained, wrenched his knee badly. He asked Aspinall to tell Hamilton that 'he was going to do his best, but if the enemy turned out to be holding a strong line of entrenchments it would be impossible to dislodge him till the arrival on shore of many more guns.' It was clear to Aspinall that Reed had been telling Stopford all about set-piece attacks in France, of which Stopford knew nothing. Once more, Aspinall stressed the need for rapid forward movement after the landings. Although he left feeling that he had made his point, he was not to know that Stopford had already settled for a much more limited aim and would be happy merely to get ashore; the capture of the Chocolate and W Hills would be no more than a bonus.

After dark on 6 August the armada carrying the 11th Division closed with the coast. In the lead were ten destroyers, each carrying almost a thousand men, with trawlers and ramped lighters in tow. More boats followed. Further back were the transports bringing two brigades of the 10th Division from Mitylene. At 9.30 p.m., still undetected from the shore in the pitch darkness, the destroyers silently dropped anchor and the men transhipped into the lighters and picket boats which were to ferry them ashore. Not for them the agonizing crawl in rowing boats such as had taken the Anzacs and the 29th Division to their beaches on 25 April. The 'beetles' were a huge advance; armoured against small arms fire and capable of carrying 500 men apiece, they offered the prospect of setting the troops ashore dryshod. Apart from the low throb of their engines they approached the beach in silence. The troops had been warned not to fire their rifles until daylight and to use the bayonet only. They wore white armbands as a means of recognition in the dark.

There was no response from the shore until the first lighter grounded and within thirty minutes four battalions were ashore and making for their first objectives. Two marched off to the east to guard the right flank of the landings and two, the 6th Yorkshires (Green Howards) and the 9th West Yorkshires, made for the low humpback of Lala Baba, silhouetted against the night sky less than a mile ahead. Once its Turkish garrison, estimated as a rifle company, had been dislodged, the battalions were to move north, cross the Cut, and link forces with the 34th Brigade, which was to land inside Suvla Bay on A beach. Together, the combined force would assault Hill 10 and march at once around the northern edge of the Salt Lake to seize Chocolate and W Hills before daylight. On the map this may have seemed perfectly feasible; it was to prove well beyond the capacity of 11th Division.

As the 6th Yorkshires moved in towards Lala Baba they were conscious that they were the first of Kitchener's New Army to go into battle, and all ranks resolved to give of their best. However, conditions were totally unlike anything encountered in their months of training at home. They were already extremely tired, for the day had started on Imbros with some vigorous training and only after lunch was the news broken to all ranks that they were to embark that afternoon for Gallipoli. Many were sick and all were suffering acutely from vaccine reactions. No maps were issued until late in the day and when it was realized that a night landing was contemplated it was discovered that few of the officers had received training in the use of the prismatic compass; indeed, there was a distinct shortage of these essential bits of equipment. Apart from one shambolic exercise a few days earlier on Imbros, the brigade had never attempted a night march across open country. The battalions had left their camps late in the afternoon and then marched to the boats; there followed a three-hour voyage in the dark, during which the troops had time to think of what might lie ahead. As a result, they were tired and tense on arrival off Suvla.

Some minutes after the landing, a red signal flare rose above Lala Baba, announcing that the Turks had been roused. The Yorkshiremen moved eagerly forward, still in silence, and got on to the top of Lala Baba, where a bloody fight ensued before the Turkish garrison withdrew in the direction of the Salt Lake. As a result of their inexperience the attackers suffered heavy casualties, particularly amongst junior officers, easily recognizable as such even in the dark; the white armbands also made things easier for the Turks. In the aftermath of the assault the Yorkshires fell into the vacated enemy trenches and tried to reorganize, a task made harder by the state of shock into which many of the men now lapsed, and the unpleasant discovery that many of the junior officers, whose courage far exceeded their military prudence, had fallen.

By midnight, 34 Brigade was coming ashore in Suvla Bay, but things began to go badly wrong when some of the lighters went aground on uncharted reefs. The troops had to go over the side into six feet of water and as many were non-swimmers there were scenes of panic and confusion until ropes had been rigged to help them ashore. They were also now under increasingly heavy small arms fire and casualties began to mount even before contact was made with the enemy. Soon, soldiers were disregarding orders, blazing away with their rifles in all directions, and there were numerous cases of units firing on each other as their officers vainly endeavoured to restore order.

On the beach, groups of men were setting forth hopefully inland, some getting immediately lost. Many men were landed south of the Cut instead of to the north and units became inextricably mixed. One unit, the 11th Manchesters, stayed together and resolutely set off up the Kiretch Tepe ridge, aiming to get as far along it as possible by first light. Their machine-gun officer had already shown his worth by recovering a Maxim which had fallen off a lighter into deep water, cleaning it on the beach with the contents of his men's water-bottles and getting it into action up on the ridge. (He was killed a few days later.) The battalion had covered nearly two miles along the crest when they were brought to an abrupt and bloody halt by well-posted Turkish gendarmerie.

At 3 a.m. on the 7th, most of Brigadier-General Sitwell's 34th Brigade was still afloat. The 9th Lancashire Fusiliers were casting around vainly trying to identify Hill 10. With the aid of the newly risen moon Turkish snipers were taking steady toll, killing the commanding officer of the Fusiliers and adding to the general agitation and confusion. In the hour before dawn, when British troops should have been fast approaching the Anafarta foothills, two brigades were stationary in the area of Lala Baba, the Cut, and the beach. There was no sign of forward movement and only half the division was ashore. Many units were still marooned on boats aground well out in the bay. Sitwell managed to get on to the beach at 3.30 a.m., by which time his brigade was hopelessly disorganized. Neither he nor his staff could identify Hill 10, their objective. Even in daylight it is hard to pick out and on that night it eluded detection for several hours.

Brigadier-General Haggard of 32nd Brigade now sent some of his troops from Lala Baba as directed, to assist Sitwell who was launching the bewildered remnants of the 9th Lancashire Fusiliers in an attack on a sand dune which he firmly believed to be Hill 10. When the Fusiliers got on to this feature they found that Hill 10 was still 400 yards away, its garrison firing briskly at them and causing yet more casualties. Piecemeal attacks were now being made by small bodies of men at any Turkish positions, real or imaginary, and there were more fights between sub-units of the same battalions.

At GHQ, Hamilton had spent an anxious night waiting for news from IX Corps. A cable had been laid across from Imbros to Suvla before midnight and Hamilton's staff watched the telegraph dial for the first twitch announcing a signal. None came. On board the sloop *Jonquil*, which had dropped anchor in Suvla Bay shortly after midnight, Stopford decided that as all appeared quiet apart from odd bursts of firing, he would sleep on deck alongside Rear-Admiral Christian, in command of the naval force. Hammersley got ashore shortly after this, already displaying ominous signs of nervous stress, and after setting up his divisional headquarters on Lala Baba, ordered Haggard to send all available troops to the assistance of the floundering Sitwell. No attempt was made by Stopford's headquarters to send an officer ashore to find out what was happening; the corps staff, like their commander, had a tranquil night.

Dawn broke to reveal a sorry scene. The bay was filling up with transports and warships and the beaches were still under effective rifle fire. Gaggles of leaderless men were wandering around looking for their units. Instead of being firmly installed on Chocolate Hill, Hammersley's division was only partly on land, huddled around the beaches in great confusion. Its commander seemed oblivious to events around him. Stopford, afloat in his sloop, was totally out of touch and exercising no control over the mounting shambles. The naval officer in command of the armoured lighters – the 'beetles' – was none other than Commander Unwin, lately of the *River Clyde*. As daylight revealed the chaotic scene in the bay he started to sort things out. Grounded lighters and trawlers had to be towed into deeper water, and safe routes sounded to the beach so that disembarkation could continue.

At 2 a.m. there had been a flutter of excitement at GHQ when at long last, after four hours of silence, the telegraph sprang into life. Each word of the message from Suvla was read as it came through: 'A little shelling at A beach has stopped and all quiet at B.' That was all. There was no originator's identification, neither was the signal addressed to anyone in particular. It was in fact no more than the work of a bored telegraphist sitting in the dark on Nibrunesi Point, chatting up his colleague on Imbros. For the rest of the night the telegraph remained silent. It was enough, however, to convince the ever-optimistic Hamilton that the landings had gone according to plan.

On the opposite side, Liman was much better informed. He received a message from Willmer early on the 7th telling him all he needed to know: the British had landed at 9.30 the previous evening

and had taken Lala Baba whose garrison had withdrawn to the line
Kiretch Tepe–Chocolate Hill, where they confidently awaited developments. The disembarkation, according to Willmer, was continuing
and he urgently called for reinforcements.

At daybreak on the 7th, more troops were arriving in Suvla Bay,
having sailed overnight from Mitylene. These were two brigades of
Mahon's 10th (Irish) Division, the third brigade having been
detached to Anzac to take part in the main attack there. Instead of dis-
embarking both brigades on A beach as planned, one was put ashore
to the south of the Cut. At this stage the division was temporarily
under the command of one of its brigade commanders, Brigadier-
General Hill who, apart from knowing that he was required to march
up Kiretch Tepe and take over from the Manchesters, had no idea as
to where they were. At Mitylene he had been completely out of touch
with Mahon and had received no instructions or maps from him, or
from Hammersley's 11th Division, under whose command he now
found himself. When Mahon arrived he was in an ambiguous position: ashore at Suvla, a senior lieutenant-general, with none of his
three brigades under command. Strings of conflicting orders now
found one of Hill's brigades on the far side of Lala Baba, where it was
to remain detached for some days, and the other at the northern
extremity of Suvla Bay.

Mahon's division, when he recovered partial command, therefore
comprised only three infantry battalions, the divisional pioneer battalion and three companies of engineers. The divisional artillery was
still in Egypt, and the 10th (Irish) Division was fated never to fight as
a complete formation while at Gallipoli. Mahon, never one to suffer
fools gladly, was already fuming at the incompetence of his superior
headquarters and of his fellow divisional commanders. His despair
was shared by many of his junior officers. Lieutenant Douglas Piggis,
commanding a platoon of the 5th Royal Irish Fusiliers in Hill's 31st
Brigade, wondered:

> How GHQ thought that to land the whole of the 11th Division in the
> dark on a strange shore and a few hours afterward, land two brigades
> of the 10th Division on top of them could possibly be successful passes
> the comprehension of even a junior officer . . . At the actual landing my
> battalion lost the senior major, two captains and the adjutant killed
> and 12 officers wounded. I never saw my colonel for two days.

From his vantage point on Lala Baba, where he enjoyed an excellent panoramic view of the whole Suvla area, Haggard could see
Sitwell's brigade wandering around at the north end of the bay

looking for something to attack. Along the beach north of the Cut the 5th Dorsets and 8th Northumberland Fusiliers had dug themselves in, for no apparent reason, on the edge of the beach, having made no attempt to advance inland. Hill 10, at 5.30 a.m., was still held by the Turks, although Sitwell was convinced that his men had captured it. A hesitant move inland was under way by 8 a.m. but in the area of the Cut a disorganized mass of men was still milling aimlessly around, occasionally lying down as distant shrapnel bursts were seen. Lala Baba was packed with units of 33 Brigade. As the morning wore on it was clear that the Turks had pulled back to take up new defensive positions on the Chocolate and W Hills. There were now almost no enemy troops on the plain and nothing to stop a general advance. Despite this, 11th Division did not stir.

Hammersley now issued a series of contradictory orders. At 8 a.m. he ordered 32nd and 34th Brigades forward to 'push on vigorously to Chocolate Hill' whilst Hill's 31st Brigade was to protect their flank. No move, however, was to take place until Hill's battalions were in position. At this point several well-aimed shells landed on Hammersley's headquarters, killing and wounding a number of officers and soldiers in front of him. The *Official History* confines itself to saying that Hammersley 'was naturally much shaken'. In fact, his nerves, never strong, began finally to collapse from that moment. He cancelled the earlier order. Haggard and Hill were now to advance on Chocolate Hill, but no mention was made of Sitwell's brigade.

At 8.45 a.m. Hill, now thoroughly concerned, came in person to Hammersley for instructions; he was told to link up with Haggard north of the Cut and advance with him to Chocolate Hill. Hill pointed out that as he was actually part of Mahon's 10th Division, he ought to revert to its command. This was ignored by Hammersley, who issued yet more orders to Haggard just after 9 a.m., conflicting with those just given to Hill.

Haggard was now alongside Sitwell, who was issuing orders on his own initiative, being the senior of the two. He was upset that Haggard's latest instructions made no provision for his brigade and shortly thereafter cancelled the orders he had just issued, and declined to take any further action. In his subsequent evidence before the Dardanelles Commission Hill stated that Sitwell now told him that 34th Brigade was incapable of advancing because its battalions had suffered very heavily during the night and were 'much done up'. Haggard was now in an embarrassing position: technically he was under Sitwell's command, but Sitwell had elected to do nothing; Haggard therefore obeyed what he took to be his last orders from

Hammersley, which were to attack Chocolate Hill with the four rifle companies immediately available to him.

All this time, the two battalions sent south-east from B beach before midnight to set up a line of defence covering the right flank of the landings had achieved their objective and were only one and a half miles from Chocolate Hill, which they could have occupied without a fight until 6 a.m. by marching for less than forty-five minutes. On the far side of the Salt Lake, brigade commanders were arguing furiously over the next stage in the operation; it was abundantly clear that 11th Division had ceased to exercise control, if it ever had done. As Haggard, Sitwell and Hill could not reach agreement, the advance came to a halt; the troops sat down and brewed up. In the fierce sun they soon became dehydrated and listless. Water-bottles were dry by mid-morning.

Desultory enemy artillery fire began to inflict casualties. Haggard, who had been hit by a spent bullet early in the morning (he had pulled it out of his thigh and carried on), was now seriously hit by a shell splinter and had to be carried off. Sitwell was again offering every excuse he could find for not going forward; water shortage and the heat were now added to what he claimed were 'heavy losses'. He also declared that his brigade no longer had any offensive capability, despite patrol reports now reaching him that the plain ahead was virtually free of Turks. Hill was still edging forward at the north-east edge of the Salt Lake, even though Sitwell's inertia had left his flank wide open on the left. Hammersley then issued an order prohibiting all forward movement. A new attack was to be made at 5.30 p.m.

All over the beach-head commanding officers and staff officers dashed around, wild with frustration as they sought to locate their scattered units and bring them under control. More battalions were being fed in and two were now seen taking a short cut across the open surface of the lake to join Hill's right flank. Together they all moved towards Chocolate Hill and the final attack went in at last light. More by luck and the dogged bravery of the infantry it succeeded, and the Turks were driven off the hilltop as darkness fell. IX Corps' timetable was now running eighteen hours behind schedule.

Five battalions had become intermixed on the summit of Chocolate Hill and the night was spent in sorting them out. The men, dog-tired, dropped into trenches filled with Turkish and British corpses and had to be kicked into activity. With dawn came the frightening realization that it had been a very costly operation. Hill's brigade had lost 20 officers and 400 men and the two battalions of 33rd Brigade which had joined the attack had lost between them 7 officers and 226 men.

These casualties had been inflicted by no more than 500 Turks and a few field guns.

Lieutenant Piggis' platoon of Royal Irish Fusiliers had been in the thick of this fight: 'My platoon fought their way through shelling and hidden snipers to Chocolate Hill at about 7 p.m. . . . Major Johnston told me to line the hill, find out whether there were any troops on our left and dig in until morning.' This they did, under heavy fire from Green Hill, less than 400 yards away, and from strong Turkish positions on Scimitar Hill. Next morning the Irish took Green Hill and spent an unpleasant day there without reinforcement, ammunition or water. There was universal execration of Hamilton for not sacking the corps commander on the spot.

It was apparent to all ranks that the campaign was being grossly mismanaged. Piggis recorded:

> My brigade was on board the SS *Andania* from 6 July to 7 August, with one route march through Alexandria . . . the officers were allowed to land [at Suvla] in officers' uniform, Sam Browne belt and all – they were picked off by plucky snipers camouflaged in the stunted oak trees and scrub on the left of the Salt Lake . . . by 16 August my battalion was reduced to the colonel, the new adjutant, another officer and myself, and about 180 men.

On the left flank of the Suvla beach-head, while the muddled attack on Chocolate Hill was taking place, there had been long delays as the rump of 10th Division got ashore, formed up and then set off hopefully along the Kiretch Tepe ridge. To begin with, the order to land was countermanded and some units had to go back on to the trawlers. Their bemused commanding officers were reluctant to disembark again when ordered to do so until an exasperated Commodore Keyes appeared and told them that as their brigade commander, Nichol, was ashore and waiting, it might be a good idea to join him on the beach. The 6th Munsters therefore came ashore late in the morning, but in doing so, detonated some landmines on the beach; this delayed the disembarkation of the 7th Munsters who beached at 1 p.m. The 5th Royal Irish, the divisional pioneers, came ashore at teatime and some of Mahon's troops did not arrive until early on the 8th.

The two Munster battalions moved up the ridge during the afternoon and duly caught up with the Manchesters, who were at their last gasp following their splendid effort of the previous night. Many of the men had been without water since shortly after landing and were in a very bad way. In less than twenty-four hours the battalion had lost 15 officers and over 200 men; the stunned survivors were sent back to the beach and the Munsters dug in without pressing the resolute Turkish gendarmerie, whose main defence works were actually another 400 yards further along the ridge. Water-bottles were empty, and men were discarding kit, such as heavy wirecutters and pickaxes, which would be badly needed in the days ahead. Fortunately, it was possible to obtain limited supplies of drinking water from a destroyer which came close in to the foot of the cliff below the Munsters' positions.

In its first twenty-four hours ashore IX Corps achieved very little but lost 100 officers and 1,600 men to a Turkish defence at no time numbering more than 1,500 soldiers and gendarmes. Willmer had fought a copybook action and had disengaged effectively.

The navy's landing plans had turned out as disastrously as the army's. Rear-Admiral Christian had openly expressed his doubts as to the feasibility of the landings, but gained confidence when initial opposition turned out to be light. His plans began to come apart with the unexpected grounding of many of the lighters out in the bay. This forced last-minute changes of landing beaches and a consequent mixing-up of battalions, leading to prolonged delays and loss of operational efficiency. No guns were brought ashore on 7 August, and only 50 mules.

Christian, like Stopford, seems to have suffered from a lack of urgency. In particular, the water lighters brought across from Imbros under tow early on the 7th went aground well offshore and because of delays in freeing them, no bulk supplies of water came shore until much later in the day. By then, groups of thirst-maddened men were wandering around the beaches, at times fighting each other in their search for water. Elsewhere the water situation was at least partly met by the discovery of wells in the Lala Baba and Kiretch Tepe areas. The forward troops, however, were suffering dreadfully as the result of a lack of mules to take water supplies to the firing line and many soldiers had been reduced to drinking their own urine by the end of the day.

When Stopford's first situation report arrived at GHQ at noon, its news was already several hours old; nonetheless Hamilton was dismayed to learn that Hill 10 had still not been taken and that most of IX Corps was still in the immediate area of the beaches. Even so, Hamilton neither said nor did anything at this point to prod Stopford into action. At 4.20 p.m. he could bear the suspense no longer and at his direction Braithwaite telegraphed Stopford: 'Have only received one telegram from you. Chief glad to hear enemy opposition weakening and knows you will take advantage of this to push on rapidly.' If Braithwaite or Hamilton thought that this would have a quickening effect on Stopford they were in for an unpleasant shock on the following day.

At first light on 7 August the three Turkish battalions summoned from Bulair fell in and immediately set out for Suvla. Liman, now certain of the British plan, ordered Feizi Bey to alert two more of his divisions at Bulair and get them moving at once in the wake of the first three battalions. To sustain the defence until the arrival of these reinforcements, Willmer was given several squadrons of cavalry for dismounted use in the Anafarta area. They had deployed there by midnight on the 7th as the Turks displaced from Chocolate Hill prepared their defences carefully to meet a further British advance. Willmer had watched the hesitant forward progress of IX Corps from an observation post near Anafarta village for most of the day. He noted, with a professional's cold detachment, all the signs of ill-trained troops: bunching, poor fieldcraft, reckless exposure, and apparent lack of co-ordinated effort.

The entire front held by Willmer's little force of some 1,100 bayonets extended for over two and a half miles and all along it an army corps was being easily restrained. The British artillery had been ineffectual and the fire support of the fleet had caused neither damage nor casualties. As the sun went down, the three battalions which had marched all day from Bulair in blinding sun arrived in bivouacs about four miles behind the Anafarta ridge. They had covered well over thirty miles between dawn and dusk over poor tracks and were exhausted. Willmer allowed them a good night's rest as their reward. Further back down the peninsula marched the two divisions alerted by Liman. Unless the British got to the top of the ridge early on the 8th their battle would be lost.

Had he but known it, Stopford still had victory in his grasp. He vastly outnumbered Willmer and with reasonable urgency could have been on the ridge by last light on the 7th in some strength, only twelve hours later than planned. But inertia had set in. The troops were tired, baffled, dehydrated and hungry. They were also aware that monstrous mismanagement was depriving them of what might once have been a famous victory.

# 25

# *The Struggle on the Heights*

The great thing now was to push on everyone, at all
costs. Alas! it was not done.

Major Allanson, 1/6th Gurkhas

BY MID-MORNING on 7 August several battles had already taken place
on the Sari Bair ridge and its approaches. A dreadful silence reigned
over Baby 700 and the Nek following the destruction there of the
Light Horse, whose bodies lay in piles on the narrow strip of ground
in front of the Turkish trenches. At 6.30 a.m. Johnston's New
Zealanders began to move forward again. With Brigade HQ, the
Auckland and Wellington battalions pressed on to the point known
as the Apex, where they were pinned down by heavy Turkish fire.

Despite the crucial hours already lost, Johnston ordered both battalions to halt and dig in, pending the arrival of reinforcements. Little
did he realize that his other two battalions were at that moment on
the move and struggling up to join him. The Turks were desperately
holding on, heavily outnumbered and on the point of breaking; but
Mustafa Kemal's headquarters was close at hand on the far side of
Battleship Hill and from here he ran the battle. By 10 a.m., Johnston's
chance had gone for ever and the Turks were holding the crest in
overwhelming strength. Despite this, the Auckland battalion gallantly attacked at 10.15. They lost 250 men in the three assaulting rifle
companies but managed to secure a foothold on the Pinnacle.

Major-General Cox, commanding the 29th Indian Brigade, realized
the urgency of the situation, and obtained permission to call up
Godley's reserve brigade to augment his drive for Hill Q and Point
971. This was Baldwin's 39th Brigade of untried Kitchener battalions:
the 9th Royal Warwicks, 7th Gloucesters, 9th Worcesters and 7th
North Staffords. Owing to lack of experience, the difficulty of

navigating in this tumbled country, and the unmitigated chaos reign-
ing on the lower slopes of the hills, only one of the battalions, the 7th
Gloucesters, reached Cox. The others, led astray by poor guides and
conflicting instructions, had marched off in almost the opposite
direction and soon became hopelessly embroiled in the mass of
humanity and animals struggling in the nullahs. It was almost dark
when they were found and marshalled into position, and it was clear
from their condition that they could not be used offensively until the
following day.

Godley's HQ, still far away at No. 2 Outpost, was completely out
of touch with the battle, reliant on information many hours old. The
night of 7/8 August was one of unimaginable confusion as formations and units tried to reorganize and resupply in the dark, harassed
continually by Turkish artillery fire and the ever-present snipers who
punished anyone rash enough to show a light.

On the spurs above the Aghyl Dere the men of the 29th Indian
Brigade grappled as best they could with a situation for which even
their experience on the North-West Frontier had not prepared them.
Second-Lieutenant Savory's battalion, the 14th Sikhs, recovered from
its terrible experiences in Gully Ravine, had recently spent several
weeks on Imbros, training and absorbing new drafts. Amongst these
was an entire rifle company from the State Forces of Patiala, who, as
Savory noted, were 'magnificent men but poorly trained'. There was
a new Subahdar-Major to replace the one killed on 4 June. Sham
Singh turned out to be 'a tower of strength. Tall, soldierly, dignified,
strict . . . the *beau idéal* of the Sikh (or any other) soldier.' Savory and
his fellow officers explored the island and found a tiny monastery
high in the hills where they went as often as possible to enjoy the
tranquillity, home-made bread and wine, and hours of silent medita-
tion and prayer before returning to the slaughter on Gallipoli. It was
an idyllic interlude and Savory would remember to the end of his
long life the sound of the chapel bell as it tolled for evening prayers.

The 14th Sikhs arrived at Anzac early on 6 August and went into
hiding at once. Consequently, none of the officers had any knowledge of the terrain over which they would be called to fight within
hours. They first took part in the initially successful attacks on the
Turkish outposts. A German officer was captured in his pyjamas and
the Sikhs almost succeeded in rushing a Turkish battery as it lim-
bered up and got away. Then the guides lost their way and at first
light on 7 August they were still far from their objective. The men
were tiring and there was no one from higher headquarters to give
orders to the battalions jammed in the nullah.

During the night of 7/8 August orders were received for resumption of the attack at 4.15 a.m. The battalion was still scattered and there was no liaison with flanking units. It was decided to use only two companies, under Major MacLean; but Savory did not find him until 3.30 a.m. The orders were for an assault on Hill Q with the 5th Gurkha Rifles, with the Australian 4th Brigade on the left. Nobody knew what or where Hill Q was, for it was not marked as such on the maps issued. The men were still asleep where they had dropped at last light and many had to be physically kicked into action. Talking quietly with MacLean, Savory was shocked when the major showed him a box of opium tablets, which he carried in case he was seriously wounded and out of reach of stretcher bearers, to end his own life rather than lie out in agony for days. He agreed to administer them, however, if MacLean was unable to do so himself.

At 4.15 a.m. the advance got under way; not directly towards Hill Q but up the Abdul Rahman Spur. This was well off course, but the Australians and Sikhs pushed on with fixed bayonets. Suddenly they were confronted with a deep ravine. At this moment the Turks opened up a devastating fire. MacLean fell, muttering about his opium pills, then died. Savory was now alone, the only British officer in the battalion as far as he could see. Shell scrapes were dug and the men lay down, most to fall asleep immediately despite the hellish noise.

With full daylight came a magnificent view of the fleet in Suvla Bay, from whence came no sounds of battle. Up to the right a continuous roar of firing floated down from Chunuk Bair. Then the Sikhs and Australians came under close-range artillery fire. The exhausted Australians began to fall back on the left and the Sikhs fell back too. Soon, they were on their original start line. Out of MacLean's two companies only one officer – Savory – was on his feet, with 69 men. The remnants of the battalion were now mingled with the Australians and the rest of the day was spent in reorganizing. During the night of 8/9 August these remnants struggled back once more up to the head of the Aghyl Dere, immediately below Sari Bair.

Not until the early morning of 9 August did the 14th Sikhs receive any replenishment of water, rations or ammunition, when the battalion's mules managed to get as far as the entrance to the Aghyl Dere. Savory now concentrated on getting these up to what was left of his men, making numerous journeys up and down the Aghyl Dere with the mules. After dark there were numerous alarms and during one of these a rabble of British troops came down the nullah in full flight without their weapons, led by a red-headed officer. Savory vainly

ordered them to stop, then drew his revolver and blazed away ineffectually at the rapidly disappearing officer. As he forced his way up
the Aghyl Dere against the press of officers and men deserting their
posts he felt that the scene resembled the bursting of a dam. It was
appalling, and he was not surprised, further up the valley, to come
across the commanding officer of a Gurkha battalion and a wounded
subaltern of his own regiment sitting side by side, weeping uncon-
trollably. That night, Savory visited the British battalion placed in
reserve behind the 14th Sikhs. Under a tarpaulin the commanding
officer sat with some of his officers. They offered Savory some rum;
he then noticed that one of those present was the embarrassed red-
headed officer at whom he had so recently emptied his revolver.

The fate of the 6th Gurkhas, watched from below by Savory and
hundreds of others, resulted from orders given to Major Allanson,
their commanding officer, to attack over the crest at first light on the
8th. He was told that extra British battalions from the 39th Brigade
would be made available in his support, but in the confused situation
most did not reach him where he lay with his men within a hundred
yards of the crest line. One unit which did was part of the 8th
Warwicks, in which Lieutenant William Slim was commanding a
company as its sole surviving officer. Slim took his men over to report
to Allanson and realized he was in the company of professionals.
What he saw in the next few hours would change his life and leave
him with the ambition – duly consummated – to soldier with
Gurkhas for the rest of his days.

On Allanson's right the revived New Zealanders, in the form of
Malone's fine Wellington battalion, had managed to gain a foothold
on Chunuk Bair, where the Turkish garrison had been blasted out of
their shallow trenches by naval gunfire. The Wellingtons took their
chance, leaped into the vacated trenches and began frantically to dig,
knowing that they would be counter-attacked in strength.

Things had not gone well for Monash and his 4th Australian
Brigade, which had made another drive for Point 971 but walked into
devastating machine-gun fire. It was the first time that Australians
had been seen to flinch, then turn tail; but these were not the men of
25 April, and in any case they had been driven far beyond what
should be expected of any troops. Early in the afternoon, therefore,
it was decided to postpone the main attack on the summit until the
following day.

The New Zealanders held out grimly on Chunuk Bair. They were
alone now, for the Gloucesters on their immediate left had been
overrun after a stubborn fight which later drew the unqualified

admiration of their opponents. The Wellingtons were forced to yield some of the summit but, helped by survivors of the Gloucesters and by the Royal Welsh Fusiliers, continued to beat off every attack. The Turks charged again and again and the shallow trenches became clogged with the dead. A terrible blow was sustained when a mis-placed salvo from the fleet mortally wounded the gallant Malone. Not till last light was it possible for the Wellington Mounted Rifles and the Otago battalion to get up to the relief of Chunuk Bair, where only 70 men of Malone's battalion were still on their feet. The Royal Welsh Fusiliers had lost 17 officers and 400 men and the 8th Gloucesters all their officers and nearly 400 soldiers. Of all the Kitchener units at Gallipoli, theirs had been the cruellest introduction to war.

In his autobiographical notes, Mustafa Kemal gives an insight into the qualities that made the Turkish peasant soldier such a formidable opponent at Gallipoli. Of the great Turkish charges earlier in the summer at Quinn's and Courtney's, when the Australians had stood up on their parapets for a better sight of the masses charging towards them, Kemal writes:

> We are not concerned with acts of individual heroism but I cannot pass on without telling you of the happenings . . . The distance between opposing trenches was 8 metres, that is to say death was almost certain. Those in the first trench all succumbed, knowing that they could not be saved. Those in the second trench took their place. But with what enviable calmness and confidence! They saw the dying, they knew that they would die in about three minutes, but they showed not the least dismay, there was no wavering! Those who could read prepared to enter Paradise with the Koran in their hands; those who could not, recited the Martyrs' Prayer as they went forward. This is a remarkable and praiseworthy example of the morale of the Turkish soldier. You must realize that it was this high morale that won the Dardanelles campaign.

At an early stage on the night of 6/7 August, Mustafa Kemal real-ized that the British aim was to extend their left flank in order to break the Anzac deadlock. He had for some time been training his subordinates with war games based on a British landing north of Ari Burnu and a 'left hook' attempt. Despite his strong representations, none of his superior Turkish generals was inclined to support this view. He identified the chief threat to the main Turkish position as stemming from the long re-entrant reaching down from Chunuk Bair towards Hill 60 and correctly foresaw the attack which would be launched (disastrously, as it turned out) by the British and Australians around the flank of Hill 971 in August. He took great pains to familiarize himself with every detail of the ground and was thus in a far better position to fight the battle, when it came, than the likes of Godley, Cox or Johnston. Kemal became exasperated beyond measure when his corps commander, after a heated discussion of likely future British moves, patted him on the shoulder and told him not to worry, for the British would not and could not bring such an operation off. As Kemal wrote later, 'Seeing that it was impossible to put over my point of view, I felt it unnecessary to propose the argument any further. I confined myself to saying, "God willing, Sir, things will turn out as you expect."'

Kemal had placed his division at a high state of readiness during the night of 6/7 August and spent a sleepless night at the end of a telephone line in a forward observation post. Early in the morning the Australians attacked and were thrown back everywhere. Although Kannengiesser managed to hold the vital high ground, there were signs that the Turkish 9th Division was cracking and Kemal's 19th Division was threatened by the advance towards Chunuk Bair. As telephone lines began to fail, units of other divisions were sending panicky messages to 19th Division.

By first light on 8 August, Kemal knew that the New Zealanders had got up on to Chunuk Bair because his ADC, sent there to investigate, was killed at once. A second party confirmed the worst. A huge fight was raging on the summit and his own headquarters was under accurate small arms fire. On his own initiative, and as the chain of command had clearly broken down, he sent a message to Essad Pasha, commander of the Northern Group, earnestly requesting that the army commander be informed and that it was essential 'for the security of the nation' that something was done immediately to secure the high ground. Perhaps, at this moment, he had detected a slackening of resolution in the Turkish High Command and sensed that his moment had come. Later in the day he managed to get to a telephone, over which he spoke with Liman. He gave his assessment of the situation, that not a moment could be spared if defeat was to be averted, and that unified command of the situation was essential. He was now emboldened to propose himself as overall tactical commander. When Liman suggested that he would have too many troops under command, Kemal replied crisply that there could hardly be enough.

At 5.55 p.m. on 8 August Liman ordered Essad Pasha to throw the

7th Division, the leading reinforcement from Bulair, straight off the line of march into the attack at Anafarta. The attack did not get off its start line. Kemal later found out that Feizi Bey, bringing the reinforcements from Bulair, received Liman's order and passed it on to the divisional commander who pleaded that his troops were prostrate after their forced march and in no state for battle. Feizi reported this to Liman, who sacked him on the spot, giving the command at Anafarta to Mustafa Kemal.

Kemal's first task was to mount an attack at dawn on the 9th. As he wrote in his memoir: 'Thus to take on the responsibility for a new task with troops I did not know and in a completely vague and unknown situation was no mean task . . . I however accepted this responsibility with pride.' Handing over his division to Colonel Sefik Bey, commander of the 27th Regiment, he briefed him carefully before going across to Anafarta. He had not slept for three days and nights and was kept going with injections given by his personal medical officer, Hussein Bey.

All eyes and hopes were now on Chunuk Bair and the fortunes of the New Zealanders. The 4th Australian Brigade could not help them as it was still immobile amongst the nullahs and spurs below Point 971. All over the battlefield, British, Australian, New Zealand and Indian soldiers were moving as if in a nightmare, filthy, unshaven, bleeding and bewildered. The dead, men and animals alike, lay where they had fallen, unburied and unknown. Stretcher bearers fought against torrents of humanity in the congested ravines as they tried to carry the wounded down for some basic first aid before returning to the beaches, where the evacuation system once more threatened to break down, leaving them in their hundreds on the shore, subjected to the merciless shrapnel. Stragglers, many without weapons or equipment, were making their way off the summits, unrestrained by regimental police posted to turn them back but themselves long since drawn fatally into the bloodbath. Bearer parties and mules struggled up the gullies, laden with water, rations and ammunition. Over all was the stench of death, dust, smoke, flies, an overwhelming airless heat, and the unremitting thunder of battle.

At dawn on the 9th the New Zealanders were still holding on at Chunuk Bair. Further over to the left, Allanson's Gurkhas and Slim's Warwicks, with two companies of South Lancashires in reserve – some 450 bayonets in all – were pressed against the side of the steep hill only a hundred paces from the summit of Hill Q. Late the previous evening Allanson had received a message from Cox which made it quite clear that he was to do much more than merely support the attack on Hill Q; he was actually to carry it out, with whatever troops he could muster. 'By 5.15 a.m.,' the message went on, 'when bombardment ceases, it must be your aim to have the whole regiment close under the steep crest within assaulting distance and ready to join in the charge. Any British troops with you, you must take up with you in similar manner; orders to that effect have been issued to the troops of the 39th Brigade.' Allanson sent down for more water, rations and ammunition but was told that if he wanted them, he must provide his own carrying parties. Resigned to what he had to do, he despatched a final prophetic message just before midnight: 'Please note my position carefully; some of these naval high explosives are coming frightfully close to us and it is important tomorrow's support should not catch us.'

Allanson spent most of the hours of darkness going around the units on either flank of his battalion, asking for all the support they could muster in the morning. He had 300 Gurkhas to seize 300 yards of Turkish trench on the summit; he was sure that if he got into the enemy trenches he would be promptly counter-attacked with bombs, but felt that his soldiers could deal with this. All he wanted was the assurance that substantial reserves, in the form of 39th Brigade's infantry, were at hand in case of crisis. Apart from the South Lancashires and the company of Warwicks, however, he had been unable to convince the commanding officers of the British battalions that they should commit their units unconditionally to the attack. They were apologetic, but had no orders. Neither had Allanson; but at least he knew what was needed and did his best to bring it off. During the night a confusing order did reach him: he was to try to get up on to Point 971 after the barrage lifted at 5.15. Hill Q was to be tackled by five fresh British battalions. In default of a visit to the front line by any senior officer, Allanson felt he was being lumbered with responsibility for the entire attack.

Battalion HQ of the 1/6th Gurkhas spent a sleepless night; the Turks had discovered how close to the summit they were and kept them under continual fire. At 4.30 a.m. Allanson was poised for the attack:

> The roar of the artillery preparation was enormous; the hill was almost leaping underneath one. I recognized that if we flew up the hill the moment it stopped we ought to get to the top . . . I had my watch out, 5.15 a.m. I never saw such artillery preparation; the trenches were being torn to pieces; the accuracy was marvellous . . . 5.18, it had not

stopped and I wondered if my watch was wrong. 5.20, silence. I waited three minutes to be certain . . . then off we dashed all hand in hand, a most perfect advance and a wonderful sight.

(Although Allanson was unaware of it, Godley, who had at last left his headquarters at No. 2 Outpost, was afloat in a destroyer and, with all his staff, was watching the Gurkhas through field glasses.)

The Turks were ready for them at the top of the hill and savage hand-to-hand fighting broke out, kukri versus bayonet. It went on for at least ten minutes. Allanson noted that 'blood was flying about like spray from a hair-wash bottle'. Fists, teeth, clubbed rifles and entrenching tools were now being used. Suddenly the Turks broke and ran. Allanson and the survivors stood gasping on the summit. For a few tantalizing minutes they had a view for which thousands had already died: the entire Turkish rear areas spread out below, with guns, staff cars, gallopers, columns of infantry frantically marching to the sound of the guns; and further away, seductive in the early morning light, the silver-grey waters of the Narrows, only four miles distant.

Catastrophe was violent and quick. As the Gurkhas attempted to consolidate their gain, a salvo of heavy artillery landed in their midst. Allanson, to his dying day, would assert that it came from the guns of the fleet; but as he was clearly over on the reverse slope, where high velocity naval guns would not have been able to place their fire, it seems far more likely that these shells came from a 'friendly' battery controlled by observers further down Pine Ridge, who would have seen tiny figures moving on the upper slopes but would have assumed that they were Turks. Allanson remained on the crest for a few more minutes with a handful of dazed survivors, but then had to retire. No other units had been able to get up in his support and he appeared to be the only officer still on his feet, albeit bleeding heavily from a bayonet wound. Slim had also been brought down; his batman supported him all the way down to the dressing station, then bravely returned up the hill to his death.

The British brigade tasked for the attack on Point 971 had meanwhile gone hopelessly adrift; it eventually arrived in the area of flat ground known as the Farm, below Chunuk Bair, where stood a small shepherds' enclosure. Here the Turks stood their ground and another bloody fight took place.

As Allanson made his way down the hill for medical treatment he received first aid from Captain Phipson, the battalion medical officer, who had set up his aid post just below the lip of the hillside. Phipson,

as the only surviving British officer, now found himself in command
of what was left of the 1/6th Gurkhas. Earlier, he had been knocked
off his feet by the six mighty explosions of the salvo which did for the
assaulting group, and he now had to cope with the flood of casualties resulting from this and the earlier fight at the top. Those hit by
the shells were a ghastly yellow colour, the result of the lyddite filling
which led Allanson to believe that the shells were from the fleet.
Allanson's last words to Phipson as he was carried away were 'Do all
you can to help Gambarsing Pun'. This was the Gurkha Subedar-
Major, an old and experienced soldier who now, to Phipson's relief,
took over as *de facto* commanding officer, as the officer sent to relieve
Allanson, Major Tomes of the 53rd Sikhs, was killed within half an
hour.

After caring for all the wounded, Phipson tore off his Red Cross
brassard and, brandishing a revolver, set off to find reinforcements.
A short way down the hill he came on a battalion of Kitchener troops

> comfortably disposed in a small open glade . . . having a hearty meal
> from steaming field kettles . . . I explained our situation to the CO, who,
> in answer to my earnest request for reinforcement, firmly and rather
> indignantly refused, saying he could not think of disturbing his 'lads'
> who had not eaten a square meal since breakfast that morning.

In disgust, Phipson gave up and returned to his battalion. When he
sent messages to the units still in position on his flanks – the 4th South
Wales Borderers, 9th Worcesters and 6th South Lancashires – they
replied that they had either retired, or were about to, or believed that
they were about to be attacked. It was now well into the evening;
Phipson sent a message to brigade headquarters, where Allanson
was still debriefing and receiving medical attention. The reply came
that every effort would be made to relieve the Gurkhas that night.

Phipson and the remnants of the battalion spent another sleepless
night, continuously sniped and bombed by the Turks, who at times
got to within thirty yards. Early on the morning of the 10th, a
message came from HQ 29 Brigade: Phipson was to retire on to the
next main position held by friendly troops. At this point, Gambarsing
came into his own. Schooled on the North-West Frontier, he knew the
drills for evacuating pickets by rote and performed them to perfec-
tion, explaining each step patiently to the doctor:

> I marvelled at the precision with which he described the different
> phases of the retirement and the proper precautions to be taken; such
> as the removal and disposal of the bolts of rifles which could not be

taken, of surplus ammunition, collection of stores, destruction of equipment, and the timing of the movement itself . . . to retire 900 feet down a rocky declivity, intersected by deep and narrow gullies, many of them choked with corpses, and the infinitely difficult job of carrying down the wounded . . .

It is doubtful if any other unit under Birdwood's command on that terrible evening behaved with the classic professionalism of the 1/6th Gurkha Rifles.

Whilst the Gurkhas were fighting their way up to Hill Q the battle for Chunuk Bair continued. By first light on 9 August the Turks were massing for a decisive counter-attack to sweep the New Zealanders off their toe-hold. Hamilton came across from Imbros and Suvla during the morning for an urgent consultation at No. 2 Outpost with Birdwood and the divisional commanders at Anzac. He was near despair after the events of the previous two days at Suvla and knew that all remaining hope of success lay with a breakthrough at Anzac; to this end he even offered to divert the newly arrived 54th Division, straight off the boat, in order to maintain momentum at Anzac; the offer was declined on the grounds that the injection of yet another division into the grossly congested beach-head would place intolerable strains on the water supply. Birdwood made a counter-proposal: that the 54th should be deployed from the Suvla beach-head in an attack on the Anafarta ridge, where IX Corps was stalled at the bottom of the foothills, apparently unable to move forward.

The command structure at Anzac now verged on the bizarre. Two Major-Generals – Godley and Shaw (the newly arrived commander of the 13th Division) – sat uneasily alongside each other; Johnston was placed under Shaw's command for the time being, pending the relief of the New Zealanders on Chunuk Bair by Kitchener battalions on the night of 9/10 August. Unfortunately, the fighting of the past thirty-six hours had resulted in a total mix of units and the tenuous communications system, reliant on telephone cable and runners, was on the verge of complete breakdown.

After dark on 9 August, the battered Auckland and Otago battalions were relieved on Chunuk Bair by the 6th Loyal North Lancashires. The New Zealanders' casualties had been appalling: in Auckland, 12 officers and 308 men; in Otago, 17 and over 300; and of the 173 officers and men of the Wellington Mounted Rifles who had gone into the fight, only 63 remained unwounded. Two and a half companies of the 5th Wiltshires were brought up to support the

Loyals but so great was the congestion in the corpse-jammed trenches at the summit that they had to remain just below the crest. The Wiltshires had not slept for nearly three days and as soon as they arrived they piled arms, took off their equipment and fell exhausted to the ground without attempting to dig in.

Dawn on the 10th found the Loyals still in possession of the trenches vacated by the New Zealanders. Some survivors of the Wellington battalion were posted at the Apex, with elements of the 6th Leinsters from 29th Brigade (from Mahon's Irish division, part of which was five miles away at Suvla, on Kiretch Tepe ridge). In addition, the massed machine-guns of the New Zealand Brigade were sited at Apex to give close support to the Loyals. The crucial point in the British defence was therefore held by a *mélange* of units drawn from four different brigades and three divisions. The senior commanders had never met each other and Shaw in particular was a total stranger to Anzac, with no personal knowledge whatever of the terrain in which his troops were fighting.

Further around to the left flank, in the area of the Farm, a similarly anarchic situation obtained. Here were units of Baldwin's Brigade, mingled with the 10th Hampshires (29th Brigade), the rest of 5th Wiltshire (40th Brigade), the 6th Royal Irish Rifles (29th Brigade) and one and a half companies of the 9th Royal Warwicks (39th Brigade). Two brigade headquarters were sited yards from each other on the edge of the Farm plateau. On the opposite side of the Aghyl Dere were the 6th East Lancashires (38th Brigade) and the rest of 10th Hampshires. Between this group of loosely associated battalions was Monash's 4th Australian Brigade and a mixture of Gurkhas, elements of 39th Brigade, the rest of the Warwicks, and fragments of the 6th South Lancashires, 9th Worcesters and 7th North Staffords. If ever there was a prescription for military confusion, it lay here.

Godley's command, clear-cut on the evening of the 6th when the columns had set off so confidently for the flank march, had effectively disintegrated. It was no longer able to offer a co-ordinated defence or mount any form of attack. The outcome now depended entirely on the fortunes and courage of individual soldiers and their immediate leaders; it was a soldiers' battle with no perceptible chain of command. The troops were tired, hungry, thirsty and, in some units, demoralized.

Shortly after dawn on the 10th, the great Turkish counter-attack was launched. Despite fierce resistance, the Loyals were overwhelmed by sheer weight of numbers on top of Chunuk Bair; their commanding officer and nine other officers, with nearly 500 men, were never seen again. As the survivors tumbled down the reverse slope, they found the Wiltshires still not under arms and with rifles piled. Both units continued down the hillside in disarray. The Turks also got back on to the Pinnacle, but then the New Zealand machine-guns and the Leinsters at Apex caught them in the open and wrought great execution.

As the Turkish tide swept the Loyals and the Wiltshires away down the reverse slope of Chunuk Bair, another full-scale assault, Mustafa Kemal's right wing, descended like an avalanche over the flank of Chunuk Bair and on to the Farm. There were so few survivors here that no clear account can ever be given of what happened. Baldwin fell in close combat alongside his brigade major. The Warwicks – or what remained of them – were wiped out. The headquarters of 29th Brigade was overrun and every one of its officers killed or wounded. It is probable that the slaughter around the Farm that terrible morning surpassed even that at the Nek or in the Turkish attacks on Pine Ridge earlier in the summer. Brigade and battalion commanders fought and died shoulder to shoulder with their troops to show how the often reviled Kitchener units could behave in battle. The Turks' casualties were horrific, for as their massed ranks emerged over the skyline they presented a target which the guns of the fleet could not miss.

Meanwhile, Captain Phipson and the devoted Subedar-Major were extricating the survivors of the 1/6th Gurkhas off Hill Q. The situation was now critical and Birdwood threw the 5th Connaught Rangers in at the Farm; they arrived there in the afternoon, having marched round from Lone Pine, and reoccupied the plateau, rescuing large numbers of wounded who had been abandoned there. The Farm, however, was totally exposed to fire from above; the Rangers' position was untenable and they were taken off to the spur running to the north-west and known as Cheshire Ridge.

By last light on the 10th Birdwood realized that his attack had failed, with more than 12,000 casualties. The fate of the wounded was so appalling as to exceed the worst that had occurred on 25 April. As nearly all the battle casualties had occurred high up on the ridgeline, the problems of getting them down to the beach were immense. No man on earth could be expected to perform what unit stretcher bearers had to do, without respite, for over four days and nights. As Savory and others observed, the nullahs leading up to the firing line were clogged with stretcher cases, many *in extremis*, awaiting collection from regimental aid posts, where men like Phipson worked

unceasingly to save as many lives as possible under conditions
redolent of a mediaeval butcher's shambles.

In addition to the wounded streaming down from the heights there
was the no less pressing requirement to tend and evacuate rocketing
numbers of seriously sick. In the week of the Sari Bair fighting, over
10,000 of these had to be added to the toll of battle. At the beaches
there were insufficient small boats to take casualties out to the hospital ships and converted transports waiting offshore. Once aboard
the latter, the wounded fared little better than those of the April landings, and the passage to Alexandria was punctuated by numerous
burials at sea. Although Hamilton's estimate of casualties had
proved more accurate than that of the pessimistic Birrell, it was the
inadequate provision of hospital shipping that did for so many who
might otherwise have survived. Much of the problem undoubtedly
stemmed from the curious system arranged for control of casualty
evacuation which had brought Sir James Porter out as Principal
Hospital Transport Officer. The War Office had never been happy
over his appointment (which, curiously enough, can be seen in hind-
sight as a laudable attempt at 'joint command') and he was quietly
removed back to England in November.

The battle for Chunuk Bair and the Sari Bair ridge had been lost,
and with it the last real hope of victory at Gallipoli. Hamilton's spirit
could have been broken, but if it was, he gave no outward sign. On
the evening of the 10th, as the curtain came down on the great battle,
he wrote in his diary: 'The Turks knew they were done unless they
could quickly knock us off Chunuk Bair. So they have done so. Never
mind – never say die.' But in his heart, taking into account what had
occurred over the last sixty hours at Suvla, he must have known that
defeat stared him in the face.

# 26

# Fiasco at Suvla – II

No information as to the operations and plan of
action was mentioned and no information was given
as to what our side was trying to do.

> Commanding officer, British infantry
> battalion at Suvla

ALTHOUGH CHOCOLATE AND W Hills were in British hands by last light
on the 7th, the following day saw a display of military incompetence
which, with the failure of the great Anzac offensive, was to spell the
doom of the entire expedition.

Dawn on the 8th found Stopford well rested after his night on the
deck of the *Jonquil*. All was quiet on shore, with only the occasional
crack of a distant rifle to suggest that military operations were in
progress. Hammersley had at last caught up with all his brigade commanders, but when he suggested that a forward move should be
attempted they declined; none of them had yet managed to locate all
his battalions, and Mahon, with one brigade perched up on Kiretch
Tepe ridge, one wandering around the shores of the Salt Lake and
another engulfed in the struggle at Anzac, could barely trust himself
to speak to his fellow divisional commander. So for the time being,
the corps remained motionless in the area of the bay, despite the fact
that it could have walked almost unopposed up on to the Tekke Tepe
ridge, beckoning invitingly across the plain, only four miles distant.

In default of action, Stopford issued an order of the day congratu-
lating his troops; he also contacted Hamilton on the barely used telegraph to tell him how well the landings had gone, despite 'strenuous
opposition'. He also added that he now intended to consolidate
ashore and land the supplies, ammunition and other stores still afloat
in the bay. Hamilton responded in a message reflecting little anxiety:
'You and your troops have done splendidly. Please tell Hammersley
how much we hope from his able and rapid advance.'

The morning continued; stores began to come ashore, and a water lighter was brought close enough in to the beach for a hose to be connected to a prefabricated tank. Unfortunately, there were still many leaderless men wandering around the foreshore and these closed in on the pipeline, in many cases cutting holes in it from which to fill their water-bottles. Discipline was restored after a while, but the general impression was one of near anarchy and a sad lack of junior leadership.

During the morning Hamilton became uneasy. There were still no signs of energetic activity from Suvla and the sun was high in the sky. Lieutenant-Colonel Aspinall was sent over to report on Stopford's progress. With him went Lieutenant-Colonel Maurice Hankey, Secretary to the Cabinet, who had been sent out from London on a fact-finding mission and in particular to ascertain whether certain adverse reports which had reached Whitehall were as accurate as it was feared they might be.

Once ashore, Aspinall and Hankey could immediately see that something was very wrong with IX Corps. In his subsequent statement before the Dardanelles Commission, Aspinall described what happened next: 'The whole bay was at peace, crowded with transports and supply ships unloading their stores without any interference by the enemy. There was no sound of firing on the shore and all round the bay were clusters of naked men bathing in the sea.' The two officers went ashore to look for Stopford's headquarters, which they presumed would already be operational. Nobody could tell them anything about it.

Aspinall set off inland, passing throngs of idle and incurious men. He was certain that the firing line was several miles ahead, but was shaken when he came across Colonel Bland, the Chief Engineer of 11th Division who, to his amazement, informed him that he was within a few hundred yards of the front. Stopford, he said, was still aboard the *Jonquil*. When Aspinall asked about the strength of the enemy, Bland replied: 'I can tell you exactly. We are being held up by three men. There is one little man with a white beard, one man in a blue coat, and one boy in shirt sleeves.' Aspinall now came across Hammersley, who horrified him by saying that 11th Division had no orders to advance until the next morning, and feared that even this might be impossible until more guns had been brought ashore.

Seriously alarmed, Aspinall at once went aboard *Jonquil*, to be greeted cheerfully by Stopford with the words, 'Well, Aspinall – the men have done splendidly and have been magnificent.'

'But', replied Aspinall, 'they haven't reached the hills.'

'No – but they are ashore' was Stopford's disarming reply.

Aspinall told him that Hamilton would be disappointed that the high ground had not been taken in accordance with his orders, and re-emphasized the absolute importance of getting on at top speed. Stopford acknowledged this but insisted that the men could not be called on to go forward again until they had been rested. Aspinall excused himself and immediately sent a telegram to GHQ, to sound the alarm: 'Just been ashore where I found all quiet. No rifle fire, no artillery fire and apparently no Turks. IX Corps resting. Feel confident that golden opportunities are being lost and look upon situation as serious.'

This signal did not reach Hamilton, for as the day dragged on without news from Stopford he had become increasingly agitated, eventually calling for the destroyer which the navy had put at his disposal in order to cross over to Suvla. He was told its fires had been drawn and that it was undergoing boiler repairs. No alternative means of transport had been arranged and it was several hours before Hamilton, on the admiral's yacht, eventually arrived at Suvla, where Aspinall met him and repeated the burden of his earlier signal.

Hamilton at once went on board the *Jonquil* and took Stopford aside for what was clearly a heated conversation. Aspinall only overheard the latter part of this; Stopford was telling Hamilton that orders had been issued for the resumption of the attack early on the following morning, the 9th. The excuse for the delay was that he wished to reorganize and rest the men (the greater proportion of whom had seen little or no fighting). When Hamilton directed that the attack was to go ahead immediately, that evening, Stopford protested that Hammersley would be unable to cancel the orders already issued and get out another set in the limited time available. Hamilton, exasperated beyond measure, now declared his intention of going ashore and finding Hammersley. He invited Stopford to accompany him, but in the event went alone, with Aspinall and one or two of the GHQ staff. Stopford is reported as having excused himself owing to the pain from his wrenched knee; later, he was to assert that Hamilton had snubbed his offer to go ashore and had deliberately left him on board.

Once ashore, Hamilton tracked Hammersley down and ordered him to resume the advance immediately, or at least very early the next morning. Hammersley had only just completed the orders drafted as the result of Stopford's earlier instructions for a resumption of the advance next day. He now told Hamilton that only one of his brigades, the 32nd, was capable of concentrating for an immediate attack. Hamilton replied that even if only one rifle company was

available, it should be got on to the top of the ridge at once.
Hammersley then told his GSO2, Major Duncan, to go to 32nd
Brigade and tell them to occupy the Tekke Tepe ridge at once, and certainly not later than first light on the 9th. Hammersley shrank from
giving 32nd Brigade a direct order to take the ridge, merely saying
that it was most important for the ridge to be occupied, even if only
with a company.

These instructions did not reach the 6th East Yorkshires, the divisional pioneer battalion selected to lead the advance, until 10 p.m.
and they did not get under way for a further six hours, owing to the
immense difficulty of pulling in their outlying platoons, widely dispersed on the plain. They had, however, already sent patrols forward
on to the ridge and these had only found a few Turkish outposts
and sentries. Lieutenant-Colonel Minogue of the West Yorkshires,
who was still in the process of taking over command of Haggard's
brigade, was preoccupied at this stage and inclined to be cautious. He
had already decided to play for safety and send not just the East
Yorkshires, but all his battalions, to the ridge. Messages were accordingly sent out to all four battalions to come back out of their forward
positions and concentrate for a general attack.

Hammersley's orders to Minogue were ambiguous. He was
directed to advance towards the ridge during the night and reconnoitre it. On the results of this, Hammersley would then plan a deliberate divisional set-piece attack the next day. With the East Yorkshires
would be a field company of engineers who would start constructing
defensive positions in the Sulajik Farm area; this was well below the
foothills, out on the open plain, and Minogue must have wondered
what Hammersley was thinking about. He went off and started to get
32nd Brigade ready to resume the advance.

It was now pitch dark. The runners carrying the messages to the
battalions got lost in the bush and it was hours before all the units
had filtered back to the forming up point in the Sulajik area. Minogue
had been told to maintain contact with the troops already installed
on Chocolate Hill, a mile or so to his right, and with elements of
34th Brigade who were deployed to his left on the lower slopes of
the Kiretch Tepe ridge. This meant that his brigade frontage was
extended to nearly two miles as the troops groped their way forward.
Dawn came, to reveal that they had a long way to go.

The East Yorkshires, led by Lieutenant-Colonel Moore, pressed on
up the hill in the growing light, but they were too late, for the Turks
had just occupied the ridge in great strength. As Moore and his headquarters party reached the summit, well ahead of the rest of the now

exhausted battalion, a mass of Turkish infantry met them head-on. Moore and those with him were overwhelmed; the colonel was captured but then put to the bayonet in cold blood, as was Major Brunner of the Engineers. The lives of the few survivors were saved only by the courageous intervention of an imam attached to the Turkish unit which now occupied the heights. The triumphant Turks poured down the hillside in pursuit of the British, who retired in disorder on the Sulajik area. The 8th West Yorkshires fared no better than the East Yorkshires when they attempted to move up the ridge, to be met by superior numbers of Turks. The situation was only saved from rout by the resolute stand of two companies of the 6th York and Lancaster. By mid-morning the British line was back on the lower slopes of the foothills where it was to stay for the remainder of the campaign.

Early on the 9th another division began to come ashore at Suvla. This was the 53rd (Welsh) Division under Major-General the Hon. John Lindley, a 55-year-old cavalryman who had commanded the division since 1913. Apart from service in South Africa he had little combat experience and his career had mainly been in staff and regimental appointments, and as Commandant of the Cavalry School. His division, like the 54th (East Anglian) which followed the 53rd ashore in the next few days, had begun the war, like the 42nd and 52nd of Helles fame, as a well-trained territorial formation. Since then, however, it had been continually 'milked' of its best units and personnel as reinforcement drafts to France. At least half the battalions now serving in the division were actually wartime creations, whose standard of training, particularly in shooting, was well below that achieved by the pre-war Territorial Force. It is therefore all the more reprehensible that these troops were flung into action at Suvla as soon as they arrived off the troopships.

In the 159th Brigade of the 53rd Division, the Brigade Major was Captain Arthur Crookenden of the Cheshires, two of whose battalions, the 4th and 7th, were serving in the brigade, together with two battalions of the Welsh Regiment. The 159th Brigade arrived off Suvla late on the evening of the 8th. All ranks were anxious to land; having spent a week at Port Said after the long voyage from England without going ashore, they were decidedly out of condition. At anchor in Suvla Bay (though no one seemed to know where they were) all lights were doused. Embarkation staff came aboard and instructed the troops to go ashore with only the equipment which could be carried by the men, who waited on deck in the dark for the lighters to take them off.

On reaching the shore, there was no indication of where the battalions were, until the brigade headquarters chief clerk found a crate of maps, which were then handed out to the officers. The brigade assembled in the lee of Lala Baba to avoid the shrapnel which continually burst overhead. In Crookenden's words:

> The military situation at this juncture beggars description. The 10th and 11th Divisions had landed two days earlier, and had been severely handled by the enemy and poorly directed. Commanders and staffs, officers and men, all showed marked signs of having reached the limit of endurance. An atmosphere of indifference, laissez-faire and chaos was the result, which was inimical, if not fatal, to action even by fresh troops. The hearts of all sank as they realized the conditions in which they were to go into battle. They had no ammunition except what they carried, no transport, no artillery. It seemed incredible.

Whilst officers and men were physically soft after a month spent on board, Crookenden considered that the 53rd was still perfectly capable of a sustained effort and that all ranks were keen to show up well in this, their first action. After a visit to the top of Lala Baba at daybreak, Crookenden began to have further misgivings. To the front, he could see the surface of the dry Salt Lake covered with wounded men being brought back from the front line. As a professional soldier he also spotted a danger sign; even the lightly afflicted 'walking wounded' were attended by several of their comrades, when they were perfectly capable of walking back unaided. He saw his divisional commander nearby and told him that the 159th Brigade was perfectly capable of crossing the lake and taking the Tekke Tepe ridge, if an hour's time could be granted for an officers' briefing on top of Lala Baba. General Lindley dismissed him brusquely; the division must move off immediately, without preliminary reconnaissance. Crookenden objected and was threatened with arrest. He was told to send two battalions off at once to find Brigadier-General Sitwell, 'somewhere in the bush ahead'.

At this stage Crookenden was unaware that the 53rd Division had been put at Hammersley's disposal by Stopford as it disembarked. Stopford had given no directive as to their use other than that 'it was hoped that they would be employed in such a way that it would be possible to gather them together at last light under their own commander, for use as a corps reserve.' Lindley was given no other orders. For the time being the new arrivals stared in disbelief at the lamentable scenes around them; stragglers who had fled the line were roaming the beach in disarray, without their weapons. Many, who had stolen jars of quartermaster's rum, were raving drunk. Here were all the signs of military collapse and imminent defeat, and the mood of general pessimism began to infect the 53rd Division before it ever got into battle. One staff officer likened the scenes on the lake to a crowd 'streaming away from a football match'.

The 4th Cheshires, in 159 Brigade, were a typical territorial unit, proud of their lineal descent from the Rifle Volunteers whose smart grey uniform with red facings they wore on parade and for 'walking out' in peacetime. Private William Courtenay had enrolled before the war. The 4th Battalion recruited in the Chester, Birkenhead and Wirral areas and its men were thus a good mix of town and country. On mobilization in August 1914 they considered themselves, with some justification, to be as good a unit as any in the Territorial Force. A flood of new volunteers quickly brought them up to war establishment and when the battalion was invited to sign for overseas service it volunteered *en masse*. The 159th Brigade was originally an all-Cheshires formation, but the needs of the Western Front led to the removal of the 5th and 6th Battalions and their replacement with Kitchener battalions of the Welsh Regiment which, though enthusiastic, lacked the thorough training of the long-standing territorial units.

When the 4th Cheshires left England for the Mediterranean they had been training hard for ten months and were as fit as they would ever be. Courtenay considered that they were 'among the best trained and disciplined of the territorial units in the country. Our ranks had been stiffened with many "old sweats" of previous wars who had been recalled to the colours in 1914. Many of them wore the ribbons of South Africa, Chitral, the Nile, Burma and the Sudan.' These old soldiers were a great benefit and 'fathered' the younger ones. It was a very close-knit and potentially effective battalion, proud of its nickname, the 'Chester Greys'.

After coming ashore near Lala Baba, Courtenay's company was marched inland within hours and flung straight into battle.

We broke up into 'artillery formation' of small columns, each on a narrow front, as we marched into action . . . passing our puny field guns and the remnants of the battle of the previous day. Mules' entrails filled every pool, and pathetic haversacks with their abandoned contents and letters from home told their own story. While on the march we had to tread warily at times to avoid stepping over the newly-dug shallow resting place of a fallen soldier . . .

As the battalion trudged over towards Chocolate Hill it was met by a constant stream of men retiring from the fight, not all of whom appeared to be wounded. None of the officers was able to find out what the battalion was supposed to be doing and the men were soon grumbling that 'they had been given better orders for a Saturday afternoon bun-struggle in Birkenhead Park.'

Eventually, Crookenden obtained a written order from HQ 53rd Division. Written on a scrap of message pad, it simply read: 'Attack the Turks.' The brigade staff blundered about in the bush until the elusive Sitwell was found, but he had no coherent orders to give. As darkness fell, three out of four battalions of 159th Brigade were 'lost'. The order which had placed the 53rd Division under the questionable command of 11th Division early in the day had proved meaningless.

Crookenden now embarked on a nightmare search of the battlefield in the dark, looking for the missing battalions. By 3 a.m. on the 10th he had only found part of the 7th Cheshires, and was now required to issue orders for a set-piece brigade attack at 6 a.m.,

> involving leapfrogging by a brigade last seen in Bedford. Boundaries and objectives were described from a map, and included such easily recognizable points as the crossings of tracks with contours! It was pitch dark, and it should also be remembered that the brigade had no transport of any sort, no arrangements for ammunition supply, no medical arrangements except the doctors' haversacks, no tools, no food, no water, nothing but what they stood in. There was no artillery.

It is not surprising that when a forward movement was undertaken by what could be found of the brigade at first light, it came to a halt in a trench packed with badly shaken men from a number of battalions, brigades and divisions, all hopelessly intermingled.

When a further order to advance was given in the afternoon, Brigadier-General Cowans of the 159th Brigade led a small number of men forward, but they were quickly killed or wounded. The fate of the wounded out in front was terrible, for a bush fire now swept across the battlefield, cremating dead and wounded alike. A few gallant men who had taken up positions ahead of the main entrenchment with its rabble of demoralized men were counter-attacked by hordes of Turks and overwhelmed as hundreds of their comrades looked on apathetically. It was a woefully conducted battle on the British part. These piecemeal attacks were easily fought off by Major Willmer's resolute Turks, and the advance withered and died. So ended the first battle for Scimitar Hill.

On their first day in action, the 4th Cheshires suffered a fate typical of that endured by the territorials at Suvla. Nine of their officers were killed and seven wounded. The chaotic nature of the fighting is revealed in the numbers of men listed as 'missing', whose bodies were never found, or who perished in the flames as the scrub caught fire. Of the 4th Cheshires alone, 289 were reported as 'missing' in addition to 20 known to have been killed and 117 wounded; some stragglers returned days later after undergoing horrific experiences. The heart had been torn out of the territorials in just one day by crass generalship and misuse of potentially fine troops, who were unable thereafter to make much of a contribution to the fighting. The 53rd Division, to all intents, had ceased to be operational within twenty-four hours of its arrival at Suvla.

Following his unsatisfactory visit ashore on the 8th, Hamilton decided to spend the night afloat in Suvla Bay in order to intervene, if necessary, in the battle on the morrow, should Stopford again display the torpor which had so far characterized his handling of IX Corps. He went ashore at 8.30 a.m. on the 9th and was amazed to find Stopford personally supervising the construction of a substantial command bunker a few hundred yards from the beach. Mahon was found up on Kiretch Tepe ridge; his depleted division, which considerably outnumbered the 500 Turkish gendarmerie opposing it, was stationary. Mahon announced that he did not intend to lose men in any more frontal attacks and was considering making a flanking movement. Hamilton forebore to comment and departed in a fast motor boat for his fateful conference with Birdwood and the divisional commanders at Anzac.

As darkness fell on 10 August, the landings at Suvla had failed irretrievably. The Turks were holding the Tekke Tepe range in strength and had halted Mahon's advance up the Kiretch Tepe. The 53rd Division was scattered all over the plain, thoroughly demoralized after its first day of battle, and the morale of IX Corps was at rock bottom. All ranks had been totally ignorant of the thoughts and aims of their generals, and had ended the day baffled and angry.

# 27

# Culling the Generals

From this moment . . . the Gallipoli story sinks into
an ugly welter of accusations, personal spite, dashed
hopes and despair.

Robert Rhodes James, *Gallipoli* (1965)

HAMILTON NOW HAD to make some urgent decisions about his generals. After visiting IX Corps on 10 August, he sat down and wrote to Stopford in a last attempt to get him moving:

I am in complete sympathy with you in the matter of all your officers and men being new to this style of warfare and without any leaven of experienced troops on which to form themselves. Still, I should be wrong if I did not express my concern at the want of energy and push displayed by the 11th Division. It cannot all be want of experience as the 13th have shown dash and self-confidence . . . Today there was nothing to stop determined commanders leading such fine men as yours. Tell me what is wrong with 11th Division. Is it the Generals or the Brigadiers or both? . . . you must get a move on or the whole plan of operations is in danger of failing . . . use your personal influence to insist on vigorous and sustained action . . . remember that the Anafarta ridge is your principal and dominant objective and it must be captured.

Within twenty-four hours Hamilton heard of the failure of the luckless 53rd Division in an almost maudlin letter from Stopford:

These troops showed no attacking spirit at all. They did not come under heavy shell fire but went back a long way at slightest provocation. Lots of men lay down behind cover etc. They went on when called upon to do so by staff and other officers but they seemed lost and under no leadership – in fact, they are not fit to put into the field without the help of regulars . . . they have no standard to go by . . . the attacking spirit was absent; chiefly owing to the want of leadership by the officers.

After reading this, Hamilton confided to his diary: 'This letter has driven me nearly to my wits' ends. Things can't be so bad! None of us have any complaint at all of the New Army troops; only of their Old Army generals.'

On the afternoon of the 10th, as the battle on Sari Bair drew to its bloody close, the 54th (East Anglian), commanded by Major-General Inglefield, started to come ashore at Suvla. Its men were treated to the same depressing sights on arrival as their immediate predecessors in the 53rd, now engulfed in the battle for the Anafarta ridge. Dead and wounded seemed to be lying all over the beaches and there was a terrible air of apathy and lack of motivation. Hamilton had issued a specific order to IX Corps that the 54th was to be kept together as a formation and not delivered piecemeal to the battle. Furthermore, it was not to be used without the express authorization of GHQ and was to be regarded as a last reserve in case of emergency. Stopford's staff chose to ignore this. They were worried by a widening gap in the line, and late in the evening of their first day ashore, no less than six battalions of the 54th were marching in pitch darkness to where the gap was believed to be. They had few maps and were led by unreliable guides. Units quickly became lost, eventually collapsing exhausted in their tracks without making contact with the enemy.

Early on the morning of 11 August, Hamilton (who had not been informed of the misuse of these battalions) gave orders for IX Corps to launch 54th Division in a general attack on the Tekke Tepe ridge at first light on the 12th. GHQ recognized that the other divisions under Stopford's command were incapable of offensive action, and the new plan provided for a frontal assault by 54th Division, its flanks protected by 10th and 11th Divisions. Later in the day Hamilton went over once more to see Stopford and to give him a lecture on the need for aggression. Stopford protested that the 53rd had failed because of their inadequate training and their dilution back at home to provide reinforcements for the Western Front, and gloomily forecast that the 54th would fare no better. Hamilton would have none of this, but gave Stopford a further twenty-four hours' grace; the attack would now be launched at dawn on the 13th.

As such an attack would involve a difficult night march up to the start lines, Stopford worried even more; nevertheless he held a planning meeting on the morning of the 12th to prepare for it. It was decided that a start line had to be established beforehand, that afternoon, well forward of the existing front line; one of 54th Division's brigades, the 163rd, was selected for this important task. Once this start line had been properly secured a brigade of 53rd Division was to come up and take over from the 163rd, who could then get on with the main attack. At dawn on the 13th, the rest of 54th Division was to sweep up and through the start line and on to the summit of the ridge.

Stopford was still uncertain that this plan would succeed, so Hamilton, instead of coercing him, agreed to a scaled-down version. The 163rd Brigade would attack another objective, the W Hills. The revised plan was promulgated to the divisional commanders at 4.15 p.m. Then it was decided that the divisional attack should be post-poned another twenty-four hours, but that 163rd Brigade's attack on the W hills should go ahead as planned that afternoon.

One of the battalions in the 163rd Brigade was the 8th Hampshires, still known by its old volunteer name, the Isle of Wight Rifles. They had come ashore at Suvla on 10 August and spent two days in reserve. There was little to encourage them as they prepared for action; 2,000 wounded were lying out on the open beach awaiting evacuation and there was little to be done for them; many died there. On the afternoon of the 12th they were summoned to attack the Turks. Bugle-Major Peachey raised a silver bugle to his lips and sounded the 'advance'; the sun, flashing on his instrument, betrayed him to the enemy and he was the first to fall.

The vaguely specified objective was the Anafarta ridge, but there were no maps. The battalion moved forward and despite heavy sniping reached a position near the village of Anafarta. After the first thousand yards it had been impossible to maintain any sort of for-mation; the advance turned into a series of short dashes by small groups, then came to a halt. About half the battalion had now been hit, and it was clear that the other battalions had fared no better. Serving in the ranks of the Isle of Wight Rifles was a would-be poet, whose commemorative verses stand as epitaph for yet another battalion thrown away:

> Let us tell how the Island Rifles, 800 of the best,
> Crossed Anafarta Valley
> To Anafarta crest.
> Our officers nobly led us,
> As we went to face the foe.
> Alas, our valiant Major fell
> And some gallant captains too.
> Norfolks, Suffolks, Hampshires,
> Formed that brigade so brave
> And they fought like true-born Britons,
> Many finding a soldier's grave.

Another battalion in the 163rd Brigade was the 5th Norfolks, one of whose rifle companies had been recruited from workers on the King's Sandringham estate. The company commander was Captain F. R. Beck MVO, the estate agent; before leaving England he was presented with an inscribed gold watch by Sir Dighton Probyn, Comptroller of the Queen Mother's Household, on behalf of Queen Alexandra. Beck carried this watch into battle on the afternoon of the 12th. The 5th Norfolks under Lieutenant-Colonel Sir Horace Proctor-Beauchamp, on the right of the line, gradually veered even further to the right and the companies became separated from each other. When last seen, the Sandringham company was advancing steadily into the heart of the Turkish positions, disappearing from view in the smoke. None of its men returned.

Beck had been issued with the wrong maps, which showed an entirely different part of the Gallipoli peninsula and were thus useless. After the war, when the War Graves Commission sent parties to locate the dead on the Gallipoli battlefields, more than a hundred bodies bearing the regimental insignia of the Norfolks were found, well inside the old Turkish positions; they had apparently been surrounded and fought until none remained alive. The only official notification received by Beck's family was that he was 'wounded and missing'.

Another futile attack had failed. Only 800 men of 163rd Brigade remained. The Isle of Wight Rifles had lost 8 officers and 300 men, and the 5th Norfolk 22 officers and over 350 men. Neither battalion became fully operational again while at Gallipoli.

After another visit to IX Corps on 13 August, Hamilton could see that Stopford was unnerved and ordered IX Corps to sort itself out, consolidating on a line as far as possible up the slopes of the Anafarta hills, and to make this line impregnable. He was now thinking of drastic changes to the high command at Suvla but made no move on that day.

Stopford ignored Hamilton's directive and ordered Mahon to attack along the Kiretch Tepe ridge with three battalions on 15 August. It was an ambitious plan, requiring the 10th Division to move along the summit and also to take Kidney Hill, a prominent hillock on the southern slopes of the main ridge. By 15 August the 10th Division had inched its way along the crest line to a point known as Jephson's Post. Two of the division's brigades, the 30th and 31st, had been grouped on the ridge and Mahon was given 162nd Brigade from the 54th Division to make up numbers and take the Kidney Hill position. Mahon placed Brigadier-General Hill in charge of the attack, but kept 162nd Brigade under his own control.

This operation might have succeeded in the first week after the landings, but the Turks had pushed in strong reinforcements for the gendarmerie who had stubbornly held up 10th Division for over a week. Five extra Turkish battalions were close at hand and a further five within reach for use if needed. By 6 p.m. very little headway had been made until the 7th Munsters made a desperate bayonet charge. For a time it seemed that success was in the offing, but at dusk the 5th Royal Inniskilling Fusiliers ran into heavy opposition, sustaining such heavy casualties that the attack had to be called off whilst attempts were made to recover the wounded left on the ground. Second-Lieutenant Lyndon spent much of the night rescuing them in the depth of the Turkish lines, to earn the first of two MCs he would gain during the war. In later years he was to say that he only got the awards 'because there was nobody else left alive to receive them'.

The 162nd Brigade advanced on the right flank along the southern slopes of the ridge towards Kidney Hill with all the enthusiasm of inexperienced troops and paid heavily for it. When the advance faltered in the afternoon the brigade commander, Brigadier-General de Winton, placed himself at the head of the leading battalion and took them forward until he was wounded. These territorials of the Bedfords and the London Regiment (Royal Fusiliers) behaved gallantly, obtaining a lodgement on Kidney Hill and holding on for many hours against repeated attacks. At 4 a.m. on the 16th the Turks launched a general attack along the ridge held by the Irish battalions, who threw rocks when their meagre supply of jam tin bombs ran out. At this critical point in the battle, with the 10th Division fighting for its life, a sensational rumour was passed round. Its commander, Mahon, had resigned under most unusual circumstances.

There was now a series of convulsions in the senior ranks of the Mediterranean Expeditionary Force, triggered earlier by a growing belief in GHQ that Egerton of 52 Lowland Division was no longer fit for command. In mid-July, as already described, Hunter-Weston, in command of VIII Corps at Helles, had found it necessary to take Egerton away temporarily from his division in the middle of a battle for an enforced rest. Early in August he was given an adverse confidential report by Major-General Douglas, in temporary command of VIII Corps pending the arrival of Lieutenant-General Davies. Meanwhile, back in England, Hunter-Weston had been to see Kitchener and briefed him on the performance of the generals at

Gallipoli – including, no doubt, Hamilton. Kitchener's reaction was to signal Hamilton on 30 August, directing him to send Egerton, who was filling a temporary post in the Egyptian base, home to England, where he became an Inspector of Military Training.

Egerton was not in fact the first to fall. First there had been Brigadier-Generals Breeks, the artillery commander, then Hendry of 157th Brigade, who was invalided off Gallipoli with fever, liver 'and other complications', with Egerton's recommendation that he be boarded and sent home. Hendry was unusual in that he was one of the first territorial officers to be given command of a brigade, but according to Egerton he was *persona non grata* and they were all jealous of him'. It is hard not to feel sorry for Egerton. He had brought an excellent division to Gallipoli to see it butchered by what he considered to be inept handling by Hunter-Weston and, briefly, de Lisle. Devoted as he was to his men, he now felt hard done by and blamed the Commander-in-Chief.

Hamilton's problems in dealing with his senior officers were exacerbated by his own generous spirit and kindness and the fact that in a small peacetime army, men got to know each other well as they ascended the promotion ladder. In mid-July Hamilton had written to Hunter-Weston about Egerton:

> I know that commander well; I looked at him, spoke to him and came to the conclusion that there was not a grain of generous inspiration in the whole of the man from the top of his head to the sole of his foot. Plenty of ability, competent at his job, an excellent disciplinarian and knowing the routine of military business from A to Z, he is no leader of men and has no capacity. Now think of it. It was not affection, but rather respect and fear on which that man's power rested. But who will respect or fear a soldier regarding whom exaggerated stories will pass around that after two days' fighting he left his division to go aboard ship, and that somebody else acted in his place? I must say that . . . it would have been better for him, and better for us, had he remained on board his ship . . . He has dined, lunched etc etc in my house I am sure a hundred times or more. I like him, and my wife and all our people like him very much also. But what is the use of all this if he is unable to lead his men victoriously against the Turk?

Following his unhappy visit to IX Corps on 13 August, Hamilton knew that Stopford would also have to go. With Kitchener's approval, he was replaced by de Lisle and a mollifying message was sent to Mahon: 'Although de Lisle is junior to you, Sir Ian hopes that you will waive your seniority and continue in command of the 10th

Division, at any rate during the present phase of operations.' Whether Hamilton knew it or not, Mahon loathed de Lisle, and this, coupled with what he regarded as his shabby treatment to date, prompted him to send a furious reply: 'I respectfully decline to waive my seniority and to serve under officer you name. Please let me know to whom I am to hand over the command of the division.' Hamilton immediately appointed Brigadier-General Hill; Mahon packed his valise and took the next boat to Mudros. Once there he had second thoughts and on 17 August, from the comfort of the headquarters ship *Aragon*, he wrote saying that he had acted hastily and did not mind waiving his seniority, but still declined 'for personal reasons' to serve under de Lisle.

Stopford was deprived of his command on the evening of 15 August, departing for England at once and taking Reed with him. His appointment in the first place was a sorry reflection on a rigidly hierarchical system which made appointments to key posts on the basis of Buggins's turn.

The next general to fall out was Lindley of the 53rd Division. When Hamilton was ashore on 18 August he received very gloomy news on the state of IX Corps from de Lisle. He had only been there a few days but reported a lamentable want of grip throughout the higher command, worse than he had dared put on paper. it would take several weeks to reorganize the corps. Hamilton told him that offensive action was needed within days, and ordered de Lisle to start planning. After the meeting Lindley asked Hamilton if he could accompany him to the beach, and as they walked 'he told me frankly that his division had gone to pieces and that he did not feel it in himself to pull it together again. Very fine of him to make a clean breast of it, I thought, and said so.' That night Hamilton signalled the War Office: 'Lindley feels he is unable to pull the division together so I have relieved him at his own request and appointed Lawrence who has done extremely well, to take over the 53rd Division.' Almost as an afterthought, Hamilton added: 'I have also been obliged to relieve Sitwell of his brigade command as he cannot be made to move.'

If Hamilton hoped that de Lisle's arrival had fired IX Corps with a new spirit, others were not so sure. For some time Captain Milward had been trying to escape from GHQ, and on 12 August he was told he was being posted as Brigade Major to the 163rd Brigade in the 54th East Anglian Division 'who have hardly been in action yet. I received this with mixed feelings.' When he joined his new brigade on the 21st it had not recovered from its terrible mauling on the Anafarta ridge and was in bad order: 'Now I find them much shaken and a general

spirit of depression exists – awful. The brigade major was hit and the
general invalided. Was almost depressed myself the first morning.'
The brigade was now commanded by Major Evans of the Wiltshires
'and a topper he is. He may stop on. I hope so.' The 4th Norfolks were
being commanded by their regular adjutant; the 5th Norfolks could
only muster six officers, the 5th Suffolk were in a similar state. The
Isle of Wight Rifles were a

> very young lot, commanded by Veasey, a lawyer. The brigade is only
> 1,800 strong. The territorial cannot stand all this with his lax discipline,
> habit of doing as he likes and inability to strictly carry out orders . . .
> the territorial is not enlisted from a class of man who is used to deny
> himself anything – no self-discipline. The general situation and state
> of feeling and depression with which I was greeted can be imagined.
> No blankets or coats yet – grilled all day, they are frozen at night.

A few days later, Milward was still finding much to criticize; when
visiting the fire trenches he 'found several men and officers without
their equipment on. They are slack. Sleeping, and officers not with
the men. But they are more cheerful, not so shaken.'

As the weeks went by and he was able to infuse the brigade with
his own professionalism, Milward warmed to the territorials, recog-
nizing their unfamiliar qualities. But the rest of the campaign would
be a dour struggle to maintain morale and survive. For many,
however, there was to be one last battle, the largest in terms of manpower to take place during the entire campaign; the attack of 21
August.

# 28

# Catastrophe at Scimitar Hill

To persevere, trusting in what hopes he has, is
courage in a man. The coward despairs.

Euripides

HAVING DECIDED TO resume the offensive, Hamilton sent a signal to
Kitchener asking somewhat optimistically for 45,000 reinforcements
to make good battle casualties and losses through sickness, as well as
several more divisions. Had these been received, Hamilton's strength
would have exceeded 95,000 men, and the lack of response indicates
that Kitchener, under constant pressure to send all available
resources to the Western Front, no longer felt he could take such
requests from Hamilton seriously.

Although de Lisle professed confidence as he worked himself in,
he had been appalled on his first tour of the corps by the condition of
its brigades in the forward area. A few days earlier Major Hore-
Ruthven had visited the front line at Braithwaite's bidding; he also
was not impressed.

I walked across the open to a line of lightly dug trenches which I, at
first, assumed was occupied by the reserves, as the men were standing
about on the top of the parapet, cooking in front of the trench, and
were not being fired on except by an occasional sniper. But little work
appeared to be going on to improve the trenches and a general air of
inaction appeared to exist. I was therefore much surprised when I was
informed that these were the front line trenches. There were no Turkish
trenches or Turks to be seen in front and the only sign of the enemy
was some desultory shelling . . . The officers in command of this part
of the line were often unaware of the positions of troops on their
flanks, and while I was there it was discovered that what for some days
had been supposed to be Turks, in Turkish trenches in the bushes on

our left front, were in reality our own men. There appeared to be no difficulty in water, rations or ammunition reaching the firing line, and pack mules were going continuously to and fro to the front trenches from the beach.

It struck Hore-Ruthven forcibly that the lassitude of the higher command had filtered down through the ranks to the firing line, that the junior officers lacked self-confidence and thus initiative as the result of their sketchy training, and that the army's training system had drained the soldiers of the desire to do anything to help themselves.

At Anzac, which he visited a few days later, Hore-Ruthven found an entirely different spirit. Cox's Indian brigade was installed in the Aghyl Dere, the scene of appalling confusion at the beginning of August. It was hard to reach the Indians because of incessant rifle and shellfire. Dead men and animals still littered the steep path, but despite their heavy losses, 29th Indian Brigade were hard at work improving their defences, cheerful, confident and ready to resume the offensive.

Second-Lieutenant Savory was now the only British officer surviving unscathed with the 14th Sikhs. After the battle of Sari Bair he set about reorganizing the unit, carrying out all the prescribed administrative procedures for the notification of casualties. At one point in the fighting, a clerk's error had resulted in his father being sent a telegram to the effect that his son was 'Missing, believed killed'. The father had written at once to the officer commanding 14th Sikhs, asking for the details of his son's presumed death. Young Savory had an agreeably warped sense of humour and saw how his father's grief could be assuaged. He sent a telegram back assuring him that Second-Lieutenant Savory was in fact alive and well, signing it 'R. Savory, 2/Lieut, Officer Commanding, 14th Sikhs.' In the following week, he warmed to his task and began to publish unit routine orders. One of these announced that a number of appointments had been made in the battalion:

Commanding Officer, 2/Lt R. A. Savory; Second in Command, 2/Lt R. A. Savory; O/C A, B, C and D companies, 2/Lt R. A. Savory; Quartermaster, 2/Lt R. A. Savory.
(Signed) R. A. Savory, 2/Lt and Adjutant

Each of these appointments entitled the holder to draw an allowance over and above his basic pay and could only be held by an officer holding the King's Commission. In a memoir, Savory later recorded that 'I was the only one present and therefore entitled to hold them all . . . Having spent four months fighting in Gallipoli I had now clearly returned to the realities of life, so I drew the cash and went to Cairo to spend it.'

As de Lisle briefly imposed his grip on IX Corps it became apparent that he was a very different character from the gentle and courteous Stopford. Birdwood, a shrewd judge of character, summed him up in a letter to his wife as 'a real thruster – everyone hates him as he is a brute, with no thoughts for others, rude to everyone and has no principles, but I believe him to be the right man in the right place, and, by his brutality, I hope he will see things through.'

The new attack was ordered for 21 August. De Lisle's new-found enthusiasm led him initially to think in terms of capturing the whole of the Tekke Tepe and Kiretch Tepe ridge lines, but Hamilton, mindful of the calamities resulting from earlier over-optimism, directed him to plan a limited advance. The object would be to secure the 'Anafarta Gap' – the saddle of ground linking the main Anafarta ridge with the high ground surmounted by Point 971 and Chunuk Bair, both of which were firmly in Turkish hands and likely to remain so unless Kitchener produced the manpower for which Hamilton had asked. It was essential, if this more limited objective was to be attained, to seize the W and Scimitar Hills; in addition, in order to make good the junction between IX Corps and the Anzac beach-head, the latter needed to be extended further round the Turkish right flank to include the feature known as Hill 60, a strongly held Turkish redoubt threatening the Anzac left flank.

In view of the drained condition of the formations involved in the recent fighting, the 29th Division was brought round from Helles and given the left hand position in the attack, with the task of moving forward from the area of Chocolate Hill and on to Scimitar Hill. In the centre, 11th Division would move on to the W Hills, and a composite brigade from Anzac, under Cox, was to capture Hill 60. In reserve would be the newly arrived 2nd Mounted Division, a yeomanry formation sent out to Egypt in April for possible use as reinforcement for Gallipoli.

The yeomanry was a curious semi-feudal relic of the militia. Officered by the aristocracy and squirearchy, it recruited mainly in rural areas, especially in the fox-hunting shires. In August 1914 its units were well below war establishment and there was a rush to join. Philip Campion, a farmer's son, went to Warwick to join the county yeomanry. Here, the recruiting and selection process was reminiscent of Shakespeare's day. The selection panel consisted of Lord

Willoughby de Broke and Colonel Charteris, who tested the candidates in horsemanship. In Campion's words:

> The horse that had passed hundreds into the Warwickshire Yeomanry was fetched out of his stables, and in turn we mounted and rode up the road and back. The horse knew the spot where he was supposed to turn back, and as he did this rather quickly, it was at this period that would-be yeomen of uncertain seat found themselves affectionately embracing the animal instead of sitting erect on its back. We succeeded in satisfying His Lordship in this respect and after a few questions such as 'What pack of hounds do you hunt with?' we passed to the doctor for examination. I regret that on acquainting His Lordship with the fact that I hunted with the Grafton I omitted to say that it was on foot.

In August, with no prior warning, the yeomanry were suddenly told to prepare for service in the dismounted role. Leaving their horses in Egypt, Campion and his comrades embarked on the Cunarder *Ascania* which took them to Mudros, where the yeomen were transferred to the cruiser *Doris* and soon found themselves ashore at Suvla, landing from 'beetles' near Lala Baba, behind which the division formed up out of sight of the Turkish observers on Tekke Tepe. It was the evening of 20 August.

On the following morning Hamilton crossed over from Imbros and took up an observation post on the Kiretch Tepe ridge. He was not in an optimistic mood, for there had been no response to his request for reinforcements and he was now even thinking, as he looked gloomily over the plain, that he would have to consider reducing his perimeter by abandoning Suvla Bay and concentrating on a slightly enlarged Anzac beach-head.

De Lisle had issued his final orders on the previous afternoon so that adequate time should be available for preparation. Because of the ammunition shortage, only half an hour's preliminary bombardment was possible. It would start at 2.30 p.m. and the infantry were to advance at 3 o'clock. The first move would be by 11th Division, who had to take some advanced Turkish trenches. Half an hour later they were to seize the W Hills whilst the 29th Division (or rather, those brigades which had managed to arrive in time after dashing around from Helles) swept forward on to Scimitar Hill. At this point the 2nd Mounted Division, equal to an infantry brigade in bayonet strength, was to move forward across the Salt Lake to Chocolate Hill where it would be close enough to exploit any success gained by 11th and 29th Divisions. On the right, Hill 60 was to be taken by Cox's scratch force drawn from four brigades – a telling commentary on the straits to which Birdwood's corps had been reduced after Sari Bair.

On paper, the artillery available in support was impressive compared to that used in earlier attacks of this scale. A total of eighty-five guns of various calibres, the battleship *Swiftsure* in Suvla Bay, three cruisers and a pair of destroyers would combine for the short barrage. Unfortunately, the weather now played an adverse part; what had started as a fine sunny day became hazy and cloudy, and visibility for the spotters on the ships deteriorated. Worse, the sun which should have been in the eyes of the Turkish defenders was obscured by cloud. The artillery preparation proved wholly inadequate. Turkish guns soon began to take their toll of the infantry packed in the forward trenches, especially in the 29th Divisional sector. When the advance began, the Turks, untouched by the British guns, were full of fight. In the 11th Division's sector the New Army battalions went forward despite heavy casualties. The adjutant of the 9th Lancashire Fusiliers noted that the men went over the top 'as one', to be greeted by heavy shrapnel and rifle fire almost at once. The battalion started the attack with seven officers but only two reached the Turkish defences and one of these was badly wounded. The signals sergeant was killed and the telephone wire he was paying out was blown apart.

Once in the Turkish trench, whose occupants were all killed, the Fusiliers set about consolidating. A drummer volunteered to take a message back to brigade and on his return reported that the 33rd Brigade which was supposed to be in contact had disappeared into the smoke and could not be found. Some men of the South Staffords now came into the trench, saying that they were all that remained of the missing 33rd. The 5th Dorsets and 9th Lancashire Fusiliers – both of which had been roughly handled in the landings of 6 August – had done remarkably well under appalling conditions.

Other units of the 11th Division were mown down by enfilading fire, the advance came to a halt and the 32nd Brigade was compelled to fall back on its start lines. The 33rd Brigade, ordered up in support, had been heavily shelled as it marched round the southern shores of the Salt Lake and became entangled with the 34th Brigade. Both formations tried to go ahead but were thrown back in growing confusion by devastating Turkish crossfire. By 5 p.m. the attack had failed.

To the left, where 29th Division was meant to capture Scimitar Hill, things were, if possible, even worse. Here, the men of the 86th Brigade had come under very heavy shellfire even before leaving their trenches and as they moved forward concealed machine-guns exacted a terrible toll. The scrub was now well alight and adding its smoke to the dust clouds that hung over the battlefield, thickening by the minute. By the time the attack had been going for an hour the slopes of Scimitar Hill were littered with British dead and wounded, and the main Turkish trenches, several hundred yards to the front, were still untouched. The 1st Royal Inniskillings now charged up the hill and reached the summit, only to be blasted off by artillery fire. It was too much for even these well-tried troops and they streamed back off the top. Then it was the turn of the Border Regiment, who also got to the top, carrying many of the Inniskillings back up with them; part of the summit was taken, but gradually the troops succumbed to sniping, machine-guns and shrapnel until only a few small groups remained on their feet.

After 5 p.m. the sky was darkened by great clouds of smoke. The 2nd Mounted Division was called forward from behind Chocolate Hill. Earlier in the afternoon they had crossed the Salt Lake from Lala Baba in open formation under heavy shrapnel fire. There were two miles to cover, but when they arrived at the foot of Chocolate Hill it was found that because of their immaculate formation and lack of bunching, casualties had been low. In the Royal Gloucestershire Hussars, a patrician yeomanry regiment, Private Lewis, in peacetime a small dairy farmer, was walking alongside his troop commander, Lieutenant the Viscount Quennington, arguing hotly with him about the sale of his milk, which he preferred to dispose of to a local dairy rather than the co-operative of which Quennington was a keen supporter. Still volubly debating milk marketing, they realized that they had arrived safely in the lee of Chocolate Hill.

Watching the 2nd Mounted Division from his perch on Kiretch Tepe ridge, Hamilton was deeply stirred. 'Such superb martial spectacles', he wrote, 'are rare in modern war.' Commodore Keyes, afloat in Suvla Bay, was equally fascinated: 'The spectacle of the yeomen of England and their fox-hunting leaders, striding in extended order across the Salt Lake and the open plain, unshaken by the gruelling they were getting from shrapnel – which caused many casualties – is a memory that will never fade.'

The attack had been followed on foot by the journalist Ellis Ashmead-Bartlett across the Salt Lake and on to the top of Chocolate Hill, where the massed machine-guns of the Royal Naval Division were firing steadily into the smoke towards the Turkish lines with the aim of subduing the opposition. It was soon clear that the initial assaults of 11th and 29th Divisions had been brought to a halt and masses of men were to be seen surging around the lower slopes of the

W and Scimitar hills. Visibility was deteriorating by the minute, and large tracts of the scrub were ablaze, in which lay hundreds of figures, some frantically trying to escape the flames, others ominously still. As the daylight began to fail, at about 4.30 p.m., the yeomanry were ordered to attack and Lord Longford's brigade started to ascend Scimitar Hill in the gathering gloom. The last thing that Ashmead-Bartlett saw before he was buried in his trench by a shell was a mass of yeomen moving steadily up the slopes into the smoke. He wrote afterwards:

> I have no idea who took part in this final advance. Probably the 2nd Yeomanry Brigade and men of the 11th Division who were lying in the scrub at the foot. The mob surged upwards. The roar of the guns, the crackle of rifle fire, the burr of the machine-guns, was incessant, and then these blurred khaki figures disappeared into the darkness and were lost to view.

The yeomanry were sent forward with no clear directive after all other attacks had failed, and in conditions of rapidly failing visibility. The commanding officer of the Sherwood Rangers Yeomanry, Lieutenant-Colonel Sir John Milbanke, had been at Harrow with Winston Churchill and the two men had remained firm friends. When ordered forward from Chocolate Hill, he gathered his officers together and told them all he knew: 'We are to take a redoubt. But I don't know where it is, and don't think anyone else does either. But in any case we are to go ahead and attack any Turks we meet.' With that, in Churchill's words, 'he led the Sherwood Rangers into the evil murk, and oblivion. On this dark battlefield of fog and flame, Brigadier-General Lord Longford, Brigadier-General Kenna VC, Colonel Sir John Milbanke VC and other Paladins fell.' Kenna was in temporary command of the yeomanry division; he had gained his VC riding, with Churchill, in the charge of the 21st Lancers at Omdurman. Longford fell at the head of the troops he was personally leading to the top of Scimitar Hill, where he was last seen alive. His brigade major died with him; their bodies were never found.

It was now 9 p.m. and the situation was totally obscure. All that had been gained was a small portion on the lower slopes of Scimitar Hill. Great fires raged on the slopes where the wounded lay helpless, and the main preoccupation was now to rescue as many of them as possible. Hamilton had left for Imbros as the light failed, still optimistic that the attack had succeeded. Brigadier-General Marshall, acting commander of 11th Division (for Hammersley had collapsed with mental prostration), now took it on himself to order all troops on the forward slopes back to their starting positions. On hearing of this, Hamilton wrote in his diary: 'I am quite confident he will be able to give good reasons for his act.'

Many notable deeds of gallantry must have passed unseen in the hours that followed. Private Potts was wounded in the thigh soon after moving forward from Chocolate Hill. For a time he lay bleeding in the scrub, then was joined by two other wounded, one of whom soon died. The two survivors lay in the open under a bush amidst heavy fire as darkness came down. It was soon intensely cold and they were in agony as their wounds congealed. A full moon shone down on the scene of carnage around them; they dared not move because the Turkish line was close by. All the next day they lay under the bush, tormented by thirst, which they tried to allay by chewing twigs. They could see stretcher bearers in the distance but the Turks would not let them near their lines, although they respected the Red Cross. Potts knew that survival depended on crawling closer to the British lines; after dark, dragging his companion Private Andrews, he began to move downhill. By dawn he had covered nearly 300 yards; the men lay up all day behind a bush, sustained by the water-bottles of dead men who lay in heaps all round their hide. Their wounds began to bleed and Potts dressed Andrews' to staunch the flow. After dark on the third night Andrews could go no further, so Potts found an entrenching shovel and dragged him on it, a few feet at a time. After dark on the fourth night Potts felt bold enough to stand up, and continued to drag Andrews to safety until they reached the British front line. For this act of endurance and self-sacrifice, Potts was awarded the VC.

On the right, where Cox's composite brigade was attacking Hill 60, a problem arose; there was little information on the extent and state of the Turkish defences, and no up-to-date aerial photography was available for planning purposes. It was assumed, wrongly as it transpired, that the Turks had ringed the summit of this none-too-prominent mound with a trench system and that possession of one part of this would lead naturally to the capture of the whole position. In the event, the Turks had laced the whole feature with a network of fire and communication trenches, making Hill 60 an extremely complex defensive system which was destined never to fall entirely into British hands.

Cox could muster what, on paper, looked like a formidable force for the attack, but the 29th Indian Brigade was heavily depleted by casualties, as was the Australian 4th Brigade, now down to 1,400 bayonets. An assortment of battalions was also available: the 5th

Connaught Rangers, five officers and some 300 men of the 10th Hampshires, and two regiments of New Zealand Mounted Rifles, now down to 200 men apiece. The troops earmarked for this desperate enterprise had still not fully recovered from their experiences a fortnight earlier on Sari Bair.

Because of the shortage of guns and ammunition the attack on Hill 60 had to make do with only thirty minutes' worth of artillery preparation, and the infantry went over the top at 3.30 p.m. The Turks were ready and opened up a deadly fire. The Australians advancing on the right were particularly hard hit, their leading wave losing 110 out of 150 men in minutes. The second wave fared no better despite the gallantry with which they advanced to almost certain death. Yet again the scrub caught fire and soon the screams of the wounded, punctuated by the sounds of their exploding ammunition pouches, could be heard all over the battlefield. When the 10th Hampshires went forward they walked straight into a Turkish artillery barrage. Three of their surviving officers fell to this, and 125 of their men. As the battalion reeled under this shock, the formidable Captain-and-Quartermaster Saunders took control, steadied the younger soldiers, and held on. Only one man of the battalion, however, managed to get forward to join the Australians and New Zealanders on Hill 60. The survivors of the Hampshires – perhaps 200 men, many of them wounded – were ordered to strengthen the Indian Brigade.

A grim fight raged all night on the western slopes of the hill, taken earlier in the day by the Connaught Rangers in a wild bayonet charge which gained the unstinting admiration of the Australians who watched it. Now the Irish were in reserve, their position on the slopes taken over by the remnants of two Gurkha battalions. At dawn on the 22nd, the 18th Australian Battalion was thrown in, its officers and men unaware that they had been detailed for a forlorn hope and under the impression that they had been called up to occupy and hold a section of captured trench. Consequently, when ordered to carry out the assault using only grenade and bayonet, the officers protested that they had no bombs. They were told that they must do their best with what they had. Nevertheless, the battalion rose from its trenches and charged with great spirit. This was a newly arrived unit, fresh from Australia; its soldiers were the fittest and most enthusiastic on the peninsula, but their attack did not get the support it needed. Hill 60 remained firmly in Turkish hands.

For another week the battle ebbed and flowed around the fatal hill; when it died down, the summit was shared by both sides, and for the rest of the campaign it was the scene of constant fighting and mining. In the words of the *Official History*:

> The bitter fighting on Hill 60, still regarded by the Australians and New Zealanders as perhaps their sternest trial at Gallipoli, had added the final straw. None of the units engaged had ever been so depleted as at the moment when the action began, and the men had only been able to carry on by sheer force of will . . . but the prolonged strain at Anzac – the fighting, the heat, the constant debilitating sickness – had made too prodigal a call upon their store of nervous energy, and at the end of August the Anzac Corps was temporarily incapable of further offensive action.

With the double failures at Scimitar Hill and Hill 60, the writing was on the wall. No further substantial reinforcements were in view; the order went out from GHQ to consolidate on the positions already gained, and to prepare for a winter campaign.

De Lisle's interregnum at IX Corps was brief, for Lieutenant-General Sir Julian Byng arrived presently from France, where he had acquired a deservedly high reputation; Hamilton had long sought his services, but it had been difficult to pluck him away from the Western Front, and now it was too late. With de Lisle's departure, Hamilton retrieved Mahon from Mudros. Hammersley was removed abruptly from command of the 11th Division on 23 August and replaced by Major-General Fanshawe, another high performer from France. The campaign was now, however, past recovery.

The most that could be hoped for was the establishment of a defensive line strong enough to deter Turkish attacks, for it was clear that there was now no hope of new divisions being sent out from home; even the flow of reinforcement drafts for the peninsula was drying up and all units faced the approaching winter at strengths well below their authorized war establishments. The 'Western' school now predominated and the national war effort was increasingly directed towards breaking the stalemate in France and Flanders. In Whitehall, the concept of the indirect approach against the Central Powers through the capture of Constantinople was quietly interred, and politicians were quick to distance themselves from any signs of support they might have displayed for the Dardanelles expedition. More significantly, forces were at work which were to ensure that Hamilton would be displaced as Commander-in-Chief before many weeks had passed.

# 29

# The Power of the Press

I could not tell lies to 'make things pleasant'.
W. H. Russell, Crimean War correspondent, 1857

ELLIS ASHMEAD-BARTLETT was an experienced journalist who had been frequently under fire during the Balkan wars and was thus prepared for action when he arrived at Gallipoli. In the early stages of the campaign he had been allowed to live afloat with the fleet, as it was the navy to which he had been originally accredited. His copy, however, which had to be submitted to the GHQ censor's office prior to despatch to London, soon began to irritate the staff with its criticism of the conduct of operations and growing undertones of pessimism.

When he returned to London at the end of May on leave, Ashmead-Bartlett made a point of contacting as many persons of influence as he could. He dined with Lady Randolph Churchill and her son Winston, still smarting over his removal from the Admiralty. Churchill was in a sulphurous mood over the Dardanelles and displayed one of his less endearing characteristics when the conversation turned to the navy's repulse at the Narrows. He was totally undismayed, it seemed to Ashmead-Bartlett, by the loss of so many battleships: 'What matters it if more ships are lost? The ships were old and useless and are not required in the North Sea.' At Churchill's insistence, Ashmead-Bartlett briefed the Prime Minister at No. 10 Downing Street. He also saw Kitchener and the slippery Colonel Repington, military correspondent of *The Times* and a strong opponent of the Dardanelles expedition, who pumped him for the sort of information that would enable him to write an article such as that which had triggered off the great shell scandal and the overhaul of Britain's war industries.

On 24 June Ashmead-Bartlett was back at Mudros where he discussed his London visit with de Robeck and Keyes. To his fury he found that GHQ had changed his terms of reference; all accredited pressmen were now to be based alongside GHQ on Imbros in the miserable, dirty and smelly headquarters camp at Kephalos, which he described as

a Via Dolorosa for the whole of GHQ. Burnt up by the sun. Blown about by the siroccos, tormented by millions of flies, they pass a miserable time, and their meals are largely composed of a fine sprinkling of sand . . . nearly everybody is at loggerheads with someone else, and a more unhappy, dusgruntled staff have never attempted to lead an army to victory.

The staff's mounting dislike for Ashmead-Bartlett was aggravated by his ostentatious life-style; with the aid of hampers of foodstuffs and wines ordered when he was in London he managed to live in some splendour amidst the squalor of Jack Churchill's badly run camp, sitting outside his tent in a silk dressing-gown sipping champagne. It was widely known in the headquarters that he had been talking to influential persons in London and that his criticisms of the conduct of the campaign were being openly discussed there. He also made himself unpopular with his reporting of the arrangements for handling reinforcement drafts on their arrival at Imbros and Lemnos, pointing out that there was no welcome for new arrivals before they were despatched to the slaughter on the peninsula, and no attempt to provide canteens and amenities for the troops. The new drafts still arrived at Mudros full of keenness and optimism, but the antiphonal shouts of 'Are we downhearted?' seldom drew any response now from the disillusioned veterans. When one shipload of reinforcements chorused the question as they arrived in the harbour, only one sepulchral voice responded from a transport laden with casualties: 'You bloody soon will be!'

The more Ashmead-Bartlett saw and heard on his visits to the peninsula (for which he now had to gain written permission from Braithwaite's staff) the more he felt that he must bring the facts before the British public. After the fruitless Krithia attacks he interviewed a number of commanding officers including one who 'complained bitterly of the manner in which his division had been led to the slaughter over and over again . . . the smell of the dead in the captured Turkish trenches was too awful for words . . . the troops now so demoralized that they are in no condition to undertake further offensive action'.

At Anzac, Ashmead-Bartlett was more favourably impressed, even though the Australians found his determined pessimism hard to stand. Godley's staff were openly critical of Hamilton's conduct of operations and of his recent official despatch, optimistic in tone and, in their opinion, bearing little resemblance to what had actually happened.

Back on Imbros he met another Royal Naval Division officer, Lieutenant-Colonel Leslie Wilson, Member of Parliament, commanding the Hawke battalion. He too was disgusted with the higher command; de Lisle's orders, he stated, were seldom intelligible or clear-cut and were generally ignored. He described vividly the destruction of the Collingwood battalion, never in action before its fatal attack, whose officers had been given no chance to look at the ground over which they were to advance. The campaign, said Wilson, was especially hard on the elderly reservists in his division, many of whom were over 50 and had never expected to serve in any capacity ashore, let alone as infantrymen. There was great resentment in the trenches over GHQ's refusal to permit a truce, such as had been arranged at Anzac, in order to bury the dead and rescue the wounded. Hunter-Weston's charm was acknowledged by all, but so was his wild optimism and penchant for ordering senseless frontal attacks in broad daylight without artillery support. Wilson reported widespread derision for Hamilton, who was said to have thrown two fine Anzac brigades away at Helles with his injunction to 'fix bayonets, slope arms, and quick march to Krithia'.

There was clearly much to report which Ashmead-Bartlett realized would never get past the censor at GHQ. He sincerely believed that the public needed to be told the truth, in the way that the pioneer war correspondent William Howard Russell's despatches to *The Times* from the Crimea in 1854 had brought home to the British nation something of the true horror of that equally mismanaged campaign. Until a suitable opportunity presented itself, he bided his time. He went across to Suvla for the landings aboard the cargo liner *Minneapolis*. Occupying a comfortable first-class cabin, he found it incongruous that as the blacked-out ship approached Suvla Bay, stewards were sweeping the stair carpets, and a polite notice gave warning that breakfast, of iced melon, fish, eggs to order and grilled bacon, would be served early in view of the landings. Going on deck he could see the heights of Sari Bair enveloped in white smoke as the battle raged there, but ashore at Suvla a sabbath calm reigned.

When he was allowed ashore he found a scene which 'resembled rather the retreat of a routed army rather than the advance of a victorious one . . . stragglers in a state of pitiful exhaustion . . . many with tongues bulging from their mouths, blackened with thirst'. Men were trying to fill water-bottles from hoses of three to four inches' diameter. Others were dead to everything and just lay on the sand. 'Water and shade now counted more with men whose objects the day before had been the Narrows and Constantinople.'

On Lala Baba, he came across Hammersley, who barely seemed to know what was happening as no communications appeared to exist down to his brigades. A solitary heliograph flickered fitfully from Chocolate Hill but its messages were indecipherable. Rumours were rife that most of the officers were dead and that troops were refusing to advance. All this time the battle thundered down from Sari Bair, a reproach to all concerned in the Suvla landings.

A day later, Ashmead-Bartlett walked over to Chocolate Hill, from where he could see the holocaust on the slopes of Scimitar Hill as flames engulfed the hundreds of wounded men lying in the open. In a memorably chilling passage he later described how, 'When the fire passed on, little mounds of scorched khaki alone marked the spot where another mismanaged soldier of the King had returned to mother earth.'

It was not only the more perceptive pressmen who were beginning to worry about the overall conduct of the campaign. An Irish peer, Lieutenant-Colonel the Lord Granard, was commanding the 5th Royal Irish, the divisional pioneer battalion in 10th Division. He was an old friend of Hamilton's, indebted to him for his first commission in the Gordons (he had later transferred to the Irish Guards). Even he, however, felt in duty bound as a Privy Councillor to write personally to the King and others to acquaint them with the true state of affairs at Suvla. He told Hamilton that he had done so: 'I think that it is only right to inform you of this, and to leave this matter in your hands, as under these circumstances you may not wish me to remain under your command.' Hamilton replied that

> In face of the enemy, Privy Councillors, private soldiers, generals, colonels, all come under the same obligations to hold together and fight. The obligations of military discipline are serious, and are not likely to be set aside. In taking the steps you have taken I believe you did not fully realize their import. I will leave it at that, subject to any action the King or Lord Kitchener may think fit to command or order.

Granard wrote back to apologize and received a typically handsome acknowledgement from Hamilton. The truth was out, however, and there was growing anxiety in London as the full measure of incompetence at Suvla emerged.

The doubters in Whitehall were given further food for thought when, in early October, Stopford, uninvited, put his account of the events at Suvla before the Dardanelles Committee. Written without Hamilton's knowledge and unseen by him, it implied that the débâcle was largely the fault of GHQ and that their estimation of only light Turkish opposition had in fact been wrong. Stopford was critical of Hamilton's conduct of operations and although he disclaimed any personal interest in composing his report, it was clear that he sought to distance himself from any allegations of incompetence. The report was laid before a panel of senior generals in Whitehall, who concluded that there was not enough to damn Hamilton out of hand and that further evidence was needed from reliable witnesses who had been present at Suvla. Kitchener now signalled Hamilton to warn him that a whispering campaign was gathering strength against him in London.

The catalyst of the events that were to lead to Hamilton's dismissal was a 29-year-old Australian journalist, Keith Arthur Murdoch, on his way to London to take up an appointment in Fleet Street. With Hamilton's somewhat reluctant permission he crossed over to Anzac where, despite an instruction issued by Birdwood before the April landings that military personnel were strictly forbidden to have any dealings with newspaper correspondents, there were many only too ready to unburden themselves to Murdoch. When he returned to Imbros, after only four days on the peninsula, he met Ashmead-Bartlett, who now saw a way to getting his unexpurgated saga of military incompetence back to London. The two correspondents agreed that Murdoch should take back with him a long report from Ashmead-Bartlett. However, when searched by military police in Marseilles, Murdoch was obliged to hand it over to the authorities.

Unfortunately for Hamilton, who had so courteously accepted him at GHQ, it was impossible to silence Murdoch, who prepared a long and highly coloured statement of his own on Gallipoli which rapidly circulated in Whitehall. He also corresponded with every influential politician he could find, including Churchill, Lloyd George, Bonar Law and the grim Sir Edward Carson, Unionist *éminence grise* of Ulster. It was now that some politicians who had kept quiet, like the devious Lloyd George, suddenly began to proclaim that they had never believed in the Dardanelles expedition. Asquith circulated Murdoch's report – still unsubstantiated by Hamilton's GHQ, which had not at this stage been consulted – and it found its way before the Committee of Imperial Defence as well as the Dardanelles Committee.

If Murdoch believed he was the bearer of revelations, he was deluding himself. A far more potent eyewitness came to London from Hamilton's GHQ at the end of August in the form of Major Guy Dawnay, a close associate of Aspinall's on the General Staff and, as such, one who had been deeply involved in the planning of all operations on the peninsula since the outset of the campaign. He came with Hamilton's blessing, ostensibly to put GHQ's case for reinforcements to the authorities in Whitehall. Like Aspinall, Dawnay had been aghast on his first visit ashore to Suvla. Both these officers had a deep affection, amounting almost to love, for Hamilton; yet they had come reluctantly to the opinion that he had ceased to act as a commander-in-chief and was no more than an impotent spectator of his subordinates' follies. They had seen all their master's despatches and knew them to be hopelessly optimistic. They felt, though for very different motives than those of Murdoch and Ashmead-Bartlett, that the truth must be known at home. Kitchener soon got to hear that Dawnay was loose in the corridors of power but was powerless to stop him seeing whom he wished, including the King, who had been getting increasingly alarmed over the Gallipoli casualty lists and was now furious with Hamilton for what he saw as his mismanagement of the entire show.

Faced with the rising tide of uneasiness in high places, Kitchener threw a final lifebelt to Hamilton, offering to replace Braithwaite, against whom the groundswell of adverse comment seemed to be directed more than anyone else. Hamilton's quixotic nature, however, would not stoop to this. Braithwaite had been Kitchener's selection, not his, but he could not bring himself to make this last gesture, signifying lack of confidence in the War Minister who had sent them both out in the first place. Hamilton also rejected any idea of an evacuation, citing the huge casualties that would attend such an attempt whilst in contact with the enemy.

Time was running out. The Dardanelles Committee met on 14 October under strained conditions; London had been raided by Zeppelins the previous night, causing little material damage but much unseemly panic. Hamilton's estimates of casualties, of up to half the force in the event of evacuation, brought more gloom. The Committee decided there and then that a new commander was required at Gallipoli. On the 16th, Hamilton received a personal cipher telegram from Kitchener. In it, he read that whilst the Government appreciated his work at Gallipoli, he was to return to London immediately, 'so that we can see you'.

## 30

# Under New Management

Do not stop an enemy on his way home.

Sun Tzu

ON RECEIPT OF Kitchener's telegram, Hamilton immediately prepared for departure. Braithwaite went with him, as General Sir Charles Monro, the replacement commander-in-chief, would bring his own chief of staff, Major-General Lynden-Bell. If Hamilton was afflicted by the situation he gave no sign and was his usual cheerful and courteous self as he bade farewell to the staff with whom he had worked since March, considerately finding a word of thanks for all.

The new commander came fresh from the Western Front where he had made a name for himself as divisional, corps and army commander. He firmly believed that Germany could only be beaten by the breaking of her armies in France and Flanders, and had consistently opposed the idea of a Dardanelles expedition. Monro insisted on an extremely thorough briefing before leaving London and arrived at Imbros with a far better understanding of the Middle Eastern theatre of operations than had been vouchsafed to Hamilton. He had also been subjected to no less than four personal sessions with Kitchener, who pressed on him the need for an immediate report as soon as he had seen conditions at Gallipoli. He was also assured in London that substantial reinforcements could be made available should he decide to reopen the offensive on the peninsula. Having committed so much effort to the Dardanelles, Kitchener now dreaded the idea of evacuation, especially if Hamilton's gloomy forecast of up to half the force being lost were to prove correct.

Monro reached Imbros on 28 October and at once impressed the GHQ staff with his decisive, personable and professional approach.

He was, they found, a harder man than the whimsical Hamilton, disinclined to spare the inefficient or incompetent whatever excuse was proffered, but with a refreshingly open mind.

Before Monro's arrival, Birdwood's opinion had been sought by the anxious Kitchener. In a long reply, Birdwood stated his view that the only residual hope of a breakthrough lay in the northern sector at Suvla, as opposed to the trench-bound stalemates at Helles and Anzac, where the Turks, enjoying numerical superiority, were content to sit the winter out. Birdwood also ventured to suggest that a landing on the Asiatic shore might allow the teeth of the batteries there to be drawn.

Military activity on the peninsula had now slowed down and the priority was to improve the exiguous entrenchments at Suvla. But there was a great increase in mining, and more sappers were brought in to reinforce the tunnellers of the Royal Naval Division at Helles, where some notable successes were achieved. There was also a trickle of reinforcements. The 2nd Mounted Division at Suvla was brought up to strength by the arrival of the Scottish Horse and Highland Mounted Brigades; a battalion of the Newfoundland Regiment also went into the line at Suvla.

Some of the veteran battalions, such as the 5th Royal Scots, were now little more than shadows, having received no fresh drafts, and were sent over to Mudros to recuperate. Many other battalions in the 53rd and 54th Divisions had been so shattered in the August offensive that, left without reinforcement, they could only be employed in menial roles such as stevedoring, portering stores up to the front from the beach, and repairing the rutted tracks to the rear of the forward positions. The 10th (Irish) Division, down to two brigades and three companies of engineers, departed for Salonika in October, still under Mahon, and there were numerous other piece-meal unit rotations. The Royal Naval Division was down to a bayonet strength of below 4,000 by the end of September when their neighbours the French at Helles began to thin out, leaving in the line only twelve battalions of shaky African and Colonial troops. By mid-October the total strength of the Allied force at Gallipoli had dropped to 114,000 against war establishments of some 200,000. Hundreds of sick were being evacuated every week without replacement and the entire force was steadily running down.

When 'resting' on Imbros and Lemnos, the troops found themselves beset by boredom in their desolate and insanitary camps. There were no YMCA or Toc H canteens, or anywhere in which the men could enjoy simple recreation, other than the small amount of organized games which their regimental officers could arrange. Depression was the overwhelming mood of all, despite the efforts of officers and chaplains to raise morale.

Throughout the campaign chaplains of all denominations had coped as best they could. They had an unpleasant duty in addition to their pastoral and sacramental roles, for theirs was the responsibility for ensuring, as far as possible, that the dead received the appropriate rites of passage and a decent burial. Their dedication on numerous occasions had been truly remarkable, as shown by the performance of the Irish priests at V beach on 25 April. Many were so emotionally damaged that they could not continue in their ministry. Others, like Father Ernest Raymond, made it their business to perpetuate the Gallipoli experience in the pages of their books. So deeply affected was Father Raymond by his experiences that he later wrote a number of profoundly moving novels based on his time at Gallipoli, giving a haunting impression of life in rest camps and in the trenches at Helles and Suvla. In *Tell England*, on the eve of an attack in which many are certain to die, 'Padre Monty', an Anglo-Catholic priest, describes to some of his unit's officers the sense of frustration felt by chaplains as they faced another battalion attack:

> I so want to be of use to all the fellows who are going over the top tomorrow. But they don't understand. They don't think of me as a priest with something to do for them that nobody else can do. They think I've done my job when I've had a hymn-singing service and preached to them . . . And all the time I want to absolve them. I want to send them on the field – white . . . but you understand, and, if you'll come to your Confession, I'll at least have done something for somebody in this scrap. You can thank Heaven that you don't feel as I do – that you've nothing positive to do tomorrow – that you're not pulling your weight. I shall just skulk about, like a dog worrying the heels of an attack.

But despite such misgivings casualties were frequent. Of one such front-line chaplain at work with the New Zealanders in the August fighting around Hill 60, Captain Twistleton of the Otago Mounted Rifles laconically reported, 'We lost our chaplain Grant, shot as he was attending to the wounded out in front of the firing line; after all, it was a fine way for a soldier priest to die.'

On arrival Monro immediately toured both Gallipoli fronts and, as bidden, sent a preliminary report back to London. Despite the bedraggled air of the troops and their appalling living conditions, he was not unduly depressed. It was too soon to make a decision on evacuation and he contented himself with asking for priority in supplies of winter equipment, especially materials for overhead cover, experienced junior leaders, and good company commanders. He was certainly a 'Westerner' but was also objective, and Churchill's waspish aphorism that 'He came, he saw, he capitulated' does Monro no justice.

The balance, however, was inexorably going in the Turks' favour. There was no hope of substantial Allied reinforcement; the artillery was still desperately short of ammunition; Bulgaria's entry into the war on the side of the Central Powers now meant that the Berlin–Sofia–Constantinople railway could be used to bring vast quantities of German munitions to the support of the Turks and – more ominously – a siege train of heavy artillery for the reduction of the Allied trench systems. It had only been a chronic shortage of field artillery that had prevented the Turks from overwhelming the shell-starved British guns on the peninsula, and the prospect of strong reinforcement for Liman's artillery was a gloomy one.

By 31 October Monro had responded at length to Kitchener: 'The troops in the peninsula, with the exception of the Australian and New Zealand Corps, are not equal to a sustained effort owing to the inexperience of their officers, the want of training of their men, and the depleted condition of many of the units.' He went on to describe the exposed tactical situation, especially at Suvla where the Turks were able to overlook much of the British rear areas, and the lack of opportunity for any use of surprise. Only a frontal attack could be carried out and its chance of success, given the prevailing numerical superiority of the Turks, was minimal. There was no room in the beach-head for the accommodation and concealment of substantial reinforcements, or for the deployment of the amount of artillery needed to support effective operations. All intelligence information pointed to the impending arrival of massive German artillery reinforcements. On purely military grounds, and in view of the continual drain of manpower due to sickness, Monro concluded that evacuation was the only course open.

Kitchener, who had all the political as well as military factors to consider, was taken aback by Monro's report. He now asked for the views of the corps commanders at Gallipoli and apart from Birdwood they backed Monro. Kitchener, striving to keep the campaign alive, returned to a plan put forward by Keyes in August, for a resumption of the naval attack, in which he was supported by

Wemyss but not de Robeck, who absolutely refused to risk his fleet again and apparently had the support of the Admiralty.

It was now that the lack of an overall joint command structure was felt more acutely than ever. Hamilton, whilst bearing the title of Commander-in-Chief, had never been able to act as such, with control over naval as well as land forces. He had in fact been no more than an army commander, working under different masters in London from de Robeck. At last aware of the root of the problem, Kitchener announced his intention of coming out to see for himself. On 3 November Monro went off to Cairo for discussions with Maxwell, never to return to the peninsula, leaving Birdwood in charge, to whom Kitchener immediately sent a cipher telegram for his eyes only. Another telegram was sent to Monro in Cairo, curtly relieving him of the Gallipoli command and appointing him to command at Salonika.

Kitchener set out from London on the evening of 4 November after sending another telegram to Birdwood exhorting him to consider holding on, 'as I regard evacuation as a frightful disaster which should be avoided at all costs'. Birdwood also received a signal from the Prime Minister assuring him that His Majesty's Government had yet to make up its collective mind over evacuation and would await Kitchener's views after his visit. At the same time, clearly hedging his bets, Asquith directed Birdwood to start making contingency plans for an evacuation.

De Robeck also had a signal, from Balfour, now First Lord of the Admiralty, recommending that after his exertions he should take a holiday and hand over to an officer who was prepared, if directed, to reopen the naval attack. De Robeck sensed that Keyes was at work somewhere in the background, for he was in London at the time. In fact, Kitchener regarded the Keyes plan for resumption of the naval attack as possibly the last hope of sustaining the campaign and had intended to meet up with the fiery commodore at Marseilles on his way out to the Dardanelles; but Keyes was unable to make this rendezvous, and by the time he got back to Mudros, Kitchener had seen enough to convince himself that withdrawal was indeed the only option.

Kitchener arrived at Mudros on 9 November. He now realized what he had asked of Hamilton back in March and that his refusal to meet the latter's urgent requests for reinforcement in August had effectively sunk the campaign. He sensed the claustrophobia of Anzac and the great distances to even the nearest island bases and was humbled. Meanwhile, the British and French governments were still examining schemes for new landings in Asia Minor, under French command, which would aim to cut the railway linking Turkey with Palestine. The idea was viewed with horror back in London but Kitchener hung on to it for as long as possible as it seemed to be the only way of countering the adverse political effects of an evacuation from Gallipoli. The very least that could happen, he felt, was an Islamic *jihad* against all British interests in the Arab world, threatening India as well.

In addition Salonika was now giving anxiety, for the collapse of Serbia had seriously altered the balance of power in the Balkans. Greece, on whose territory the allied Balkan army was living, and whose Aegean islands were the vital bases for Gallipoli and the Dardanelles, was increasingly hostile towards the Entente. So it was to Salonika that Kitchener next went, on 16 November. What he saw there convinced him that Monro had been right. Salonika needed reinforcing, and Gallipoli had to go. If the Greeks decided to support the Central Powers by any means short of declaring war against the Entente, Kitchener reckoned that the British fleet could deal with them by pulverizing all their seaports.

The opinions of the Gallipoli generals kept changing, which did little to help Kitchener. Birdwood still believed that with a general improvement in morale it was worth hanging on, a view now shared by Davies of VIII Corps who felt that the risks attending an evacuation were infinitely worse than sitting it out. He was encouraged in this by an abortive Turkish attack on the 52nd Division on 21 November in which the enemy displayed little of their old fire. It was Monro's views, however, which prevailed. Kitchener signalled London on the 22nd, recommending evacuation and tacitly admitting that if he had backed Hamilton more energetically earlier on, the situation might have been saved. The War Committee and Cabinet endorsed the decision. Monro was mollified by appointment as Commander-in-Chief Mediterranean, with responsibility for all land forces other than those in Egypt; Birdwood was confirmed in post as Commander, Dardanelles Army. Its HQ remained on Imbros, and Lieutenant-Colonel Aspinall, in the acting rank, became Brigadier-General, General Staff.

No sooner had Kitchener departed than Nature struck at Birdwood's command. For several days the south-westerly gales had been gathering strength, and on the afternoon of the 26th all shipping had to stand out to sea. Many of the flimsy piers at Anzac and Helles were washed away. On the evening of the 26th torrential rain descended on the northern sector. In the trenches at Suvla the 1st

Royal Munster Fusiliers caught its full force; Major Geddes was at battalion headquarters when he received an urgent telephone message from one of the forward companies

> requesting me to come up the line as they did not understand what was happening. There was a loud roar and before I could reach the front line – not 200 yards from battalion HQ – the rain came down like a waterspout, a solid sheet of water, unbelievable except to those present. The communication trenches were a raging torrent and impassable, and one had to proceed overland. So sudden was this phenomenal incident that men were literally drowned in their trenches, being unable to get out in time. The trenches crumpled as if made of paper. During the height of the flood a pony, a mule, a pig and two dead Turks were swept into the trenches. By daylight on the 27th the water had subsided to a depth of four feet. Towards evening the wind shifted towards the north and it became bitterly cold. Then came snow and a blizzard. On the morning of the 28th our situation was deplorable. Many lay dead from exposure. At 4 a.m. the GOC ordered a withdrawal . . . the battalion was reduced to a few officers and 68 other ranks. At nightfall the whole battalion to a man answered the call for volunteers to go and collect arms and equipment from the trenches.

The Munsters were moved back to Helles where they spent their time preparing for evacuation. When this came in January the battalion numbered just 11 officers and 75 soldiers out of a unit which had landed in April nearly a thousand strong.

The storm was worst where troops high up on the Kiretch Tepe ridge were totally exposed to the elements, and on the open Suvla Plain. Although every effort was made by the medical staff to get hundreds of frozen men into tents where they could thaw in front of fires, casualties were appalling. The Turks, if anything, underwent worse torments on the Anafarta ridge, and could be seen in the open trying, like their enemies, to warm themselves with huge bonfires. Hostilities were abandoned as both sides sought to recover. At Suvla over 5,000 cases of severe frostbite required evacuation and more than 200 men either drowned or were frozen to death at their posts.

This calamity was one of several factors which made evacuation inevitable. Even so, Wemyss and Keyes were still hard at work pressing for a resumption of the naval attack, and the fleet, under the temporary command of Wemyss, was recovering some of its old aggressive spirit. Monro was not amused by this lobbying and, as Commander-in-Chief Mediterranean, wrote an unfriendly letter to Wemyss ordering him to desist. He was convinced that evacuation was the only real option, even if it involved losing a third of his troops, and he pressed Whitehall for a final decision. On 7 December the Cabinet finally made up its mind, directing that Suvla and Anzac were to be evacuated at once; a decision would be made shortly on Helles, where some felt that a lodgement could be maintained, if only as a gesture.

What followed at Anzac and Suvla, and thereafter at Helles, must stand as one of the outstanding examples of deception combined with sound logistic planning in military history. Birdwood's staff began to realize that there was a sporting chance of getting most of the force and its equipment off the peninsula without incurring heavy losses. It would be necessary to man the fire trenches until the very last moment and then delude the Turks that they were still held in strength. Turkish suspicions had to be allayed by ensuring that the appearance of the anchorages did not show a change of pattern, for the sudden arrival of transports in broad daylight would certainly give the plan away. Daily routines had to be maintained and as the artillery were gradually thinned out, the use of dummy batteries and movement of guns by night to alternative sites would would have to be practised. There must be no perceptible change in the appearance of the many dumps, medical units and daily administrative patterns.

Anzac presented the gravest risk; here, the Turks were within yards of the forward Australian and New Zealand positions, and on Russell's Top they only needed to move forward some 300 yards in order to be able to rake most of Anzac Cove with plunging fire. To lull the enemy, Godley gave orders that there were to be long periods of total inactivity when not a shot was to be fired. If the Turks then rashly concluded that their enemies had abandoned a position and showed themselves, they were to be met by a hail of fire. Very quickly, they came to the conclusion that the Anzac positions were as strong as ever, when in fact they were being steadily evacuated until only a skeleton force remained.

At Suvla, where the November tempest had refilled the Salt Lake, the northern sector in front of the bay was virtually cut off from that adjoining Anzac, linked to each other only by a foot-bridge across the Cut. Byng therefore decided that he would have to evacuate the northern group at Suvla as a separate force. In order to stall any Turkish attempt to move forward off the Tekke Tepe and Kiretch Tepe ridges once the evacuation was detected, intermediate lines of defence were dug halfway back to the embarkation beaches, although it was recognized that if it came to an evacuation with the Turks in hot pursuit, the sacrifice of this rearguard would have to be accepted.

At the beginning of December, the Anzac–Suvla garrison amounted to some 85,000 men, 2,000 vehicles (mostly horse drawn), 5,000 animals, almost 200 guns, and vast stocks of ammunition, rations and ordnance stores. In the middle of the month a steady rearward movement was under way. Ships came in to the beaches under cover of darkness and were loaded in accordance with carefully detailed schedules under control of the chief naval beachmaster, Captain Staveley. By 18 December the garrison had been halved and the Turks suspected nothing. As even a small Turkish trench raid could reveal the true situation, all the usual artillery programmes were shot off, snipers continued to operate normally, and barbed wire was continually renewed. Men were detailed to move around and loiter in the rear areas, fires were lit in vacated medical tents and daily fatigue parties fed the incinerators to give an impression of normality.

The troops entered into the spirit of the deception and devised numerous ingenious pieces of equipment. Outstanding among these was the Australians' delayed action rifle, by which fire could be sustained from a trench long after it had been finally abandoned. A rifle was mounted on the parapet with a string attached to its trigger. This in turn was tied to an empty container suspended below the rifle, into which water slowly dripped from another container fixed above. When sufficient weight of water had dripped into the lower container the trigger was pulled. The final act in the trenches was to rig dozens of these devices, timed to discharge over a period of several hours, to simulate snipers.

By day, lighters approached the beaches and unloaded boxes filled with sand to give the appearance of routine maintenance. In order not to arouse suspicion, unwanted stores could not be burned, so together with surplus foodstuffs, all tins having been pierced, they were buried under cover of darkness. Mining continued throughout November and December on all fronts, with notable successes being achieved at Hill 60 and Anzac. The last mines, however, were designed to use up remaining stocks of explosive and timed to detonate after the last troops had left the beaches, as a final salute to the enemy.

On the night of 19/20 December only 5,000 men remained ashore at Anzac–Suvla to face 60,000 Turks. All now hung on the conduct of the final withdrawal following the evacuation of the firing trenches. There was intense competition at Anzac to serve in the rear parties.

When volunteers were called for, every man in the battalion would step forward; there was a fiercely proprietorial spirit amongst the men who had come ashore on 25 April and had been there ever since, and they were reluctant at the end to leave their dead comrades behind.

To many, it seemed that the evacuation would only be in the nick of time; the arrival of German artillery reinforcements was evident in the increased level of shelling. On the last evening, the front line troops at Anzac and Suvla prepared for the end. At Anzac, a huge mine was made ready under the Turkish position at the Nek. The floors of all forward trenches were dug up so that the departing foot-falls of the defenders would be soundless. Sandbags were wrapped round feet to make doubly sure. Barbed wire barricades laced with booby traps were readied so that the last man out of each section of trench, always an officer, could pull them across to impede pursuers.

By 10 p.m. only 1,500 picked men remained in the fire trenches and at 1.30 a.m. the final withdrawal began. The last machine-guns were taken down to the beach, fuzes lit for the mines and the wire barriers pulled across the communication trenches. Lone Pine, the linchpin of the Anzac defences and the scene of their greatest triumph, was evacuated at 2.40 a.m. At 3.30 the mine under the Turkish trenches at the Nek went up with a roar; the last files of men, carefully mustered and re-counted through successive check-points, were down at the beach. Only now were the remaining supply dumps fired. At 4 a.m. there were no living defenders ashore at Anzac. The last men off had been profoundly moved at the thought of leaving their dead comrades whose simple graves they had done their best to maintain. As one Australian soldier said to Birdwood down at the beach just before the final boat left: 'I hope *they* won't hear us marching off.' After Birdwood had embarked, Captain Staveley's naval beach party waited for a few minutes to make sure that no man remained ashore, and then put out to sea.

The Suvla evacuation, like that at Anzac, went off without enemy detection, but had its moments of anxiety when newly arrived enemy guns began to shell the embarkation beaches on the final morning. One of the piers was hit, but quickly repaired, and the firing had died down by the evening. The front trenches were vacated by 1.30 a.m. but so carefully was this done that the Turks continued to fire briskly at the empty positions for the remainder of the night. At both Anzac and Suvla the departing forces watched as a series of explosions rent the air, detonated by delay fuzes, and great fires flared ashore as the stores dumps ignited. Even so, the Germans reckoned that enough stores and provisions were left intact to feed the Turkish troops on the peninsula for several weeks. It was in the glare of the burning supply dumps that Captain Unwin's picket boat, the last to leave, sailed out into Suvla Bay.

The success of the Anzac–Suvla evacuation greatly encouraged those charged with the evacuation of Helles, although they knew that to repeat such a triumph of deception would be difficult against an enemy now thoroughly alert. The Turks could concentrate all their resources, particularly their newly augmented artillery, behind Achi Baba, and disengagement would be tricky. The French commenced their final withdrawal in mid-December and by Christmas only a single Colonial regiment remained. Whilst the loss of the Senegalese troops would not be mourned, their superb artillery had been a keystone of the defence and was sorely missed. To compensate, the hard-used 29th Division was now back at Helles, albeit a mere shadow of its former strength. The 86th Brigade was down to a bayonet strength of 1,400 and could boast of only four regular officers, of whom the most senior was a temporary major. Most of the officers and men were still suffering the effects of the recent blizzard and in very low physical condition and the brigade had lost virtually all its equipment, including spare clothing.

A debate still raged over the evacuation of Helles, which the navy wanted to retain because it would help with the continuing naval blockade of the Dardanelles. Whilst this discussion continued, General Davies, commanding VIII Corps, maintained an aggressive posture in order to convince the Turks that he had every intention of staying, but the evacuation of unwanted stores, men and animals went on as well. By the end of the month, information received from Turkish prisoners and deserters indicated that a very close watch was being kept on the British trenches and rear areas for the slightest hint of withdrawal, and that Turkish front line units were under orders to keep up constant pressure on the British positions.

Unfortunately a combination of bad weather and accidents seriously affected plans for evacuating stores and animals. The ship earmarked for the large numbers of pack animals still ashore collided with a French battleship and sank, and continuous gales lashing the embarkation beaches over the new year impeded the shipment of the huge French stockpiles at Sedd-el-Bahr. It was therefore the melancholy duty of the mule transport units to destroy hundreds of their animals which had served so patiently throughout the campaign. The Turks were to find them, lying dead in their lines, lovingly groomed and fed to the end.

As the garrison reduced to a strength of 19,000 men and 63 guns, the Turks increased their pressure at the bidding of Liman, who was determined not to let the British stay on or get away. He therefore planned an attack for 7 January at Gully Spur, preceded by a particularly heavy artillery bombardment, which descended on the British lines, held by the 13th Division, at noon. Two great Turkish mines were detonated, but when the attack came in it was so vigorously resisted that the Turks failed to press it home. In particular, the 7th North Staffords, far up on Fusilier Bluff at the northern extremity of the British position, stood their ground, inflicting hundreds of casualties on their attackers and throwing them back in confusion. They lost their commanding officer and many of their men in the process, but the Turks were induced to think that an evacuation was not imminent. In fact, it began that night.

By dawn on the 8th, there were still nearly 17,000 men ashore but it was decided to complete the operation after dark. The garrison now consisted of the greatly reduced 13th, 29th, 52nd and Royal Naval Divisions. The 52nd, as the result of its devastating casualties and lack of reinforcement, was down to less than 3,000 all ranks, and the 29th, which had been brought up to near its full war establishment of over 17,000 for the August battles, could muster only 4,145.

As night fell the front trenches began to thin out and the same measures were taken as at Anzac. The men filed out past successive check-points; fuzes were lit and barbed wire barricades drawn across the vacated trenches. Feet muffled in sandbags, the silent columns moved steadily towards the beaches. From the Asiatic shore came a steady bombardment, as had been the case every night for months. When the marching columns neared Sedd-el-Bahr, they heard the notes of a bugler posted on the ramparts, who sounded a long 'G' when he saw the flash of 'Asiatic Annie's' discharge, the signal for everyone quietly to move off the track and wait in the ditch until the shell exploded.

With the approach of darkness a great fleet of warships and transports had once more closed with the shore; this time not to land an army hopeful of victory but to save a beaten one. During the night the wind rose and at one time it seemed that the embarkation was in danger, with a heavy swell at W beach. There was also a delay at Gully Beach, where the 13th Division was to embark, when one of the 'beetles' grounded and could not be pulled off. The troops had to set out at top speed along the coastal road for W beach with Major-General Maude, their commander, at their head. On the way, Maude suddenly realized that he had left his luggage on the stranded lighter at Gully Beach and insisted on returning for it. As a result he was nearly marooned. He arrived late at W beach, triumphantly pushing a stretcher trolley bearing his bags, and was bundled aboard a boat as the fuzes were lit to blow up the remaining magazines and dumps, which went up with a gratifying roar at 3.45 a.m.

Once again, a substantial force had escaped without sustaining a single casualty. Realizing that they had been tricked, the Turks sent up dozens of alarm rockets, surging forward into the vacated trenches where they fell victims to the host of booby traps left for them, whilst the guns on the Asiatic shore blazed impotently as the fleet sailed away.

# Aftermath

There is no profit and loss account for Gallipoli.

Robert Rhodes James, *Gallipoli* (1965)

SOME OF THE shattered formations which had sweltered, fought and on occasion frozen on the peninsula went to join Monro at Salonika. Many of the Anzacs, notably the Light Horse, and the remnants of the 2nd Mounted Division, were shifted to Palestine where, reunited with their horses, they were to earn glory against the Turks in what would turn out to be the cavalry's final fling. The Anzac gunners, sappers and infantry went to the Western Front where, after a painful learning period, they became the finest assault troops in Haig's armies. The 'Incomparable 29th' also saw out the war in France and Flanders, as did the Royal Naval Division.

Almost all the warships which served in the Dardanelles were rapidly consigned to the scrapyard after Versailles. The *Queen Elizabeth* ended her distinguished career in 1945 in the fleet which bombarded the Arakan coast in Burma. Many of the 'beetles', sold off to civilian owners, plied the east coast and Thames estuary for decades, a few still operating in the gravel trade in the 1980s. One of the monitors may still be seen at Portsmouth dockyard. The *River Clyde* remained aground at Sedd-el-Bahr until 1919 when she was sold to a Spanish firm and continued to ply the Mediterranean as a tramp for another forty years, first as the *Angela*, then as the *Maruja y Aurora*.

In 1936, the Cunarder *Lancastria* was returning to England following a Dardanelles pilgrimage. On board were many of the heroes of the campaign, among them Lord Birdwood, Admiral of the Fleet Sir Roger Keyes, and Captain Unwin VC. As the ship approached

Gibraltar, her captain informed his passengers that he had sighted the old *River Clyde*, on a reciprocal course. The two captains steered their ships so that they slowly passed close to each other. The *Maruja y Aurora*'s ensign dipped in salute and the *Lancastria* returned the compliment, her decks lined with hundreds of silent and deeply moved veterans. Then the Spaniard vanished into the afternoon haze. She was sold for scrap in 1966, when she could have been purchased for a few thousand pounds by the British government as an enduring memorial to a great enterprise.

The *Goeben*, renamed *Sultan Selim*, remained at Constantinople until 1918, but in the last weeks of the war, attended by the faithful *Breslau*, now known as the *Medilli*, she made an attempt to break out of the Dardanelles and seek the open sea. Both ships struck Allied mines; the *Medilli* blew up and sank with great loss of life, but *Sultan Selim* was able to limp back to base, where, renamed again as the *Yavuz*, she remained to the end of her days as a training and depot ship of the Turkish navy.

Varied fortunes awaited the survivors of Gallipoli and the Dardanelles. Most of them were to find that the 'Land fit for Heroes' promised by Lloyd George and his ilk was a politicians' myth. Private Begbie of the Royal Scots, who had gallantly returned to the peninsula, can stand as an example. He was eventually evacuated sick and, his true age discovered, packed off home, where he served for three years until sent to France in 1918 to join the 2nd Battalion of his venerable regiment as it stood its ground in the final days of the great German offensive of that spring. He was demobilized in due course but never realized his ambition of becoming a draughtsman, for no vocational training was provided for war veterans who had loyally answered the call to arms in 1914. It was many years before he regained his confidence after the appalling scenes he had witnessed – a combat veteran at 17. After the blackness of the Great Depression he found work with the Edinburgh Bus Company for the rest of his working life. After his death his widow, 'in memory of a brave young soldier', transcribed the war journal he had kept, and deposited a copy with the Royal Scots Museum in Edinburgh Castle.

Second-Lieutenant Sinclair of the same regiment, who started his diary out of sheer boredom at Helles, prospered in later years, becoming President of Imperial Tobacco and the 1st Baron Sinclair, among many other honours and distinctions. Amongst the thousands who endured at Gallipoli was a future Prime Minister. Major Clement Attlee, interviewed in old age by Robert Rhodes James, admitted that at times he had 'rather enjoyed himself' there, and praised the strategic inspiration of Churchill whilst roundly condemning its incompetent execution. Hore-Ruthven, later Lord Gowrie, became Governor-General of Australia, where he was later followed by Field Marshal Sir William Slim; both proved to be hugely successful and popular in that appointment. Bernard Freyberg VC became Governor-General of New Zealand, having commanded the New Zealand Corps with distinction in the Second World War. 'One-arm Sutton', who had landed at Helles complete with golfclubs, continued to play the game despite his disability; in the 1920s he became a warlord in China under Sun Yat-Sen and a general in his army. In 1941 he was interned at Hong Kong and died heroically in a Japanese prison camp after giving his food rations to others that they might live.

Of the sailors, de Robeck, Wemyss and Keyes all became Admirals of the Fleet. Keyes eventually became Conservative MP for North Portsmouth; he was never a great orator, but rose in his uniform to condemn the Admiralty's conduct of the war at sea in the pregnant Commons debate of 7 May 1940 which resulted in the resignation of Neville Chamberlain as Prime Minister. Later that summer Keyes became Chief of Combined Operations, laying the foundations of the Commandos and drawing on the lessons of Gallipoli to ensure that the blunders of 1915 were never repeated. Despite this, the fiasco of Dieppe in 1942 (by which time Lord Louis Mountbatten had succeeded Keyes) showed that much still had to be learned. The old sailor was ennobled as Baron Keyes in 1943 and, though mainly as a spectator, contrived to stay near the action to the end of the war, dying in 1945 of overstrain after a tour of the Far East.

Keith Murdoch received a knighthood in due course as he prospered in the world of journalism, becoming something of an establishment figure. His son Rupert followed him into the profession and is now the proprietor of a vast media empire encompassing the London *Times* and a clutch of tabloids as well as television and radio networks worldwide.

Winston Churchill's political career suffered only temporarily; after a spell as Chancellor of the Duchy of Lancaster he departed for the Western Front to command a battalion of the Royal Scots Fusiliers but returned in 1917 as Lloyd George's Minister of Munitions. For another ten years, before going into the political wilderness in the 1930s, he held various ministerial posts in Liberal, then Conservative governments. In September 1939, however, the Admiralty made a signal to every ship in the navy: *Winston's back*. He resumed his old office as First Lord until May 1940 when he at last attained the premiership for which his whole life had prepared him.

Kitchener continued as War Minister, but his position had been fatally weakened as a result of the Gallipoli expedition. He grew apart from his Cabinet colleagues, with whom he had never been close; overwork, exacerbated by his refusal to delegate, made him even more unapproachable. He also lost his grip over GHQ in France, which pursued its own military and political course. Eventually a pretext was found to get him – at least temporarily – out of Whitehall. He was despatched on a mission to Petrograd and departed for Murmansk aboard the cruiser *Hampshire*. Shortly after putting to sea it struck a mine and sank with almost all hands, including Kitchener, and with him the Garter insignia he had intended to wear on arrival at the Russian court.

Hamilton was never actively employed again, although he offered his services on his return from the Dardanelles in any capacity thought appropriate to his talents. He spent his long retirement, until his death in 1945, caring as best he could for his former officers and men, never repining or seeking to exculpate himself, despite the frequent and often shrill judgements passed on his conduct of operations at Gallipoli. These continue to appear, from the pens of writers who have never experienced battle or the fearsome stress and loneliness of high command. In Hamilton's papers at King's College, London, however, is a letter which he clearly prized. It was addressed personally to him a year after the Anzac landings by a group of Australian soldiers, then stationed in England, who had all gone ashore at Ari Burnu. The judgement of these men, tried in the fire, is likely to endure longer than that of 'politically correct' academics and polemicists:

*18 April 1916*

The day draws near that marks Australia's first birthday. With you on 25th April last year we laid firmly the foundations of our Military History, and in a few days' time we hope to celebrate a glorious anniversary. Anzac is a topic still much discussed among us, and on this April 25th we want you to know – despite the evacuation – that you have the Confidence and Loyalty of the Men of Anzac.

May I be honest, and say what we wish to convey? We know the Naval and Military problem of the World War was given to you when the chances of success were spoilt by indiscreet management in London. We know that you considered it to be your duty to go forward with the best means placed at your disposal. We know that you could have led us forward to Constantinople, if those responsible in London could have got interested enough to provide you with the means when you asked for them. We're proud to know the reason of your recall to England . . . Finally, we know it may be 'infra dig' to write you this direct. But we feel you will accept our expressions of Loyalty and regard, in the spontaneous spirit in which they are tendered. Australians greet you.

Yours, right through,<br>2130 Bdr B. A. Clarke, AFA

My comrades endorse the above: 4469 Pte Patterson RA; 889 Tpr Campbell ALH; 5686 Dvr Kelly, 10th AASC; Tpr E. P. Nilmot 670, 2nd Signal Coy; Pte G. E. Evans, 3rd Field Ambulance

Out of nearly half a million Allied soldiers and sailors who served at Gallipoli and the Dardanelles, nearly half became casualties, through combat or sickness. Over 36,000 soldiers and sailors of the British Empire died. Although some 22,000 lie in graves within the thirty-one beautifully maintained Commonwealth war cemeteries, only 9,000 of them were ever identified; 13,000 lie in unnamed graves, commemorated by memorial stones, and 14,000 whose bodies were never found are listed on the great memorials at Helles and other sites on the peninsula. The Turkish dead were accorded scant ceremony and were generally cremated *en masse* in gullies, where their remains may still be seen bleaching in the sun. They are also honoured in a growing number of huge Turkish monuments, an idea which would not have appealed to Kemal Ataturk, who held that the Turkish army's great memorial was its soldier, the *Mehmetcik*. This idea is best expressed in the moving words he wrote on the occasion of an early battlefield pilgrimage:

Those heroes that shed their blood and lost their lives: You are now lying in the soil of a friendly country. Therefore rest in peace. There is no difference between the Johnnies and the Mehmets to us, where they lie side by side here in this country of ours. You, the mothers, who sent their sons from far away countries, wipe away your tears, your sons are now lying in our bosom and are at peace. After having lost their lives on this land they have become our sons as well.

Thousands of those who fought at Helles, Anzac and Suvla died in action on other battlefields, among them Patrick Shaw-Stewart of the Royal Naval Division who had been one of Rupert Brooke's companions and had attended his burial on Skyros. He too had been visited by premonitions of early death and his great promise was extinguished for ever in France in 1917. Whilst at Gallipoli he penned some lines of verse which typify one approach to battle:

> Was it hard, Achilles,
> So very hard to die?
> Thou knowest and I know not –
> So much the happier I.
>
> I will go back this morning,
> From Imbros, over the sea;
> Stand in the trench, Achilles,
> Flame-capped, and shout for me.

Today, the battlefields remain quietly beautiful around the year. Since the great forest fire of 1994, Anzac stands almost as it was in 1915, its dry scrub punctuated by the dazzling white stones of the cemeteries where Birdwood's men lie close to where they fell. The trench lines are still clearly visible, especially around the lip of the escarpment for which so many died. Fragments of equipment litter the area: mess tins, water-bottles, food cans, cartridge cases, innumerable shards of ASC rum jars. At Helles, the piers on the beaches are still visible, though ground down by eighty years of storm. Off W beach lies the *Majestic*, from which enterprising Turkish fishermen will undertake to retrieve mess plates and other items. To walk up Gully Ravine is a truly haunting experience; and to stand near Pink Farm and see the ground over which the battalions charged to certain destruction is to sense the futility of it all. Suvla remains alone, deserted save for the patient farmers who scratch what existence they can from the poor soil. In high summer the heat is almost unendurable, but in spring and autumn the weather is temperate. It is surely the most beautiful of all old battlegrounds. Out to sea lie the islands of Imbros and Samothrace, and to stand on the summit of the Sari Bair ridge at Point 971 and watch the sun go down behind the latter is possibly the most moving of all the many experiences to be undergone in this place. It is here that the visitor is moved to silence, to reflect that around these hills, and on the plain to the front, there died an age of innocence.

# APPENDIX I

# *Specimen Orders of Battle*

## Mediterranean Expeditionary Force

NOTE: The titles of units as in 1915 have been used throughout; hence 'Welsh' and not 'Welch', 'Yorkshire Regiment' instead of the modern 'Green Howards', etc.

| | |
|---|---|
| ANZAC | Australian and New Zealand Army Corps (also used generally to describe Australians and New Zealanders) |
| A & SH | Argyll and Sutherland Highlanders |
| Bde | Brigade (of artillery or infantry) |
| Beds | The Bedfordshire Regiment |
| Bn | Battalion (of infantry) |
| Border | The Border Regiment |
| Bty | Battery (of artillery) |
| CGS | Chief of General Staff (equivalent to modern Chief of Staff) |
| C-in-C | Commander-in-Chief |
| COLY | County of London Yeomanry |
| ConnR | Connaught Rangers |
| Coy | Company (of infantry) |
| Div | Division |
| Dublins | Royal Dublin Fusiliers |
| DWR | Duke of Wellington's Regiment (West Riding) |
| E Lancs | East Lancashire Regiment; also E Lancs Division |
| Engr(s) | Engineer(s) |
| Fd Arty | Field Artillery |
| Fd Coy | Field Company (of engineers) |
| GHQ | General Headquarters |
| Glosters | The Gloucestershire Regiment |
| GOC | General Officer Commanding |
| GR | Gurkha Rifles |
| Hants | The Hampshire Regiment |
| HLI | Highland Light Infantry |
| How | Howitzer |
| Hy | Heavy (of artillery) |
| Inniskillings | Royal Inniskilling Fusiliers |
| KOSB | King's Own Scottish Borderers |
| LF | Lancashire Fusiliers |
| Loyals | The North Lancashire Regiment |
| Manch | Manchester Regiment |
| Middx | The Middlesex Regiment |
| Mtn | Mountain (of artillery) |
| Munsters | Royal Munster Fusiliers |
| NF | Northumberland Fusiliers |
| Regt | Regiment |
| RF | Royal Fusiliers (City of London Regiment) |
| RFA | Royal Field Artillery |
| RGA | Royal Garrison Artillery |
| RHA | Royal Horse Artillery |
| RIrish | The Royal Irish Regiment |
| RIrF | Royal Irish Fusiliers |
| RIrR | Royal Irish Rifles |
| RMA | Royal Marine Artillery |
| RMLI | Royal Marine Light Infantry |
| RNAS | Royal Naval Air Service |

| | | | |
|---|---|---|---|
| RS | Royal Scots (The Royal Regiment) | Welsh | The Welsh Regiment |
| | | Worcesters | The Worcestershire Regiment |
| RSF | Royal Scots Fusiliers | Yeo | Yeomanry |
| RWF | Royal Welsh Fusiliers | Y & L | York and Lancaster Regiment |
| RWK | Royal West Kent Regiment | Yorks | The Yorkshire Regiment |
| SWB | South Wales Borderers | | (Green Howards) |
| TF | Territorial Force | | |

# A. APRIL 1915

C-in C: General Sir Ian Hamilton GCB
CGS: Major-General W. P. Braithwaite CB

*29th Division*
*GOC:* Major-General A. G. Hunter-Weston CB
*86th Brigade:* 2 RF, 1LF, 1 Munsters, 1 Dublins ('Fusilier Brigade')
*87th Brigade:* 2 SWB, 1 KOSB, 1 Inniskillings, 1 Border
*88th Brigade:* 4th Worcesters, 2 Hants, 1 Essex, 5 RS (TF)
*Artillery:* 15 Bty RHA, 17 Bde RFA, 460 How Bty RFA, 4 (Highland) Mtn Bty RGA (TF), 90 Hy Bty RGA, 14 Siege Bty RGA
*Engineers:* 2 London, 2 Lowland, 1 W Riding Fd Coys RE (TF)
*Divisional Cyclist Coy*

*Royal Naval Division*
*GOC:* Major-General A. Paris CB
*1 (Naval) Brigade:* Drake Bn, Nelson Bn, and Deal Bn RMLI
*2 (Naval) Brigade:* Howe, Anson and Hood Bns
*3 (Royal Marines) Brigade:* Chatham, Plymouth and Portsmouth Bns RMLI
*Motor Maxim Sqn RNAS:* A ground unit equipped with Maxim guns, armoured cars, and motorcycle combinations
*Artillery:* None
*Engineers:* 1 and 2 Fd Coys
*Divisional Cyclist Coy*

## AUSTRALIAN AND NEW ZEALAND ARMY CORPS (ANZAC)

*GOC:* Lieutenant-General Sir W. Birdwood KCSI
*Corps troops:* 7th Indian Mtn Arty Bde, Ceylon Planters' Rifle Corps (defence of Corps HQ)

*1st Australian Division*
*GOC:* Major-General W. J. Bridges CMG
*1st (Aust) Brigade:* 1st, 2nd, 3rd and 4th (NSW) Bns
*2nd (Aust) Brigade:* 5th, 6th, 7th and 8th (Victoria) Bns
*3rd (Aust) Brigade:* 9th (Queensland), 10th (S Australia), 11th (W Australia), 12th (S & W Australia) Bns
*Artillery:* 1st (NSW), 2nd (Victoria), 3rd (Queensland) Fd Arty Bdes
*Engineers:* 1st, 2nd and 3rd Fd Coys

*New Zealand and Australian Division*
*GOC:* Major-General Sir A. Godley KCMG CB
*NZ Brigade:* Auckland, Canterbury, Otago and Wellington Bns
*4th (Aust) Bde:* 13th (NSW), 14th (Vic)

## CORPS EXPÉDITIONNAIRE D'ORIENT

*Commander:* General d'Amade
*Metropolitan Brigade:* 175th Regiment, Regiment de Marche d'Afrique (Zouaves and Foreign Legion)

*Colonial Brigade:* Senegalese and colonial infantry
*Artillery:* Eight batteries of 75-mm quick-firing field guns

# B. AUGUST 1915

*C-in-C and CGS:* As before
*GHQ troops:* 220th and 24th Brigades RGA (three heavy and two siege batteries)
Armoured car squadron RNAS

## VIII CORPS

*GOC:* Lieutenant-General Sir F. J. Davies

*29th Division*
*GOC:* Major-General H. de B. de Lisle CB
*86th Brigade:* 2 RF, 1 LF, 1 Munsters, 1 Dublins
*87th Brigade:* 2 SWB, 1 KOSB, 1 Inniskillings, 1 Border
*88th Brigade:* 4 Worcesters, 2 Hants, 1 Essex, 5 RS (TF)
*Artillery:* 15 Bde RHA, 17 Bde RFA, 167 Bde RFA, 460 (How) Bty RFA, 90 Hy Bty RGA,
    14 Siege Bty RGA
*Engineers:* 2 London, 2 Lowland, 1 W Riding Fd Coys RE (all TF)
*Divisional Cyclist Coy*

*42nd (East Lancs) Division (TF)*
*GOC:* Major-General W. Douglas CB
*125th Brigade:* 5, 6, 7 and 8th LF
*126th Brigade:* 4 and 5 E Lancs, 7 and 10 Manch
*127th Brigade:* 5, 6, 7 and 8 Manch ('Manchester Brigade')
*Artillery:* 1, 2 and 3 E Lancs Bdes RFA (TF), 4 (How) Bde RFA (TF) (1 and 2
    Cumberland Btys)
*Engineers:* 1 and 2 E Lancs, 2 W Lancs Fd Coys RE (TF)

*52nd (Lowland) Division (TF)*
*GOC:* Major-General C. G. A. Egerton CB
*155th Brigade:* 4 and 5 RSF, 4 and 5 KOSB
*156th Brigade:* 6 and 7 RSF, 7 and 8 Scottish Rifles (Cameronians)
*157th Brigade:* 5, 6 and 7 HLI, 5 A & SH
*Artillery:* 2 Lowland Bde RFA (TF) (in Egypt), 4 How Bde RFA (TF)
*Divisional Cyclist Coy*

## IX CORPS

*GOC:* Lieutenant-General the Hon. Sir Frederick Stopford KCMG, KCVO, CB
*BGS (=Chief of Staff):* Brigadier-General H. L. Reed VC
*Corps troops:* 4 (Highland) Mtn Bde RFA (TF) (Argyllshire and Ross & Cromarty Btys)

*10th (Irish) Division*
*GOC:* Lieutenant-General Sir Bryan Mahon KCVO
*29th Brigade:* 10 Hants, 6 RIrR, 5 ConnR, 6 Leinsters
*30th Brigade:* 6 and 7 Munsters, 6 and 7 Dublins
*31st Brigade:* 5 and 6 Inniskillings, 5 and 6 RIrF
*Pioneers:* 5 RIrish
*Artillery:* 14 Bde RFA (at Mudros, then at Salonika; never landed at Suvla), 15 Bde
    RFA (half in Egypt until October 1915), 16 Bde RFA (half in Egypt, half at Helles
    until October 1915), 17 (How) Bde RFA (part only)
*Engineers:* 65, 66 and 85 Fd Coys RE
*Divisional Cyclist Coy*

APPENDIX I

*11th (Northern) Division*
*GOC:* Major-General F. Hammersley CB
*32nd Brigade:* 9 W Yorks, 6 Yorks, 8 DWR, 6 Y & L
*33rd Brigade:* 6 Lincoln, 6 Border, 7 S Stafford, 9 Sherwood Foresters
*34th Brigade:* 8 NF, 9 LF, 5 Dorset, 11 Manch
*Pioneers:* 6 E Yorks
*Artillery:* 58, 59 and 60 Fd Bdes RFA
*Engineers:* 67, 68 and 86 Fd Coys RE
*Divisional Cyclist Coy*

*13th (Western) Division*
*GOC:* Major-General F. C. Shaw CB
*38th Brigade:* 6 King's Own, 6 E Lancs, 6 S Lancs, 6 Loyals
*39th Brigade:* 9 R Warwicks, 7 Glosters, 9 Worcesters, 7 N Stafford
*40th Brigade:* 4 SWB, 8 RWF, 8 Cheshires, 5 Wilts
*Pioneers:* 8 Welsh
*Artillery:* 66 Bde RFA (detached to Helles), 67 and 68 Bdes RFA (in Egypt, then to
    Salonika; did not land at Gallipoli), 69 How Bde RFA (at Anzac)
*Engineers:* 71, 72 and 88 Fd Coys RE
*Divisional Cyclist Coy*

*53rd (Welsh) Division*
*GOC:* Major-General J. E. Lindley
*158th Brigade:* 5, 6 and 7 RWF, 1 Herefords
*159th Brigade:* 4 and 7 Cheshires, 4 and 5 Welsh
*160th Brigade:* 4 Queens, 4 R Sussex, 4 RWK, 10 Middx
*Artillery:* None
*Engineers:* 1 Welsh and 1 Cheshire Fd Coys RE
*Divisional Cyclist Coy*

*54th (East Anglian) Division (TF)*
*GOC:* Major-General F. S. Inglefield CB
*161st Brigade:* 4, 5, 6 and 7 Essex
*162nd Brigade:* 5 Bedfords, 4 Northamptons, 10 and 11 London
*163rd Brigade:* 4 and 5 Norfolk, 5 Suffolk, 8 Hants
*Artillery:* None
*Engineers:* Two East Anglian Fd Coys RE
*Divisional Cyclist Coy*

*2nd Mounted Division*
*GOC:* Major-General W. E. Peyton CB
*1st (S Midland) Brigade:* 1 R Warwicks Yeo, 1 R Gloster Hussars, 1 Worcester Yeo
*2nd Brigade:* 1 R Bucks Hussars, 1 Berks Yeo, 1 Dorset Yeo
*3rd (Notts and Derbys) Brigade:* 1 Sherwood Rangers, 1 S Notts Hussars, 1 Derbys Yeo
*4th (London) Brigade:* 1 and 3 COLY
*5th Brigade:* 1 Herts Yeo, 2 COLY (Westminster Dragoons)
*Artillery:* None
*Engineers:* None

*Royal Naval Division:* As in April

## AUSTRALIAN AND NEW ZEALAND CORPS

*GOC:* Lieutenant-General Sir W. R. Birdwood KCSI
*BGS:* Brigadier-General A. Skeen
*Corps troops:* 2nd Aust Light Horse Brigade (5, 6 and 7 Regts), 3rd Aust Light Horse
    Brigade (8, 9 and 10 Regts)

*1st Australian Division*
*GOC:* Major-General H. B. Walker DSO
*Cavalry (dismounted):* 4 (Victoria) Light Horse
*1st Australian Brigade:* 1, 2, 3 and 4 (NSW) Bns
*2nd Australian Brigade:* 5, 6, 7 and 8 (Victoria) Bns
*3rd Australian Brigade:* 9 (Queensland), 10 (S Aust), 11 (W Aust), 12 (W Aust, S Aust, and Tasmania) Bns
*Artillery:* 1, 2 and 3 Fd Artillery Bdes, Aust Arty
*Engineers:* 1, 2 and 3 Fd Coys, Aust Engineers

*New Zealand and Australian Division*
*GOC:* Major-General Sir A. Godley KCMG
*Divisional Cavalry:* Otago Mounted Rifles (dismounted)
*New Zealand Brigade:* Auckland, Canterbury, Otago and Wellington Bns
*4th Australian Brigade:* 13 (NSW), 14 (Vic), 15 (Q'ld and Tasmania), 16 (S and W Aust) Bns
*New Zealand Mounted Rifles Brigade* (dismounted): Auckland, Canterbury and Wellington Mounted Rifles
*1st Australian Light Horse Brigade* (dismounted): 1 (NSW), 2 (Q'ld), 2 (S Aust/Tasmania) Regts
*Maori detachment*
*Artillery:* 1 and 2 NZ Fd Arty Bdes (incomplete until October 1915)
*Engineers:* 1 and 2 Fd Coys NZ Engrs
*Attached to NZ/Aust Div: 29 Indian Infantry Brigade:* 14 Sikhs, 1/5 GR, 1/6 GR, 2/10 GR

*2nd Australian Division*
*GOC:* Major-General J. G. Legge
*Divisional Cavalry:* 13 (Vic) Light Horse (dismounted)
*5th Australian Brigade:* 17, 18, 19 and 20 (NSW) Bns
*6th Australian Brigade:* 21, 22, 23 and 24 (Vic) Bns
*7th Australian Brigade:* 25 (Q'ld), 26 (Q'ld/Tasmania), 27 (S Aust), 28 (W Aust) Bns
*Engineers:* 4 and 5 Fd Coys Aust Engrs

## CORPS EXPÉDITIONNAIRE D'ORIENT

*Commander:* General M. C. Bailloud
*1st Division:* 1st Metropolitan Brigade, 2nd Colonial Brigade
*2nd Division:* 3rd Metropolitan Brigade, 4th Colonial Brigade
*Artillery and Engineers:* As in April but augmented to meet requirements of the enlarged corps

*Notes*
(a) At GHQ, corps and divisional level, logistic support was provided by the Army Service Corps (rations, fodder, transport, issue of ammunition), the Ordnance Corps (clothing, and the holding of ammunition stocks, repair of equipment and weapons) and the Veterinary and Remount Services (medical care of animals, and the handling of replacements for gun-teams and pack transport). Each infantry brigade had its own medical support in the form of a field ambulance – commanded by a lieutenant-colonel of the Royal Army Medical Corps – which operated forward dressing stations for prompt treatment of battle casualties before their evacuation to the rear for further treatment and surgery.
(b) The specimen orders of battle given above are illustrative only of the general composition of the expeditionary force ashore at Gallipoli at two specific times during the campaign. As will be seen from the text, units and formations were frequently switched from Helles to Anzac and vice versa to meet tactical

requirements, and some units, such as the ill-fated Collingwood Battalion of the Royal Naval Division, came ashore after the April landings, were wiped out, and did not appear subsequently in the order of battle. Later in the year a trickle of reinforcement units not listed above arrived on the peninsula, such as the Scottish Horse Brigade and a battalion of the Newfoundland Regiment, and some formations departed before the final evacuation for redeployment to Salonika.

(c) The numerals indicating the battalion of any particular regiment have been simplified in the case of territorial units, which, as the war went on, spawned additional battalions, whose identity was denoted by a 'fractional' number: for example, the second and later battalions raised out of the 5th Royal Scots would be known as the 2/5th, 3/5th, etc. As almost all the TF battalions at Gallipoli were in fact the 'originals', and thus designated 1/5th Royal Scots, 1/8th Manchesters etc., they are here referred to throughout as 5th Royal Scots, 8th Manchesters and so on.

# APPENDIX II

# *Geographical Names*

Since the creation of the Turkish Republic the majority of place names have been changed from the predominantly Greek ones used until the fall of the Ottoman Empire. The latter are used throughout this book as they correspond with the nomenclature adopted by the official historians and by virtually every other author who has sought to record the events of the 1915–16 campaign. I trust that my Turkish friends will not therefore be affronted by this. Below is a comparative list showing the old and new names.

| *Old* | *New* |
|---|---|
| Achi Baba | Alcitepe |
| Chanak | Canakkale |
| Chunuk Bair | Conkbayiri |
| Constantinople | Istanbul |
| Dardanelles | Canakkale Bogazi |
| Gaba Tepe | Kabatepe |
| Gallipoli | Gelibolu |
| Green Hill | Mesantepe |
| Gully Ravine | Zigindere |
| Hill 10 | Softatepe |
| Imbros | Gokceada or Imroz |
| Kephalos Bay | Kefeles Liman |
| Kilid Bahr | Kilitbahir |
| Kiretch Tepe | Kirectepe |
| Koja Chemen Tepe (Pt 971) | Kocacimentepe |
| Krithia | Alcitepe |
| Krithia Valley | Kirte Dere |
| Lala Baba | Lalababa Tepe |
| Lemnos | Limnos |
| Maidos | Eceabat |
| Mudros | Moudhros |
| Nibrunesi Point | Kucukkemikli Burnu |
| Rodosto | Tekirdag |

| | |
|---|---|
| Salonika | Thessaloniki |
| Salt Lake | Tuzla Golu |
| Samothrace | Samothraki |
| Sari Sighlar Bay | Sarisiglar Koyu |
| Scimitar Hill | Yusufkuctepe |
| Sedd-el-Bahr | Seddulbahir |
| Skyros | Skiros |
| Sulajik | Sulecik |
| Suvla Plain | Anafarta Ova |
| Suvla Point | Buyukkemikli Burnu |
| Tenedos | Bozcaada |

# Bibliography

## PRIMARY SOURCES

The following list is far from comprehensive; it includes, however, those primary sources consulted. Where appropriate I have given abbreviated locations of principal documentary sources:

| | |
|---|---|
| AWM | The Australian War Memorial, Canberra |
| Churchill | The Churchill Archives, Churchill College, Cambridge |
| *Gallipolian* | Material derived from articles in *The Gallipolian*, journal of the Gallopoli Association |
| IWM | Department of Documents, Imperial War Museum, London |
| KCL | Liddell Hart Archive, King's College, London |
| LF | The Lancashire Fusiliers' Museum, Bury |
| Liddle | The Liddle Archive, University of Leeds |
| NAM | National Army Museum, London |
| RM | Royal Marines Museum, Southsea |
| RS | Museum of the Royal Scots (The Royal Regiment), Edinburgh Castle |
| SUB | The Submarine Museum, Gosport |
| SUSM | Scottish United Services Museum, Edinburgh Castle |

Ahern, Sgt (later Lt) T. P., 54th Battalion, Australian Imperial Force. Diary. AWM.

Alan-Williams, 1/1 Warwicks Yeomanry. Letter to his father. IWM.

Ataturk, Col. Mustafa Kemal Pasha (Kemal Ataturk). Memoir of the Anafarta Battle. TS, translated into English. IWM.

Atkinson, H. MS diary of a merchant seaman. IWM.

Begbie, Pte W. *See under* Royal Scots.

Best, Revd J. K. Memoir. *Gallipolian*.

Bush, Capt. Eric, DSC, RN. Miscellaneous papers including his midshipman's log. IWM. His account of the landings of 25 April, as seen by a perceptive midshipman aged 15½ who gained the DSC commanding a steam pinnace at Anzac, must rank as a classic of its kind.

Cabinet Office Papers. Miscellaneous, especially CAB 37/12A/43. (WSC's paper of February 1915 and Misc 35 (GS Dardanelles Appreciation, 1906).

Campion, P. Memoirs of a Yeoman. Papers kindly loaned by Mrs Brenda Campion (daughter).

Carr, Sgt L. Diary. LF.

Carrick, Lt-Col. Victor, DSO, VD. Memoir. AWM. A reliable source on the legend of the 'man with the donkey'.

Churchill, Maj. John (Jack). Letters. Churchill (Char 1/117).

Clarke Papers. The Essex Regiment at Suvla. KCL.

Cowtan, Pte M. Collection of letters, written c. 1952. AWM. A drily humorous account by an educated man who volunteered to serve as a medical orderly in the AIF and who gained the DCM at Anzac.

Cunliffe-Owen, Lt-Col. F. Feasibility report on operations in the Dardanelles. Liddle.

'Dardanelles Driveller'. Issue of 17 May 1915. Archive, 8201–38. RM.

Darlington, Lt-Col. Sir Henry. Letters from Gallipoli. KCL. Also published as *Letters from Helles*, London, 1930, *see below*.

De Robeck, Vice-Admiral. Miscellaneous papers. Churchill.

Dunbar-Nasmith, Vice-Admiral Sir David, VC, KCB, KCMG. Memoir. SUB.

Egerton, Maj.-Gen. G. Miscellaneous papers. SUSM.

Fisher, Admiral of the Fleet the Lord. Letters and papers. Churchill. The correspondence between Churchill and Fisher must rank as prime evidence of their stormy relationship and makes for fascinating reading.

Fox, Pte Fred. Diary. AWM.

Granard, Lt-Col. the Earl of. Evidence before Dardanelles Commission. KCL.

Haggard, Brig-Gen. Evidence before Dardanelles Commission. KCL.

Hallifax, Capt. Oswald, DSO, RN. Memoirs. SUB.

Hamilton, Gen. Sir Ian. Miscellaneous papers and correspondence. KCL. Principal sources: 6/2/1, 6/2/2, 7/2/1, 15/9/18, 15/9/21, 15/9/27, 15/9/34, 15/9/36, 16/4/4, 16/7/4, 17/3/1/5, 17/3/1/14.

Hammersley, Maj.-Gen. Evidence before Dardanelles Commission. KCL.

Hampshire Regiment. Miscellaneous papers deposited at Western Headquarters, Princess of Wales's Regiment, Winchester.

Hore-Ruthven, Lt-Col. the Hon., VC, DSO. Evidence before Dardanelles Commission. KCL.

Inglefield, Maj-Gen. F. S. Confidential report on fate of the Sandringham Company, 5 Norfolks. KCL.

Lockyer, Capt. H. C., CB, RN. Memoir written in 1936. Lockyer was the Captain of HMS *Implacable* which rendered outstanding support at close range during the landings of 25 April 1915 at Helles. KCL.

Maxwell. Letters. NAM Archive, 7402–32, Nos. 27–30. Written by the brother of Brigadier-General Frank Maxwell VC, Kitchener's erstwhile ADC. For further details of the Maxwell–Kitchener relationship I relied on a privately published family memoir, 'I am Ready', for which I am indebted to Mrs Rachel Lambert, Frank Maxwell's daughter.

Milward, Lt-Gen. Sir Clement. Journal and diaries. NAM. A remarkably candid and revealing account of the campaign as seen by the staff at various levels.

Murdoch, Pte J. Royal Scots Fusiliers. Diary. SUSM.

Murdoch, Keith. Evidence before Dardanelles Commission. KCL.

O'Neill, Prof. R. 'For Want of Critics'. The Gallipoli Lecture, Woolwich Building Socy, 1990.

Phillips, L/Cpl. Diary. LF.

Phipson, Col. E. S. Memoir. *Gallipolian*. A vivid account of the action of the 1/6th Gurkhas at Hill Q by their medical officer.

Pigge, Capt. D. Memoir. *Gallipolian*.

Plowman, Signalman. Memoir. SUB.

Powell, L/Cpl, RMA. The loss of the *Irresistible*. RM.

Redford, Maj. T. H. 8th Light Horse, AIF. Diary. AWM. Redford kept his diary until minutes before his death at the Nek and it remains an outstandingly moving and accurate account of the recruitment and training of the Light Horse and of their earlier experiences at Anzac.

Reed, Brig.-Gen. H. L., VC. Evidence before Dardanelles Commission. KCL.

Royal Scots Fusiliers. See Murdoch, Pte J.

Royal Scots Museum archive:
Orders for evacuation by CO, 7 Royal Scots.
Memoir by 2/Lt Lyall.
Memoir by Pte Begbie; transcribed for posterity by his widow 'in memory of a brave young soldier'. An outstandingly well-written narrative describing the fate of the 52nd Lowland Division as seen from the ranks.
Diary, 'C' Coy 4th Royal Scots.

Savory, Lt-Gen. Sir R., KCIE, CB, DSO, MC. Memoirs, various. *Gallipolian.* Indispensable account of life in an infantry battalion of the old Indian Army. Written with humour as well as shrewd observation and compassion.

Shuttleworth, Lt-Col. B. W. Notes on Suvla, discussed with Hamilton in 1926. KCL.

Sinclair, 2/Lt R. J. Diary, kindly loaned by Mr Alan Dowell of Linlithgow.

Stopford, Lt-Gen. Sir F. Evidence before Dardanelles Commission. *See* Hamilton Papers, 7/2/1. KCL.

——Report on Operations at Suvla. Liddle.

Twistleton, Capt. F. M., Otago Mounted Rifles. Memoir. Liddle. Vivid descriptions of the highly successful New Zealanders' patrolling on the left flank of Anzac and the fighting at Hill 60.

War Council Minutes. Various, November 1914–March 1915. KCL.

# SECONDARY SOURCES

Ashmead-Bartlett, E. *The Uncensored Dardanelles.* London, undated. A vivid if highly subjective account by a brilliant pressman whose activities alienated him from Hamilton's staff.

Aspinall-Oglander, Brig.-Gen. C. F. *History of the Great War, based on Official Documents: Military Operations Gallipoli,* Vols I and II, with appendices. London, 1924–30.

Attlee, Clement R. *As It Happened* (autobiography). London, 1954.

Bean, C. E. W. *The Story of Anzac* (Australian Official History). Sydney, NSW, 1921. The outstanding official history of the Great War, scrupulously researched and objectively written.

——(ed.). *The Anzac Book.* Published in the field, 1915.

Bigwood, G. *Lancashire Fusiliers in Gallipoli: an epic of heroism.* London, 1916.

Blenkinsop, Maj.-Gen. Sir L. J. and Rainey, Lt-Col. J. W. (eds). *History of the Great War, based on Official Documents: Veterinary Services.* London, 1928.

Brooke, R. *Collected Poems.* London, 1918.

Butler, A. G. *Official History of Australian Medical Services 1914–1918.* Canberra (AWM), 1930.

Calwell, Maj.-Gen. Sir C. E. *The Dardanelles.* London, 1919.

Churchill, W. S. *The World Crisis,* Vol. II. London, 1923.

Corbett, Sir Julian. *History of the Great War, based on Official Documents: Naval Operations.* London, 1921.

Crookenden, A. *The History of the Cheshire Regiment in the Great War.* Chester, ?1934. The author was the Brigade Major of 159 Brigade at Suvla and an eyewitness of its chaotic execution and of the fate of a territorial and a New Army battalion of his own regiment.

*Daily Mail.* Various issues of 1915, including despatches, heavily censored, from Ashmead-Bartlett and others, as well as much lurid copy composed in the safety of Fleet Street.

Dardanelles Commission. Final Report and Appendix. London (HMSO), 1921.

Darlington, Lt-Col. Sir H. *Letters from Helles.* London, 1936.

Davies, Harry. *Allanson of the 6th.* Worcester, 1990.

*Dictionary of National Biography.*

Drew, Lt H. T. B. (ed.). *The War Effort of New Zealand.* 1928.

Fuller, Maj.-Gen. J. F. C. *Decisive Battles of the Western World,* Vol. III. London, 1956.

Gillon, Capt. Stair. *The King's Own Scottish Borderers in the Great War.* London, 1930.

Hallam, Douglas. 'Quinn's and Courtney's'. *Blackwood's Magazine,* London, March 1939.

Hamilton, General Sir Ian. *Gallipoli Diary.* London, 1920. Although a fascinating insight into his complex and sensitive character, it has to be treated with care as a source. Much was added and subtracted by Hamilton before publication.

Hamilton, I. B. M. *The Happy Warrior: a life of General Sir Ian Hamilton.* London, 1966.

Harries-Jenkins, G. *The Army and Victorian Society.* London, 1977.

Haythornthwaite, P. J. *The World War I Source Book.* London, 1992. A triumph of eclecticism, containing a wealth of information on equipment.

Holloway, S. M. 'From Trench and Turret'. RM Museum publication. Includes the memoir of Lt Lamplough, who took part in the earlier landings at Sedd-el-Bahr which were intended to neutralize the outer batteries.

James, Robert Rhodes. *Gallipoli.* London, 1965. Scrupulously fair, a scholarly account that is likely to remain the standard non-official history.

Jerrold, D. *The Royal Naval Division.* London, 1933.

Kannengiesser, Maj.-Gen. H. (trans. Maj. C. J. P. Ball). *The Campaign in Gallipoli.* London, 1927.

Keyes, Admiral of the Fleet Sir R. *Naval Memoirs.* London, 1934. Of great interest concerning the evolution of the submarine service and its treatment of Lord Fisher, as well as Keyes' experiences as naval Chief of Staff at the Dardanelles.

Laffin, John. *Damn the Dardanelles.* London, 1980. Eminently readable account, highly critical of the British high command, less so of the Australian leaders and troops.

Legg, Frank. *The Gordon Bennett Story.* Sydney, NSW, 1965.

Liddell Hart, B. *History of the First World War.* London, 1970.

Liman von Sanders, Field Marshal Otto. *Five Years in Turkey.* US Naval Academy, Annapolis, 1927.

Mackenzie, C. *Gallipoli Memories.* London, 1929.

MacPherson, Maj.-Gen. and Mitchell, Maj. T. J. *History of the Great War: Medical Services,* Vol. II. London (HMSO), 1924.

Magnus, P. *Kitchener: Portrait of an Imperialist.* London, 1958.

Masefield, J. *Gallipoli.* London, 1916. Written more as propaganda than as an objective account, it is nevertheless full of haunting imagery.

Massie, Robert K. *Dreadnought: Britain, Germany and the coming of the First World War.* London, 1992.

Moorehead, Alan. *Gallipoli.* London, 1956. Superbly written, but derivative and laced with subjective opinions.

Moorhouse, Geoffrey. *Hell's Foundations. A Town, its Myths and Gallipoli: Bury and the Lancashire Fusiliers.* London, 1992.

Morten, J. C. (ed. S. Morten). *I remain, your son Jack.* Manchester, 1993.

Mure, Maj. A. *With the Incomparable 29th.* London, 1919.

Murray, J. *Gallipoli as I saw it.* London, 1965. A remarkable narrative describing life in the ranks of the Royal Naval Division. As a leading seaman, Murray, an ex-miner, was employed at Helles in the construction of mine galleries under the Turkish lines.

Nock, O. S. *Historic Railway Disasters*. London, 1966.

North, J. *Gallipoli: the fading vision*. London, 1936.

Perry, F. W. *The Commonwealth Armies: manpower and organization in two World Wars*. Manchester, 1988.

Quigley, D. J. *Princess Beatrice's Isle of Wight Rifles*. Privately published, undated.

Raymond, Revd Ernest. *Tell England: a study in a generation*. London, 1922.

Repington, Lt-Col. C. A. à Court. *The First World War 1914–18: personal experiences*. London, 1921.

Ross, J. *The Myth of the Digger: the Australian soldier in two World Wars*. Sydney, NSW, 1985.

Scott, Ernest. *The Official History of Australia in the War, 1914–18*, Vol. XI: *Australia during the War*. Sydney, NSW, 1936.

Steel, Nigel. *The Battlefields of Gallipoli: then and now*. London, 1990.

Sutton, F. A. *One-Arm Sutton*. London, 1933.

Taylor, Phil, and Cupper, Pam. *Gallipoli: a battlefield guide*. Canberra (ACT), 1989.

Thompson, Lt-Col. R. R. *The 52nd (Lowland) Division, 1914–1918*. Glasgow, 1923.

*The Times History of the War*, Vol. V. London, 1915.

*War Illustrated*. Issues of 10 April, 15 May, 12 June, 26 June, 24 July, 2 August and 21 August 1915.

# Index